Ethics Goes to the M(

MW00649127

Movies hold a mirror up to us, portraying the complexities of human reality through their characters and stories. And they vividly illustrate moral theories that address questions about how we are to live and what sort of people we ought to be. In this book, Christopher Falzon uses movies to provide a rich survey of moral positions as they have emerged through history. These include the ethics of the ancient world, medieval ethics, Enlightenment and Kantian ethics, existentialist ethics and the ethics of the other. Each theory is explained in detail, using a number of examples from the book's wide selection of movies. The discussion draws on a range of recent and not-so-recent films, from Hollywood blockbusters to art-house cinema.

Key Features

- In addition to covering thinkers one would expect in an introduction to ethics (e.g., Plato, Aristotle, Kant), the book discusses less canonical figures in detail as well (e.g., Marcuse, Foucault, Habermas).
- Similarly, the book examines both major ethical theories (e.g., Kantianism, utilitarianism, virtue ethics) and theories too often glossed over in introductory texts (e.g., Stoicism, Epicureanism, Habermas's discourse ethics and Nietzschean ethics).
- A wide range of movies are discussed, from Hollywood blockbusters and classics like *The Dark Knight, Casablanca* and *Dirty Harry* to lesser known films like *Force Majeure* and *Under the Skin.*
- At the end of each chapter a focus on two feature films is included, with a plot summary and interpretations of several key scenes with a time marker indicating when in the film the scenes occur.
- A Filmography includes all movies discussed in the book and a Glossary covers key philosophical terms and figures; both with corresponding page numbers.

Christopher Falzon is a Senior Lecturer in Philosophy at the University of Newcastle, Australia. He is the author of *Foucault and Social Dialogue* (1998) and *Philosophy Goes to the Movies* (3rd edition, 2014), and the co-editor of *Foucault and Philosophy* (2010) and *A Blackwell Companion to Foucault* (2013).

Ethics Goes to the Movies

An Introduction to Moral Philosophy

Christopher Falzon

Routledge
Taylor & Francis Group

NEW YORK AND LONDON

First published 2019
by Routledge
52 Vanderbilt Avenue, New York, NY 10017

and by Routledge
2 Park Square, Milton Park, Abingdon, Oxon, OX14 4RN

Routledge is an imprint of the Taylor & Francis Group, an informa business

Library of Congress Cataloging-in-Publication Data
A catalog record for this title has been requested

ISBN: 978-1-138-93819-9 (hbk)
ISBN: 978-1-138-93820-5 (pbk)
ISBN: 978-1-315-67580-0 (ebk)

Typeset in Times New Roman
by Deanta Global Publishing Services, Chennai, India

Printed and bound by CPI Group (UK) Ltd, Croydon, CR0 4YY

Contents

Acknowledgments

I would like to thank my colleagues William Herfel, Joe Mintoff, Michael Newton, Timothy O'Leary, Sarah Rice and Tim Stanley who were kind enough to read through various chapters and to give me the benefit of their special expertise; Tim Madigan and an anonymous reviewer for their tremendously helpful comments on the text as a whole; Penny Craswell for casting her expert eye over the text and saving it from all sorts of inelegancies; and Andy Beck, my editor at Routledge, for his ongoing support and patience. This book is dedicated to Penny Craswell, who has also been very patient.

Introduction
Rear Window Ethics

'We've become a race of peeping Toms. What people ought to do is get outside their own house and look in for a change. Yes, sir. How's that for a bit of home-spun philosophy?' So says visiting insurance nurse Stella about the activities of her charge, L.B. 'Jeff' Jefferies, in Hitchcock's classic *Rear Window*. Wheelchair-bound with a broken leg, cooped up with nothing to do, he has taken to passing the time by staring out of the rear window of his apartment, watching the neighbours in his block go about their lives. As is well-known, *Rear Window* unfolds as a murder mystery as Jeff tries to work out if the bedridden woman across the way has been murdered by her husband. But the film also includes some reflection on what Jeff himself is doing in the film. Stella is sure that there's something prob-lematic about Jeff's obsessive neighbour-watching. She thinks that those who indulge in such activity really ought to stop and think about what they are doing. Even Jeff comes to wonder about his activity, at least for a moment. As he says later to his girlfriend Lisa, who has her own concerns, 'I wonder if it's ethical to watch a man with binoculars, and a long-focus lens … Do you suppose it's ethical even if you prove he didn't commit a crime? As Lisa says, it's a question of 'rear window ethics'.

So, ethical reflection is coming into this film at a number of levels. Stella and Lisa wonder about the ethics of Jeff's behaviour, as does he. In addition, the viewer may have their own thoughts about Jeff's activity. Is all this surveillance justified in the interests of solving a crime or is that simply an excuse to look? Is Jeff a detective or a pervert, or perhaps a bit of both? And these are interesting questions for the viewer to consider since *Rear Window* can readily be seen as offering a metaphor for cinema and movie-watching. The scenes in the apartment windows are like silent movies. Jeff himself is very much like a moviegoer, the immobilised watcher who watches, unseen, in the dark. For their part, the mov-iegoer is able to secretly go places and watch things that they would not ordinarily be able to in real life. In considering the ethics of Jeff's activities, the viewer is also in a position to think about the ethics of their own movie-watching activity. Is watching movies a form of voyeurism? Can it amount to the violation or exploi-tation of those being watched? These concerns and questions notwithstanding, everyone involved in *Rear Window* is completely absorbed in the activity they are raising questions about. Whatever his misgivings, Jeff can't tear himself away from the window; and despite their initial concerns, Stella and Lisa are quickly drawn into Jeff's surveillance activities. And so, of course, are the film's viewers. As Pauline Kael pointed out many years ago, it is precisely 'the opening into other, forbidden or surprising kinds of experience' that draws viewers to the movies in the first place (Kael 1970, 105).

If what the film is showing us provokes ethical questions and concerns in characters and viewers alike, the viewer is also, uniquely, in a position to use the film to explore these ethical views and concerns, to interrogate them in the light of the film experience. This book is a more extended and systematic version of that exercise. It is an introduction to ethical thinking, in particular the kind of systematic ethical thinking that has been undertaken for centuries by philosophers. And it makes use of some recent and not-so-recent films to illustrate and explore some of the key theories, arguments and problems that have emerged in the history of ethics. I should say that using film for the purpose of exploring various aspects of philosophy is not an especially novel thing to do. Films, along with television, have enjoyed a good deal of popularity in recent years as an avenue for talking about philosophical positions and issues. There are many books that have gone down this avenue, including a number of excellent introductions to ethics. What this book does that might be new is to take this approach in relation to an entire history of ethical thinking.

Considering ethical thinking historically means that there is a progression of ideas to consider, and a natural logic to the ordering of the ideas, since later accounts respond to, contend with or distance themselves from earlier ones. But we are not simply visiting a dusty museum of superseded thoughts. The history of ethical thinking is also a history of the present, insofar as these ideas continue to speak to and inform contemporary ways of thinking. And films are a useful medium to employ in exploring the contemporary relevance of these ideas because films are inevitably contemporary in their content and references. This is not to forget all the changes in context, outlook and style that have occurred over the last hundred years or so of film history. For all that, film remains a modern art. Even history films have to speak to and resonate with modern audiences, which is why they can so readily introduce anachronistic elements into their portrayals of historical figures and events. A film like *Agora*, for example, might be seen as reading the early modern confrontation between science and dogmatic religion back into the confrontation between classical antiquity and a rising Christianity. Even in this, the film is providing a measure of how certain ideas and viewpoints have become a part of contemporary ways of thinking. And in using films to talk about views that have emerged in the history of ethical thinking, one has a measure not only of how far these historical views continue to speak to contemporary experience, but also how these views have entered into and become part of that experience.

This is not to reduce the films being discussed here to no more than means for talking about ethics. First, any use of films to talk about ethics is at the same time a way of talking about the films. Seeing a character or their actions as providing an illustration or instantiation of some ethical view or concept is already a way of thinking about what is going on in the film. Moreover, ethical views or ideas may be invoked or alluded to in the film by the characters themselves in talking about other characters or themselves. This makes talking about these views very much a matter of talking about the film. Beyond this, the film is going to be more than just a means for discussing ethics simply because talking about a film in terms of its philosophical or ethical relevance can never really exhaust what is going on in the film. A film is not an ethical treatise, a philosophical work. It has a life of its own and there will always be more going on in it than the illustration or instantiation of ethical views. There will be the story to get on with, and lives to portray, and non-philosophical concerns, artistic, dramatic or comic concerns are going to come into play in terms of what is being presented.

By the same token, that a film has a life of its own, and will be governed significantly by non-philosophical concerns, is not incompatible with a film having philosophical or ethical content. It would be odd to argue that films, simply by virtue of having non-philosophical concerns, are unable to engage with such content. Indeed, this can be expressed more positively: that a film is irreducible to any philosophical or ethical ideas it might illustrate or instantiate arguably means that there is room in film for a critical engagement with these ideas. Certainly, a film may be set up to do little more than promote a certain viewpoint or way of thinking. There are plenty of didactic, moralistic and propagandistic films of this sort. But films can also reflect on and challenge the perspectives and positions they portray in various ways, through playfulness, irony, even downright subversion (see Stam 2000, 139; Wilson 1986, 13). And it can be very much part of their artistry, drama or comedy that they do so.

So, the suggestion is that reflection on philosophical or ethical ideas might take place through the workings of a film, which is able to portray these ideas in various lights, positive or negative. The philosophical text is not the only context in which such critical reflection can take place. Admittedly, this book does not go too far down this path. That is, it does not seek to explore how a film might be philosophical or ethical in its own right, without in any way serving to illustrate or engage with philosophical or ethical positions in the literature. No doubt, like Hitchcock's notion of pure cinema, there is pure film-philosophy, pure cinematic ethics. This is not the concern of the present book. The overriding purpose here remains that of introducing ethical positions from the history of ethical thinking, so the films remain to that degree subordinated to the philosophy. Nonetheless, films are not subordinate insofar as they have resources to reflect on any ethical views they might be thought to illustrate or instantiate, to interrogate them even as they portray them. These ideas are not only concretely illustrated in the films but also, in being refracted through the lens of cinematic experience, are able to be studied from a number of different angles.

The aim here as mentioned is to use films to talk about an entire history of ethics. That a historical film can readily introduce anachronistic elements into its picture of the past reminds us that any history is going to be, to some extent, a 'history of the past in terms of the present'. One can safely assume that the history of ethical thinking is far messier than what is being portrayed in this book, which is a more or less smooth and continuous progression from ancient thinking to recent ethical thought. But in the end, the same could probably be said of any history. This does not necessarily make the history wrong, only necessarily partial. It should just be kept in mind that the history of ethics being presented here is not the whole story. Apart from anything else, there are some glaring omissions, such as Emotivism and other ethical views from twentieth-century analytic philosophy; as well as the moral views of Pragmatist figures like John Dewey. Most obviously, it is very much a story of one tradition of ethical thinking only, namely, Western ethical thinking. It has nothing to say about non-Western ethics. And with regard to the discussion of religious ethics, the religion is restricted to the Christianity that happened to become dominant in the West in the medieval period.

What Is Ethics?

I have been referring rather vaguely to ethical thinking and to unspecified ethical theories, positions, views and ideas that we will be exploring. Before proceeding any further, it will be useful to consider what might be understood by the notion of ethics. No special distinction is being made between ethics and morality here. One term comes from the Greek (*ethos*) and the other from Latin (*mores*), meaning customs, manners or social norms. And while there are of course ethical theories, and a history of such theories, ethics is not something we encounter first as abstract theory, 'moral philosophy', a branch of philosophy. Rather it is in the first instance something utterly practical, very much part of everyday life. One does not need to be a philosopher to be acquainted with it. Living a life is enough. Ethics here is thinking about how we should live that life and what sort of person we ought to be. And the ethical dimension of everyday life is the more or less organised framework of norms, values and commitments that embody our sense of how we ought to live, the sort of life we aspire to, in terms of which we ordinarily think about what to do, make our decisions and act.

A life without such a framework, in which we just did whatever we were moved to do by immediate wants and desires, would be at the very least an underdeveloped one. Very young children might qualify. They are not yet responsible moral agents, able to play a role in the dramas of life. But while some adults do of course act childishly, a framework of norms and values is not something moral agents can easily do without. We cannot lead our lives without making choices that show we think that some things are more important than others. Ordinarily, we are committed to being a certain sort of person, to living a certain kind of life; and this requires us to adhere to a framework of justification and criticism, the 'horizon of evaluation' in terms of which we reflect and weigh up the choices and actions we undertake. This set of commitments and values is central to who we are, our 'identity'. Such an orienting framework is necessary if we are to be agents at all. To lose it would not amount to a liberation but a terrifying experience of disintegration. It would be precisely an 'identity crisis', a breakdown, a catastrophic loss of orientation. In such a state, we would no longer know where we stood, how to choose, what actions to pursue and we would be crippled as agents (see Taylor 1985a, 34–35).

Thus, ethics, understood as a set of values or ideals concerning how to live that goes beyond mere survival, is not an optional extra but an essential part of being a functioning human being, a responsible moral agent. It defines who one is and where one stands in the world, and at the same time, what one aspires to or transcends oneself towards. Whatever particular form it takes, ethics always involves some form of self-transcendence or self-overcoming. We can equally say that it is a distinguishing mark of human beings that they are the creatures for whom the ethical question can arise: how should I live? What kind of life do I want? (Malik 2014, 184). While this is the kind of question one might associate particularly with twentieth-century existentialism, it would be better to say that existentialism is the philosophy especially concerned with asking this distinctively human question. It is also the question that was especially important to the Greeks, right at the beginning of systematic moral reflection. Socrates, in Plato's *Republic* says that 'we are discussing no small matter, but how we ought to live'. It is not perhaps the kind of question that can be associated so readily with modern moral philosophy to the extent that the latter has been a highly theoretical exploration of grounds or basic principles underlying moral judgements.

So, ethics is not in the first instance a matter of philosophical theory, but something to be lived. As James Griffin suggests, ethics in this sense of a lived ethics appears early in the life of a culture (Griffin 2015, 1). As a culture develops, roles are established that involve adherence to particular norms of behaviour. And individuals are inculcated into that culture, developing as individuals in the process insofar as they imbibe its norms in the course of socialisation. They are then able to take part in that society, play various roles within it, participate in its dramas. This is not to say that life is simply the slavish reproduction of pre-existing formulae, of the customary ways of doing things that we may have absorbed from our culture. Otherwise, morality would never change or evolve. But nor however are we ever completely our own creation, however much we might like to imagine ourselves so. We inevitably acquire some kind of ethical framework for living from our culture in the course of growing up, in the process of becoming who we are. However, this ethical apparatus is also something that gets put to the test in the course of living, sometimes being modified or even coming completely undone in the process.

What about the various philosophical theories of ethics, the history of which is the subject of this book? These ethical theories are not entirely distinct from lived ethics, but rather, parasitic upon it. What usually happens is that philosophers come along and try to provide lived ethics with foundations, to discern what characterises or underpins moral judgements, to bring ethics under a set of simple rules or principles. What these days is known as normative ethical theory aims to produce some kind of coherent, systematic account of what makes moral judgements correct, in terms of some fundamental principle that defines a feature common to all correct moral judgements. On the basis of some such principle, philosophers have been inspired to justify, affirm and also criticise, even try to reform, existing values, norms and ways of behaving.

But it is important to stress that ethics does not wait for philosophers to provide it with theoretical foundations. That sort of theorising happens after the event, the event being the moral training that starts in early childhood. Equally, a connection to life is necessary even for the most general ethical theory. Sometimes these theories claim to rely on intuitions about the nature of the good, access to divine revelation or the deliverances of pure reason in order to arrive in an *a priori* manner at principles that can provide a foundation for lived ethics. But however it might be arrived at, a general theory of ethics without any intrinsic reference to life would be empty and irrelevant. Equally, no matter how abstract, ethical theories generally involve some idea of how to live, bound up with a broad conception of what it is to be a human being and also of the larger world in which one exists. Even a highly theoretical account like that of the eighteenth-century philosopher Kant in the end exhorts us to live a certain way, to be what we are, namely rational beings whose reason lifts us above nature, and to never fall below that to become a mere thing, pushed around by natural forces.

Nonetheless, it is an occupational hazard for theoretical accounts that in their efforts to systematise lived ethics, or to subordinate it to simple rules or principles, life can end up being subordinated to theory, leaving us with an ethics that is unliveable, and hence inhuman. How else could there emerge such improbably superhuman figures as the entirely rational Kantian agent, or for that matter, the god-like Stoic sage or the all-knowing utilitarian calculator? This inhumanity is a problem for an ethical theory. As one commentator puts it, 'if ethics retreats to a fantasy world, providing dictates that could guide only the infinitely rational, impartial, all-knowing agent, then it loses its interest and value to our societies' (Hayward 2017). It is an at least necessary condition for any conception of how we ought to live that it is physically and psychologically possible for human beings to live in the way prescribed.

It is true that ethics involves the aspiration to certain ideals of behaviour. To that extent it is a form of transcendence, of going beyond or overcoming oneself. And every person who aspires to be a certain sort of person, to live a certain life, engages in this transcendence. This is why a moral agent cannot be reduced to a thing, and ethics cannot be exhaustively accounted for in purely objective, scientific terms. But nor can we entirely transcend our bodies, become pure subjects. The physical and psychological capacities of human beings always have a bearing on ethical life. Perhaps some people can rise higher than others, so we cannot judge what human beings are capable of just by what the 'ordinary person' can manage. But whatever the case, none of us can aspire to what is physically or psychologically beyond human beings as such. This suggests that the constraints on ethics are ultimately practical. Ethics should concern itself with what falls within the limits of human capacity (see Hayward 2017). A theory-driven ethics that is not ultimately grounded in human life and what human beings are capable of achieving is not only of no positive use or value. It can indeed be positively dangerous. It can become a tool for terrorising life, a basis for tormenting or brutalising people insofar as they fall short, as they inevitably must, of the impossible ethical ideal.

Film as Experimental

If ethical positions have a fundamental connection to the practical, and to what people are capable of doing in practice, they are not immune from being put to the test of experience, the practical experience of living. For a lived ethics, merely to live is to put oneself to the test. And what is being put to the test in these 'experiments in living', to borrow a notion from John Stuart Mill, is not some hypothesis or theory, but we ourselves, as defined by the values or ideals that constitute our identity as moral agents.

Most straightforwardly, we can be put to the test as moral agents simply by encountering challenging circumstances, which concretely pose the question of whether we are able to live up to our defining ideals in practice. These are not experiments concerned with exploring human biology or psychology, but with human beings as moral subjects; though once again, human biology and psychology have a role to play since they provide the capacities we have to work with as moral beings and the ultimate constraints on the sort of person we can be. Further, if even general ethical theories and positions have to have some connection to the practical and can only require of people what they are capable of doing if they are going to be meaningful, they are similarly not immune from the test of experience. If an ethical theory was to formulate an ideal of conduct that could only be attained by a superhuman being, and which no ordinary human being could live up to in practice, that would be a significant problem for the theory. To that extent, even abstract moral theories are at risk of disconfirmation in the light of experience and the experiment of trying to live the theory in practice affords us the opportunity to reflect on the theory in question.

Experiments in living are intrinsically dangerous in the sense that they expose us to the possibility of failure. Most straightforwardly, there is the risk of falling short of our defining ideals in practice. The stakes in such experiments are not simply epistemological. Failure to conform to expectations represents not just disconfirmation but self-betrayal, an occasion for guilt, embarrassment and humiliation – not to mention an opportunity for lying and self-deception as one tries to preserve one's conception of oneself, and one's estimation in the eyes of others. The connections between experiment, experience and danger are reflected in the very language we use. Experiment and experience once meant the same thing, and they share the Latin root *expereri* (to try, to test), which is itself linked to the word for danger (*periculum*).

We can, however, envisage experiments in living in which we are removed from the lives being lived and the risks this experimentation entails. We can envisage hypothetical scenarios, fictional stories or narratives, which provide an occasion for reflecting in an extended way on possible forms of life and views about how one should live. Being fictional here does not amount to being false, only to that which is 'fictioned', that is, fabricated or constructed (see O'Leary 2009, 86–88). This is one way of thinking about the function of the fictive arts, including films as a contemporary art form. Like novels and plays, films can be seen as offering experimental scenarios in which moral agents, ideals and views of life can be explored and tested. Narrative film seems particularly well-placed to run such virtual experiments. It is an art form that engages directly with experience, that confronts the viewer in a visceral way, as well as being able to portray relatable characters with some structure of values, ideals and commitments, experimental subjects able to be put to the test.

With respect to ethical theories, these as noted must also have some connection with the practical. They have to be able to be lived in practice. So even a highly theoretical account like Kant's exhorts us to live a certain way, to live up to a certain ideal of conduct, to be a certain kind of character. As such, through characters, actions and lives that illustrate or embody them, ethical theories can be concretely portrayed in film; and we can also ask critical questions about them. The question might be posed for example as to whether it is possible in practice for human beings to live up to the ideal of how to live, or be the kind of ideal character, that is envisioned in the theory. Or we might consider how far a complex human and moral reality that is being portrayed in the film can be captured by the theory. And it may be that the theory is going to be found wanting or inadequate when put to the test of experience in these ways.

Of course, a film can also be questioned in connection with the ideas and positions that it portrays. Insofar as the film invokes a theoretical view or position, the position may be misconstrued or oversimplified. As an instance, Nietzsche, part of whose 'posthumous life' has been in the movies, and one of the few philosophers to make regular appearances there, is regularly misrepresented. Aside from this, a film may portray undeveloped characters and contrived, unrealistic scenarios. It may recycle well-worn cinematic conventions and stock characters, so that in the end it only references other films, a movie universe with movie heroes and villains. Or it may uncritically take on and amplify conventional views circulating through the culture that offers a mythological or ideologically distorted view of the world or of ourselves. In this role, the film acts as no more than a means of perpetuating these views and is essentially part of the problem. But while films may be constructed to do no more than confirm, reproduce and reinforce prevailing myths, they are also able to invoke aspects of our experience that resist and go beyond such representations, reminding us that experience that is richer, more diverse or more complex than these representations allow. In so doing, they can challenge not only those cultural myths but also film's sometime complicity in perpetuating them. This is the experimental film as both cultural critique and cinematic self-critique.

Film understood as experimental, in this broad sense of offering a narrative through which characters, ethical positions or forms of thinking can be critically examined, explored and tested, has affinities with the thought experiments found within philosophical texts. These too are fictional narratives, hypothetical scenarios offering a mode of critical reflection. That is an aspect that some film philosophers have emphasised, arguing that it makes sense to think of some fiction films as working in ways that philosophical thought experiments do, questioning existing views, posing counter-examples, exploring what is essential to a concept and so on; and in that regard, as not only capable of illustrating philosophical ideas and themes, but of 'doing philosophy' (Wartenberg 2007, 67). However, there are also some significant differences between film and philosophical thought experiments, one being that film is more emphatically invested in experience. Whereas the philosophical thought experiment is austere and sketchy, the film narrative is richly detailed. Where philosophical experiments focus on concepts rather than people, and don't engage the audience, cinematic narratives give access to conduct, characters and extended stories involving the audience in their characters' lives and fate. And unlike even literary narratives, films do not merely describe but show things in detail, especially faces, gestures and conduct, communicating their significance directly.

These differences have led some to argue that there are too many disanalogies for film to be understood as philosophising or reflecting in this way (see Wartenberg 2011, 19–21). But rather than trying to judge film in terms of the narrow model of the philosophical thought experiment, it seems more fruitful to argue that the differences film as film brings to the table, particularly the ability to show experience in a richly detailed way, enhance its capacity to engage in narrative experimentation, to invoke challenging experiences, in ways that go beyond what is possible within the philosophical text. As Damien Cox and Michael Levine put it, through its relative richness of detail, film can 'sometimes provide nuanced investigation of fundamental features of experience well beyond the ordinary achievements of written philosophical texts, and in doing so robustly refute hollow and simplistic ways of understanding life' (Cox and Levine 2012, 12). In other words, film precisely as film is well placed to present experimental scenarios in which moral theories and forms of understanding can be put to the test of experience. And the experiment in question is not the abstract thought experiment but the concrete experiment in living.

Exploring Ethics Through Film

In this book, then, we will be turning to a range of films to illustrate and explore key theories, arguments and problems in the history of ethics. What will continually be to the forefront, even with respect to abstract ethical theory, is how these positions address the question of how we are to live and what sort of person we should be. This way of thinking about ethics is very different from the 'metaethics' that was the focus of much twentieth-century moral philosophy in the analytic tradition. Metaethics, theorising about moral theorising, asks very general philosophical questions about moral knowledge, such as: can we have moral knowledge, can we know what is right or wrong, or is morality a matter of personal opinion, a purely subjective affair? And if we can have knowledge of what is right and wrong, how do we acquire it? It also asks about the meaning of various moral terms, such as good or evil, right or wrong; and about the nature of justification in ethics, questions such as: how do we justify moral judgements, how do we justify thinking that a particular judgement is right or wrong?

Metaethics is evidently at some distance from any practical concerns about how to live. This is not to say that meta-ethical themes will be absent from this book. However, dealing with them in a separate section runs the risk of compounding this remoteness and ending up with a very abstract discussion. Accordingly, any meta-ethical questions will be addressed in a way that is integrated into the discussion of the various ethical theories and positions. The discussion in the book will primarily take the form of a survey of moral theories and positions as they have emerged historically, from ancient to medieval to modern thought. These theories and positions will be given a relatively detailed examination, and narrative fiction films will be drawn on in order to illustrate and explore these positions. At the end of each chapter, two of the films that have made an appearance in the discussion, a classic film and a more recent one, will be given a more systematic examination, with an outline of their plot, identification of key scenes with timings and an indication of the themes that the films address. At the end of the book there is a filmography and a glossary of the main ethical notions and thinkers appearing in the book.

What follows is a 'preview of coming attractions', as Lisa from *Rear Window* might put it: a quick survey of the various ethical positions we will be looking at in the book, along with the elements of film form that seem especially relevant to their portrayal and exploration. We will begin in Chapter One with the ethical thinking of ancient Greece and Rome, of Plato, Aristotle, Epictetus and Epicurus amongst others. Here, the central ethical notion is virtue, the morally praiseworthy quality of character; and the ideal is to have a character that embodies the various virtues. The different ethical accounts of the ancient world seek to give some kind of reflective account of the virtues, what they are and why they are important to pursue, usually tying them to some notion of human nature. They agree in holding that being virtuous is bound up with achieving happiness, in the sense of fulfilment or well-being. The various films used to discuss these notions provide narratives through which they can be portrayed and explored. To make use of narratives in this way is very much to follow in the footsteps of Plato. Right at the start of systematic reflection on ethics, Plato makes conspicuous use of literary narratives, thought experiments, little stories like the ring of Gyges and the Myth of the Cave, in his dialogues. Through these narratives he contemplates various philosophical questions, such as the nature of morality, even the nature of philosophical enlightenment itself.

Ironically, Plato is also the thinker who wants to exclude narratives from philosophy. He wants to establish the narrative that philosophy arises through the rejection of narrative, the old Greek myths, in favour of a rational discourse devoted to universal truths (see Derrida 1993; Wartenberg 2007, 21). In this spirit, he will ban the epic poets, the artists, from the ideal society he portrays in the *Republic*. He thus introduces an opposition between philosophy and the fictive arts that continues to colour thinking about the relationship between philosophy and film. But he also succeeds despite himself in showing how fictional narratives might be useful for exploring philosophical and ethical matters. The narratives portrayed in the Cave-like space of the modern cinema are no exception to this.

Films to be discussed in connection with ancient Greek and Roman ethics include monster movies, movies of excess and obsession, and Jane Austen adaptations: *Under the Skin, Dr Jekyll and Mr Hyde, Blue Velvet, Scarface, Goodfellas, Wall Street, The Wolf of Wall Street, Vertigo, Mulholland Drive, Pride and Prejudice* and *Sense and Sensibility*, amongst others.

In Chapter Two, we turn to religious ethics, specifically that based on the Christianity that emerged as the classical world declined and remained central to the Western outlook until the end of the medieval period. In this way of thinking, virtue and self-perfection remain important, but it is virtue grounded in a transcendental God, and which is a means to the end of becoming one with this figure. Here, morality as a set of God-given rules for living points towards a transcendental ideal beyond this world, beyond ordinary life and comprehension. With narrative films that help to explore religious ethics, what is of particular relevance is that film tells its stories by way of cinematic images, the potent combinations of sight and sound specific to the medium. These provide the opportunity not only for film to tell its stories in a distinctively visual way but also, if the image comes to be given primacy over narrative coherence, to create emotional and visceral significance that transcends narrative meaning (see Vass 2005). Amongst other things, the image that transcends narrative can be used to evoke transcendental, even mystical religious experiences that go beyond the ordinary world of narrative logic, producing a direct emotional effect in the viewer. The 'surveying God's creation' sequence in *The Tree of Life* represents an extended example. Films to be considered in connection with religious ethics include biblical epics and more quietly religious films, as well as meditations on murder, identity, death and loss: *The Passion of Joan of Arc, Babette's Feast, Noah, Frailty, Crimes and Misdemeanors, Match Point, The Crying Game, Shadowlands* and *The Tree of Life*.

Chapter Three brings us to the ethics of the early modern era, the seventeenth and eighteenth centuries primarily, with figures like Hobbes, Holbach, Bentham and Mill coming to the fore. Here, God is no longer the basis for ethics, which is now understood to be grounded in human beings. Human beings themselves are understood in a down-to-earth, naturalistic way, as creatures driven to seek pleasure and to avoid pain. This view of the human being emerges out of the new scientific world-view, a thoroughly 'disenchanted', no-nonsense view of nature, based on unprejudiced observation and experiment rather than dogma and traditional belief. On this view, human beings are not fundamentally different from any other object in the natural world, and equally the product of natural forces. So whereas in the older religious picture, human beings were subservient to a transcendent God, in the new scientific picture, human beings are subservient to nature, and in particular to their own nature as pleasure-driven animals.

There is a parallel with film here. Beyond the combination of narrative and cinematic image, film can also be seen as a combination of the constructed and the photographic. As we have seen, the cinematic image can express something out of this world, but it can also be understood as photographically capturing the utterly down-to-earth. Film theorist V.F. Perkins offers a general description of the film medium in these terms: 'the fiction film exploits the possibilities of synthesis between photographic realism and dramatic illusion'. For Perkins, film's conquest of the visual world 'extends in two opposite directions. The first ... gives it the power to "possess" the real world by capturing its appearance. The second ... permits the representation of an ideal image, ordered by the film-maker's will and imagination' (Perkins 1972, 60). The documentary and the cartoon or fantasy film occupy the purely reproductive and purely imaginative extremes respectively, with the photographic narrative film standing in a compromise position between them. The aim of the narrative film is still to present a reality, but the film's realism depends on the completeness of its illusion, the coherence of its fictioned world, story and characters, and the invisibility of its visual style. Here, the cinematic image is subordinated to the telling of the story, the vehicle through which the narrative content is made visible.

In as much as the film's narrative is organised around a central protagonist who motivates the story, the world that it shows is oriented towards revealing the character's journey, struggle or development. As such, film is able to portray a narrative space that is both a photographically captured reality and shaped by the character's viewpoint and concerns. However, the camera can also detach itself from the protagonist's point of view, revealing a world that is altogether outside their viewpoint, potentially undercutting it or highlighting its limitations. When this latter aspect is in the ascendant we have unembellished, almost anthropological films, unsentimentally recording human behaviour from an objective point of view. This allows characters to be presented largely as victims of their nature or circumstances, driven by compelling impulses or environmental factors. Such films are useful in the exploration of early modern forms of ethics, such as utilitarianism, which similarly presuppose a scientific view of the world, in which human beings are seen as natural objects driven by impulses and shaped by environmental factors. Relevant films here include action crime thrillers and superhero movies, anthropological films and comedies: *Dirty Harry, LA Confidential, I, Robot, The Dark Knight, The Lord of the Flies, Wild Child, Educating Rita* and *Simon of the Desert*.

In Chapter Four, we come to Kant's moral thinking, which arises partly in reaction to the scientific ethics of the eighteenth century. For Kant, the human being is not primarily a natural object, determined by external forces, but an active, organising subject. Moral rules are generated by human beings, through their own rationality, which is what lifts them above nature. Kant's vision of the heroic individual was in turn developed by his nineteenth-century successors into a comprehensive vision of history as a story of humanity's self-development, towards a social existence rationally organised with 'will and consciousness'. Again, there is a parallel with cinema in the manner in which film involves not only photographic realism but also the construction of a dramatic illusion, an ideal image 'ordered by the film-maker's will and imagination'. As a constructed reality, film is able to portray the world from the point of view of its protagonists, as a narrative oriented around their development, informed by their subjectivity. To that extent, they are not victims of their nature or circumstances. Even in the face of a hostile world, even if they are entirely alone and without support, they are able to make a stand. Films to be discussed in relation to Kant and his successors include a number of westerns and science fiction films: *High Noon, 3:10 to Yuma, The Searchers, No Country for Old Men, Rise of the Planet of the Apes, Blade Runner, Blade Runner 2049, Ex Machina, Fahrenheit 45* and *Alphaville*.

In Chapter Five, we will turn to ethics as it appears in two other nineteenth-century thinkers, Nietzsche and Kierkegaard, and their successors the twentieth-century existentialists, Sartre and de Beauvoir. In existentialist ethics, even more emphatically than with Kant, the focus is on the individual subject and ethical values are understood to be freely created by this subject. For Nietzsche, the creation of values is the task of the 'supermen', the strong few. For the existentialists what is required of all individuals is that they be 'authentic', that they acknowledge their freedom and responsibility for themselves. Existentialist philosophy seeks to emphasise human subjectivity and freedom in the face of forms of thinking that deny subjectivity and view human beings as mere objects. Beyond the narrative and the image, the constructed and the photographic, a relevant aspect of film here is its capacity to evoke subjective experience, a personal point of view. Films make it possible for the viewer to experience a character's world, the subjective experience that eludes scientific or objective ways of understanding life. Existentialism stands against quantifying, impersonal accounts that objectify human beings and eliminate any trace of subjectivity. In this respect, film is not only able to portray existentialist themes, but also, like other art-forms such as literature and plays that were often employed by the existentialists themselves, can play a direct role in the existentialist effort to preserve the subjective in the face of objective thinking. Films to be considered here include Nietzschean epics and films of existential anxiety: *Baby Face, Rope, Fight Club, The Matrix, The Seventh Seal* and *The Truman Show*, amongst others.

In Chapter Six, we turn to what can be termed the ethics of the other, a loose term to cover various ethical approaches that emerged for the most part in the twentieth century. These include Gilligan's feminist ethics of care, Levinas's ethics of the other, and, it is going to be suggested, Foucault's ethics. In general, the ethics of the other means turning away from the modern focus on the subject, Kant's heroic individual and the subjectivity of existentialism. This is not, however, a turn to an ethics based on a transcendental God, or a scientific view of nature and human nature, but rather, to one based on the other person that the self encounters in ordinary experience. Instead of the existentialist concern with having the right relation with oneself, personal authenticity, the focus is now on having a proper relationship with the other. The problem remains objectification, but this is now the objectification of the other at the hands of the self. For this ethics of the other, rather than objectifying the other, reducing them to an instrument for one's own interests, or absorbing them into the existing categories of one's thinking, one needs to acknowledge them in their otherness, care for or take responsibility for them.

As we have seen, film's capacity to evoke personal, subjective experience plays a role in its portrayal of existentialist ethics. Of particular relevance for exploring this ethics of the other cinematically is film's capacity to evoke non-subjective experience, to 'open up a sense of otherness in a broad sense, bringing us into sometimes intimate contact with realities we could not otherwise conceive' (Richardson 2010, x). This is Kael's idea of film as 'the opening into other, forbidden or surprising kinds of experience'. In a fundamental sense, this is experience itself, experience as the 'limit-transcending, challenging event', that conflicts with and disrupts our familiar ways of viewing the world. This sort of experience can be distinguished from experience in the more mundane sense of the 'long term, background experience that we share with our culture and our time', the historically dominant manner of viewing the world (see O'Leary 2009, 6–7). Film can certainly present us with the experience of a familiar world that embodies and confirms all our preconceptions; but it can also bring us face to face with this other kind of experience, the singular, dangerous experience that confronts and challenges our thinking, and raises the question of how one ought to respond to it. Films to be considered in this connection include a number of war movies, some more science fiction films and a ski movie: *Schindler's List, Casablanca, The Third Man, Aliens, Children of Men, Being John Malkovich* and *Force Majeure*.

So much for the preview of coming attractions. We can now move on to the feature presentation, the exploration of the history of ethical thinking with the help of film. One final word of warning. In the upcoming discussion of the films, there will not be any 'spoiler alerts'. Main plot twists and endings are going to be discussed throughout the text. With that in mind, let's start with the exploration of ancient ethics.

1   Excess and Obsession
Ancient Ethics

In Jonathon Glazer's 2013 *Under the Skin*, a remarkable and rather disturbing scene unfolds in a quiet, understated way. On a beach, a woman watches a swimmer emerge from the ocean and walk towards her. The two of them are alone except for a family further down the beach. The family's dog is swimming in the rough surf. Suddenly there is the sound of screaming. The dog is in trouble. A woman is in the water, swimming out, trying to rescue the dog. Now she is also in trouble. Her husband dives in after her, their baby left on the beach. The swimmer runs back into the ocean to rescue the husband, who once brought back to the beach immediately breaks free and goes back into the water to try to save his wife. The woman with whom the scene began has a different reaction. She watches the tragedy unfold impassively, with complete indifference. Then she walks down to the swimmer, who has returned to the beach and is lying exhausted on the sand. She picks up a rock and strikes him with it, and then drags him off the beach, leaving the crying baby to its fate, which is very likely death from exposure.

The film's premise is that the woman, played by Scarlett Johansson, is in reality an alien in a woman's skin, here to hunt humans, men in particular (Figure 1.1). The alien predator amongst us is the basis for any number of films. But what is interesting about *Under the Skin* is that it seems to depict a genuinely alien perspective on the human world. And what characterises the alienness of this perspective is that it is one of absolute amorality, portraying how things might look if one had no moral concerns at all. The drowning family is of no concern. The swimmer who heroically tried to rescue them is no more than a convenient source of food. The baby is a mere detail in the background and can be left to die. It may be that such amorality is so foreign to ordinary ways of thinking that it is only really intelligible from the perspective of an alien. But we can turn this around, look on ourselves as the alien beings for a moment, and ask why it is that these beings should view things in moral terms. What's in it for us? Why should we 'do the right thing' rather than just what happens to be in our interests?

Figure 1.1 The alien on the prowl in *Under the Skin* (Jonathon Glazer, 2013. Credit: A24/ Photofest).

Why Be Moral?

'Why be moral?' is perhaps the ultimate metaethical question. Philosophical thinking about ethics is typically divided into two areas. Normative ethics is concerned with producing theories about what we ought, morally speaking, to do, theories that allow us to make substantive moral judgements. Metaethical reflection asks general questions about the nature of the moral judgements we make and perhaps the biggest metaethical question is why be moral at all? What reasons are there for me personally to be moral, even when it does not appear to be in my individual interest to do the right thing? And why should people in general be moral, i.e., why should a society adopt the institution of morality?

In the first instance, it might be thought that we are only moral beings because if we do not do the right thing, we will be found out and punished. But suppose we could do whatever we wanted and be sure of getting away with it? What reasons could we have then for being moral? This is a question that was posed very early in the history of philosophy by the Ancient Greek philosopher Plato (c.428–347 BCE), in one of his dialogues, *The Republic*. And he posed the question through a story, the story of the ring of Gyges, about a shepherd who discovers a ring that enables him to become invisible. With this power, he is able to seduce the queen, plot with her to kill the king and take over the kingdom, becoming wealthy and powerful in the process. He can do all of this without fear of detection or punishment. So he is in a position to pursue and satisfy all his desires, regardless of moral constraints, and he does very well indeed out of it. This raises the question – what reason could Gyges possibly have for not doing what benefits him, doing what is in his interests? Why should he bother, under these circumstances, to do the right thing? As Plato phrases it, why would anyone bother to remain within the boundaries of moral behaviour 'when he is able to take whatever he wants from the market-stalls without fear of being discovered, to enter houses and sleep with whomever he chooses, to kill and release from prison anyone he wants, and generally to act like a god among men' (Plato 1993, 260c; using the standardised pagination for works by Plato)?

The tale of Gyges continues to resonate 2000 years later, although the media available for storytelling has changed somewhat in the meantime. Fast forward to the present, and we have a story that would make a reasonable plot for a film, and that film could be taken to raise similar questions about why one should bother to act morally. In contemporary cinematic stories, it is likely to be scientists rather than shepherds who discover the secret of invisibility, but this does not stop events taking a familiar path. Whatever noble aspirations the scientists might have had at the beginning, once they have this power their aspirations typically give way to various sorts of wickedness as soon as they realise how much they can get away with. Films with this theme range from the classic *The Invisible Man* (Jack Griffin, 1933), where the chemist (Claude Rains) who has discovered the invisibility formula resolves to dominate the world through a reign of terror, to the more recent remake, *Hollow Man* (Paul Verhoeven, 2000), where the wickedness that ensues, including voyeurism and murder, is presented in meticulous detail.

You might want to take an optimistic view of these scenarios, highlighting various mitigating circumstances. Perhaps the scientist behaves badly because the process that makes them invisible also drives them crazy, as in the original *Invisible Man* film. Or perhaps they were simply bad people to begin with, as in the later version where the main character, Sebastian Caine (Kevin Bacon), is shown to have questionable traits like overweening arrogance long before the invisibility process that turns him into a monster. Given this, perhaps the bad behaviour of the character who discovers invisibility is not a reflection of human nature as such, but only the nature of the particular individual involved or as a result of the invisibility process. This also seems to be the case with the ring of invisibility that features in Peter Jackson's *The Lord of the Rings* (2001–2003) and *The Hobbit* (2012–2014) films. In these sagas, based on the J.R.R. Tolkien novels, we do not simply have a magical ring that confers invisibility, as in the Gyges story, but one that exerts an evil force that corrupts the wearer. Here once again we can blame any bad behaviour on the invisibility process.

But even if we were to accept this, there are other kinds of invisibility where these considerations don't arise, and yet the question of why one should bother to be moral remains. Why do the right thing, for example, if you found that your day was mysteriously repeating over and over, with the actions of the previous day erased each time, so that only you remembered them, meaning that you could do whatever you liked without any real consequences? This is the predicament that weatherman Phil (Bill Murray) finds himself in *Groundhog Day* (Harold Ramis, 1993). Although the character is certainly grumpy and cynical, he is not an especially bad person, even when he has the opportunity to be so. Nonetheless, under those circumstances, the question inevitably arises – why not be as gluttonous, lecherous or villainous as you like? Phil's first response to his situation is very much like that of a modern-day Gyges. He proclaims: 'I'm not going to live by their rules any more', meaning the rules of ordinary, well-behaved citizens, and sets out on a night of mayhem.

If *Groundhog Day* relies on a fantasy device to achieve its state of figurative invisibility, there are more down-to-earth forms one can consider. What if, like the perfidious eye doctor in Woody Allen's *Crimes and Misdemeanors* (1989), you have the wealth and social standing to cover up any crimes you might commit, including adultery, fraud, even murder? Or if, in the criminal world, you have the kind of power that allows you to act with complete impunity, doing whatever you like without having to worry about public scrutiny or legal prosecution, like the gangsters Tony Montana in *Scarface* (Brian de Palma, 1983) or Henry Hill in *Goodfellas* (Martin Scorsese, 1990). Or suppose you have the kind of financial clout that allows you to do much the same in the business world, like the businessmen Gordon Gekko in *Wall Street* (Oliver Stone, 1987) or the Jordan Belfort character in *The Wolf of Wall Street* (Martin Scorsese, 2013). These characters all raise the question of the moment. Why abide by moral constraints if you have nothing to lose by doing whatever is in your immediate interests? Why not take the opportunity to fulfil every wish, no matter how extreme?

If these are all Gyges-like scenarios that have been portrayed and explored in various films, it is worth adding that film itself might be seen as offering the prospect of unlimited wish-fulfilment for the moviegoer, the satisfaction of any desire without danger to oneself. Every movie is a virtual world, a hypothetical situation in which anything that one desires can potentially be realised, at least in visual terms. Any scenario is possible, and more importantly, can be safely enjoyed by the film-goer, watching invisibly in the dark. Those in the movie audience, it turns out, are the original invisible men and women. Naturally, the representative power of cinema being what it is, the idea of film as an avenue for wish-fulfilment for the viewer has itself been represented in film, as early as *Sherlock Jr* (Buster Keaton, 1924). In the film, Keaton, a lowly film projectionist and hopeless would-be amateur detective, falls asleep and dreams of entering the film he has been projecting. Here, he becomes Sherlock Jr, the greatest detective in the world.

Having said that, it is not clear that we always wish for the unlimited satisfaction of our desires, the absence of any moral constraints; or indeed that we look to films only to gratify our desires, wishes and fantasies. The prospect of there being no moral constraints, no consequences for transgression, might in fact be a profoundly disturbing prospect. We might desperately wish for there to be a moral universe, like the rabbi, Ben (Sam Waterston), in *Crimes and Misdemeanours*, who insists that without some kind of moral order that acts of wickedness violate, the world would be a dark, meaningless and terrifying place. A moral universe can certainly be portrayed within film, a world where good prospers, and even if it experiences some reverses along the way, will ultimately prevail over evil; and where those who do wrong, even if they fail to see the light and join the side of good by the last act, are at least going to be found out and punished by the end. There are many films in which an essentially moral world is reassuringly confirmed in these ways. Indeed, this is pretty much the standard Hollywood scenario. And there is clearly an appetite for such films, even if part of their appeal might be the pleasure of seeing the bad guys violating all moral norms and standards, indulging in all the forbidden appetites, before being inevitably and properly called to account for their transgressions.

We know however that in real life things don't always work out this way, that good does not always prevail and that the bad guys don't always get their comeuppance. Indeed, like Gyges, they often do very well. And there are plenty of 'realistic' films that serve to remind us precisely of this. In so doing, they raise with renewed force the question of why one should be moral. One of the pleasures of *Crimes and Misdemeanors* is that it is quite conscious of its distance from the Hollywood moral universe. The main character, the ophthalmologist Judah Rosenthal (Martin Landau), contrives after some agonising to have his mistress killed when she threatens to expose their affair and ruin his comfortable life; and in the end he gets away with it, even prospers by it. It's a stark repudiation of the conventional Hollywood story and the film itself comments on this. At the end of the film, the murderous eye doctor meets the director, playing a failed filmmaker, at a wedding, and recounts his story in the guise of a possible film plot. Allen's character replies that it would be a better story if the murderer was wracked with guilt and driven to give himself up. The doctor's reply is that this is what happens in the movies, not in real life: 'If you want a happy ending, you should go see a Hollywood movie'. The film's ending is astonishingly bleak, and if on one level it might be regarded as offering a gloomy, pessimistic view of human nature, it might just as easily be seen as presenting a realistic one, stripped of all comforting illusions.

A similarly pessimistic, or realistic, vision is evident in Roman Polanski's neo-noir *Chinatown* (1974), which revives forties film noir themes but gives them a darker twist. In classic film noir like John Huston's *The Maltese Falcon* (1941), society might be corrupt and evil, and the private investigator who brings it to light may themselves be flawed, but in the end, they usually manage to bring about some degree of justice. In *Chinatown*, there is no triumph of any sort. When LA private eye Jake Gittes (Jack Nicholson) stumbles on a network of graft, murder and incest, presided over by evil businessman Noah Cross (played by John Huston, no less), neither he nor the police have the power to do anything about it. Worse, Gittes himself ends up causing the death of the woman he is trying to protect from Cross's predations and Cross escapes any punishment. In a similar way, the classic western undergoes a reality check in *No Country for Old Men* (Joel and Ethan Coen, 2007). The decent western hero who fights for what is right, and who traditionally triumphs over evil through perseverance and resourcefulness, appears here in the figure of sheriff Ed Bell (Tommy Lee Jones). However, Bell finds himself 'over-matched' by the new, brutal forms of drug-related crime he is confronting. He is unable to protect 'his people', cowboy-adventurer Lewellyn Moss (Josh Brolin) or his wife Carla Jean (Kelly Macdonald), from retribution, after Moss happens upon a large amount of money from a drug deal gone wrong. And he is unable to bring to justice the chief agent of that retribution, the terrifying hitman Anton Chigurh (Javier Bardem). In the end, all sheriff Bell can do is escape into retirement from an evil that he cannot defeat.

As a final variation on this theme, David Lynch's *Blue Velvet* (1989) simultaneously foregrounds a standard Hollywood story of good triumphing over evil and subverts it. On the face of it, the film is a conventional story of evil being properly punished, as clean-cut hero Jeffrey (Kyle McLachlan) manages in the end to defeat sadistic gangster Frank Booth (Dennis Hopper). But the hero finds he has affinities with the evil Frank, being similarly drawn to nightclub singer Dorothy Vallens (Isabella Rossellini) who represents the prospect of illicit, perverse sex. Moreover, the 'good world' that Jeffrey leaves and to which he eventually returns, represented in the picture-perfect images of the town with which the film begins and ends, is shown to be an impossible idealisation, a comforting veneer that hides a much darker reality that is always just below the surface. Under the manicured lawns, there are hideous insects. If we are going to be realistic, we need to acknowledge that wrongdoing is not always found out and punished, that people can and do get away with evil, and often do very well out of it. So, is it true that the only reason people adhere to moral standards is because of fear of being caught and punished otherwise? Or can we give a better answer to the question of why we should be moral?

One response might be that even if we can avoid external scrutiny and punishment, we will suffer punishment at our own hands for evil deeds, through guilt and remorse. On this view it is our conscience that keeps us behaving ethically. We have an internal moral sense, whether this is something inbuilt or inculcated in us through our upbringing. However, even if conscience is a psychological reality, it is certainly possible to imagine it absent. Lack of conscience, the absence of any moral constraints on one's actions and a willingness to do whatever furthers one's interests, is the familiar mark of the movie psychopath. But it might also be argued that despite the prevalence of such figures in film, this conscience-less, amoral kind of outlook is in reality relatively rare in individuals. It is a strange way of being, marking the conscienceless individual as 'other', not like the ordinary human being, and more appropriately embodied as the mysterious viewpoint of an alien, as in *Under the Skin*. It is an outlook, however, that might be more prevalent at the institutional level. The documentary *The Corporation* (Mark Achbar, Jennifer Abbott, 2003) makes the case that were the modern corporation a legal person, an actual person, the kind of person it would typically be is one that is utterly self-interested, deceitful, callous, without guilt, willing to break social rules for its own ends – in short, a psychopath. The amoral corporation is itself a familiar character in films, from *Alien* (Ridley Scott, 1979) to *Robocop* (Paul Verhoeven, 1987). But typically in these films, the corporation is pitted against human characters that we can identify with. Those characters who act in its name have sold their souls and ceased to be human. In the case of *Alien* this is quite literally so, since the 'company man', the villainous Ash (Ian Holm), turns out to be an android.

At the same time, there is perhaps something a little convenient about this relegation of evil to the alien psychopath or the inhuman corporation. The very notion of 'evil', as immoral behaviour that seems so bad that it can only come

from some conscienceless other, may be a convenient way of distancing ourselves from actions that after all are in the last analysis committed by human
beings like us (see Morton 2004, 4–5, 93–94). It is far more disturbing to think
that terrible things might be done by people we can relate to, people who are
not monsters or sadists but to all intents and purposes ordinary individuals. The
controversy over twentieth-century philosopher Hannah Arendt's notion of the
'banality of evil' was precisely of this nature. Arendt introduced the notion in
her book *Eichmann in Jerusalem*, based on her coverage of ex-Nazi Eichmann's
1961 trial in Jerusalem. The controversy was over the idea that a participant in the
Holocaust, a mid-level administrator responsible for organising transportation of
Jews to Nazi death camps, might not be crazy, or a monster, but a normal person,
indeed a nobody, a mediocrity. Margarethe von Trotta's *Hannah Arendt* (2012)
depicts Arendt (played by Barbara Sukowa) covering the Eichmann trial and the
subsequent furore over her book. In it, she is presented defending her position
in a climactic public lecture: 'I wrote no defense of Eichmann, but I did try to
reconcile the shocking mediocrity of the man with his staggering deeds. Trying to
understand him is not the same thing as forgiveness'.

It might be imagined that one's conscience would stop them from participating
in such horrors. It is easy to think that there is some kind of moral instinct in us
that would have compelled us to do the right thing, had we been German citizens
during the Nazi period. Arendt herself reports that Eichmann had the opportunity
to see the death camps in operation and was repelled by them, but soon after
began his duties administering transportation. He had a conscience, she suggests,
but it 'functioned in the expected way for about four weeks, whereupon it began
to function the other way around' (Arendt 2006, 95). For Arendt, this turnaround
is the real root of Eichmann's evil. It amounts to him ceasing to think for himself
or to see the world beyond the dictates of Nazi policy. In so doing, he ceased to
see things from the standpoint of other people and to adopt a moral understanding of what he had done to them. Giving himself to the movement, his guiding
principles became efficiency and obedience in the name of the great cause. One's
conscience can no doubt always be recalibrated in this way, so that one overcomes
one's ordinary repugnance to crime in order to perform what one understands to
be an important task requiring great courage.

Moreover, even those whose consciences function in the 'expected way' may
be less constrained by it than they imagine. This is what the eye doctor Judah
discovers in *Crimes and Misdemeanors*. Recounting his supposed movie plot to
Cliff at the end of the film, he indicates that while he suffered terrible guilt at first
over what he had done, to the point where he was on the verge of confessing to
the police, that guilt gradually diminished over time; and though he occasionally
has a bad moment, he has learned to live with what he has done. After all, as he
points out, people learn to live with all sorts of terrible sins. And apart from all
this, even if conscience does work as expected to prod us and keep us more or
less on the straight and narrow, we might still want to know why we should obey
our consciences, what reasons we might have for doing so. We need to look more
closely at the issue.

Plato's Moral Theory

This brings us back to Plato, who presents the original invisibility story, the story of Gyges. The rest of the *Republic* is, in effect, Plato's answer to the question the story poses, of why we should be moral even if we can get away with being immoral. In this, Plato wants to reject the view of morality and of human nature that the story implies: that the only reason to abide by moral standards is to avoid being caught and punished for transgressing them. Along with that, he rejects the idea that we are essentially creatures driven by our desires, with morality being merely an external constraint that limits their satisfaction. Plato acknowledges that human beings have desires, but he does not think we are just creatures of desire. He thinks that there are in fact different parts to our makeup. He points out that we often experience mental conflicts and argues that these conflicts reflect this internal complexity. Someone who is thirsty but knows the water is poisoned both wants to drink the water and stops themselves from drinking, which suggests to Plato that one part of the person just wants to drink, but another, different part is more wisely and sensibly commanding them not to drink (see Plato 1993, 435c–441c). Move forward now to David Fincher's *Fight Club* (1999), and we see such internal compartmentalisation in dramatically exaggerated form. The film's unnamed narrator (Edward Norton), with a responsible job and a well-furnished apartment, finds that a side of his personality at odds with his ordinary, responsible self, has taken on a life of its own. He finds himself confronted by his alter-ego, the anarchic and dangerous Tyler Durden (Brad Pitt), for whom jobs and apartments are merely shackles to be thrown off at the earliest opportunity. If Durden ultimately turns out to be a delusion on the narrator's part, this only underscores that the split is really internal, between different parts of his personality.

The move from experiencing internal conflicts to imagining that there are literally different parts operating within ourselves is clearly not a large one. On the basis of such conflicts, Plato argues that the self, or soul (a term that is without religious overtones for Plato) has three distinct parts: a rational part, a desiring element and a spirited part. Reason is the part of the soul that knows reality, calculates and makes decisions. Its proper role is to rule the desiring part. Desire is the irrational, appetitive part of the soul, made up of instinctive cravings and urges. It includes all the physical desires, such as hunger, thirst and sexual desire, as well as the desire for money. Properly speaking, it should be regulated by reason. To this, Plato adds a spirited part, which is manifested in feelings of self-disgust, shame, courage, indignation and strength of will. The spirited part's role is to provide reason with the force it needs to govern desire. This picture provides the basis for Plato's view of morality. Being moral for Plato is not just a matter of submitting to external constraints that stop you pursuing what is in your self-interest. It certainly involves controlling and regulating your immediate desires, but by themselves, these desires cannot be trusted to pursue what is in your interests. You may want to do all sorts of things that you know, rationally, are bad for you, like drinking the water you know to be poisonous. The rational part looks at the overall picture, at what is good for the self as a whole and for each part. So, if I am really self-interested, I must be ruled by the rational part; I must have a properly balanced soul, and, for Plato, having this inner balance is what it is to be moral.

What this means is that for Plato, being moral, instead of being opposed to self-interest, is in fact very much in the interests of the self. It means having a well-ordered soul, in which each part plays its proper role in the whole. The proper role of the rational part is to govern the other parts of the soul; the spirited part's role is to provide reason with the force it needs to govern; and the appetitive part should be controlled and regulated by reason. Moral goodness thus amounts to a kind of mental health or well-being, which is clearly beneficial for its possessor. It is also an enjoyable state to be in, and so Plato can argue that the moral life is a happy one. With this picture of the moral human being, Plato introduces an influential conception of human nature, the idea of human existence as essentially a struggle between reason and desire, a struggle that reason ought to win. For Plato and many who come after him, reason is the 'higher' part of the human being and desires are the primitive, irrational and chaotic 'lower' part. In these accounts, we are typically identified most closely with our higher, rational part. While desires are still seen as part of us, they are often seen as less central, to an extent alien to us, an unfortunate accompaniment that is perhaps part of our animal heritage, and certainly needing to be kept in check by the rational self. If the desiring side of our makeup were allowed to have its way, our inner balance would be overthrown. We would be enslaved to our appetites and passions, which without any constraint would become tyrannical.

We can see more clearly how having such an inner balance amounts to being a morally good person insofar as Plato relates this harmony to our having recognisable virtues, morally admirable character traits. In the well-ordered state, we would have the virtues of justice, courage, temperance and wisdom, which are the central elements of Platonic morality. We would be wise because the ruling element possesses knowledge of what is good for each part and for the whole; temperate, or self-controlled, because desire and pleasure are tempered by the rule of reason; and brave because the spirited part allows us to pursue the precepts of reason and to overcome the distractions of pain and pleasure. Finally, we would have the overall virtue of being just, where justice is understood not in the modern sense of having equality of opportunity or outcome, but in terms of something's being well-balanced, each part playing its proper role in the whole. So understood, being just for Plato is synonymous with being moral. Being moral in this way, with the proper balance of reason, desire and courage, is also a prerequisite for playing one's proper role in society (443d-e). And having the proper balance of parts, with each part playing its proper role, also characterises the just or good society, the republic that gives Plato's dialogue its title. The tripartite self becomes a microcosm of the tripartite society, whose corresponding parts are the ruling class, the workers and the soldiers. The just society is the one in which each social group plays its proper role: that of the workers being to serve the rulers, the rulers to control the workers and the soldiers to do the bidding of the rulers and enforce their rule. Once again, justice has nothing to do with equality. It amounts to a morality that consists in playing your proper part in the whole.

Returning to the individual case, the relation between inner balance and morality is also illuminated when we consider the alternative, when we fail to have this inner balance. Corresponding to the virtues are various vices, such as foolishness, cowardice and self-indulgence, all of which are reflections of disharmony in the soul, of injustice. As is often the case with this reason-centred sort of picture, immorality is seen to arise above all if one's desires and appetites escape the control of reason. If your desires are not under the control of your reason, if you lack self-control, you won't be able to pursue your true interests. You won't be able to do what is good for you overall, but instead will be subject to the psychological tyranny of your desires, which will grow out of all proportion. You will be the victim of your appetites, desiring ever more in the way of food, drink, material goods, wealth and so on, falling prey to all manner of addictions and obsessions. Others will suffer as well, since you will be driven to satisfy yourself at their expense, for example, by seeking the unlimited sexual pleasure that can only be had through force or deception. Given that morality amounts to a kind of mental health or well-being, the immoral person is unbalanced, mentally disordered, and the thoroughly immoral person is on the verge of being insane.

This is an influential conception of evil, or at least, morally bad behaviour. Being self-indulgent, ruled by one's appetites and blind to the needs of others, is certainly a conventional way of thinking about what being a bad person involves. The bad children in *Willy Wonka and the Chocolate Factory* (Mel Stuart, 1971) are bad in precisely this way: Augustus and Veruca are greedy and demanding, Violet and Mike are addicted to the point of obsession with chewing gum and television. They have not improved in the Tim Burton remake, *Charlie and the Chocolate Factory* (2005). Mike is now obsessed with video games. Of course, they are only children, not yet being fully developed adults, and so have the excuse of not yet being mature. A crucial part of this development is learning to govern one's desires, in the way that Charlie (Peter Ostrum, and in the remake, Freddie Highmore), the one 'good' and also most grown-up child does. At the same time, in their subjection to their appetites, these little monsters have something in common with the classic movie monsters of early cinema, the monsters that seem to personify unleashed desire beyond the control of reason. A defining mark of the monster is that it is utterly self-seeking, wholly concerned with satisfying its appetites. There is the wicked Mr Hyde of Jekyll and Hyde fame, the werewolf, the classic vampire, all grotesque figures that have been literally deformed by the appetites that consume them. The cinematic vampire in particular provides an enduring image of a creature completely given over to its desires, although as we will see, there have also been some interesting variations on the theme, including the vampire who strives to manage and control their blood lust and to be good.

These movie monsters are inhuman, and generally speaking have to be hunted down and destroyed. As always, it is convenient to ascribe wicked acts to something that is 'other', not like us. Yet they are not entirely alien to us. They all relate in some way to the human psyche, or at least a certain understanding of it. In particular, the monster can be taken to represent the dangerous desires within us that strive to escape our control and which we must struggle to keep in check if we are not to find ourselves being taken over by them. Even the vampire, perhaps the most alien of these figures, provides a metaphor for human addiction, for being entirely given over to one's appetites. In the case of the more complex and reflective vampire who struggles to control their urges, there is an image of the human struggle to master desire. These monsters may also be explicitly linked to the human to the extent that they emerge out of us or take us over. Struggling to prevent their emergence, or being taken over by them, once again dramatises the Platonic picture of the individual as engaged in a battle to control their desires and appetites, and of the consequences of losing control. The monster, all appetite, unleashed on the world to commit every kind of mayhem in pursuit of its needs, exemplifies the idea of immoral behaviour as being a matter of unchecked desire.

The Jekyll and Hyde story, popular in the thirties and early forties, but also present in one form or another in a number of more recent films, points very clearly to such a view of the self and of what constitutes immoral behaviour. The two best known classic versions are those of Rouben Mamoulian (1932) and Victor Fleming (1941). Both films open with Dr Jekyll (Fredric March and Spencer Tracy respectively) holding forth on the 'dual nature of man', as composed in Platonic fashion of good and evil parts chained together in the soul, constantly battling one another. In the films, we see the dire consequences when Dr Jekyll invents a potion to separate the two halves of his nature. The intention is to free humans from their 'evil side' so that the good in people will be able to develop unhindered. Instead, it is the evil side that is freed and Jekyll turns into the grotesque, murderous Mr Hyde. In Mamoulian's film (see Figure 1.2), the evil side is explicitly characterised in terms of 'elementary instincts inherited from an animal past'. In both films, it is identified with desire and appetites, particularly those of a sexual nature. It manifests itself in Dr Jekyll in the desires he struggles to repress when, though engaged to be married to a 'good woman' (Rose Hobart and Lana Turner respectively), he meets a 'bad' one, Ivy Pierson (Miriam Hopkins and Ingrid Bergman).

Fleming's 1941 version of the story is itself more 'repressed' than the earlier 1932 film, more toned down in its sexual content. This no doubt reflects the arrival in Hollywood of the Hays Code, the set of industry moral guidelines designed to rehabilitate the industry's image, which was enforced after 1934. Ivy Pierson, a prostitute in Mamoulian's version, becomes a barmaid in Fleming's remake, with the implication of prostitution being omitted. Ivy's flirtation with Jekyll is more overtly sexual in the earlier film than in the later one. Nonetheless, the 1941 film still manages to smuggle in some surprisingly frank sexual imagery, particularly in the Tracy Jekyll's first transformation scene. One of the images Fleming employs here is that of a horseman and his steeds, an image also used by Plato. Jekyll experiences himself as a charioteer whipping two horses, which dissolve into his fiancée and the barmaid Ivy. But this is not a representation of reason striving to control the other parts of the soul, as it is in Plato. The image has in fact been subverted in the film to become a metaphor for the unleashing of Jekyll's desires for sexual possession and domination. For both films, desire,

Figure 1.2 The 'dual nature of man' in Mamoulian's version of Dr Jekyll and
       Mr Hyde (Rouben Mamoulian, 1931. Credit: Paramount Pictures/
       Photofest).

completely unleashed as it is in the figure of Mr Hyde, is hideous, bestial, the
source of all kinds of wickedness. This follows the lines of the Platonic picture,
for which evil arises when desire escapes from the control of reason.

While these are films from an earlier era, the Jekyll and Hyde scenario has
proved to be remarkably resonant and adaptable. It can be seen for example in
Blue Velvet, where the decent, clean-cut hero Jeffrey, like Dr Jekyll, struggles to
control his lower appetites. Despite being involved with the equally good, clean-
cut Sandy (Laura Dern), he similarly finds himself drawn to the 'bad' woman, in
this case, nightclub singer Dorothy and the prospect of illicit sex. What he is in
danger of becoming, his Mr Hyde, is represented by the sadistic gangster Frank
who is terrorising Dorothy and sexually exploiting her. Like Mr Hyde, the evil
Frank personifies desire unleashed. He is consumed with uncontrollable desire
and aggression. Confronting this monster is enough to make Jeffrey draw back
from the brink and return to the 'good' side. The Jekyll and Hyde theme is also
evident in *Fight Club*, where the straitlaced narrator finds himself confronted by

his alter-ego Tyler Durden. Durden rejects conventional norms of moral behaviour and embodies all the narrator's liberated desires and appetites. It's a case of 'Dr Jackass and Mr Hyde', as the narrator's girlfriend Marla (Helena Bonham Carter) puts it. In this version, she is playing both the good woman and the bad one. As in the original Jekyll and Hyde story, the alter-ego is revealed at the end to have been an aspect of the narrator; although in this case, it also turns out to be a surprise to the narrator himself, as well as to the audience.

In all of these stories there is a frank acknowledgement by the characters of the attractiveness of their life of liberated desires, at least initially: the intoxicating pleasure Jekyll feels in becoming Hyde, the thrill of illicit sexual activity that Jeffrey experiences in *Blue Velvet* and the exhilarating liberation the narrator experiences in adopting Durden's anarchic lifestyle in *Fight Club*. However, this initial attractiveness quickly turns into the miseries of addiction. In each case, the hero becomes increasingly subordinated to their unleashed desires, which become ever more demanding and tyrannical. Jekyll becomes increasingly subject to the ever more uncontrollable Hyde. In *Blue Velvet*, Jeffrey not only has to wrestle with the dark desires within himself, but also has to deal with the terrifying Frank, the image of what Jeffrey is in danger of becoming if he stays on this path, someone entirely given over to their desires and impulses. The troubled Frank seems the very embodiment of addiction as he sucks on the bottles of mysterious gas that he carries with him. In *Fight Club*, the narrator's alter-ego Durden becomes increasingly oppressive towards those around him, and eventually sets about terrorising the narrator himself. In the slavery to desire, and lack of inner peace, that these films dramatise, Plato's idea of immoral behaviour as psychologically costly for the individual is clearly illustrated.

Plato puts a good deal of weight on the psychological costs of immorality, understood in terms of having an unbalanced personality, in making his case for it being very much in our interest to be moral. Outside of the extreme scenarios of internal imbalance dramatised in the monster movie and its variants, where the costs are clearly apparent, we might also expect them to be evident in the post-seventies 'cinema of excess', with its lurid portrayals of materialist excess, greed and conspicuous consumption. Many of these films feature gangsters or businessmen who through their power or financial clout are able to act with complete impunity and satisfy all desires without consequences or repercussions from the authorities. A number of these films of excess have been mentioned already. They include Brian de Palma's remake of *Scarface*, as well as Martin Scorsese's *Goodfellas* and *Wolf of Wall Street*.

In de Palma's gleefully over-the-top *Scarface*, Tony Montana (Al Pacino) is an escapee from communist Cuba who decides on a life of crime, becoming a successful drug dealer and making it big in eighties Miami. Part gangster and part businessman, he is able through his criminal activities to indulge all his appetites, which, like the film itself, become ever more extravagant and excessive: endless cars, a garishly luxurious mansion, a spectacular bathtub and mountains of cocaine. He is unhindered by moral considerations and does very well out of it. Yet there are undoubtedly costs to all this. He does not 'get away with it'. *Scarface* remains a cautionary tale, if a little operatic in the telling. Eventually,

Montana's criminal lifestyle catches up with him and he is killed in a shoot-out after the Colombian drug cartel he has fallen out with invades his mansion. Along the way, through his obsession with money and possessions, he alienates his family and friends, ending up isolated and alone. More importantly, in a reassuring confirmation of Plato's predictions, there is internal disquiet as well. When his friend Manny tells him he should be happy with what he has, he says he 'wants what's coming to me ... the world and everything in it'. He simply cannot be content with what he has; he constantly wants more, but the more he has, the more paranoid and distrustful he becomes, the more anxious that what he has is going to be taken from him. And no matter how much his desires are satisfied, he cannot find satisfaction or fulfilment. In the restaurant scene towards the end of the film, Tony, in a rare reflective moment, wonders glumly whether there is any point to his life of endless eating and drinking, sex and drugs.

In Platonic terms, the root cause of Tony Montana's unhappiness is spiritual imbalance, his unchecked desires ruling over the other parts of his soul. It is useful to compare him with the Henry Hill character (played by Ray Liotta) in *Goodfellas*. This is Martin Scorsese's quasi-documentary-style film of mafia informant Hill, based on the latter's memoir. In the film, Hill, who as far back as he can remember 'always wanted to be a gangster', rises in the ranks of the mob to enjoy all that the gangster lifestyle has to offer. Along with his new girlfriend Karen (Lorraine Bracco), we experience the exhilaration and seductiveness of this life. In the bravura shot of the couple making their way into the Copacabana nightclub, the money, power and privilege that he enjoys is on full display. Like Montana, Hill ends up with the cars, the lavish house and endless drugs. However, the tale is less cautionary than *Scarface* in the sense that Hill manages to get away with it at the end of the film. At least, he avoids being killed by his criminal compatriots, by informing on them and going into a witness protection program. And moreover, he is not fundamentally unhappy during his life as a gangster. On the contrary, he fully embraces its privileges and pleasures. What makes him most unhappy is his new situation, which means that he can no longer enjoy the unlimited pleasures of the gangster life where 'everything I wanted was a phone call away', and now has to 'wait in line like everyone else'.

In a similar vein, and also based on the memoirs of a real-life figure, Scorsese's later film *Wolf of Wall Street* presents the story of nineties businessman Jordan Belfort (played by Leonardo DiCaprio), who founds his own stockbroking firm and makes a fortune defrauding investors out of millions. Out of this, Belfort and his employees are able to enjoy a lifestyle of staggering excess, with seemingly boundless money, sex and drugs to keep them going. At the same time, as with *Goodfellas*, there seems to be little psychological cost to all this excess for the protagonist. In the end, the FBI catches up with him and closes down his operation, but he agrees to inform on colleagues to buy a lighter sentence; and after his release, we see him running seminars on sales techniques to transfixed audiences. Certainly, in pursuing his hedonistic lifestyle he destroys his relationship with his wife and family. However, he does not seem to experience any inner conflict or dissatisfaction. Indeed, much of the film's comedy comes from the way he so wholeheartedly embraces his lifestyle of consumption. At worst, the relentless pleasure-seeking is shown to be physically draining, as the film attests with its close-ups of bloodshot eyes and drooling faces. The lack of any fundamental dissatisfaction or unhappiness in the protagonists of these two Scorsese films as compared with a film like *Scarface* perhaps mark them out as representative of a new kind of 'cinema of excess' (see Black, 2014).

The two Scorsese films themselves do not make any explicit judgement on the actions of their main characters, being content simply to show what they do, although this is by no means equivalent to an endorsement. Nonetheless, what also seems evident is that the protagonists in both *Goodfellas* and *Wolf of Wall Street* have no obvious reason to be moral. Indeed, they actively despise those who follow the rules, live ordinary lives, work in traditional jobs and so on; and by refusing to be bound by conventional rules or moral constraints, following only their self-interest, they do very well, for a time at least. Nor, although the law does catch up with them both eventually, do they suffer any particularly terrible punishment in the course of the film. And what in particular seems to be conspicuously absent in both cases is any psychological cost for their behaviour, any internal conflict or enslavement to appetites, in apparent conflict with Plato's claim that the immoral person is inevitably unhappy. Is this a limitation in the portrayal of these characters, a failure of dramatic imagination; or is it in fact a more 'realistic' view of human beings than Plato's?

Certainly from a modern perspective, the idea of a life devoted to the satisfaction of one's appetites and the pursuit of individual self-interest seems more plausible than it would have been for Plato. Plato's thinking as we have seen is steeped in a morality where the ruling idea is that parts play their proper role in the larger whole, the individual in society as well as the parts within the individual. As such, a life dominated by desire and self-interest is likely to appear as akin to madness (see Malik 2014, 31). However, one of the features of modern thinking, since the seventeenth-century philosopher Hobbes at least, has been a down-to-earth view of the human being as primarily a creature of desire, driven fundamentally by egoistic self-interest. From this point of view, the unapologetically self-interested gangster or businessman is really just the natural human being, the human being stripped of all pretence or external trappings, who no longer subscribes to what Hobbes calls the social contract. This is the mutual agreement we make to constrain our individual appetites in order to be able to enjoy the benefits of an organised social life.

We will return to the discussion of the early modern individual and its implications for ethical thinking in Chapter Three. For the moment, it can simply be noted that while the Hobbesian notion of the human being as primarily a creature of desire might seem more down to earth, or realistic, it is also quite crude and reductive. The Platonic picture at least acknowledges a richer picture of human existence, one in which it is possible to experience internal conflict, and one can become enslaved to one's own appetites. These phenomena have themselves been interpreted by Plato in terms of a philosophical notion of what human beings most essentially are, creatures with internally balanced souls. This is a normative conception of human nature in which the good life is understood as the most fully developed human life, where human beings are most fully realised. What then of characters like *Goodfellas'* Henry Hill and *Wolf of Wall Street's* Jordan Belfort? One could argue that they do not constitute a counter-example to Plato's account. Regardless of how they feel, no matter how satisfied they declare themselves with their lives, they might nonetheless still be 'objectively' unhappy, living a less than fully human life. However, this also means that we can no longer support this philosophical conception of human nature by reference to the feelings of individuals themselves.

What remains clear is that for Plato, morality is not an arbitrary ideal. It is bound up with a certain conception of the self, of our nature. Being moral is a matter of living in accordance with our nature. The virtuous human being is the one that is most fulfilled as a human being. At the same time, it can be argued that Plato's ethics is not in the last analysis a morality of self-fulfilment or self-realisation. For Plato, being moral is a reflection of a larger, 'transcendental' order. This is the world of the 'Forms', the timeless, unchanging essences of things that exist in a non-natural realm, beyond the ordinary, shifting world that we experience in everyday life. These include the Forms of the moral virtues, Wisdom, Courage, Temperance and the overarching Form of justice. And these Forms are themselves variations of the ultimate Form of the Good. Individual harmony, the balanced state of the just individual, mirrors the larger harmonious order of the world of Forms. The ultimate basis of morality for Plato, then, is not to be found in human nature but in his conception of ultimate reality, the transcendental world of the Forms.

As such, Plato's moral position can be characterised as an 'objectivist non-naturalism', in which there are objective but otherworldly moral standards or laws. For Plato, there is one universal, objective form of the good life, which the rational part of our soul can discover by coming to know the forms. Reason in his account has two functions, to control the lower parts of the soul and to know the truth about reality, the transcendental forms that ultimately ground moral judgements. Accordingly, discovering the good life is a rational task, like determining the principles of mathematics. Through this knowledge, the rational part knows how to do what is good for the person overall. At times, Plato goes so far as to suggest that you can only be truly virtuous if you have knowledge of the forms (Plato 1993, 517c), though elsewhere he concedes that one could still acquire justice and live the good life by imitating those with knowledge of the good. However, he does acknowledge that knowledge alone is not sufficient for virtuous behaviour. To be virtuous we must not only understand what is good overall for us, but also have mastery over ourselves, so the appetites agree with the guidance provided by the rational part of the soul. We need, that is, to develop virtuous habits, in the sense of making the appetites docile and compliant so that they will obey reason's commands.

Despite these qualifications, some have still found Plato's account too rationalistic, too focused on making ethics a matter of reason and knowledge. Can we know what the right thing to do is, in the way that we can have mathematical or scientific knowledge? Is establishing the right thing to do, or the proper life to lead, anything like gaining knowledge of the world? And is there really only one correct answer to what it is to lead the good life, as Plato seems to imply? Couldn't there be a number of ways in which one can be good? Plato's emphasis on reason might be thought overly rationalistic in another way. His view that reason needs to be firmly in charge means that his notion of inner mental harmony is a repressive, authoritarian one, marked by suspicion and hostility towards desire. For Plato, being moral, living the good life, requires us to firmly control our desires. However, this kind of moral authoritarianism might be thought less a recipe for inner harmony and mental health than itself a source of unbalance and illness. And underlying this is a narrow identification of human beings with their rationality, the desires being marginalised as the primitive, irrational lower part of our makeup. In another dialogue, Plato presents the rational soul as imprisoned by the body, which corrupts it with bodily needs and desires, and stands in the way of its knowing the truth about reality. The philosopher longs for the purification of the soul from the body, which comes only with death. Only as pure mind can we behold the transcendent Forms, things in their purest form. For the soul that is still imprisoned in the body, reason needs to keep desire firmly under control (Plato 2003, 77a–84b). We may wonder however whether this is a particularly healthy conception of human nature, given that it sets us in such stark opposition with ourselves.

From the modern perspective at least, even if we don't want to go so far as to say with Hobbes that human beings are no more than creatures of desire, we are still more inclined to see desires as an important and legitimate part of our makeup. As such, we are more likely to see dangers in excessive repression or self-denial. This is evident in the cinematic representations of the Jekyll and Hyde story. Even if the Mamoulian and Fleming versions demonise desire as belonging to our evil side, an obstacle to being good, and portray the dangers of it getting out of control in the figure of Mr Hyde, the films also betray a modern sensibility in presenting Dr Jekyll as a vigorous, passionate man who is frustrated by the oppressive strictures of Victorian society. It is suggested in both cases that Jekyll is being driven to despair by being forced to endure a long engagement to his fiancé. The reimagining of the story in *Blue Velvet* portrays the indispensability of desire even more forcefully. Its hero Jeffrey manages to put his own perverse desires behind him to overcome his evil side and to kill his alter-ego Frank Booth. On one level it is a happy ending, with good triumphing resoundingly over evil. But as noted earlier, the good, decent world that Jeffrey leaves and eventually returns to, represented in the picture-perfect images of the town at the beginning and end of the film, is, it is being suggested, an unreal idealisation. Just beneath the surface, the film suggests, there remain primal desires and instincts that we cannot disown, that are part of who we are and which we have to learn to deal with.

This is not, however, to advocate the complete liberation of desires from control. The Mr Hyde and Frank Booth characters also embody the idea that desire unconstrained is chaotic, threatening and at odds with sociability. Arguably one cannot be a properly developed human being, able to function in a rule-governed society, without some kind of ordering of desires, some sort of moral self-mastery. Nonetheless, Plato comes across as rather authoritarian in this regard, demanding the strict mastery of desires, and it is easy to imagine that beyond a certain point such self-mastery is going to become harmful and self-destructive. The cost of excessive self-control features in another, even more recent, iteration of the Jekyll and Hyde story, *Black Swan* (Darren Aronofsky, 2010). The film focuses on ballerina Nina Sayers (Natalie Portman), who is obsessed with perfection and maintains a rigorous self-control, at the cost of being profoundly emotionally repressed. As the innocent 'sweet girl', she is ideal for the gentle white swan role in her company's production of Swan Lake, but she is unable to embrace the sensuality needed to play the seductive black swan role that accompanies it. Under the strain of trying to master both roles, she suffers a breakdown and her 'Hyde' element emerges. The sensuality that she so rigorously represses in herself is projected onto another dancer, Lily (Mila Kunis), who figures as her alter-ego in fantasies that Nina is increasingly unable to distinguish from reality. As always, Hyde is eventually overcome, in this case by Nina herself, who kills Lily in the dressing room and goes on to deliver a perfect performance. She seems to have finally appropriated her dark side and channelled it into her performance. But by this stage, we cannot tell whether she really killed her friend or was in reality alone and injured herself, at last able to dance the role but eventually succumbing to the self-inflicted wound.

Just as desire may not simply be a source of evil that requires one to exercise strict control and regulation, rigorous self-control and self-regulation may not necessarily result in someone's being good. Plato may equate being morally good with having a well-ordered self, but there is nothing in self-mastery itself that implies that one has to be morally good. Someone could have a harmonious, balanced self in the Platonic sense of being in control of oneself, but not be morally good. Quite the contrary; it is entirely possible to single-mindedly pursue evil. Indeed, it may be that the greatest crimes involve not unchecked appetite but self-mastery and single-mindedness, and are quite impossible without these things. Here we arrive at what in relation to film is sometimes referred to as the unconventional portrayal of evil. If the classic bad guy is the one who satisfies their own desires without regard for others, often at their expense, and the monster is the creature who has become wholly consumed by their desires and appetites, there is another figure to consider: the monster whose wicked actions are the outcome of the most consummate self-discipline and self-control.

In the gangster genre, and providing a sharp contrast to the desire-driven hedonism of Tony Montana and Henry Hill, the monster of iron self-control finds a representative figure in Michael Corleone (Al Pacino). The main protagonist in *The Godfather* trilogy (Francis Ford Coppola, 1972, 1974, 1990), Michael takes over the family business after an assassination attempt on his father. In the process, Michael is transformed from the war hero who had no interest in the 'family business' at the start of the first *Godfather*, into a cold, calculating, mafia don, far more ruthless than his father, by the end of the second. His transformation is complete when, at the end of *Godfather II*, he has his brother Fredo (John Cazale) killed for a transgression against the family committed years before. He has become a monster, but a monster with the iron self-control not only to have his brother executed, but to pretend to forgive him and involve him in the family's life during the intervening years, all the while waiting for their mother's death in order to act.

This peculiar combination of extreme self-control and diabolical evil provides an added dimension to the movie psychopath, who might otherwise be no more than a nondescript force of nature, a relentless killing machine in the conventional horror/slasher film mould. The combination may be seen in the figure of Hannibal Lecter in *Silence of the Lambs* (Jonathon Demme, 1991). Lecter's murderous cannibal is the epitome of self-control, his absolute self-possession evident, as Yvonne Tasker points out, in the slow, deliberate way he blinks (Tasker 2002, 8). His crimes are controlled and meticulous, without the slightest passion or even, it would appear, any measurable change of heart rate, as indicated by one especially gruesome incident that is mentioned rather than shown. This sets into relief the almost sentimental attachment he forms with FBI agent Clarice Starling (Jodie Foster), who has enlisted his formidable analytical skills to help her catch another serial killer, Buffalo Bill (Ted Levine).

An even more uncompromising representative of self-controlled evil, without any of Lecter's redeeming sentimentality, is the hitman Chigurh in the neo-western *No Country for Old Men*. Chigurh has no interest in money or material things and nor does he exhibit the slightest passion or personal desire. He is terrifying because he embodies almost inhuman self-control, pursuing his murderous mission so relentlessly that he even astounds other contract killers. As one, Woody Harrelson's Carson Wells, puts it: 'You can't make a deal with him. Even if you gave him the money he'd still kill you. He's a peculiar man. You could even say that he has principles. Principles that transcend money or drugs or anything like that. He's not like you. He's not even like me'. As Jeffrey Adams points out, Chigurh is like a lawman dispensing a higher form of justice, single-mindedly upholding his mysterious principles with the dedication and personal integrity usually associated with the western hero (see Adams 2015, 186). He is, in short, that combination of principled self-mastery and absolute evil so difficult to fit into the Platonic account of morality.

A more recognisable Platonic character is the person who behaves badly because they lack self-mastery, whose desires overwhelm them and compel them to act in ways contrary to what they know to be right. This is the situation for example when the male hero is unable to resist the woman he knows to be 'dangerous' or 'forbidden'. This figure is already visible in the classic Jekyll and Hyde films of the thirties and forties, in Miriam Hopkins' bar singer and Ingrid Bergman's barmaid; the forbidden woman arousing in Dr Jekyll the desires that he struggles to suppress, and counterposed to the 'good woman' that he is engaged to be married to. The seductive femme fatale is a stock character of forties and fifties film noir and reappears in neo-noir films like *Basic Instinct* (Paul Verhoeven, 1992), which draws on and breathes new life into the noir conventions. There, detective Nick Curran (Michael Douglas), against his better judgement, is drawn to murder suspect Catherine Trammell (Sharon Stone). In the process, he also returns to a host of addictive behaviours he has been trying to overcome, particularly drinking and smoking. His self-mastery has been comprehensively undermined.

Everything so far has been considered from the male perspective that is so often given priority in film. But if we turn our attention to source of all this male discord, we find once again, a figure that is difficult to incorporate within the Platonic picture. Trammell remains closer to the psychopath who combines iron self-control with evil. From a Platonic point of view, the more intelligible female evil-doer would be the 'monstrous feminine' kind of character, the woman consumed by desire and obsession to the point of madness. Representatives would be the obsessive stalker Evelyn Draper (Jessica Walter) in *Play Misty for Me* (Clint Eastwood, 1971) or the vengeful book editor Alex Forrest (Glenn Close) in *Fatal Attraction (*Adrian Lyne, 1987). *Basic Instinct*'s Trammell departs from the Platonic picture of evil in another way. Not only is she in complete control of herself, but her self-control does not involve the rather ascetic self-mastery that we find in Lecter or Chigurh. Rather than repression and abstinence, it involves her being in full control of her sexuality, which she uses to manipulate those who aspire to possess and control her, like the hapless detective Curran. This also represents a refusal on her part to be subordinated to traditional norms of female behaviour.

In this, the Trammell character builds on classic femme fatales like Barbara Stanwyck's Phyllis Dietrichson in *Double Indemnity* (Billy Wilder, 1944). The classic femme fatale represents desire that refuses to be subordinated to and constrained by the traditional norms of 'good' female behaviour, the moral norms associated with marriage and family life. She is a threat to the status quo and to the male hero precisely because she takes control of her sexuality and directs it in terms of her own choosing. In this way, in *Double Indemnity*, Dietrichson is able to manipulate insurance agent Walter Neff (Fred MacMurray) into helping her get rid of her indifferent husband and escape a stifling, joyless marriage. This might be seen as another case of the evil that results when desire escapes from the constraints of morality, in this instance in the form of female desire that is no longer channelled into marriage and family. It could also be seen as a refusal on the part of women to submit to the constraints of traditional moral norms, a challenging of the norms themselves in the name of liberation. We will return to the theme of morality as a means of social constraint, tied up with oppressive social relationships, in Chapter Six.

Aristotle and Virtue Ethics

At this point, let us turn to the moral thinking of Plato's student Aristotle (384–322 BCE). These days Aristotle is particularly associated with virtue ethics, but broadly speaking all ancient ethics is concerned with virtue, with what sort of person to be and what sorts of morally praiseworthy qualities of character, or virtues, to acquire. The word ethics itself derives from the Greek word for character, ethos; and the Greek word for virtue, *arete*, means that at which a thing excels, the goodness of a thing, which is bound up with the idea of the thing's fulfilling its purpose or function. Originally, the virtuous character was the individual who performed their particular role well. The scope of ethics was confined to the particular role that one fulfilled in society. For example, the soldier's role is to defend one's country, and the skills or virtues needed to be a good soldier are things like physical strength, courage, skill in using weapons and so on. These are the warrior virtues celebrated in Homer's *Iliad*, the tale of the Trojan War. The development introduced by Plato's teacher Socrates (470–399 BCE), was to go beyond the ethics of particular roles and argue that there were virtues pertaining to being a good person as such. Virtues like courage, temperance, wisdom and justice enable one to perform the role of being a human being well. And in becoming a person who embodies all the virtues, we will achieve *eudaimonia* or happiness. Happiness is not understood here in the modern sense of a pleasant state, but rather as a state of objective fulfilment, realising one's nature, genuinely achieving one's potential as a human being. For ancient Greek and Roman thought in general, the life of virtue is the happiest, most fulfilled human life and is the life lived in accordance with human nature. It is, in short, the good life.

Socrates is the first moral philosopher, in the sense of being the first to think rigorously about human nature and ethics, about how we ought to live; as well as the first philosophical martyr, his philosophical activities eventually leading to his being put on trial and condemned to death. The traditional story at least is that he infuriated the powerful in Ancient Athens, deflating their pomposity by demonstrating that they were too ignorant to know how little they knew. Although he wrote nothing, Plato gives him a voice by making him a character in his dialogues. The dialogues relating to Socrates' trial and death, *Euthyphro*, *Apology*, *Crito* and *Phaedo*, in turn provide the dialogue for Roberto Rossellini's austere but powerful *Socrates* (1971), the director following Plato in turning Socrates (played by Jean Sylvere) into a speaking character, though the constraints of the cinematic medium mean that the Socratic dialogues inevitably appear in a shortened form. Nonetheless, the film provides a dramatic supplement to the dialogues, as well as portraying many details of ancient Greek life, including the workings of the Athenian legal system. To the extent that Socrates' views can be distinguished from those imposed on him by Plato, he is the first to argue that the best, happiest human life is the life of virtue. Virtue or moral goodness is essentially doing what promotes the soul's health and well-being, the soul being something like the intellectual and moral force that makes a human being a real person. Its well-being is the only thing that really matters. And once we know what is virtuous, which in Socratic terms is to understand the correct definition that captures the essential nature of the good, of courage, justice and other virtues, we will act in a virtuous way. People do evil things because they do not know what is in their interest, and so mistakenly believe that cheating and harming others will benefit them.

This provides the starting point for Plato's account of the virtuous life as the means to human fulfilment. Plato both moves in a more abstract direction, identifying the essential nature of the virtues with timeless, perfect forms that exist in an otherworldly realm, and turns away from Socrates' abstractly intellectualistic account to insist that over and above knowledge of the virtues, one must have control over one's appetites and desires in order to be virtuous. But the heart of Plato's account remains the Socratic idea that the moral life is the genuinely fulfilling life for the human being, and it is in these terms that Plato argues that it is in the interests of human beings to be moral. For Aristotle also, the traditionally good and virtuous life is the one we have good reason to follow, because it is the happiest, most fulfilling life, and happiness is the proper end of human existence. His *Nicomachean Ethics* aims to articulate this view. At the same time, Aristotle does not think that knowing these reasons, or for that matter attending a philosopher's lectures on ethics, is going to make someone a good person. That is the result of the kind of moral training one usually gets from parents, which has to start in early childhood so that the young person acquires habits of good behaviour. However, a person may come to wonder why they have been brought up to behave in one way rather than another. This is where Aristotle's lectures on ethics come in, providing an explanation as to why his students have been brought up as they were, a theoretical backing to a process of moral training that has already largely been completed.

For Aristotle as for Plato, it is ultimately in one's self-interest to be moral, since the virtuous life is the happiest life, in which human beings most fully realise or fulfil themselves. But we cannot achieve such happiness through a life of self-centred pleasure-seeking. Like Plato, Aristotle thinks that we are not just creatures of desire who will find happiness in a life dedicated to the pursuit of pleasure. For Aristotle, specifically human fulfilment involves realising what is distinctive of human beings and not shared by other living things. What distinguishes humans is not that they are alive, can grow and reproduce, all of which they share with plants and animals; nor that they have desires, feelings, emotions and sensations, which animals also have. What is distinctive is that human beings possess reason. Thus, for Aristotle, fulfilment consists of activity, feeling and acting, in accord with reason. And rational activity is activity in accord with virtue. Says Aristotle: 'Happiness is an activity of the soul in accord with perfect virtue' (Aristotle 2004, 27). In addition, we need what Aristotle calls 'external goods' to be truly fulfilled. We need friends, wealth, power, good birth, good children and good looks. It is hard to be happy, Aristotle thinks, if you are born ugly, born to a humble position or have disappointing children. These are things that we do not have control over, so there is also a degree of luck involved here.

With Aristotle's central claim that human beings find happiness or fulfilment in rational activity, it might seem that we are just back with Plato's reason-centred view of the human being and his rationalistic ethics. However, there is a significant difference. Plato gives us a picture of reason as locked in a battle with desire and feeling, a battle that reason has to win. For him, the well-balanced self, the self of justice, is the one in which reason subordinates and represses desires and feelings. But Aristotle argues that there does not need to be this antagonism. Rather than being opposed to reason, feelings themselves can be more or less rational, more or less reasonable. What makes feelings unreasonable is that they are felt in the wrong degree, felt too strongly, or not sufficiently, for the occasion.

So they are irrational in the sense of being inappropriate to the occasion, either in the sense that we feel too much or too little given the circumstances. Feelings, and the actions that express them, are reasonable insofar as they 'observe the mean' between excess, too much feeling, and deficiency, too little. And for Aristotle this is what moral virtue amounts to. When we have come to habitually feel and act in accordance with the mean, we are behaving virtuously.

Aristotle's list of virtues includes the traditional Platonic virtues of wisdom, justice, courage and temperance, but he expands it to include things like generosity, wit, good temper, magnanimity (having the right amount of self-worth) and friendliness. He also shares Plato's view that we are essentially social animals, meant to live in society. The virtues themselves, including generosity and good temper, are clearly social in character. If the ethical ideal is happiness or flourishing, the virtues enable individuals to flourish in a community. Indeed, for Aristotle, there is a direct link between ethics and politics, the latter being the question of what form of social and political community would best allow us to fulfil ourselves. To put this another way, politics for Aristotle is profoundly ethical, concerned with the good of the individual from the point of view of the community, whereas ethics looks at it from the individual's point of view.

So, how do the virtues as Aristotle conceives of them involve observing the mean? Take the virtue of courage for example. Someone who is excessively afraid and stands up to nothing becomes a coward, whilst someone who lacks fear and marches up to every danger becomes reckless or foolhardy. The virtue of courage is the mean between the vices of cowardice (excess) and recklessness (deficiency). The pathological deficiency of fear is evident in the reckless bravado exhibited by *Scarface*'s Tony Montana in almost everything he does, making him come across at times as a little crazy. His recklessness and risk-taking gets him to the top, although it also precipitates his downfall and death. At the other end of the spectrum, exhibiting excessive fear, is the cowardly father Tomas (Johannes Bah Kuhnke) in *Force Majeure* (Ruben Östlund, 2014). At the upmarket ski lodge restaurant where he is having lunch with his family, when it looks like a controlled avalanche is coming too close, he panics and flees, abandoning his family (though remembering to grab his phone) while his wife Ebba (Lisa Loven Kongsli) courageously stays to protect the children.

Much of *Force Majeure* is devoted to a dissection of Tomas's unfortunate behaviour, enabling further insight into the Aristotelian notions of vice and virtue. His friend Mats (Kristofer Hivju) tries to explain his behaviour by arguing that in extreme situations we are all apt to do things 'instinctively' that we cannot help and that we cannot really be blamed for such acts. His wife, however, has a different opinion: 'I can't identify with anyone who would trample on their own kids to survive. My problem is that my natural focus is on my children, while Tomas's natural focus is away from us'. Her view is that in this action, Tomas has revealed his bad character. This is closer to the Aristotelian position. For Aristotle, being good is not a matter of thinking how to behave before acting; nor is an action undertaken without thinking necessarily outside ethical consideration. The good person is precisely the one who does not have to think. Being good involves practicing being good until one has cultivated the habits of goodness, and they have become 'second nature'. When we have become habituated to responding appropriately to our circumstances, we have acquired moral virtues and a good character. Similarly, vice is not a matter of a single bad act, but a habitual disposition to behave in a bad way. As such, an unthinking, 'natural' action can reveal your bad character. That certainly seems to be Ebba's interpretation, that Tomas's action reveals his less than ideal character – a person who is not only given to excessive fear in a crisis but who 'loves himself and his phone more than he loves his wife and family' (see Baggini, 2015).

Thus, being moral for Aristotle is not a matter of following certain rules but becoming a certain sort of person. When a way of acting has become ingrained in us, through repeated actions, it becomes part of who we are, and we become a good person. *Groundhog Day*, with its endlessly repeating day, provides the opportunity for its central character Phil to become a good person in this sense. Indeed, this is the process of character development in the film, which can also be seen as solving the problem of how to represent the repetition that builds character and inculcates virtues in an enjoyably cinematic way. Phil's initial response to his situation, as noted earlier, is the Gyges-like one; if I can do whatever I like without consequences, why should I follow the rules? Why not be as gluttonous or lecherous as I like? But tiring of the pursuit of immediate appetites and pleasures, in keeping with Plato and Aristotle's contention that a life devoted to mere pleasure is ultimately unsatisfying for a human being, he looks for a more profound kind of fulfilment, the sort to be found in becoming morally good. And he does not achieve this state simply by doing good deeds. He performs a number of good deeds to impress his work colleague Rita (Andie MacDowell), to whom he has become attracted, but she sees through this for the performance that it is. Rather, he achieves it by making himself into a person who is disposed to be good, a virtuous person, where the reward is in the fulfilment itself – although this transformation has the convenient side-effect of finally impressing Rita.

As with Plato, there is a wider view of the world underpinning Aristotle's conception of morality. In Plato's non-naturalist morality, the internal harmony that characterises the moral person reflects the harmony of the forms that exist beyond the world that we experience. To live virtuously is to live our lives in accordance with these transcendental forms. For Aristotle, things in the world also have forms or essences, but these do not exist in a separate, unworldly realm. Rather, they are the internal organisation of things themselves. All things in nature have a form that organises the material making them up, giving them the capacities that they have; and all things inherently strive to realise their form, which is to say, to exercise their distinctive capacities successfully. The goal that things strive for, the realisation of their form, is what Aristotle calls the thing's *telos*. In the case of human beings, their essential nature or form, the distinctively human capacity, is to act rationally; and their *telos*, ultimate goal or summum bonum, namely happiness or fulfilment, is successfully acting in accordance with reason. Morality is all about fulfilling one's own nature. We can thus broadly characterise Aristotle's ethics as 'naturalistic'. It is entirely grounded in nature, built into our biology.

From a modern perspective that sees nature in terms of mechanical interactions, Aristotle's teleological vision of the natural world as a network of things striving to realise their inherent form or nature seems exotic. But Aristotle cannot believe that the observable structure and regularities of the world could arise from undirected, random mechanical interactions.

Aristotle is evidently more down to earth, more this-world oriented, than Plato. This difference is reflected in their respective understandings of the human being. Where Plato sees the rational self or soul as distinct from the body and its irrational desires, for Aristotle, the soul is the form of the body, inseparable from it. It is that which organises the body's material, giving it the capacity to grow and reproduce, to sense, feel and desire, as well as the distinctively human capacity to be rational. Fulfilment for human beings is the realisation of this capacity for rational activity, which includes bringing one's feelings, emotions and desires under rational control, feeling and acting in accordance with the mean, being morally virtuous. One question remains: how do we tell where the mean lies? As with Plato, it seems that for Aristotle we can know what counts as moral behaviour. Unlike Plato, this is not a purely intellectual appreciation of absolute moral truths, but rather a practical wisdom or know-how. To know what to do in this sense is simply to know, in a particular situation, what one should do. We acquire this wisdom through moral training, being properly brought up in a civilised community, through which we develop an intuitive feeling for what the mean is, what feelings are reasonable or appropriate in a particular situation. Aristotle does, however, follow Plato in holding that we can have an understanding of what is appropriate in the situation yet still act immorally. There is such a thing as moral weakness in which we know what is right but do the wrong thing anyway. Knowledge alone is not enough for moral behaviour; there needs to be a sound training in good habits when we are young, so that when we come to understand what the mean is for us, we will also have the self-control to follow it.

Now let us turn to some of the questions arising from the Aristotelian account. For Aristotle, being virtuous is an all-or-nothing affair. You cannot be courageous and temperate while choosing not to be magnanimous or good-tempered. To be truly virtuous is to exhibit all the virtues. This is because all the virtues come from the same source, namely one's character, understood as a unity. This idea of the 'unity of the virtues' is also held by Plato and later on by the Stoics. The problem is that it seems quite unrealistic. Most people, arguably, are more likely to be a mixture of good and bad, virtues and vices. It is entirely plausible to imagine someone who is courageous, but also mercenary and arrogant, like Oskar Schindler, the German industrialist who, though himself a Nazi, saved many Jews from the death camps by employing them in his factories. He is portrayed convincingly as such by Liam Neeson in *Schindler's List* (Steven Spielberg, 1993).

Facing the film's flawed hero is the villain of Spielberg's film, the concentration camp commandant Amon Goeth (Ralph Fiennes). Though also based on a real historical figure, who was reportedly extreme even by Nazi standards, Goeth comes close to being the one-dimensionally evil 'movie Nazi'. He is monstrous, out of control, ruled by sadistic impulses, almost a paradigm of Platonic evil.

Given the kind of planning and organisation required for a crime as enormous as the Holocaust, it suddenly becomes intelligible that a more important role might have been played by dutiful, organised, mediocre bureaucrats like Eichmann. There is nothing banal about Goeth's evil, except its utter casualness. Yet even Goeth, at least as portrayed in the film, is not an entirely one-dimensional character. He suffers from internal conflict when he is momentarily torn between desire and disgust for his Jewish maid Helen (Embeth Davidtz). And after a conversation with Schindler about real power being tempered by mercy, he is impressed enough to go around the camp for a short while pardoning some minor infractions. But each time his wickedness reasserts itself and he crushes the contrary tendency in himself.

Hitchcock makes use of this complexity of character to great effect in *Notorious* (1946). In this film, the villain, Nazi Alex Sebastian (Claude Rains), is far more appealing than the hero, US government agent T.R. Devlin (Cary Grant). Sebastian is the leader of a group of Nazis hiding out in a house in Rio de Janeiro after the war. In the film, Ingrid Bergman's Alicia Huberman is notorious because she is the daughter of a convicted Nazi spy. She parties and drinks to forget her circumstances and falls in love with Devlin, who has been instructed to recruit her as a spy. Devlin in turn falls for Alicia but is instructed by his superiors to persuade her to infiltrate the Nazi group by seducing Sebastian. Although ostensibly the villain of the piece, Sebastian elicits the audience's sympathy because he is far from being a straightforwardly wicked character, a monster. He has some entirely decent qualities, including a genuine love for Alicia. As Hitchcock himself notes, Sebastian probably loves Alicia more honestly and deeply than Devlin does (see Truffaut 1986, 247). For his part, Devlin, though ostensibly on the side of the good, not only exploits Alicia's affection in order to manipulate her into seducing Sebastian, but also treats her jealously and spitefully when she does what he requests, to the point where he becomes a deeply unsympathetic character. In this manner, Hitchcock exploits complexity of character to make the audience feel sympathy for the villain, as well as some revulsion towards the hero.

Mindful that characters can be complex in this way, we might want to revise our view of Tomas in *Force Majeure*. Whatever his wife thinks, perhaps he has not simply revealed his bad character through his cowardly action. Perhaps like most people he is a mixture of good and bad, in many situations a good husband and caring father who is also on occasion cowardly and self-centred. A more severe critic might go even further and question the very idea that people have a consistent character, in the sense of a set of stable, ongoing dispositions of any sort to behave in certain ways across different situations. According to the so-called 'situationist' view, which comes out of experimental social psychology, we tend to underestimate how much a person's behaviour varies from situation to situation, and to ascribe behaviour like honesty or cowardice to an underlying character. On this view, our behaviour can be better explained not in terms of persisting character traits but as ways in which we typically respond to different kinds of situation (see Appiah 2010, 44ff). One is simply the same person in different circumstances. Thus, someone may be honest at home, but dishonest at work. The famous obedience experiments of Stanley Milgram (dramatised in Michael Almereyda's 2015 film *Experimenter*) suggest that many people, even if perfectly decent in ordinary life, will go along with the requests of an authority figure in a white coat to administer dangerous electric shocks to a stranger. For the situationist, this is evidence that it is circumstances that dictate behaviour, not some underlying character. The Milgram experiments began in 1961, a year after Eichmann's trial in Jerusalem, with the intention of exploring the apparent willingness of many ordinary people to follow orders and become complicit in wartime atrocities. In the right circumstances, they seemed to suggest, people are capable of anything.

However, it might also be argued that this situationist view fails to capture our behaviour. Not everyone went along with the experimenter's commands in the Milgram experiments, and many who did protested, convinced of the wrongness of what they were doing. And not everybody went along with the Nazi program; some like Schindler stood against fascism and behaved heroically. It might be argued, on equally empirical grounds, that we don't simply respond in different ways to different situations, but also judge what we do in the light of some persisting conception of who we are and what we stand for. Thus, it is possible to act badly, but also feel that in our actions we have betrayed ourselves. And on closer inspection, this does seem to be the case in *Force Majeure*. Tomas himself is far from content with his conduct during the avalanche incident. Later, wallowing in self-pity, he says that he 'hates the person who materialised' and can't forgive him. He finds his conduct despicable, shameful, and not only because he has embarrassed himself before others, but because he has fundamentally betrayed himself. His behaviour in the film suggests that he is operating with a certain character ideal, something like the 'proper man', the patriarch in a nuclear family, who takes care of his family, protects his wife and children, and so on. This is the ideal that he has failed to live up to.

Moreover, nothing in what the situationist says undermines the claim that it would be better if someone were, say, a proper man who looks after his family; or that this is a character ideal that someone might aspire to, even if it is not easy and they all-too-readily fall short in practice. We may, of course, fall short more often than we care to admit, even to ourselves. That is, it may be that we quite routinely reinterpret, edit out or selectively ignore things we do, in order to preserve our sense of who we are, morally speaking. This is what Tomas does initially in *Force Majeure*. He pretends to himself that he did not run away in panic and rejects his wife's less-than-flattering account of the incident until the phone he was using to take a video at the time reveals the unfortunate truth. Once again, none of this implies that we should take a reductive path and view the character ideal as an illusion, hiding a real diversity of behaviour. Indeed, the reality of this character ideal is manifest precisely in the way that, even if we don't act in conformity with it, we try to interpret our behaviour as being consistent with it. So, on the basis of all this, it seems possible to argue not so much that people have a character with persistent dispositions, as that they typically aspire to be some sort of character, to embody certain ideals in their behaviour even if they sometimes fall short of this character ideal. As Aristotle himself acknowledges, acquiring virtue is difficult, it involves effort and can take a long time, and many never attain it.

A further feature of Aristotle's picture that has raised questions is his idea that there are different forms of human nature and different forms of fulfilment. All human beings possess reason. It is the defining feature of human nature, and for Aristotle, the virtuous life through which human beings find fulfilment consists of activity in accordance with reason. However, he holds that some human beings, women and 'natural slaves' by nature have a lesser degree of reason and that the proper role of women is to obey men, and of natural slaves, to obey those who are by nature masters. As such, it would seem, the fully human life can only be lived by members of a particular social group, the free-born male citizen of fourth-century Athens. The virtues that Aristotle cites, including courage, good temper and magnanimity, through which one supposedly finds fulfilment as a human being, are very much the virtues associated with this particular social group. This in turn might be taken to indicate that the virtues that Aristotle ascribes, as reflective of human nature, in fact reflect a specific social role and that talking in terms of different natures only serves to legitimise a particular social hierarchy. This is a danger for this way of thinking, though admittedly the idea of a human nature with distinctively human capacities could also be used to criticise social arrangements on the ground that they prevented some groups of people from properly exercising their capacities and living a fully human life.

Jane Austen's virtuous heroines would no doubt have something to say about Aristotle's effective exclusion of women from the realm of the fully human. Austen herself has been described as 'the last great representative of the classical tradition of the virtues' (MacIntyre 1981, 226). At the same time, however, the virtues her heroines typically strive to exhibit are clearly socially and historically specific. They are those of the nineteenth-century English middle-class female, very different from the male-oriented, aristocratic virtues that Aristotle promotes in the *Nicomachean Ethics*. For Austen's heroines, they include propriety, modesty, prudence, constancy and above all amiability, in the sense of civility to family, friends and strangers (see la Rocca 85, Rodham 2013). They are the virtues cultivated for example by Elizabeth Bennett, the heroine of *Pride and Prejudice*, and championed by her against what she sees as the arrogance and vanity of the male aristocrats of her own time, Mr Darcy chief among them.

No doubt these virtues also reflect the constraints of a particular social milieu. For all her independence, forthrightness and strength of will, Elizabeth has to operate within the same social constraints as other women of her class in nineteenth-century Regency England. Modern cinematic portrayals of the character have tended to underplay the constraints in favour of the independence. In the 2005 Joe Wright version of *Pride and Prejudice*, it is very much the independence that prevails. Elizabeth (Keira Knightley) is presented as a relatively free spirit, less subordinated to social norms than her sisters, and able to observe their marital pursuits with some detachment. She is most comfortable roaming around in the countryside and running through fields, at least when no one else is around to see her. The overall result, however, is an Elizabeth who comes across more like a contemporary teenager than a person of the time. Conformity to social constraints is much more evident in the 1940 Hollywood version, directed by Robert Z. Leonard.

Here, events have been transposed to a slightly later time period to allow for more opulent costumes. As the opening scene makes clear, this Elizabeth is very much part of the town world of shopping and husband hunting, and much less distinguishable from her sisters in this regard (see Fraiman 2010). Even here, however, as Sue Parrill notes, the actress Greer Garson plays Bennett 'broadly, with the bold looks and casual manners of a modern woman' (Parrill 2002, 52).

A feature of the Aristotelian account that is clearly evident in Austen's writing is the understanding of feeling as morally relevant, as not something opposed to reason and needing to be suppressed, but as able to be integrated with it (see Ely 1995, 94–95; Lara 1998, 95). In *Sense and Sensibility*, Aristotle's happy integration of reason and feeling is represented by Elinor Dashwood. In the novel, Austen describes her as possessing 'excellent heart; – her disposition was affectionate, and her feelings were strong; but she knew how to govern them' (Austen 2011, 8). As Gilbert Ryle puts it, she is 'sensitive *and* sensible' (Ryle 2006, 287). Having resolved to give up Edward, the object of her affections, for reasons of propriety, she certainly feels the loss keenly, but she is not overwhelmed by her feelings. In this, she is contrasted instructively with her sister Marianne who believes that feelings should govern reason and be masters over what we do. In the Ang Lee's 1995 film version, Marianne thoroughly embodies this philosophy of sensibility at the expense of sense. For her, love has to be of the crazed, consuming variety: 'To love is to burn, to be on fire, all made of passion, of adoration, of sacrifice!' A case can perhaps be made for considering the film Elinor, played by Emma Thompson, more as Marianne's opposite, a representative of sense at the expense of sensibility. In this reading, Elinor is sensible to the point of being repressed, unswervingly dedicated to the proper codes and behaviours, on constant guard against the eruption of feeling and sensibility (Köhler-Ryan and Palmer 2013, 51–55). Thompson, who wrote the screenplay, gives the character some uncharacteristic scenes of emotional outburst that are not present in the novel, presumably to show clearly that Elinor is indeed a woman of feeling (see Parill 2002, 34). But this does rather suggest a character whose long-suppressed feelings have finally been able to burst forth, rather than one whose feelings are integrated with their reason.

Marianne's conception of love incorporates the 'romantic' view of feeling, romanticism being understood here as the nineteenth-century reaction to the preceding century's supposed overemphasis on dry rationality. According to the romantic conception, reason should keep out of the way of feeling and leave room for the latter's free and spontaneous expression. For Marianne, the only alternative to this is to devalue feeling in favour of reason, and for her this is what 'being moral' amounts to, the repression of one's emotions and feelings for the sake of a supposedly higher moral demand. This is also what she thinks her sister Elinor is doing: 'Always resignation and acceptance! Always prudence and honour and duty! Elinor, where is your heart?' In fact, however, the repression of desire and its spontaneous expression are two sides of the same coin. Both views share the idea that reason and feeling are in fundamental opposition to one another. And whatever Marianne thinks, the accusation is manifestly unfair.

Although sensible and restrained, Elinor is clearly not without feelings, even in the film. Her response to Marianne: 'what do you know of my heart? ... had I not been bound to silence I could have provided proof enough of a broken heart, even for you'. In the novel it is clear that whatever Marianne thinks, her sister in fact stands for a third alternative, which is the Aristotelian integration of reason and feeling. Tellingly, Elinor does not grow or develop as a character in the story, and this is because morally speaking she has already arrived. It is Marianne who has to undergo growth, eventually realising that Elinor was right and that she should have been more like her (see Lara 1998, 95–96).

Stoicism

After Plato and Aristotle, two schools of ethical thinking became prominent, Stoicism and Epicureanism. Both originated in Greek civilisation and underwent further development during the Roman period. Both are eudaimonistic, arguing that the aim of life is to attain happiness. Where Plato identifies happiness with justice, and Aristotle with the integration of reason and feeling, these schools identify it particularly with inner peace, tranquillity or contentment. And both provide the individual with strategies for finding tranquillity and contentment in a world that is often uncertain and beyond their control. Broadly, tranquillity in both cases requires some form of detachment or withdrawal from the world, along with a transformation of those inner emotions, feelings and desires that have the power to disturb us. Finally, both schools thought that the virtues were essential to attaining the life of happy tranquillity and contentment.

Stoicism was the most influential ethical doctrine in the ancient world before the advent of Christianity. It originated with the Greek thinker Zeno of Citium (334–262 BCE), and was later developed in the Roman period by the Greek ex-slave Epictetus (55–135), where it became the default ethical position for the upper classes, all the way up to the emperor. Many of Epictetus's ideas, formulated in his *Enchiridion* ('handbook' or 'manual'), are echoed in the *Meditations* of the Roman Emperor Marcus Aurelius (121–180). Central to Stoicism was the idea that we achieve happiness by 'learning to live with the inevitable'. There is a great deal in the world that we cannot control, that is fated to happen regardless of what we might want. The reasonable thing to do is to accept it, to 'live in agreement with nature'. While this might sound like a doctrine of resignation, the Stoics put a positive spin on this to the extent that they understood the universe to have an underlying ordering principle or logos, which accounts for its structure and regularities. Like Aristotle, the Stoics could not believe that the structure and regularities of the world could arise from undirected, random processes. Rather, nature is a well-ordered system in which everything has its proper place and relation with its environment. This larger order is understood in entirely naturalistic terms. Although the Stoics identify the logos with God, there is no appeal to an otherworldly realm, in the manner of Plato. This is a God that is inherent in the world, imbuing it with order and meaning. Logos is also identified with reason; the world is a rationally ordered system.

Since everything that happens is supposed to be, the rational thing for individuals to do is to accept this, to conform their will with the events that are destined to occur in the universe, to train themselves to desire what the universe allows and not pursue what it does not. To do so is to live in agreement with one's own nature, because for the Stoics, as for Plato and Aristotle, what distinguishes human beings is that they have the capacity to reason. Like all living things, humans eat, grow and reproduce, and, like animals, they have capacities for sense perception, desire and locomotion, and take care of their offspring, but what is uniquely human is the capacity for reason. In living in accordance with our nature as rational beings, we will attain happiness. Stoicism is another eudaimonistic ethical theory, in which the proper goal of human endeavour is happiness or flourishing, and in which the happiest, most fulfilled human life is the one lived in accordance with our rational nature. Acting rationally in the various areas of human conduct is equivalent to abiding by moral virtues, which for Stoicism are the classic virtues of wisdom, temperance, courage and justice. Wisdom is the virtue of feeling and acting rationally, being in harmony with one's nature. Feeling and acting rationally in situations where one might feel fear or be tempted by pleasure defines the virtues of courage and temperance. Acting rationally with regard to other people is the virtue of justice, living in harmony with others, wishing them to be happy and flourish. All four virtues are conceived by Stoicism as being interdependent.

For Stoicism, then, in order to have a fulfilling life, we should pursue whatever cultivates and preserves virtue. The virtues enable individuals to live contented, fulfilled lives. Stoicism is however distinctive amongst ancient schools in insisting that virtue is the *only* thing needed for happiness. Whereas for Aristotle, having external goods like health, wealth, good looks, friends and the like is necessary for full happiness, the Stoic view is that happiness does not depend in any way on external circumstances, which we cannot control and which are a matter of luck. We should be concerned only with what is in our control, namely our inner mental judgements, opinions, attitudes, desires and actions. Everything else falls into the class of 'indifferents'; they neither contribute nor detract from the happy life. The Stoics were not entirely dismissive of external circumstances. They argued for a class of 'preferred indifferents', things like life, health, strength, prosperity, friends and family and a good reputation. These promote the natural condition of the person so it is usually rational to prefer them to 'dispreferred indifferents' like death, disease, pain, ugliness, weakness and poverty. However, even preferred indifferents remain indifferents. We should not be upset if we don't have these things, or if we lose them. Happiness lies in learning to be indifferent to the external circumstances beyond one's control, learning that one can be happy and fulfilled regardless of our material circumstances.

As such, becoming virtuous, rational in feeling and action, involves radically transforming our emotional life. For the Stoics, emotion or passion is a psychic disturbance that is contrary to reason. We should act purely on the basis of reason, not emotion. Even Plato, for all his hostility to desire and emotion, saw these as part of the psyche, to be controlled by reason, not extirpated. Aristotle of course thought that emotion and feeling had a place in the rational organism provided it was reasonable or appropriate to the situation. For Stoicism, a significant amount of emotional life needs to be removed. One can have certain mild 'rational' emotions, like joy, kindliness or cheerfulness, but we need to free ourselves from disturbing emotions like distress, jealousy, pity, grief, worry, fear and panic; appetite which includes yearning, anger and passionate love; and pleasure or irrational elation over what seems worth choosing. All of these disturbing emotions are based on mistaken judgements about the importance of external things like wealth, health, good looks, a happy family life, and so on. We mistakenly take these things to be important and become emotionally attached to them. But although we cannot control them, we can control our judgements about them. We can learn to be indifferent to our circumstances, to calmly accept them. Here, the therapeutic aspect of Stoicism is evident. Stoicism recommends various exercises to achieve this healthy indifference. We will thereby be cleansed of all the fears and anxieties that ordinary people suffer, and attain *apatheia*, the state of freedom from disturbing emotions. This for Stoicism is the happy, fulfilled life, the life of virtue. The Roman Stoics, in particular, emphasised the tranquillity that will result from the virtuous life.

Being stoic has come to mean being able to grit one's teeth, suppress one's feelings and endure adversity without complaint. However, it is not so much about suppressing as not having the relevant feelings, being indifferent. As John Sellars argues, this is why we cannot really see Maximus (Russell Crowe), the hero of Ridley Scott's historical epic *Gladiator* (2000), as a Stoic figure. Though a protégé of Marcus Aurelius (played by Richard Harris), he does not inherit the emperor's Stoic outlook. After Aurelius's successor Commodus has Maximus's wife and family killed, he is exiled, captured by slavers and trained to fight as a gladiator. But rather than accepting his new circumstances, he plots to return to Rome to kill Commodus (Joaquin Phoenix), in order to exact revenge. The Stoic view is that one's close relations are amongst the external things that are not necessary for one's happiness. What Maximus needs to do is free himself from the passionate desire for vengeance, the disturbing emotion tied up with his attachment to his family. The same can be said for the Bride (Uma Thurman) in *Kill Bill* (Quentin Tarantino, 2003). She endures a great deal, but her actions are driven by the desire for revenge against Bill and the assassination squad who attacked her and left her for dead, and in the second part of the film, the additional desire to rescue her daughter from Bill's clutches. Getting to the point where the mind only makes rational judgements about the importance of external objects requires considerable mental discipline and that discipline requires a lifetime of training and practice. Epictetus recommends various exercises to cultivate it: for example, when we kiss our child, remember she is mortal and not something we own, silently reflect on the possibility she may die tomorrow; as we go about our day, periodically pause to reflect on the fact that we will not live forever and that this day could be our last; and so on (Epictetus 2008, 222).

Thus, the vengeance-driven action hero, no matter how heroically enduring they may be in the pursuit of their goal, does not qualify as a Stoic figure, since they are too passionate, too attached to external things. A much more unprepossessing figure can come closer to the Stoic ideal, at least with respect to displaying the right kind of attitude towards externalities that cannot be controlled. In Spielberg's *Bridge of Spies* (2015), set at the height of the Cold War, the Russian spy Rudolf Abel (Mark Rylance), having been arrested by the US authorities, radiates an extraordinary calm despite difficult circumstances. Each time he is asked by his lawyer James Donovan (Tom Hanks) whether he is worried about the prospect of being found guilty and going to the electric chair, he replies in a deadpan manner, 'would it help?' This is Stoic indifference in essence; it is pointless to worry about what we cannot control. As noted, getting to the desired Stoic state of tranquil indifference is not easy. If we lived in perfect accord with nature, behaved purely rationally, we would be what the Stoics called a perfect wise man, a sage. Sages are completely virtuous and do not suffer from any mistaken emotions. They do not desire the things that people ordinarily regard as indispensable for happiness, like prosperity, fame, romantic love, social success and so on. They recognise that these external goods, over which non-Stoics suffer anxiety, fear, disappointment and desire, are not necessary for the good life; only virtue is required for that. As a result, the sage acquires a kind of psychic invulnerability. They cannot be harmed, no matter how dire their circumstances. They could lose everything, wealth, friends, family, reputation, life, without compromising their happiness, since they have everything they need for their happiness within them. As the Stoics themselves recognised, few could be said to have reached this ideal, though most saw Socrates as having come close. He demonstrated extraordinary equanimity while on trial for his life and calm acceptance of his fate once condemned to death. These qualities are eminently on show in Rossellini's *Socrates*, which is itself filmed in a calm, serene style, without melodrama, befitting its subject.

A potential criticism of Stoicism is that it focuses too much on acceptance of external circumstances and on changing oneself, leading to passivity and inaction. For the Stoics themselves, indifference does not mean inaction. Stoic detachment is compatible with involvement in everyday life, in society. The Stoic can take full part in life, marry and have a family, engage in politics, and so on. The attitude of indifference towards externals does not preclude the energetic pursuit of preferred indifferents, of things like prosperity, health, friends, life and so on. But it remains the case that the Stoic should not be disappointed if they don't achieve these things or if they lose them. These things are not necessary for happiness; only virtue is necessary for that and this is what we should focus our attention on cultivating. Still, we might wonder if this is a sustainable position. It might be thought that there is a conflict between the Stoic ideal of indifference to externals and our unavoidable involvement in social affairs. Can we really pursue external things without being emotionally attached to them, and without being disappointed if we fail to achieve them, or lose them? By the same token, is it possible to detach ourselves from our ordinary needs and concerns for family and friends, for fame, prosperity, health and so on, and still be motivated to act?

Over and above this, the radical transformation in emotional life required in order to become virtuous in the Stoic sense is perhaps only attainable by a superhuman figure, someone far removed from ordinary humanity. As such, the

Stoic ideal seems to be in conflict with the often-repeated insistence in ancient ethics that the best human life is the one lived in accordance with human nature. Lack of a rich emotional life is ordinarily more likely to be taken as a marker of the inhuman, as in *Invasion of the Body Snatchers* (Don Siegel, 1956). There the transformation is not effected through Stoic therapies but alien intervention. The inhabitants of a California town are replaced by duplicates grown in pods, their minds absorbed into the new bodies while they sleep, and their old bodies destroyed. The replacements have the same memories, habits and mannerisms as the original, but they no longer feel love, grief or hope. From a Stoic point of view, one could see this as an improvement. Stoicism may not advocate the rejection of all emotion, but it does seem to want to remove a significant portion of emotional life. Yet the film's main characters, Miles and Becky, refuse the pod peoples' offer to join them precisely because it would mean giving up the ability to love and have feelings. For them, as for the audience, there is something profoundly inhuman about the absence of emotional life. It is what above all marks the pod people as alien, even though they are in so many ways identical to the individuals they have replaced.

Epicureanism

Epicurean thinking, the main rival to Stoicism, was founded by the Greek thinker Epicurus (341–c270 BCE), and later developed by the Roman poet Lucretius (c98–c55 BCE). Epicureanism is another eudaimonistic ethical theory, holding that the goal of human endeavour is happiness or fulfilment. It is distinctive however in holding that the happy life for human beings is the life of pleasure, free of any pain or suffering. This sort of ethical view is sometimes called 'egoistic hedonism', the doctrine that the only thing intrinsically valuable is one's own pleasure, and that everything else is valuable only as a means of securing pleasure for oneself. In this, Epicureanism departs from much of ancient ethics, which follows Plato, Aristotle and Stoicism in holding that happiness in the proper sense requires us to rise above the pursuit of mere pleasure, mere desire-satisfaction, in order to live a virtuous life. However, as we will see, Epicureanism is by no means a straightforwardly hedonistic position, advocating a life of unbridled excess. Epicurus recommends limiting one's desires as the best means of securing pleasure for oneself.

This is an ethics that is once again based on human nature, but unlike much of ancient ethics, human nature is understood as primarily pleasure-seeking rather than rational. The Epicureans saw this view as supported by empirical observation, arguing that pleasure is the only thing that people do, as a matter of fact, value for its own sake. This can be confirmed by observing infants who instinctively seek pleasure and avoid pain, and it is just as true of adults, although they have more complicated beliefs about what will bring them pleasure. The Epicureans insisted that all activity, even apparently self-sacrificing behaviour performed solely for the sake of virtue, is in fact directed towards getting pleasure for oneself. Shocking though this view must have been for their contemporaries, it is far more plausible to a modern audience. As noted, a feature of modern thought since the seventeenth century and Thomas Hobbes is the idea that human beings are fundamentally self-interested creatures driven by desire, seeking the pleasurable satisfaction of our desires. In embracing this doctrine, Epicureanism has a surprisingly modern feel about it, although as we will see in Chapter Three, Hobbes builds a rather different picture of morality on this basis.

Another feature of Epicureanism that has surprisingly modern resonances is that it rests on an entirely materialist view of nature, as involving nothing but the blind interactions of particles. This wholly materialistic vision of the world will not reappear in Europe until the seventeenth century, when the foundations for the modern scientific worldview are laid. It is also a departure from much of ancient ethics. Certainly, Aristotle and the Stoics offer naturalistic accounts in the sense that they don't appeal to any otherworldly ordering principles, such as Plato's Forms. However, neither Aristotle nor the Stoics could quite accept that the structured world could arise from undirected processes. They envisaged ordering principles that are inherent in nature, Aristotle's forms and the Stoics' logos. For Epicureanism, there is no such internal ordering principle in nature; all phenomena are the result of the random, fortuitous interactions of atoms. Thus, for the Epicureans, there is nothing to imbue the world with order and meaning. The universe is a chaotic, meaningless place, indifferent to human hopes and concerns. There are gods, but they don't intervene in human affairs. We are alone in the world and our only guide for how to act is our own pleasure. Epicureanism tells us how to be happy in this world on the basis of a strictly materialist view of nature, and a correspondingly down-to-earth view of human beings as creatures who seek pleasure and want to avoid pain.

One might suppose that, given this view of human nature, and the ethical view based on it, namely that pleasure is the only thing that is good in itself, what Epicureanism is counselling is unlimited pleasure-seeking, decadent sensualism. This indeed was how Epicureanism was characterised by its bitter rivals the Stoics, and later on by the Christians. And nowadays that is precisely what 'epicurean' has come to mean, the self-indulgent seeker of pleasurable delights, devoted to sensual enjoyment, especially fine food and drink. On this view, the modern heroes of Epicureanism would be those who have the power to indulge all of their desires, like the avaricious gangsters of the *Scarface* variety or the unapologetically hedonistic stockbrokers in *The Wolf of Wall Street*. In this view, Epicureanism is nothing less than an ethics of conspicuous consumption, of capitalism's consumerist culture. However, unlimited pleasure-seeking is very far from what Epicureanism calls for. What Epicurus counsels is in fact something quite austere and restrained, what might be termed 'negative hedonism'. And Epicureanism also offers a possible standpoint for the moral critique of modern consumerism as trenchant as anything that might emerge out of Platonic thinking.

It's true that, for Epicurus, the happy, fulfilled life is the pleasant life, and virtues like courage and moderation are only valuable insofar as they are a means to pleasure. And this is another significant departure from most ancient ethical thinking, for which pleasure is usually something to be sacrificed for the sake of virtue, the only thing good in itself. Now, it is pleasure that is the only good in itself. But if pleasure is the satisfaction of your desires, there are at least two ways you can ensure that you are satisfied to the maximum degree. You can strive to acquire the power to shape the world so you can get whatever you want, like Tony Montana or Jordan Belfort. This, however, is a problematic strategy, as the world does not always cooperate in satisfying us; and even if we are successful, too much indulgence has its own painful consequences for the body, as is all too clearly apparent to the bleary-eyed heroes of the cinema of excess. Alternatively, you can limit your desires to simple ones that can be easily satisfied. That way you will be able to be completely happy, completely free of pain and suffering, regardless of your circumstances. This is the path that Epicurus recommends. For him, the best sort of pleasure is the kind that involves no pain. Happiness here can be best understood in negative terms, as freedom from suffering, from the suffering caused by overindulgence and from the frustration of not being able to satisfy one's desires. The Epicureans called it *ataraxia*, meaning peace of mind, serenity or tranquillity. This is not unlike the Stoic goal of *apatheia*, unsurprisingly as the Roman Stoics appropriated the notion from their Epicurean rivals.

So rather than promoting the unlimited pursuit of pleasure, the Epicurean focus is on sensibly limiting ourselves to simple desires for things we cannot do without, what Epicurus calls 'natural and necessary desires' for food, drink and shelter, which can be easily satisfied, and without which, we would suffer. One needs to be more cautious about 'natural but unnecessary' desires, such as a taste for rich food when simple food will do. Habitually pursuing these unnecessary things sets one up for pain and distress, because they can be hard to acquire which will be frustrating and potentially harmful, like the rich food that gives you indigestion. And one should altogether avoid 'vain and empty' desires, for political power, money, fame, designer goods and the like. These desires are not natural to human beings but are inculcated by society and involve false beliefs about what we need. Not only are these things unnecessary for our survival, the more one has of them, the more one wants, making the desire for them impossible to satisfy and leading to endless frustration and discontentment. Thus, Epicureanism advocates reducing your desires to a minimum core, which can then be easily satisfied. It turns out that we don't need much to be happy; a simple diet, basic accommodation and perhaps a few good friends will be enough. And in restricting ourselves to simple pleasures, we will no longer dependent for our happiness on a world that we cannot control, which we cannot rely on to cooperate in the satisfaction of our desires. To this end. Epicureanism, alone among the ancient schools, advocates actual withdrawal from involvement in social and political life. Plato and Aristotle both view human beings as essentially social animals who flourish best in a properly organised community. Even Stoicism, which advocates detachment from an uncertain world understands this detachment to be compatible with continued involvement in society. Not so Epicureanism. As Luke Slattery puts it 'whereas the Stoic withdraws into a fortified self or inner citadel … the Epicurean picks up his bags and quits the city' (Slattery 2012, 4).

Yet, as Slattery goes on to note, Epicureanism also contains the seeds of a radical social and political critique. In advocating a life of simple pleasures, Epicureanism emerges as implicitly critical of modern consumerism and its requirement of endless consumption. From this perspective, the modern advertising that fuels consumption is a concerted effort to implant 'natural but unnecessary' and 'vain and empty' desires in people, to convince them that satisfying these desires will make them happy and that the discontent or frustration that is inevitably going to arise from the pursuit of these sorts of desires can only be cured by yet more consumption. Epicurus insists that 'it is not continuous drinkings and revellings, nor the satisfaction of lusts, nor the enjoyment of fish and other luxuries of the wealthy table, which produce the pleasant life, but sober reasoning, searching out the motives for all choice and avoidance' (Epicurus 2006, 454–455). Grotesque images of overindulgence in the 'luxuries of the wealthy table' have provided a handy metaphor for the excesses of modern life in a number of socially critical films. *La Grande Bouffe* (Marco Ferreri, 1973) protests against consumerist hedonism, portraying a group of friends who decide to kill themselves in the most hedonistic way possible, eating their way through meal after meal of increasingly exotic food. In *The Cook, The Thief, His Wife and Her Lover* (Peter Greenaway, 1989), the greed of the entrepreneurial classes in the Margaret Thatcher era is distilled into the figure of the thief, a brutal criminal who presides over obscenely lavish banquets in a London restaurant.

The heroes of Epicureanism are those who are content with the simple pleasures, though their conspicuous lack of interest in acquisition and consumption is liable to mark them out as eccentric in the present context. Morgan Rempel has argued convincingly that one character who might be thought to approach the ideal of Epicurean sage is Jeffrey 'The Dude' Lebowski from *The Big Lebowski* (Joel and Ethan Coen, 1998). He has achieved his tranquillity in the midst of contemporary Los Angeles by giving up any desire for wealth, achievement, a partner or clean clothing. He is content to spend his time bowling, smoking dope, living in his modest apartment and driving an old car. From an Epicurean point of view, the key point here is that The Dude is not happy despite his reduced circumstances, but because of them (see Rempel 2012, 67ff). A similar tranquillity seems to be achieved by the teenage runaways in *Moonrise Kingdom* (Wes Anderson, 2012). In their case, it literally requires them to pick up their bags and quit the city. On the fictional island of New Penzance, in the 1960s, 12-year-olds Suzy (Kara Hayward) and Sam (Jared Gilman), who have fallen in love, pack their bags and run away from town to set up camp together in the small cove they name Moonrise Kingdom. There they are happy enough living in the tent Sam has brought, with Suzy's six stolen books, a portable record player, binoculars and each other's company. Their innocent affection for one another adds to the tranquillity of the moment, which is only disturbed when the frantic adults finally locate their campsite. The matter of love, however, raises some new issues. Love is something that is potentially problematic from the Epicurean point of view. The danger with romantic love for the Epicurean lies in the way lovers can become obsessed with one another, in ways that profoundly threaten any possibility of contentment and tranquillity.

Two centuries after Epicurus, the Roman poet Lucretius, in his Epicurean philosophical poem 'On the Nature of Things', argues against indulging in romantic love. While ordinary sexual desire is relatively easy to satisfy, romantic love for Lucretius is a psychological obsession that disorders the mind. It drives people to ruin their reputations, neglect their duties and waste their money lavishing gifts on their beloved. It is nourished by distorted perceptions of the object of their affection. Their ordinary attributes are idealised, producing an illusory image of perfection that no person can possibly live up to. The impossible romantic ideal of a complete union with another who is a model of perfection only leads to unrealistic expectations and frustration for all concerned. As long as you are afflicted with this sickness, you will have no peace or tranquillity. Even if your beloved is absent, you will still be tormented by images of them and have no peace (see Lucretius 1951, 162–167). This is the passionate, consuming love celebrated by the romantic Marianne in *Sense and Sensibility*; but for the Epicurean, it is a mental affliction that ruins happiness and peace of mind. Lucretius suggests therapies through which we might rid ourselves of the romantic sickness, should we be unlucky enough to contract it. For example, he suggests that you should concentrate on the beloved's faults of mind and body so you no longer have an idealised, distorted image of them. More positively, you should learn to love the imperfect. If you want to be happy, you need to go for realistic love based on character and habitual affection, rather than blind passion (Lucretius 1951, 170).

Seen as a love story, Hitchcock's *Vertigo* (1958) portrays many of the pathological features of love described by Lucretius. San Francisco detective John 'Scottie' Ferguson (James Stewart) has become romantically involved with Madeleine Elster (Kim Novak). She is the apparently suicidal woman whose husband has asked him to follow, and after Scottie saves her from a suicide attempt, he inevitably falls for her. Their growing closeness dominates the first part of the film. After her apparent suicide at the clock tower, however, Scottie becomes tormented by her image, imagining that he sees her in their favourite restaurant, in front of the apartment building where she lived and on the street. When he meets a woman, Judy, who resembles her, he tries to transform her into the ideal he obsesses over, demanding that she dress and wear her hair as Madeleine did. Here the distorting idealisation of the other becomes akin to the Pygmalion pattern in which the protagonist, usually male, tries to mould a female to fit an ideal. The whole situation is complicated in that Judy really is his lost Madeleine; her charade as the suicidal wife was part of his client's plot to get away with murdering his real wife. But having fallen in love with Scottie, she hopes that he will now love her for herself. Unfortunately, she is caught up in Scottie's obsession. He can only love her if she becomes his ideal Madeleine, a woman who was never real. From here the film spirals to its tragic conclusion, the real death of Madeleine/Judy, driven by Scottie's obsessive desire for an impossibly idealised other.

Noel Carroll argues that *Vertigo* not only offers an analysis of love and its pathologies, but also illuminates a distinction between normal and pathological love. All romantic love involves a degree of fantasy, an idealisation of the other, in which the participants imagine themselves two parts of a larger whole. And this idealisation is unproblematic, to the extent that it remains based in the other's reality and encourages them to bring out their best. It becomes pathological when the fantasy takes over, and the other is no longer seen as they are in any respect but becomes completely subject to distorting idealisation. In these terms, Carroll sees the first part of *Vertigo* as portraying a normal form of love and the second as lurching into the pathological variety (see Carroll 2007). From this perspective, Lucretius's dismissal of all romantic love as a dangerous sickness could be questioned as overemphasising its pathological forms. But even if we accept this, he can still be seen as calling attention to a pathology that is an inherent possibility in love relationships. *Vertigo* itself shows how readily love can turn into something obsessive and pathological, and how the potentiality of its doing so is present right from the start. The impossible ideal of a perfect union with one's ideal soulmate that fuels such obsessions is itself promoted through the fairy-tale images of romantic love peddled by Hollywood films (Stephens 2010, 86). But even within the Hollywood system, films like *Vertigo* have drawn attention to the more pathological aspects of romantic passion, and in so doing, have also raised questions about Hollywood's own pathological romanticism.

To that extent, *Vertigo* can be seen as offering a Lucretian critique of romantic love as a sickness, 'with its demand for perfect union and its tendency to construct the loved one as an idealized fantasy figure' (Wood 2002, 385). It also offers a commentary on the idealised Hollywood notion of love and the cinematic construction of women as impossible fantasy figures. It is worth noting that in Lucretius's account of the pathologies of love, while the lovesick party is clearly male, and the object of their obsession female, there is nothing to say that this necessarily has to be so. As far as Lucretius is concerned, the roles could in principle be reversed. It could just as easily be a woman who has become obsessed over an impossibly idealised male. And the obsessed woman can also be found in Hollywood films. For instance, there is the delusional Evelyn Draper in *Play Misty for Me*, whose obsession with disc jockey Dave Garver (Clint Eastwood) tips over into crazed violence. This is a scenario that is repeated later on, almost note for note, in *Fatal Attraction*. But it also says a good deal about Hollywood that these stories of female obsession are told very much from the male perspective, in terms of male panic over the threat posed by women who are not compliant, who refuse to go along with male requirements and obediently disappear if they are no longer needed. This anxiety frames the representation of these women as versions of the 'monstrous feminine'.

Mulholland Drive (2001), David Lynch's 'love story in the city of dreams', offers a corrective here in that it tells the story of romantic obsession from the point of view of Hollywood starlet Diane Selwyn (Naomi Watts). The object of obsession, however, remains a woman, in a further departure from Hollywood norms. Diane not only creates an impossibly idealised image of her girlfriend Camilla Rhodes (Laura Harring) but an entire fantasy or dream world that appears to occupy the first two-thirds of the film. In this dream, Diane recreates their relationship in an idealised form in which she is successful Hollywood new-comer Betty, and Camilla, an amnesiac car accident victim, Rita, whom she is helping to search for her true identity. The story unfolds as a sunny neo-noir, with Betty as the detective and Rita as her 'friend fatale'. The dream is happy, a Hollywood movie-style romance, but there are intimations that it is unreal and a different reality lies under the surface. This is so most wrenchingly in the 'Club Silencio' scene, where the couple's bliss is destroyed as it is somehow indicated that their entire relationship is an illusion. Soon afterward the dream evaporates. The last part of the film is Diane's bleak reality as a failed starlet, bitter at having been abandoned by Camilla, who got the lead role in the movie that would have brought Diane fame, and who, after enduring multiple humiliations at Camilla's hands, Diane has had murdered. This is the grim place, the 'boulevard of broken dreams' that Diane has tried to escape from in the dream, and from which she will eventually escape more permanently by killing herself.

The preceding represents a straightforward reading of the film, which has a complex structure. However, much of the complexity has to do with the film's subversion not only of the ideal images that it presents but of the distinction between ideal and real itself. There is no hard and fast division between the beautiful dream and the unpleasant reality. The one bleeds into the other. Even in the sunny, romantic part of the film, which is largely coherent, even hyper-realistic, there are ugly and disturbing episodes, such as a confrontation with the evil hobo who lurks behind the diner. In the final scene, the distinction between ideal and real collapses altogether, leaving us with two violently opposed images: the dead body of Diane, who has just shot herself, over which float images of the blissfully happy Betty and Rita from Diane's dream (see Vass 2000; Sinnerbrink 2005). Overall, *Mulholland Drive*, like *Vertigo,* is both a story of romantic obsession in which reality is displaced by delusional images of perfection that people cannot possibly live up to and a commentary on Hollywood's own contribution to the production of such fantasies, its construction of women as impossible fantasy figures. *Mulholland* Drive goes further in criticising the Hollywood system itself, subverting Hollywood's self-image as the place of dreams, the 'dream factory', by pointing to the brutal mechanics of a male-dominated industry and the exploitative reality that greets actresses seeking to make it there. Diane's dream is also the compensatory delusion of someone who has been destroyed by the industry.

To return to Epicureanism, we can finish with some questions that arise in connection with this ethical position. As we will see, similar concerns arise with more recent forms of pleasure-based ethics. Regarding Epicureanism's psychological hedonism, its view of human nature, is it really the case that we are primarily motivated by the desire for pleasure? Can this view be maintained without becoming trivial and unfalsifiable, as when we hold that even the most selfless acts are 'really' performed because they give us pleasure? Questions can also be raised about Epicureanism's ethical hedonism, its view that pleasure is the only worthwhile goal, the only thing that people should strive for, and the idea that the happy life is above all the pleasant one. It might be argued that human beings characteristically value things over and above pleasure. They typically aspire to certain virtues or ideals of character and feel badly if they fall short of these ideals. As such, purely pleasure-based accounts of morality might not be able to address the full range of moral experience. There are times, arguably, when being moral might involve putting constraints on desire, and not simply in order to ensure maximum satisfaction in the longer term; times when doing what we ought to do might be at the expense of pleasure. Certainly, Plato, Aristotle and Stoicism lined up against the Epicurean idea that a life of pleasure could constitute a fully realised human life. Of course, even Epicureanism turns its back on the life of pleasure to the extent that it counsels not unlimited pleasure-seeking but restricting oneself to those desires that can be easily satisfied. Its peculiar achievement is to fashion a pleasure-based morality of restraint. But it is not clear that it can account for situations where being moral requires not merely restraint of pleasure but downright suffering and pain.

Whatever the debates between the various ancient schools, by the third century AD, in the declining period of the Roman empire, they were displaced by Neoplatonism, a revived version of Plato's ideas developed particularly by the Roman thinker Plotinus (205–270). Plotinus construed the universe as an 'emanation' of the One or God, a transcendental first principle that is above material being, a higher reality, the notion being derived from Plato's supreme Form of the good. For Plotinus, the One can be apprehended by the human soul as a presence transcending all knowing. Itself absolutely perfect and good, it brings about increasing imperfect forms of existence, with physical matter being the lowest form. Because human beings are attached to the material, the physical body, they are open to evil. In order to flourish, the soul or mind needs to purge itself of the bodily, this purging to be achieved through the virtues. The happy life is very much a matter of turning away from this world in order to contemplate and ultimately return as a disembodied soul to higher unity with the One. Neoplatonism also appropriated elements of Stoic ethics, to the extent that Stoic ethics teaches us to get rid of disturbing passions.

Neoplatonism also looks forward to the Christian era. From our vantage point in the present, we are perhaps apt to see the transition from the classical to the Christian era as the triumph of dogmatic religion over the reason, critical reflection and independent scientific enquiry, which will only return with the collapse of the medieval worldview. The film *Agora* (Alejandro Amenábar, 2009) might serve as an example. It deals with the final years of philosopher-scientist Hypatia (c.370–415), director of the Neoplatonist school in Roman Alexandria, murdered by a Christian mob led by fanatical monks. The film portrays Hypatia as an independent thinker, affirming her known interest in mathematics and astronomy, and imagining her to have anticipated key discoveries the seventeenth-century scientific revolution such as the sun-centred view of the solar system and the elliptical orbits of the planets. By contrast, the Christianity that is coming into ascendancy demands unswerving belief in the word of God as revealed in the scriptures and submission to the authority of priests. The impression is of an abrupt transition into dogmatic religion. What is obscured here is the manner in which Christianity incorporated many classical ideas into its developing worldview. In particular, many Neoplatonic ideas were appropriated in the theology of Augustine, Christianity's first great synthesiser. Hypatia herself was by all accounts a Neoplatonist in philosophical matters, her mathematical and astronomical investigations serving as a pathway to the contemplation of the higher reality envisaged in the Neoplatonic account (see Sharpe 2012, 35).

Hypatia is also said to have lectured on *apatheia*, freedom from the tyranny of emotions that served to distract the mind from contemplation of the cosmos; and she was widely known for her sage-like equanimity. We can see something of this ideal of equanimity, familiar from Stoicism, in Amenábar's film, which imagines Hypatia being mercifully euthanised by her slave before the Christians have a chance to murder her. Faced with the inevitable, she calmly assents to this loving gesture. As Matthew Sharpe notes, the film itself employs a tech-nique similar to that recommended by the Stoics to promote such philosophical detachment and acceptance, namely trying to see things from the point of view of nature as a whole rather than from one's limited perspective, in order to recognise how we are but small, temporary elements of a larger order beyond our control. As the Stoic emperor Marcus Aurelius urges, assuming this point of view will help us to attain the appropriate indifference towards our circum-stances, their 'calm acceptance' (Marcus Aurelius 2006, 90; see Sellars 2006 126–127). The film encourages this larger point of view by placing the events that it portrays within such a large perspective, its first shot beginning from far out in space, then revealing the earth's globe and moving in on ancient Alexandria, and the last shot pulling back from the events in Alexandria to a view from space (see Sharpe 2012, 42).

However, these events are to be viewed, the death of Hypatia provides a con-venient marker for the end of the classical era and the beginning of the Christian era, and it is to the moral thinking of the Christian era that we now turn.

FEATURE FILMS: *DR JEKYLL AND MR HYDE* AND *UNDER THE SKIN*

Dr Jekyll and Mr Hyde

Robert Louis Stevenson's Jekyll and Hyde story has been filmed many times. Robert Mamoulian's 1931 *Dr Jekyll and Mr Hyde* was remade by Victor Fleming in 1941. Being made after the institution of the Hays Code, Fleming's film is less sexually explicit than its predecessor. However, despite being made by a different studio (MGM rather than Paramount), it is very similar to its predecessor in plot and screenplay. Concerned that audiences might compare the two versions, MGM acquired the rights to the 1931 film and kept it out of circulation for decades.

Plot

Dr Henry Jekyll, a doctor in Victorian London, is certain that within each person there is both good and evil, and that science offers the possibility of freeing us from the evil side of our makeup. In Mamoulian's version, the film opens with Jekyll (Fredric March), heading off to give a lecture to this effect to colleagues and friends. In Fleming's version, the story opens with a congregation at a church service, with Dr Jekyll (Spencer Tracy) in attendance. The service is disturbed by a madman in the grip of his evil side.

In the Mamoulian version, Jekyll arrives late for a dinner party at the home of fiancée Muriel Carew (Rose Hobart), daughter of Brigadier General Sir Danvers Carew (Halliwell Hobbes). After the others have left, Jekyll asks Danvers' permission to bring forward their wedding date, but Danvers refuses. In Fleming's remake, Jekyll holds forth about the dual nature of man at a dinner party hosted by a Mrs Marley. In attendance is his fiancé, now called Beatrix Emery (Lana Turner) and her father Charles Emery (Donald Crisp).

In the Mamoulian film, Jekyll, while walking home with his colleague, Dr John Lanyon (Holmes Herbert), spots a prostitute, Ivy Pierson (Miriam Hopkins), being attacked by a man outside her boarding house. He drives the man away and carries Ivy up to her room. Ivy tries to seduce Jekyll, but Jekyll fights temptation and leaves with Lanyon (Ian Hunter). In Fleming's version, Ivy (Ingrid Bergman) is a barmaid and singer, with no implication of prostitution.

Jekyll develops a drug that releases the evil side in himself, becoming Hyde. In the Mamoulian version, the physical transformation when Jekyll transforms into Hyde is striking. In the Fleming version, there is less physical change. The remainder of Fleming's film largely follows the lines of the Mamoulian version, which runs as follows. Hyde returns to Ivy's boarding house and offers to look after her financial needs in return for her company but treats her cruelly. He remains at her boarding house until he discovers that Muriel and her father are returning to London. He leaves Ivy but threatens that he will be back. Guilt-ridden over Hyde's treatment of Ivy, Jekyll has his servant deliver money to her. Ivy goes to see Jekyll, hoping he can free her from the abusive Hyde. She recognises Jekyll as the man who saved her from the attack outside her boarding house. Jekyll promises Ivy she won't have to worry about Hyde anymore.

En route to a party at the Carews' home to celebrate their return, Jekyll changes spontaneously into Hyde. Hyde goes to confront Ivy about seeing Jekyll and murders her. He returns to Jekyll's house but his servant refuses to admit him. He writes a letter to his colleague Lanyon from Jekyll, asking him to get chemicals and have them waiting at Lanyon's home. When Hyde arrives, Lanyon produces a gun and demands Hyde take him to Jekyll. Hyde drinks the formula and turns back into Jekyll. Jekyll decides he must call off the wedding to Muriel for her own safety.

Jekyll goes to the Carews' to tell Muriel he cannot be with her anymore. After leaving, he changes into Hyde again, comes back into the house and attacks Muriel. When her father intervenes, Hyde kills him using Jekyll's cane, then runs off towards Jekyll's home lab to mix a new formula to change himself back. Standing over Danvers' body with the police, Lanyon recognises Jekyll's cane and agrees to take the police to its owner. The police arrive at Jekyll's lab looking for Hyde and find only Jekyll, but Lanyon tells them that Jekyll is the man they are looking for. Jekyll changes into Hyde before their eyes. He attacks Lanyon, then tries to escape from the police but is shot. As he lies dead, he transforms one last time back into Jekyll.

Key Scenes

1   Mamoulian's version opens with an extended point-of-view shot that arrives in front of a mirror, revealing the point of view to be that of Dr Jekyll himself [1.10–4.37]. In this way, we in the audience are identified with him, and his nature with ours. Jekyll heads off to give a lecture on human nature, in which the 'soul of man' is said to consist of two sides, the 'good' side and the 'bad' or 'evil' side, engaged in an eternal struggle [4.18–6.33]. In Fleming's version, the good and evil sides of the human being are portrayed visually, the story opening with a church service, linking the good side with religion, interrupted by a madman who is wholly given over to the evil side [1.20–4.25].

2   In Fleming's version, the references to religion continue. Jekyll presents his view of the duality of human nature at the dinner party, describing two parts, good and evil, 'chained together in the soul' where they constantly fight one another. This version is distinguished by religious references invoked by Jekyll himself: 'we all have an evil side … why, as Christians we admit that man is created weak'. In response to Jekyll's claims that science will free human beings from their evil side, the bishop asks whether it is wise to tamper with the problem of good co-existing with evil in the human soul. Instead he invokes the need for God's grace to help human beings

overcome their physical appetites and aid them in their struggle against evil [9.30–14.05].

3 In both films, Jekyll acknowledges the need to keep physical desires under control. In Mamoulian's version, Jekyll uses the incident with Ivy to re-emphasise his view of the two competing sides of human nature. He tells Lanyon that his sexual attraction to Ivy was a matter of 'elementary instinct ... we may control our actions but not our instincts', but he still thinks that it would be better to be rid of these desires. He longs to be 'clean, not only in my conduct but in my innermost thoughts and desires' [18.17–23.30]. In Fleming's version, Jekyll comments afterwards that it was only a momentary 'attack' from his evil side, which he feels perfectly capable of repelling [18.28–28.14]. Since Fleming's film was made post-Code, the scene with Ivy is less sexually explicit than in Mamoulian's version. The sexual aspects of the scene have been suppressed by the film itself.

4 Both films also suggest that desires have a legitimate role in our makeup and that excessive repression has costs. In both versions, Jekyll is a vigorous man frustrated by a repressive society, embodied in the fiancée's father. In the Mamoulian version, the father prevents the couple from bringing the marriage date forward, making Jekyll receptive to the temptations of more available women. In this connection, Jekyll asks Lanyon if a 'man dying of thirst' can 'forget water' [22.40–22.47]. In Fleming's version, Jekyll is also frustrated by a repressive society, the father even looking on disapprovingly at his public displays of affection towards his fiancé [4.26–5.35].

5 However, neither film endorses the uninhibited expression of the instincts, represented by the violent, sadistic personage who emerges when Jekyll drinks his formula. In the Mamoulian film, when Jekyll first drinks the formula and turns into Hyde, there is montage of disapproving faces together with images of desire and its frustration. Certainly, in becoming Hyde, Jekyll feels powerful and uninhibited, and rails against the social constraints on the instincts: 'You hypocrites, deniers of life. If you could see me now ... what would you think?' [26.40–29.30]. But Hyde goes on to demonstrate the dangers of fully unleashed desire.

6 Hyde cannot be identified with Nietzsche's '*ubermensch*'. For Nietzsche also, the ideal is not the uninhibited expression of instinct, which for him would amount to a reversion to the status of a brute. In keeping with this, when Jekyll becomes Hyde in the Mamoulian's version, he looks decidedly bestial and primitive.

7   In the Fleming version, there is less of a physical change in appearance during the transformation scene. This is, however, one time where Fleming's film is racier than the Mamoulian version. As Jekyll turns into Hyde, he experiences erotic hallucinations, in particular, the horseman and his steeds image, which leave no doubt that forbidden instinctual and sexual desires are finding expression [33.04–34.46].

Under the Skin

Under the Skin is a 2013 science fiction film directed by Jonathon Glazer (*Sexy Beast, Birth*). In this film, the 'monster inside' is an intelligent alien, in the guise of a woman who is driving around Scotland, stalking and killing working-class men. This is a science fiction film without big-budget special effects, relentlessly realistic. Many roles are played by non-actors and there are unscripted encounters with men on the street, filmed with hidden cameras.

Plot

In Glasgow, a motorcyclist (Jeremy McWilliams) retrieves a dead woman (Lynsey Taylor Mackay) from the roadside and puts her in the back of a van. A woman (Scarlett Johansson) puts on her clothes. The woman drives the van around Scotland, picking up men. She lures a man (Joe Szula) into a house. As he undresses, following the woman into a dark place, he is submerged in a black liquid.

At a beach, the woman tries to pick up a swimmer (Kryštof Hádek), who runs off to help a couple in trouble in rough sea. When he returns exhausted and unsuccessful, the woman strikes his head with a rock, drags him to the van and drives away, ignoring the couple's baby. The next day, the woman listens to a radio report about the missing family. The woman then visits a nightclub and picks up another man (Paul Brannigan). At the house, he follows her into the void and is submerged in the liquid. Suspended beneath the surface, he sees the swimmer floating beside him, alive but bloated. When he touches him, the swimmer's body collapses and a red substance empties out through a trough.

The woman seduces a facially-disfigured man (Adam Pearson) but lets him leave after catching herself in a mirror. The motorcyclist intercepts the man and bundles him into a car, then sets out in pursuit of the woman. In the Scottish Highlands, the woman abandons the van in the fog. She walks to a restaurant and tries to eat a piece of cake but cannot and spits it out. At a bus stop, she meets a man (Michael Moreland) who offers to help her. At his house, they eat and watch television. Alone in her room, she examines her body in a mirror. They visit a ruined castle. Back at his house, they kiss and begin to have sex, but the woman stops abruptly and examines her genitals.

The woman wanders in a forest, meets a commercial logger (Dave Acton) and finds a place to sleep. She awakes to find the man molesting her. She runs into the wilderness but he catches and attempts to rape her. He tears her skin, revealing the featureless body of the alien. As the alien extricates herself from the skin, the man douses her in petrol and burns her alive.

Key Scenes

1   As the alien sets out on her mission, to lure and entrap men, there is an extended point-of-view shot in which we follow her through a shopping mall, and later we view the world through the windows of the van she is driving [10.10–13.25]. In this manner, we are identified with her point of view; but at the same time, it is a perspective that seems strange because it is, unusually in cinematic terms, a female gaze that objectifies men and reduces them to prey. In this manner, the film conveys the sense of an alien perspective on the world. This is also an ironic comment on gender relations: a woman could only act like this and get away with it if she were an alien.

2   In the scene at the beach, the sense of an alien perspective on the world is reinforced. The woman strikes the swimmer with a rock and drags him to her van, leaving the baby of the couple the swimmer had tried to save crying on the beach. The scene is shot in an objective, anthropological way. No particular attention is paid to the baby, who is left in the background of the shot, a mere detail, reflecting the woman's own lack of interest in it [22.37–28.06]. In this scene, a sense of the alienness of the woman's perspective is conveyed through its absolute amorality, so remote from ordinary human ways of responding to such a situation.

3   There are now hints that the woman is no longer a pure predator. She is presented walking in the street as if being watched rather than watching. When she falls, passers-by gather around her to help her up. This is followed by multiple scenes of people interacting on the streets, eventually forming a golden aura around her face, as if she is starting to be drawn to humanity, wanting to belong [44.40–47.48].

4   The woman picks up her last victim, a facially-disfigured man and, though talking with him sympathetically, brings him to the house for consumption. However, after examining herself at length in a

mirror, she lets him go. We have so far seen portions of her face
in the van's rear-view mirror, but this is the first time her entire face
appears in a reflected image. It does not seem to be a moment of
self-discovery, but rather the point where she tries to identify with
the woman she is in the eyes of others [59.44–1.01.55].

5   After this, her point of view is no longer dominant. She appears
increasingly as a figure in the landscape [1.04.40–1.07.13; also
1.09.08–1.10.13]. This also marks a shift in her relations with others. She ceases to be a predator of men; instead, she becomes
their prey. Now, instead of picking up and luring men to her
house, she is picked up by a man, and invited to stay in his house
[1.13.25–1.14.09]. He is kind and wants to help her, but this could
also be seen as a form of male predation. Now she has to be
carried over puddles [1.19.15–1.19.48] and helped downstairs
[1.20.09–1.22.04]. Again, there is an ironic reference to gender
relations. To identify as a human female is to no longer be a predatory subject but to become the object of prey.

6   There are further mirror scenes at the man's house [1.14.07–1.14.10;
1.16.13–1.18.04]. The attempt to identify with the woman she is in
the eyes of others may represent a form of self-deception, insofar as
it constitutes an attempt to deny her own alienness. That alienness
continues to intrude. In the restaurant, she gags on a piece of cake
she tries to eat [1.07.23–1.09.07]; at the man's house, she taps the
wrong rhythm to the music [1.14.44–1.15.37]; sex is incomprehensible to her [1.22.19–1.26.36]. In the end, she is unable to lead this
human life and flees into the forest.

7   This only makes her more vulnerable to attack. After the predatory logger tries to rape her, he discovers the alien under her skin
and runs off. She discards her human skin, fully revealing her alien
form. She spends some time contemplating her face, which she now
holds in her hands. This may constitute a final recognition that the
human female she wanted to identify with was only a mask, skin-
deep [1.37.47–1.39.30].

2   Sin and Self-Denial
Religious Ethics

At the end of Abel Ferrara's *The Addiction* (1995), a young woman lies on a hospital bed. She has asked for the blinds to be opened and is now waiting for the sunlight to fall on her. Kathleen Conklin (Lili Taylor) is a vampire who has come to be horrified by her addiction to blood and no longer wants to submit to it (Figure 2.1). As a vampire, she knows how to do away with herself.

Figure 2.1 Kathleen the vampire in *The Addiction* (Abel Ferrara, 1995. Credit: October Films/Photofest).

But Casanova (Annabella Sciorra), the vampire who originally bit her, has entered the room and abruptly closes the blinds. 'It's not that easy' she says. 'To find rest takes a real genius'. But now as Kathleen lies alone in the gloom, she has another visitor. A priest enters and asks how she is. She whispers that she wants to make a confession and asks for God's forgiveness. The priest absolves her, administers a communion wafer and she becomes still, in repose as we hear her say 'Amen' in voiceover. She is seemingly released, at rest at last. In the film's final scene, we see Kathleen in a cemetery, leaving a flower on her own grave and then walking off as the camera pans upwards to a sculpture of a crucifix. Over this we hear her in voice-over, saying 'To face what we are in the end, we stand before the light. And our true nature is revealed. Self-revelation is annihilation of the self'. With this scene, this grittily realist film's narrative has given way to imagery filled with intimations of the transcendental. In accepting God, Kathleen has been annihilated as a vampire and has transcended her addiction. Thus, the vampire returns to our discussion, only now in a form coloured by religious considerations. It is the religious, specifically Christian, view of ethics and human nature that is the subject of this chapter.

Divine Command

With the rise of Christianity, which emerged out of a first-century Jewish movement to become the dominant worldview in the West, especially in the medieval period, a new stream was injected into ethical thinking, a religious conception of morality that turned on a single transcendent deity existing in a realm beyond this one. Gone is the profusion of rather worldly gods that populated the ancient world. In the Christian view, the world is understood to be subject to a supernatural ordering principle, itself personified as a divine being that creates the world and is able to intervene in it. The focus in ethical thinking is on how human beings are related to this divine being, which is greatly superior to them in power, goodness and wisdom, indeed all-good as well as all-knowing and all-powerful. As has been noted, Christianity incorporated a great many classical ideas into its worldview, particularly from Greek philosophy. This notion of a transcendental being is informed by Plato's Form of the Good, the overarching Form in his unworldly sphere of perfect Forms. But where the Good is an abstract ideal for Plato, the Christian God is personal. As with Plato, for Christianity there is one universal, objective form of the good life. The Christian God issues commands for the universe as a whole and human beings in particular. Being good is a matter of obeying those commands, submitting to them, bringing your will into line with God's. Evil is turning away from God, trying to determine your own fate and thinking that you are self-sufficient. Left to your own devices, you will fall prey to the cruelty and evil that arises from your own corrupted nature.

Even today there are many for whom morality seems impossible without a Christian religious basis and for whom the modern 'materialist' or scientific view of the universe consequently represents a profound problem. This is the position famously expressed by Dmitri Karamazov in Dostoevsky's novel *The Brothers Karamazov*, when the character proclaims that 'Without God ... everything is permitted' (Dostoevsky 1990, 589). Or, as expressed by Sonia (Diane Keaton) in Woody Allen's Russian novels parody *Love and Death* (1975), 'let's say there is no God and each man is free to do exactly as he chooses, well, what prevents you from murdering someone?' It's a question that as we will see, haunts a number of the characters in his subsequent films. The more general concern being expressed here is that not only would one have no motivation to be ethical if God did not exist, but there would be no basis for the rules of morality. However, it should already be apparent that, even if religious systems typically dispense morality, morality does not necessarily depend on religion. In the West, ancient Greek and Roman ethical positions justifying moral judgements developed prior to and independently of Christianity, indeed of any religious standpoint. Epicureanism in particular developed an ethical position on the basis of an aggressively materialist view of the world, a reason perhaps for Christianity's particular hostility towards it. In the end, morality only depends necessarily on the Christian God to the extent that one will only accept as morality a Christian conception of morality. In other words, that is a view that presupposes what it is arguing for, a God-centred conception of the world and morality.

In this God-centred understanding, emerging out of both the Jewish and Christian traditions, God is envisaged as a lawgiver, handing down laws. The Hollywood biblical epic provides a spectacular visual representation of this. Moral laws are literally etched into stone by God from on high in *The Ten Commandments* (Cecil B. DeMille 1956; see Mitchell 2009, 489). On this understanding, in order to guide us in the right way of living, God has formulated certain rules or commands, epitomised by the Ten Commandments, that we ought to obey. We are not compelled to obey them, because we have been created as free agents, and so we can know what we should do and yet choose not to abide by it. It is up to us to decide whether to accept or reject these rules. Nonetheless, these rules tell us how we ought to live. This is a rule-based or 'deontological' conception of morality, one characterised by universal moral laws. The virtue ethics of the ancient world does not disappear. The ideal remains virtuous behaviour, but whereas in ancient ethics the focus was primarily on living in accordance with one's nature, now right living becomes a matter of following external standards, the divine commandments, conforming to the will of God, whether embodied in the revelations of the bible, the authority of the church or the inner voice of one's conscience. Virtues are now the states of character that help us to do God's will (van Hooft 2006, 84). In terms of predecessors in ancient thought, this picture is closest to Plato's, insofar as for Plato the ultimate basis of morality is not to be found in human nature but in the transcendental world of the Forms. It can similarly be seen as a non-naturalist notion of ethics only now moral values are dependent on a supernatural deity. To distinguish it, we can characterise this as a 'supernaturalist' conception of morality.

A more mundane version would have it that moral rules that evolved out of ancient communal life came to be understood as having been laid down by God.

But in the religious view at least, moral rules are God's commandments. This view has been spelt out as the 'divine command' theory of morality, for which the morally right thing to do is whatever is commanded by God, and morally wrong means that which is forbidden by God. This construction also provides us with a new sort of reason to be moral. Plato's Gyges story raises the question of why we should be moral if we can commit immoral acts without any chance of being observed and punished. On the religious account, even if we are invisible to those around us, we can never ultimately escape being seen and judged. Judah, the doctor in Allen's *Crimes and Misdemeanors*, may have wealth and social standing to arrange for his mistress's murder and cover up his involvement, but he is haunted by memories of his father and his religious upbringing. In particular he recalls his father saying that God sees everything and that those who are righteous will be rewarded while those who are wicked will be punished for eternity. We may thus have a reason to do the right thing, constrained by the threat of divine punishment or at least by the promptings of our own conscience – whether the latter is understood as the voice of God within or internalised parental admonitions.

The idea that moral rules are an expression of God's will is not, however, without its problems. Apart from anything else, this view of morality depends on a belief in God and the validity of the scriptures. If this belief is questioned, it is undermined. So it is for the murderous doctor in *Crimes and Misdemeanors*. For Judah, despite the residual religious orientation that derives from his upbringing, and the internal struggles that he has to undergo as a result, he insists that he is in the end a 'man of science', that there is no God watching and judging, and that there is no divine punishment to contend with. The scientific view of the world is understood here to undermine the religious perspective, with large implications if religion is taken to be the basis for morality. Without it there is only our conscience stopping us from acting purely in our own self-interest and Judah finds that conscience is not as powerful a constraint on behaviour as one might imagine. Here, we are back on the couch at the end of film, with Judah, having gotten away with murder, telling his story to filmmaker Cliff in the guise of a movie plot. Cliff suggests that a more believable scenario would be to have the protagonist being driven by guilt to turn themselves in, an allusion to the plot of Dostoevsky's *Crime and Punishment*. Judah's response is to dismisses this as something that happens in the movies, not in real life. In reality, people can live with all sorts of sins.

Allen's more recent *Match Point* (2005) explores similar themes but with God even more conclusively out of the picture. This time the character who gets away with murder is Chris (Jonathan Rhys Meyers), an ex-tennis star. Having married into a wealthy family, he, like Judah, does away with a mistress who is threatening his privileged life. Here, the religious dimension has been more starkly eclipsed. There are no troubling flashbacks to a religious upbringing. Early in the film, over dinner, Chris relates dismissively how his father found religion when he lost both his legs and insists that 'scientists are confirming more and more that all existence is here by blind chance'. Once again, the modern scientific view of the world is seen as excluding a religious perspective, which is significant if morality is understood to be impossible without God. Nor is Chris greatly troubled by guilt or remorse at what he has done. Conscience remains a weak force. In a later dream sequence, he confesses to his victim Nola (Scarlett Johansson) that he did feel guilt, but you can learn to push it under the rug and go on. Like Judah in *Crimes and Misdemeanors*, he sees himself as having done what had to be done to protect his interests, making pure self-interest the ruling determinant of his behaviour. In another echo of the earlier film, *Match Point* makes a jokey reference to Dostoevsky's *Crime and Punishment* with a shot early on of Chris reading the book in bed, and, presumably perplexed by the protagonist Raskolnikov's actions, turning to a *Companion to Dostoevsky* for explanation.

Match Point can be taken to dramatise, even more emphatically than *Crimes and Misdemeanors*, the Dostoevskian concern that without God everything is permissible. Equally, it highlights the problem that to understand ethics as necessarily based on religion makes one vulnerable as a moral being if one loses one's faith. But there also internal problems with the religious conception of ethics. In its divine command form, in which the morally good thing to do is whatever is commanded by God, it is not clear how we are to establish what God's will actually is, what God in fact commands. The scriptures are not always consistent and are open to interpretation, as are miracles, dreams and other signs that might be invoked to support claims regarding God's will. The problem becomes especially acute if the will of God is invoked in order to justify what to ordinary observers might seem to be evil, cruel or in other ways morally questionable acts. How do we know that those who invoke this justification are not simply mistaken, deluded, mentally ill or perhaps just finding a convenient rationalisation for what they do? The more extreme the actions, the more likely we are to think that something like this is going on. The person themselves might be absolutely sincere in their beliefs about what God is commanding them to do, but such claims not only make it possible for them to justify extreme acts to themselves, as being in the name of a higher power, but also serve to insulate their actions from critical examination. As Voltaire puts it in his 1764 *Philosophical Dictionary*, 'What can you say to a man who tells you he prefers obeying God rather than men, and that as a result he's certain he'll go to heaven if he cuts your throat?' (Voltaire 2011, 138)

A case in point, the biblical story of Abraham presents a picture of someone who believes that he has divine justification (via angelic command) for killing his son, however reluctant he might be to do so. For all his certainty, it would be natural for others to suppose that this must be the belief of a delusional individual, perhaps one suffering from a mental illness. This is certainly our natural assumption when presented with the homicidal father (Bill Paxton) in *Frailty* (Bill Paxton, 2001), who one night informs his children that he has been visited by an angel and given the mission of destroying demons disguised as human beings. There is also an Abrahamic element here, in that he also indicates that the angel told him that his older son, Fenton, is a demon as well, though he refuses to kill him. We can sympathise with Fenton, who thinks that his father has 'gone crazy', and that his younger brother, Adam, who claims to be sharing some of his father's visions, has been brainwashed by him. The film is able to exploit the audience's presuppositions by eventually making it apparent that the father was in fact telling the truth; and also revealing that the narrator of the story, which we were led to believe was Fenton, was in fact Adam, who did indeed share the father's visions. At the same time, film has the advantage of being able to give the viewer God-like access to the world it creates. In this case, we are given access to enough information to know that the father is not crazy, that he really is on a mission from God. For ordinary human beings, without any God-like access to the transcendental, it remains unclear how we can ever know what the will of God might be, or whether anyone who claims to be following God's commands is indeed doing so.

By way of comparison, *The Passion of Joan of Arc* (Carl Theodor Dreyer, 1928) seems to bring us face to face with the religious mission that infuses the life of the central character. The film follows Joan of Arc's 1431 trial for heresy, her interrogation, torture and eventual execution, based on a transcript of the actual trial. Here there is a dramatic portrayal of someone who fervently believes themselves to be on a mission from God. Through stylistic means, particularly the repeated, almost obsessive close-ups of actor Maria Falconetti's expressive face, what is communicated is the character's absolute commitment to a religious experience, regardless of the consequences of doing so. In this way, the film conveys the reality and certainty of religious experience, at least for the person directly involved. Yet despite that, it remains the case that there is nothing approaching certainty for the viewer here. In contrast to *Frailty*, what is absent is any 'objective' filmic validation of Joan's belief, any revelation to the audience allowing us to see that she was indeed acting in God's name. The film does not portray the transcendental and we are not given access to transcendental experiences themselves or even indirect evidence of them. The character can certainly be seen as somehow communicating an experience of something beyond that cannot be conveyed through words. Someone who already believes might be predisposed to view what is being presented this way. Or we may simply see an extraordinary evocation of religious fervour, as something akin to madness. And in the end, it remains possible to ask whether we are gazing on the face of a saint or someone who is simply insane.

So these are some of the problems with the divine command view to do with what we can know of the basis for its moral claims, but a further kind of problem has to with the very notion of moral goodness or rightness it involves. Inasmuch as the belief that one is following God's commands provides a justification for the actions one undertakes, it is not an objection to what they are doing that their action might seem evil or terrible. If it is commanded by God, it is morally right. By definition, what is morally right is what God commands, and what is wrong is what he forbids. Thus, the homicidal father in *Frailty* can quite rightly say he is doing the morally good thing, however horrible it might appear to others, insofar as it has been commanded by God. In principle anything, no matter how seemingly reprehensible, is morally right provided God commands it. To that extent, the problem is not so much that without God everything is permissible, as that if there is a God, then anything is permitted. In practical terms, the person who believes that God is on their side is capable of anything, in the name of the higher law. Belief in a higher justice will enable one to overcome the moral qualms most would ordinarily feel about killing and other extreme acts (see Zizek 2012; Ignatieff 2013).

We might protest that surely a good God would not command terrible things, that there would be limits to what a genuinely good God would command. But now we are in the realm of the Euthyphro problem, so-called because it was raised by Plato in his dialogue *Euthyphro*. In the dialogue, Socrates and Euthyphro are discussing piety, and Socrates asks whether the gods love the pious because it is the pious or whether the pious is pious only because it is loved by the gods (Plato 2003, 10a). This is now our question: is something right because God commands it or does God command it because it is right? The problem is, there are problems with both alternatives. If something is right because God commands it, there is no moral limit to what God can command. *Frailty*'s homicidal father insists that 'destroying demons is a good thing. Killing people is bad', but while he may want to draw the line at doing away with people, were he to be commanded by God to kill indiscriminately, he could not object on the grounds that such an action was evil. God's command would make it good. But if there is no reason why God cannot command any act, including indiscriminate murder, this also means that God's commands are completely arbitrary. He has no more reason to command an action than to forbid it. Moreover, the very idea that God is good is destroyed on this view. If good and bad are determined by God's will, then to say that God's commands are good is only to say that God's commands are commanded by God, which is an empty statement. Thus, while we might look for guidance to rules of morality handed down by God from on high, if right and wrong are whatever God determines them to be, they become a matter of arbitrary choice, and the firm foundation God is supposed to provide for morality evaporates away.

The alternative is to drop the idea that an action is right because God commands it and to hold instead that God commands an action because it is right. In this view, God has the infinite wisdom to know what is right and what is wrong, and in the light of this knowledge, commands the right conduct. This avoids the arbitrariness of the first option. However, this approach has its own difficulties, severe ones because it seems to make a religion-based conception of morality unnecessary. Now, God is no longer required in order to make an action right or wrong, to justify moral judgements. There are objective standards of right and wrong that are independent of God's will, that God himself has to adhere to. And as such, what is distinctively theological about this account of morality seems to disappear. We have effectively abandoned the divine command theory of morality.

Augustine

A key architect of the Christian world view, and Christian ethics in particular, is Augustine (354–430 AD), bishop of Hippo, in what is now Algeria. Living in the dying days of the Roman empire, around the same time as Hypatia, Augustine articulates a unified doctrine for the emerging religion, drawing on both Plato and

Neoplatonism. The two-level view of reality as material existence and a higher, transcendental reality that these views share is transmuted into the idea of God as a transcendent, immaterial reality existing eternally outside of space and time, but also the source of everything that comes below. Against this background, Augustine formulates a Christianised version of eudaimonistic virtue ethics, bound up with a version of the divine command theory. Once again, all human beings are understood to seek happiness, 'beatitude' in Augustine's terms. Only now, real happiness for a human being consists in enjoyment of God, which is the reward for being virtuous in this life. God provides the rules we must adhere to if we are to attain this reward and virtue consists in successfully following the rules. Morality thus takes the form of conforming to the prescriptions of the divine law, the unchanging and eternal ideals, articulated in the scriptures, that are also imprinted on the human mind. As such, we have reasons to be moral over and above the fear of divine punishment if we do not. Being moral, following the rules, being virtuous in this life, is a condition for human happiness, the ultimate happiness of being one with God in the next. Thus, as with ancient ethics, the goal for human beings remains happiness, the fulfilled life. Only now that happiness requires that we follow God's commands and fulfilment takes the form of the ultimate union with God.

Virtue here includes the classic virtues celebrated by the Greeks, wisdom, justice, courage and temperance or self-denial, but also virtues that are foreign to Greek thinking but praised in the New Testament, namely faith, hope and charity. Charity is an orientation towards the good or well-being of others. The addition of these new virtues by Augustine is the point where altruism enters significantly into moral thinking, though the term itself was not coined until the nineteenth century by August Comte. It is not that ancient ethics was self-centred, concerned only with the individual and their happiness. What seems new with Christianity however, is the increasing importance of the ideal of selflessness, sacrificing oneself, putting the needs and interests of others above one's own, the altruism that nowadays is practically synonymous with being moral. With Augustine, altruism in the form of Christian charity is the preeminent virtue, the most important of a number of forms of behaviour commanded by God, the pursuit of which will lead to eternal salvation. For the moment, however, we are going to focus on another aspect of Augustine's moral picture, which is the supreme importance of self-denial, the renunciation of desire.

One important thing that God's rules commanded was to go against one's feelings, desires and appetites. They are too strongly attached to the things of this world and this is an avowedly supernatural conception of morality. Being moral, attaining Christian goodness and virtue, is very much bound up with rising above the physical appetites, denying our love for sensual pleasures, rejecting attachment to this world, in order to reach God in the next. Desire, which connects us to the material world, stands in the way of goodness, and ultimately of salvation, and needs to be overcome. We can see in this the reappearance, with Augustine at the start of the Christian era, of Plato's picture of human life as a struggle to overcome and control desire. Augustine also takes from Plato the view that the self is an immaterial soul that can think, the 'inner person'; and the idea of human being as the combination of a rational soul and a mortal and earthly body. There is, however, one important difference. For Plato, the good life depends on reason having the dominant position. For Augustine, the most important feature of the soul, ethically speaking, is not reason but the will, the ability to choose between the lower goods, the objects of the bodily pleasures and appetites, or the higher goods of virtue and God. In his autobiographical *Confessions*, Augustine details his own addiction to bodily pleasures in his youth, before he overcame them with his eventual conversion to Christianity.

Thus, being moral on this account requires us to overcome our desiring nature, for the sake of ultimate union with God, in which the immaterial soul, finally free of the body, will go to heaven. At the same time, Augustine is extremely pessimistic about the prospects for most of us managing to achieve this self-denial and attain virtue. Whereas for the ancient world virtue was generally seen as being within the power of human beings to achieve, albeit with difficulty, for Augustine, it is virtually impossible. As far as the appetites are concerned, he has a keen appreciation of human weakness of will. To say he is suspicious of desire is an understatement. He seems to have been terrified of the pleasures of the flesh, the physical desires that persistently refuse to be constrained by the will, which he calls 'concupiscence'. For him, desire is an internal compulsion that human beings by themselves are too weak to overcome or break free from in order to choose the good. Human beings are constantly attracted towards evil, the excessive satisfaction of their lower desires for material things and pleasures. Why do people find it so difficult to choose the good? For Augustine, it is a matter of human nature. Human beings are inherently depraved, constitutionally inclined towards indulging their physical desires.

This inherent human predisposition towards evil is in turn understood as a sickness that is part of humanity's 'fallen' condition. Human beings had inherited the original sin of the first parents, Adam and Eve, who disobeyed God and were thrown out of the Garden of Eden as a result. The biblical story, which had been dismissed or treated as an allegory by earlier commentators, was turned by Augustine into a founding myth. Or as one commentator puts it, Augustine 'rescued Adam and Eve from obscurity, devised the doctrine of original sin—and the rest is sexual history' (Greenblatt 2017). Before the fall, 'though they [human beings] carried about an animal body, they yet felt in it no disobedience moving against themselves' (Augustine 2015, 202). Now, the individual is 'disobedient to himself' (Augustine 1958, 313). Because of Adam and Eve's original rebellion, every individual is now plagued by rebellious appetites and passions. Now, says Augustine in *City of God*, the individual is 'disobedient to himself' (Augustine 1958, 313). Their will has been corrupted, they lack the capacity to choose the good, and are incapable of obeying God's laws without otherworldly assistance, in the form of the grace of God. Virtue is only possible now as a gift from God. There may be saintly humans, but they are only good by virtue of God's grace, something that can be given but cannot be earned. In the end, only a few will be saved; most will continue to sin and end up in hell. In this manner, Augustine introduces the abiding religious notion of human beings as fundamentally corrupted by their physical appetites, constitutionally given over to the sin and evil that are associated especially with the pleasures of the flesh. Much of this thinking was reaffirmed by the Protestant reformers in the sixteenth century, of which we will see more later.

There are recognisable features of this Augustinian account in Fleming's *Dr Jekyll and Mr Hyde*. This film has already been discussed as a representation of Plato's picture of human nature as a battle between reason and desire. Over and above this, it also has distinct religious overtones, and indeed, features that are characteristic of the Augustinian appropriation of Plato's picture of human nature. Human beings are presented as striving to be good, where this is identified with Christian virtuousness as well as Victorian propriety; and there is also an evil side in all of us, identified particularly with physical appetites, which are nonetheless strangely attractive and constantly threaten to undermine our efforts to be good. Spencer Tracy's Dr Jekyll discusses his picture of human nature over the dinner table in explicitly religious terms, insisting that 'we all have an evil side ... why, as Christians we admit that man is created weak'. He envisages the soul as a battleground in which good and evil, chained together, fight for supremacy. This is not to discount the modern sensibility that also runs through the film. The bishop invokes the need for God's grace to overcome our physical appetites, suggesting that there is a 'higher source' from which human beings can find aid in their struggle against evil. Dr Jekyll, more up to date, insists that human beings will be assisted in choosing the good not by otherworldly grace but by this-worldly medical science. Science will free human beings from their evil side so that the good can develop unhindered.

As indicated in the earlier discussion, the *Dr Jekyll and Mr Hyde* films are also modern to the extent that there is a readiness to see desire as having a legitimate role in the human makeup and its excessive suppression as damaging. This is evident in Mamoulian's pre-Code version of the Jekyll and Hyde story. Fredric March's Jekyll clearly wants to marry his fiancé as soon as possible but is being made to wait by her father. Frustrated, he is attracted to a prostitute, who flirts with him in a remarkably erotic scene. He is still capable of expressing Victorian sentiments, saying of his impending marriage that he wants to be 'clean, not only in my conduct but in my innermost thoughts and desires'. Nonetheless, on first becoming Hyde he rages against the constraints of propriety: 'You hypocrites, deniers of life. If you could see me now ... what would you think?' It might be thought that the Fleming version is going to be more conservative, appearing as it does after the enforcement of the Hays Code. Certainly, there is the overt religious content and the object of Jekyll's forbidden desire is now a barmaid. But it is clear that Tracy's Jekyll is also being frustrated by a repressive society, his fiancé's straitlaced father insisting in delaying his marriage and looking on disapprovingly at his public displays of affection. The film also rather subversively co-opts both Platonic and religious symbolism to depict unleashed desire. As Jekyll turns into Hyde for the first time, there are the revealing hallucinatory images. As noted earlier, Plato's horseman and horses image of human nature appears as a coachman whipping horses that turn into his fiancé and the barmaid, the image becoming a metaphor for Jekyll's desires for sexual domination. There are also images of a whirlpool and mud, images that Augustine uses in his *Confessions* to describe the sexual impulses that dominated what to him was his debauched youth (see Augustine 1961, 41, 55).

Here we can also return to our discussion of *The Addiction*. The vampire, as another monstrous embodiment of unconstrained desire, is given a thoroughly Augustinian interpretation in this film. The scene described at the start of the chapter is the culmination of a story that begins with Kathleen, an idealistic philosophy student appalled by a world that could allow evils such as the Holocaust and war crimes, being turned into a vampire and becoming everything she hates. As a vampire, she cannot help committing evil acts and the film suggests that in this she is really no different to the rest of humanity. All human beings have an innate predisposition towards evil. We have seen the vampire as a representation of the Platonic conception of evil, in terms of being dominated by one's desires and appetites. Now, resurrected in a more religious register, the vampire has become a metaphor for the evil at the very heart of a corrupt human nature. It is a fateful addiction to evil that can only be overcome in the end through the saving grace of a Christian God. This gloomy Augustinian view of human nature is summed up by the vampire Casanova who originally bit Kathleen, as she lectures her in the hospital room: 'we're not evil because of the evil we do, but we do evil because we are evil … What choices do such people have? It's not like we have any options'. It is the priest, the next visitor, who provides Kathleen with her only way of escape. The focus of the film, then, is very much on human nature as fundamentally corrupted by the physical appetites, inherently given over to sin and evil, and too weak to resist without divine assistance.

There is no sense here of physical desire being a legitimate part of our makeup. In line with the Augustinian account, it remains something that we need to overcome. For the early Church in general, desire is viewed with deep hostility, a sign of corruption, an evil we must struggle against; or at the very least, a distraction from higher spiritual concerns, keeping us tied to this world. Any moral improvement that might be possible in this world involves denying or suppressing one's desires. Consequently, in early Church writings and practices, there is a strong emphasis on asceticism, the extreme renunciation of worldly desires. Amongst the more spectacular expressions of this was the ascetic saint Simeon Stylites, who in the fifth century spent 37 years living on a platform atop a pillar in the Syrian desert. We will have occasion to revisit the Christian ascetic atop his pillar in the next chapter, with the help of Luis Bunuel's *Simon of the Desert* (1965), whose central character is loosely based on this historical figure. The film, while not being unsympathetic to its central character, finds his exorbitant self-denial irresistibly comic. Even if this extreme behaviour represents something of a high point in the history of Christian asceticism, in the broader history of Christian thought, goodness and virtue have always seemed to require a generous dose of self-denial and privation. And here lies a problem. Particularly from a modern point of view, this self-denial, like the authoritarian suppression of desire in Plato that it echoes, is liable to come across as repressive and unhealthy, bordering on self-mutilation.

Nonetheless, the attitude persists, extending even to the modern Antipodes. For the priests and brothers running the fifties Catholic boys' boarding school in *The Devil's Playground* (Fred Schepisi, 1976), any unseemly desires in their charges have to be identified and stamped out wherever possible. The most fanatical amongst them, Brother Francine (Arthur Dignam), tells the boys, 'your body is your worst enemy ... you must be on guard against your senses at all times'. Naturally, he is also the one most tormented by the desires he is trying to forbid in others, reduced to anguish in the mundane circumstances of a visit to the public swimming pool and tormented at night by lurid dreams. Others on the teaching staff talk more matter-of-factly about the strange requirements of their profession and its probably futile efforts to stamp out what is surely a natural part of the human makeup. Nonetheless, the institution is dedicated to teaching its charges to suppress their desires. The hero, 13-year old Tom (Simon Burke) spends long hours praying for guidance, terrified and ashamed by his 'impure' thoughts. In the end, he runs away from the school, escaping not from his desires but from the tyranny of the institution that demonises them.

This is not to discount the religious film that celebrates the satisfaction of desires. In *Babette's Feast* (Gabriel Axel, 1987), two sisters, Martine (Birgitte Federspiel) and Philippa (Bodil Kjer), live in a small village in nineteenth-century Denmark. They are members of a strict, puritanical Protestant sect founded by their father and have lived lives marked by deep self-denial and sacrifice for others. Now elderly, their father dead, they take in a Parisian refugee, Babette (Stéphane Audran), to work as a housekeeper. When Babette wins the lottery, she decides to spend it on a sumptuous banquet for the sisters and the other towns-people. These people are initially scandalised by the prospect of this 'satanic Sabbath', which represents to them the evil of indulgence. However, as the meal itself proceeds, they cannot help taking enjoyment from it, and in the process loosen up and become more human, able to express love and mercy. The film might be seen as a critique of religious self-denial, which has clearly cost the sisters a great deal and a reminder of the pleasures of this life. However, it could also be read in religious terms as a film in which the episode of earthly satisfaction, the feast, is invested with value as symbolising the 'heavenly banquet', a premonition of the other-worldly fulfilment that will be a reward for the self-denial in this one (see Wright 1997). Still, precisely by being reduced to a symbol of other-worldly satisfaction, the feast is no antidote to religious self-denial in this world, no cure for the Augustinian hostility towards physical desires.

A further issue from the modern point of view is the Augustinian representation of human beings as not only corrupted by their physical desires, but also as having limited prospects of overcoming this corruption. It seems that on this view moral improvement is simply not possible by human means. It is only with divine assistance that any improvement is going to be possible, and even then, only after death. In *The Addiction*, the only people in the film who are able to resist the vampires are the priest and a man handing out religious pamphlets. They have presumably been lucky enough to be fortified by God's grace. For those who have not been so strengthened there is no hope of escaping evil and corruption. The vampires are representative of the rest of us, addicted by nature to evil, powerless to fight against it. For the modern sensibility, this extreme pessimism about the prospects of improvement is one of the most problematic features of the Augustinian view. The idea that human beings are intrinsically depraved and corrupt seems to condemn them to evil, leaving little hope of progress in this world or the next. Indeed, being good seems so far out of reach of human beings as to make any aspiration to moral goodness meaningless. If as the vampire Casanova says, we 'do evil because we are evil', if we have no choice in the matter and if we are only made moral by God's grace, which may be given but not earned, we might wonder whether there is any point in talking about morality at all (see Malik 2014, 71).

Finally, we have to return to the problem noted earlier, that evil might arise not from being under the sway of one's lower desires and instincts, but from the virtuous, self-controlled individual who takes themselves to be acting in order to please God. As with Plato's account, rigorous self-control and the denial of desire is perfectly compatible with evil behaviour. Self-control allows one to pursue one's tasks with especial single-mindedness, bringing about the suppression of any feelings of compassion or sympathy that might otherwise moderate one's actions. This is another concern highlighted by early modern critics of religion like Michel de Montaigne, the sixteenth-century philosopher-essayist. He fills his essays with examples of people acting cruelly, not because of an excessive pursuit of physical pleasures, but because they think they have a higher mandate for what they do. In his essay 'On Moderation', he mentions the notion 'which was universally embraced by all religions … which leads us to think that we can please Heaven and Nature by our murders and our massacres' (Montaigne 2003, 226). Two hundred years later, Voltaire's comments on the dangers of fanaticism in the *Philosophical Dictionary* will express similar concerns.

The potential for murderous behaviour in this way of thinking is dramatised in Darren Aronofsky's *Noah* (2014). The film, essentially a revival of the old Hollywood biblical epic, reimagines the biblical story of the flood, but it does so in a grimly realistic way. It does not hold back from showing the flood itself as an act of spectacular brutality, a genocidal act that does away indiscriminately with innocent and guilty, young and old alike. More to the point, Noah (Russell Crowe) himself comes across as a religious fanatic, inexpressive and driven, convinced that the human race is inherently wicked and ought to die out. This attitude extends to his own family; he does not want them to produce any offspring. In keeping with this, when his adopted daughter Ila (Emma Watson) produces two children he resolves to murder them, despite his family's protests. He only refrains from doing so at the last moment, and this is the point where he ceases to be a vehicle of blind religious certainty and feeling and humanity reassert themselves.

There is a further suggestion here that religion might be not only unnecessary for but in some cases positively inimical to moral behaviour and that human beings might have a better chance of behaving decently without it. In having Noah contemplate killing his granddaughters, the film is not being particularly faithful to the biblical story. Indeed, it is incorporating a version of the Abraham story into the story of Noah. But the Abraham story can itself be seen as a testament to fanaticism and the willingness to murder even those closest to you in the name of religious belief. In Abraham's case, there is no saving intervention of feeling or humanity. The protagonist would have gone through with the murder had he not been stopped, and he is only stopped by divine intervention, the same intervention that set the events in motion in the first place. Once again, it seems that with God anything is permitted. In the extremity of his behaviour, Abraham will continue to be of interest to later commentators on the human condition such as Kierkegaard and Sartre, as we will see in Chapter Five.

Aquinas and Natural Law

We move forward now to the thirteenth century and to another key figure in the development of the Christian worldview and religious ethics. This is Thomas Aquinas (1225–1274), perhaps the pre-eminent philosopher of the middle ages. At the height of the medieval period, in thirteenth-century Italy, Aquinas rewrote Christian theology with his monumental *Summa Theologica* (literally, a summary of theology). At one level, the picture being presented here is similar to Augustine's. It is also a Christianised eudaimonistic account. Human beings seek happiness or fulfilment, which is understood ultimately as union with God, the transcendent figure that is all-knowing, all-powerful and all-good. Attaining this ideal is a matter of following God's rules and the moral virtues are states of character that help us to do so.

However, there is a marked shift in orientation with Aquinas. Where Augustine's ethics is transcendental, Aquinas's is more down to earth, more naturalistic. For Augustine, following God's rules requires that we detach ourselves from the world and from our corrupted bodily natures. For Aquinas, it means following the natural inclinations of our natures, our bodies. Overall, Aquinas is far less critical of the body and bodily appetites than Augustine. Moral directives, God's commands, are embedded in nature and in human nature. Certain ways of acting are morally good because they are the natural thing to do for human beings and others are to be rejected as unnatural. Another key difference is that whereas for Augustine what was most important ethically speaking was the will, backed up by faith, Aquinas puts the focus back on reason. The rules of Christian morality might still be based on the revelations of the bible and Church tradition, but Aquinas argued that reason could provide a basis for these precepts. Rational insight into our own nature is going to provide the basis for the moral prescriptions of Christianity.

This is still a divine command view of morality, but the divine commands are now understood to be imbued in nature itself. There is a God-given moral structure to the universe, an 'eternal law' inherent in nature and human nature. Our reason enables us to discern this order in nature and in the inclinations of our own nature, and by reflecting on them, we can derive the principles of natural law. As Aquinas puts it: 'the natural law is nothing other than the participation in eternal law on the part of the rational creature' (Aquinas 1998, 620). Thus, where Augustine counsels us to reject this world in order to turn towards God, Aquinas argues that God manifests himself through worldly things, and by understanding this world, we can understand God and the moral rules he prescribes for us. To that extent, Augustine's supernaturalism turns into a form of naturalism.

Underlying this change is a shift in philosophical inspiration. Where Augustine drew on Plato who looked to the transcendental Forms, Aquinas is influenced by the more this-worldly oriented Aristotle, whose writings had been recently rediscovered by the West. Aquinas's vision of nature is a Christianisation of Aristotle's view that all things, animate and inanimate, have an inbuilt purpose that they are designed to realise, a goal that is proper to the kind of thing they are. With Aquinas this inbuilt purpose comes to be understood as God's purpose, built into the nature of everything that God has created. In fulfilling their nature and purpose, doing what comes naturally, they are playing their proper role in God's comprehensive plan for the world. Here Aquinas is also drawing on the Stoic idea that there is a rational order to nature, a logos. For Aquinas, a rational God makes the world act in accordance with laws. And while non-human things obey these laws blindly, human beings have been given reason that enables them to discover and explicitly formulate these laws, which tell them how we ought to act, in the form of the natural law. This is discussed in particular in Questions 91 to 94 of Part 1 of Part 2 of *Summa Theologica* (Aquinas 1998, 611–652).

In this manner, the divine command theory is turned into the idea that there is a natural law inherent in things and human nature, expressing God's will for creation. Though coming from a different religious tradition, something like this is articulated in *Crimes and Misdemeanors*. It is another of the moral perspectives considered by the eye doctor, Judah, as he contemplates having his mistress killed. Responding to Judah's questions, which are couched as general inquiries, his patient and friend rabbi Ben argues that he needs to believe there is a 'moral structure' in the universe, which acts of wickedness violate (Figure 2.2). If there

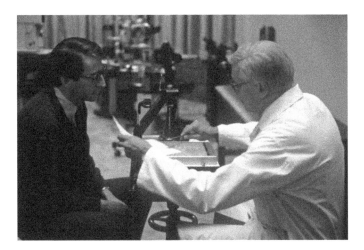

Figure 2.2 The rabbi and the eye doctor in *Crimes and Misdemeanors* (Woody Allen, 1989. Credit: Orion/Photofest).

were no such moral order, the rabbi insists, the world would be a bleak, empty, meaningless place. At the same time, the eye doctor, as a self-described man of science, cannot believe in such an order. Here is an impending problem for the natural law account. It is radically at odds with the modern scientific conception of nature, understood as a realm of mechanically interacting particles, empty of value and purpose. And this is seemingly confirmed when Judah escapes punishment for his crime.

Whether the recognition that there is no moral order to violate, that the universe is indifferent and meaningless helps Judah to come to terms with his crime or in fact represents the real punishment for what he has done, is another question (see Pappas 2004). Filmmaker Cliff suggests the latter when he meets the eye doctor at the wedding that closes the film. As he remarks in response to Judah's 'great story for a movie', if the murderer succeeds in getting away with murder, then surely 'his worst beliefs are realized'. His punishment might be the very fact that he is not punished. Perhaps acknowledging this, Judah certainly replies by saying 'Well, I said it was a chilling story, didn't I?' Nonetheless, he does not in the end seem overly concerned, getting up soon after to rejoin his wife and family, happy enough to be able to return to his privileged life.

By the time we get to Allen's *Match Point*, any idea of larger moral order has disappeared in favour of the scientific view of nature as meaningless and indifferent to human existence, which is actively opposed to a religious view from the start. As the protagonist Chris remarks early on in the discussion over dinner, 'it seems scientists are confirming more and more that all existence is here by blind chance. No purpose, no design … faith is the path of least resistance'. There is constant reference to the role of chance and lack of design in the universe. By implication, we can no longer speak of any God-given moral order in the universe. This, it would seem, leaves the behaviour of the participants to be dictated entirely by their greed, lust and self-interest. From the point of view of his self-interest, Chris is able to regard Nola's murder as 'necessary'. Yet even here there are echoes of the lost moral order. After the murder, Chris muses that 'it would be fitting if I were apprehended and punished. At least there would be some small sign of justice, some small measure of hope for the possibility of meaning'. But no such punishment eventuates. There is evidently a large gap between the idea of nature as morally structured and the scientific view. Aquinas may present us with a naturalistic notion of morality, but the conception of nature involved is quite unlike the modern scientific understanding. It is the Christianised version of Aristotle's notion of nature as imbued with value and purpose.

Let's look more closely at Aquinas's notion of a God-given moral order inherent in nature. Aquinas thinks that we can look to our own nature for moral guidance. Human beings have inbuilt purposes, fundamental tendencies or inclinations that they can rationally comprehend and articulate in the form of explicit rules of conduct. This is the natural law that tells them how they ought to act. This is not however to say that we should simply surrender ourselves to our desires and feelings. Our inclinations, Aquinas thinks, remain subject to the corruption of our sinful nature. Here he adopts Augustine's doctrine of original sin to explain why human beings do not automatically follow the laws of their nature, though without going quite as far as Augustine in regarding humans as completely corrupted. Rather, we have to be critical about the inclinations we pursue. We first have to recognise the 'natural purpose' of the inclination, through our reason, and only act on it to the extent that that purpose is respected. Inclinations belong to the natural law only insofar as they are 'ruled by reason', seeking what reason determines to be their proper purpose, the one appropriate to our nature. Thus, what Aquinas calls the sense appetites, 'concupiscible' appetites like love and the desire for pleasure, and 'irascible' appetites like fear and the desire to shun pain, are a legitimate part of our make-up, but they have to be pursued appropriately. The good person is the one whose desires have been trained by reason to seek their appropriate objects, with virtue being the settled disposition to so behave. Habitually appropriate concupiscible appetite is the virtue of temperance, habitually appropriate irascible appetite is the virtue of courage, and so on.

Being virtuous thus amounts to conforming to the rule of reason, which directs human beings to behave in accordance with their proper, God-given nature and purposes. Aquinas's account of virtue clearly builds on Aristotle's picture. And like Aristotle, Aquinas thinks that through virtuous behaviour we will attain our ultimate goal or end. Where Aristotle identifies this supreme good with *eudaimonia*, happiness, the good life here on earth, Aquinas like Augustine calls it beatitude or blessedness, and for him perfect happiness, the ultimate end, is to be found in possessing God, the most perfect being, the supreme and infinite good. For Aquinas, knowing is a form of possessing, and so to possess God is to know God, to have the intellectual and direct knowledge of God that we will attain in the afterlife. In doing so, we will realise ourselves in the fullest way, and attain beatitude. As Aquinas puts it in *Summa Contra Gentiles*, 'man's ultimate felicity consists only in the contemplation of God' (Aquinas 1956, 125).

Thus, for Aquinas, as for Augustine, the ultimate human goal, happiness, consists in union with God; and the virtuous life is the means to this end. Like Augustine, he does not think we can attain perfect happiness in this lifetime. However, unlike his predecessor, Aquinas does think we can make some moral progress in this world. We can achieve an imperfect happiness through the exercise of the 'cardinal virtues', prudence, justice, courage and temperance, through which we order our desires and appetites. But it remains the case that true happiness will have to wait for the next world. And to get there we will also need to have the 'theological virtues' of faith, hope and charity, which orient our activities towards uniting with God in the next world. These virtues are not acquired by education or practice, but only as a gift from God. Thus, even in Aquinas there remains a role for God's grace.

Before proceeding further, there are a couple of issues worth noting. First of all, we might wonder if the moral ideal being presented by Aquinas is in fact an inhuman one, one that is beyond the capacity of human beings to attain. Aquinas holds that while we may make some moral progress and attain a degree of happiness in this life, one can only achieve complete happiness and fulfilment in the afterlife. And it might be thought that this is not a human conception of happiness, because it is not a happiness that one can attain as a human being. One has to die, to cease being human, in order to attain it. This is the paradox that Kathleen discovers at the end of *The Addiction*, that moral progress is only possible at the cost of 'annihilation of the self'. Secondly, and this is not unrelated, there is some conflict in Aquinas's account between the Christian doctrine of a non-bodily soul able to survive death that he espouses and the Aristotelian picture that he wants to build on. Aquinas accepts Aristotle's idea of the soul as the form of the body, organising the matter of the body and making it possible for the body to exercise various capacities. But if so, how can mind and body come apart in the way required in order to be able to talk of a soul capable of persisting after the decay of the body? Aquinas says that the highest activities of the human soul, the intellectual operations, are intrinsically independent of the body and can survive death, but it is hard to reconcile this view with the Aristotelian doctrine that he appropriates.

These issues notwithstanding, the preceding picture provides the background for Aquinas's natural law view of morality. It is worth noting that natural law for Aquinas is the basis not only of ethics but politics. With Aristotle, Aquinas sees human beings as essentially social animals; human beings have a natural inclination to live in society, and the fully human life to be part of a community. Moreover, for Aquinas, natural law dictates that the best political regime is the monarchy, the monarch's rule of society mirroring the manner in which the universe is ruled by God. But staying with ethics for the time being, on the basis of natural law, some ways of acting can be said to be morally right because they are natural, in keeping with our nature, while others are wrong because they are unnatural. But even though the basis for morality is now to be found in our own nature and inclinations, there remains plenty of opportunity for the religious condemnation of desire, to the extent that the desires are understood to be directed towards inappropriate objects. To follow those desires is to act contrary to our nature. In this manner, for example, the natural law account has been used to support the longstanding religious tradition of condemning as immoral any sexual activity not undertaken for the purpose of reproduction. It can be argued from the natural law perspective that the proper, God-given purpose of sex is procreation. Human beings have been given sexuality in order to reproduce, so anything that frustrates the proper purpose of sexuality is unnatural and wrong, including contraception and homosexuality. Aquinas himself condemns 'that two men should seek sexual union, which especially is called a vice against nature' for this reason (Aquinas 1998, 647).

Naturally, this raises a number of questions. Natural law is not based on nature as observed so much as nature as interpreted by reason, a human nature or essence designed by God. Appealing to the fact that people happen to have certain desires is not sufficient to deem them natural to human beings, in this sense. That requires interpreting the desires that we have. We then have the problem of how to determine which desires are proper to our nature. To put this a different way, as Richard Norman notes, human beings in practice have all sorts of desires and inclinations and are capable of pursuing all sorts of purposes. It is not clear how we can identify, out of all the possible purposes we can pursue, the ones that are proper or natural to us. To take the case of sexuality, human beings can employ their sexuality for many purposes, including sheer enjoyment. Why shouldn't that, rather than reproduction, be the natural purpose of sexuality? (see Norman 1998, 33). All of which is to say, the problem that moralities based on God's will have, that of determining what God's will actually is, persists even if that will is understood to express itself in the way our nature is designed.

It also seems that Aquinas is vulnerable to the kind of criticism that can be applied to Aristotle when the latter says that some human beings, such as women and 'natural slaves', are fitted by nature to obey those who are by nature masters. Aquinas himself rejected the idea that slavery is justified by natural law, since all men are equal by nature (Aquinas 1998, 651). There were no natural slaves, though he also thought that slavery could be legitimate as a matter of human law. However, he does argue in Part 1, Question 92, that women are naturally subject to men, because in men, 'reason predominates'. The general concern remains that in making these claims about what is justified by nature, how do we know that we aren't in fact smuggling in a value judgement about how people ought to act, a particular cultural view about the activities that people should engage in or the roles they should play? Talk of certain roles being natural can be used to give a specious justification for what are in fact historically emergent arrangements, such as the place of women or the institution of slavery – although in fairness, the argument can also run the other way. That is, one can also invoke natural law in order to criticise particular social roles and practices. Both sides of the equation are evident in Steven Spielberg's *Lincoln* (2012), which features scenes in the American Congress where different factions, battling over the question of slavery, invoke natural law both in support of slavery and against it. In this context, anti-slavery Republican Thaddeus Stevens (Tommy Lee Jones) gets one of the best lines. To an opponent who suggests that ending slavery 'affronts natural law' and is 'insulting to God', he responds with: 'What violates natural law? Slavery, and you, *Pendleton*, you insult God. You unnatural noise'.

Nonetheless, claims that certain roles or practices are proper to people, or particular groups of people, because they are natural, have to recognise that 'natural' is a morally loaded term here, not a matter of straightforwardly observable fact. This is not to say that our nature has no bearing on notions of how we ought to act. Even if we consider our nature in relatively neutral terms, as the biological makeup and capacities distinctive of our species, this surely sets some limits to what we can aspire to morally. If ethics concerns how we should live, it cannot ignore the limits of what we as human beings are in fact capable of doing. A complete disconnection between the two is played for comic effect in *The Life of Brian* (Terry Jones, 1979). In comedy troupe Monty Python's religious satire, Brian (Graham Chapman), born just down the road from Jesus, joins a revolutionary group, the 'People's Front of Judea', who are opposed to the Roman occupation. His fellow revolutionary Stan (Eric Idle) demands that the other members recognise his right to have babies, a moral aspiration that as Reg (John Cleese), the group's commander points out, is somewhat undermined by his inability as a biological male to reproduce. A moral claim is meaningless if it is entirely incompatible with one's physical makeup and capacities. But even if we take into account a requirement that moral aspirations have to be compatible with what we are capable of doing, this does not get us very far in determining what those aspirations should be. As already noted, the capacities we have can be exercised in many different ways, so it is difficult to see them as providing any guidance as to the right way to behave.

The idea that there are deep-seated desires or inclinations in people's makeup, natural tendencies towards 'the good', appears in Neil Jordan's *The Crying Game* (1992). At the end of the film, ex-IRA terrorist Fergus (Stephen Rea), explains why he has nobly taken the rap for his lover Dil (Jaye Davidson) and gone to jail. He tells the story of the scorpion who asks a frog to carry it across the river, pointing out that if it were to sting the frog, they would both drown. Halfway across, the scorpion does sting the frog, and to the frog's protests, says 'I can't help it, it's in my nature'. One reading of this story is as a suggestion that behind Fergus's noble act of self-sacrifice there is a fundamental tendency or inclination towards the good in his nature. It outweighs even his own self-interest. This reading is reinforced by Fergus's behaviour earlier in the film, while he is still a member of the IRA, the militant group fighting at the time against British rule in Ireland. Despite strict IRA rules about dealing with captives, Fergus befriends the kidnapped British soldier Jody (Forrest Whitaker) that he is supposed to be guarding. And he is unable to shoot his prisoner when he tries to escape, as Jody realises: 'I know you won't shoot me because you can't help it. It's part of your nature to be a good person'. Indeed, his escaping prisoner is killed not by Fergus but, perversely, by a British army truck out searching for him.

But though one might hope to see, in such fundamental tendencies and inclinations, a natural basis for moral behaviour, things are not so straightforward. Even if there are fundamental tendencies in people's behaviour, these are likely to be more diverse than the religious moralist would want to allow. When a guilt-stricken Fergus comes to London to find Dil, Jody's girlfriend, and becomes attracted to her, he gets a surprise when she turns out to be transgender. It would seem that it is Dil's deep-seated inclination to be a woman despite being born biologically male. Moreover, Fergus finds that he is strongly inclined to continue to pursue a relationship with Dil, despite some initial misgivings. As we've seen, he eventually goes so far as to take the rap for her and go to prison because, as he explains, like the scorpion, it is his nature to do so. But it is not clear that the particular inclinations being exhibited by Dil, and by Fergus in relation to Dil when he gets over his shock, would be seen as by Aquinas as pointing in the direction of moral behaviour. They would more likely be viewed as unnatural inclinations. This indicates not only that fundamental inclinations are diverse, but also, once again, that there is an element of interpretation involved in talk of desires and inclinations being natural and unnatural.

Indeed, it is arguably a feature of the developed moral agent that they are not simply moved by desires, but reflectively interpret or evaluate their desires and impulses in the light of various norms or ideals of behaviour. These norms may in turn have been internalised from one's culture in the process of growing up. As such, it might be quite literally the case that in speaking of certain desires as being reflective of our God-given nature, we are in fact presenting what are in fact particular cultural views about the activities that people should engage in or the roles they should play. At the same time, as the characters in *The Crying Game* indicate, individuals are far from being the mere products of 'cultural programming'. They can readily come to explore directions that are at odds with prevailing social norms and which may not meet with mainstream social approval. And if nothing else, this speaks to the plasticity of human nature, the degree to which a relatively complex creature is able to take a wide variety of forms. On this understanding, the story of the scorpion that Fergus tells at the end of the film is in fact ironic. We do not have a relatively fixed nature that determines what we do or narrowly limits what we might strive for. Fergus himself demonstrates this in his continuing attachment to Dil, pursuing a direction that is at odds with his earlier sexual orientation; as indeed does Dil, who is reinventing herself as a woman.

A further issue for Aquinas's natural law account is, as already noted, that the particular conception of nature that it depends on comes into question in the modern era, with the rise of the scientific worldview. This is the scientific world of *Crimes and Misdemeanors* and *Match Point*, which seems to exclude not only God but also the idea that things in the world are designed by God with inbuilt purposes. The natural law account comes under direct attack by the twentieth-century existentialist Jean-Paul Sartre in his 'Existentialism is a Humanism' (Sartre 1975), where he argues that human beings could only be thought of as existing for a purpose if they were the product of some divine artisan, in the same way that an object of manufacture can be said to have a purpose since it has been made by an artisan with a definite purpose in mind. If there is no God, human beings have no such God-given nature or purpose. Sartre's own view is that this amounts to a liberation for human beings. He mentions the Dostoevskian idea that if there is no God, everything is permitted, but he does not think that this means there is no longer any morality, value or purpose. Rather, it means that human beings are free to choose themselves and responsible for whatever morality they subscribe to and purposes they pursue. From this perspective, what Dil and Fergus demonstrate is the human being's lack of any pre-given nature or essence. Rather than being defined through biological maleness or heterosexual orientation, they are free to determine themselves as they see fit. On that reading, the scorpion story turns out to be a form of bad faith or self-deception on Fergus's part, a way of denying his freedom to himself, pretending that he cannot help doing what he does. But this is to get ahead of ourselves. We will return to Sartre's account in Chapter Five.

For all its potential criticisms, Aquinas's natural law approach remains dominant within Catholic moral thinking. Within Christianity, however, it was opposed by the Protestant reformers of the sixteenth century, who instigated the Reformation in protest to what they saw as the errors and decadence of the Catholic church. Amongst other things, Protestantism returned to Augustine's conception of the world as utterly fallen, of human beings as fundamentally corrupted and completely dependent on God for the attainment of goodness. And against

Aquinas's rationalism, his belief that rational insight into our own nature can provide the basis for Christianity's moral prescriptions 'the protestant reformers followed Augustine in subordinating reason to will. Man in his inmost essence is will, and can either rebel against the divine law, or humbly and obediently submit' (Burtt 1951, 153). It is this gloomy Augustinian view, revived by Protestantism, and exported to the new world, that finds expression in the nineties New York of *The Addiction*, with its view of human beings as inherently sinful, addicted to evil and weak. It is in this spirit that Casanova tells Kathleen, 'We sin because we are sinners. We do evil because we are evil. What choices do such people have? We have no options'. In the end, the only chance Kathleen has of being able to reject evil is with God's help.

The Problem of Evil

As should be clear, there are a number of problems arising in connection with religious ethics in its various forms. Issues arise especially around the question of how we can know what counts as good behaviour, given that it is founded in a supernatural principle; even if that principle is understood to be manifest in the design of things, as with Aquinas. We can also go further and ask whether moral considerations might not actually call the existence of that supernatural principle into question. If the contention that without God everything is permitted is a kind of moral argument for believing in God, there is also a kind of moral argument for positively disbelieving in God. This involves the 'problem of evil'. The problem of evil, first pointed out in fact by Epicurus, is a problem of consistency. If God is omnipotent or all-powerful, and also benevolent or all-good, why is there evil in the world? How can a benevolent, all-powerful God allow evil to go on, whether 'moral evil', humanly produced horrors like cruelty and war, or 'natural evil', disease, famine and other natural disasters? It is hard to reconcile the two, and for some, the presence of such evil represents an argument against the very existence of God. A good, all-powerful God would not allow evil things to happen, and since evil things do happen, perhaps, as the German philosopher Nietzsche put it in *Ecce Homo*, 'God's only excuse is that he does not exist' (Nietzsche 1989, 244).

Naturally, from a Christian point of view, a less drastic response to the problem of evil would be preferable. One might try to deny the presence of evil in the world, but one of the basic beliefs of the Christian tradition is that evil, both moral and natural, exists, or to be precise, for Augustine and Aquinas, evil exists parasitically as a 'privation' or lack of the good, when a thing falls short of what it ought to be. This does not, however make evil unreal, so the problem of evil persists. Alternatively, one might try to modify the way God is understood, perhaps arguing that God is not good, but an evil deity who enjoys the suffering of humanity. But this would be to abandon a significant aspect of the Christian conception of God. To deny that God is all-powerful is similarly to go against a central element in Christian theology, in which God is seen as being able to do anything (or in some versions, everything except what is logically impossible, such as making

2 plus 2 equals 5). In all these cases, the proposed modifications might resolve the problem of evil, but they also mean that the traditional notion of God would be significantly damaged and diminished.

It would seem that if we are to avoid the argument from evil, and hold onto the traditional Christian conception of God, we have to find a way of reconciling an omnipotent, all-good God with the presence of worldly evil. The area of theology that tries to do this is known as theodicy. The classic attempt to reconcile the two, which goes back to Augustine, and which is also pursued by Aquinas, and more recently by Alvin Plantinga (see Plantinga 1977), is the 'free will' solution. That is, since God created human beings with free will, it is they, not God, who choose to bring evil into the world. Free will allows us to turn away from God, to choose to pursue inappropriate objects or purposes. Yet the free will response is not without its problems. First of all, if God is omnipotent, why couldn't he have created us in such a way that we always freely choose the good? Another objection to the free will solution is that it leads to the paradox of omnipotence. That is, if God created us with a totally free will, then he cannot be omnipotent since there is something, namely human free will, that he cannot control. And if he does have control but refrains from using it when people commit evil acts, then in what sense can he be said to be benevolent? Finally, resorting to free will would at best allow us to deal with moral evil, the evil that comes through human actions. It does not help us come to terms with natural evil, for example the earthquake or tsunami that causes untold death and suffering. How could a good and all-powerful God allow devastating natural catastrophes to happen?

Another strategy for reconciling God and evil is to hold that bad things that happen are really for the best in the longer term, that they are somehow part of God's plan for the world and ourselves, even if we cannot comprehend what that plan might be. In this way, worldly evil can be made ultimately consistent with the existence of a benevolent God, perhaps even a necessary part of the story. In this approach, the existence of God, rather than being challenged by the presence of evil, is something that is required in order to make sense of what would otherwise to be senseless pain and suffering. This seems to be the view of Antonius Block (Max von Sydow), the knight in Ingmar Bergman's *The Seventh Seal* (1957). The film is set in fourteenth-century Sweden. The knight has returned from the Crusades to find the Black Death ravaging the country. Faced with this catastrophic situation, Block looks to God to try to find some point to the terrible suffering he sees all around him. He is desperate for a sign of God's existence because otherwise 'life is a preposterous horror. No man can live faced with Death knowing everything is nothingness'.

At the same time, even if Block thinks a God is required to make sense of suffering and death, he refuses to retreat into faith. In this, he evinces a distinctly modern sensibility. He needs to have real evidence of God's existence, a sign. The problem is that no sign of God's existence is forthcoming. God remains silent and does not respond to the knight's prayers. What Block finds instead is a good deal of suffering that is provoked by people's attempts to reconcile their impending death with their religious beliefs. For the procession of flagellants that Block encounters, the plague is God's punishment for their sins, which they are trying to purge. For others, the plague is the work of the devil, in league with witches who must be destroyed. In an episode that recalls Dreyer's *Passion of Joan of Arc*, the knight comes across a young woman condemned to be burnt at the stake for witchcraft. Still searching for answers, he wants, through her, to ask Satan about God. She says that you can find God in the eyes of another human being, but when he looks into her eyes all he can see is 'terror, nothing else'. For the knight's atheistic squire Jons (Gunnar Bjönstrand), there was never anything to see. Religion is a lie that priests and fanatics take advantage of to exploit and persecute people. He also has a fine line in dry humour. When Death, personified in this film as the classic black-cowled figure, finally comes for them in the knight's castle, Block calls out for a God, who 'must exist somewhere', to have mercy on them. But Jons corrects him: 'You'll find no one that listens to your complaint or is moved by your suffering. I had a herb to purge your anxiety over the eternal. Now it's too late. Feel in this final minute the triumph of rolling your eyes and moving your toes'.

A more recent attempt to reconcile God and worldly evil by arguing that evil is for the best in the long run has been to argue that it is required because it makes it possible for us to perfect ourselves, to become good people, which is what God ultimately wants (see Hick 1990, 44ff). On this view, human beings are not fully completed creations but need to undergo a process of moral development, and in order for that to happen, there has to be evil in the world. If the earth were free of suffering, pain and death, and nothing we did had any bad consequences for ourselves or others, we would not have any reason to try to be good, courageous, honest and kind, or to take responsibility for our actions. This world would be pleasant, but there would be no possibility of character development. It is because the world is not like this that we are able to develop moral character. Yet even if one were to accept this, the critic might still ask why a good and all-powerful God allows quite so much evil and does not step in to reduce it. Dealing with evil may indeed be character-building, but the amount of moral and natural evil in the world is surely far in excess of what might be required for such a task.

Moreover, the same evil that we are trying to account for in terms of character-building may have the effect of undermining the argument, making it seem like an empty rationalisation. This is especially if we are faced with concrete rather than merely theoretical evil. A version of the idea of pain and suffering as facilitating character development appears in the work of the Christian apologist C.S. Lewis and is evident in a film based on his life, *Shadowlands* (Richard Attenborough, 1993). Early on in the film, Lewis (played by Anthony Hopkins) delivers a practiced lecture in which he argues that God allows suffering because 'we are like blocks of stone out of which the sculptor carves the forms of man. Blows of his chisel, which hurt us so much, are what make us perfect'. But while this position on coming to terms with suffering might be easy enough to argue for in the abstract, it becomes much harder to maintain in the face of the experience of the real thing. Already, during the lecture, the camera picks out one woman in the audience who, presumably having dealt with real suffering, looks decidedly dubious about the argument Lewis is presenting.

As the film proceeds, Lewis himself is confronted with the direct, brutal experience of suffering, when he has to endure the death of his new wife Joy Gresham (Debra Winger) from cancer. It is a changed Lewis by the end, who is now afraid 'that suffering is just suffering after all. No cause. No purpose. No pattern', or as Antonius Block put it, that 'life is a preposterous horror'. The old answer now seems empty. 'Just don't tell me it's all for the best', he tells his colleagues. Lewis does not quite seem to have abandoned his beliefs, or even the idea that suffering is somehow for our own good, but at the very least his picture of God has changed, from the sculptor chiselling humanity, to a vivisectionist, cruelly performing experiments on live animals. It is hard to stomach. As he goes on to say, 'We are the creatures, aren't we? We're the rats in the cosmic laboratory. I've no doubt that the experiment is for our own good, but it still makes God the vivisectionist, doesn't it? It won't do. It's this bloody awful mess, and that's all there is to it'. In tracing the undermining of the character's original complacency, the film is able to catch not only the intellectual but also emotional aspect of the problem of evil. More broadly it demonstrates the capacity of film to is evoke experiences that are able to challenge a particular understanding of life, to reveal it to be ultimately hollow and simplistic. As the character puts it, 'I've just come up against a bit of experience'.

In the end, not merely the character-building story but any attempt by theodicy to make sense of evil, pain and suffering in a way consistent with a benevolent, all-powerful God is in danger of looking like hollow rationalisation when we are confronted with concrete examples of suffering. It may be that the only way of coming to terms with evil in a theistic context is in a non-rational manner. This is one way of understanding Terrence Malick's *Tree of Life* (2011). The film turns on the struggle of protagonist Jack O'Brien (Sean Penn) to come to terms with the death of his brother, some years previously, in unspecified circumstances. He is losing faith in God and thinks about the suffering of his mother (Jessica Chastain) when his brother died, and her own spiritual crisis in the face of this seemingly senseless loss. This leads him to broader reflections on the relation between human beings and the universe, and the film follows suit, in a very cinematic way. In an extended series of wordless images that go far beyond ordinary narrative, the film evokes the larger cosmic context, portraying no less than the formation of the stars, the development of life on earth, the birth of morality, the extinction of the dinosaurs and ultimately the end of the earth.

This sequence has drawn comparisons with the 'through the Stargate' sequence at the end of Kubrick's *2001: A Space Odyssey* (1968), in which astronaut Bowman (Keir Dullea) journeys 'beyond the stars'. In that case however, the experience relates to a process of self-transcendence and self-transformation, assisted by alien forces, through which the astronaut progresses to the final stage of human evolution and becomes the 'transhuman' Starchild. Malik's film is evoking a different kind of transcendental vision, one that emphasises the smallness and limitation of human existence. We are, as it were, granted a God's-eye vision of the whole of nature, as if God is showing us the wonders of creation. The film opens with a line from the biblical book of Job, the righteous individual who nonetheless lost his wealth and children. When Job asks God why he suffers these calamities, he does not receive a direct answer but is simply reminded of his ignorance: 'where were you when I laid the foundations of the earth ... when the morning stars sang together?' By showing the creation of the world, *Tree of Life* seems to make sense of God's response. Human suffering is placed in a cosmic context. There is an acknowledgement that the cosmos is filled with arbitrary violence, death and destruction, but also a suggestion that these things might be part of a larger whole that is filled with sublime beauty. A theist might appeal to this larger vision to argue that the world God has created is filled not only with suffering but also magnificence and that the beauty of the world provides some compensation for human suffering, making it bearable. Suffering thus becomes comprehensible from a perspective that greatly exceeds our own.

Yet this way of coming to terms with suffering and evil in a theistic context depends on abandoning rational argument, in favour of appeal to a quasi-mystical vision of the world as a whole that is as far beyond ordinary human understanding as Malick's sumptuous images are beyond the limits of rational narrative. Malick's God's-eye cinematic vision notwithstanding, it remains unclear how finite human beings can have access to a perspective that so surpasses their own. Even Aquinas, who stands at the high point of the medieval attempt to reconcile Christian religion with reason, argued that there were limits to what reason could establish in this area. He thought that certain 'preambles of faith', for example, the existence of God, and some things about God's nature, could be proved by unaided human reason; but also, that other religious doctrines such as the Trinity and Incarnation are beyond human reason. These doctrines, the 'articles of faith', could only be known to humans because God has revealed them to us. They are matters of pure faith. Faith is precisely a position we take towards a claim that is not demonstrable by reason, a belief in truths revealed through scriptures or the teachings of a church, or through special experiences of some sort. But reason is also a source of authority on which our beliefs can rest, something that plays a significant role in our lives, and if we are unwilling simply to turn our back on rational considerations, appeal to the transrational no longer suffices. The tenor of thinking in the modern period has been to question any resort to faith and to emphasise rational accountability, especially reason as exemplified in science and scientific method.

From such a rationalistic perspective, the problem of evil remains difficult to resolve. Overall, whatever strategies we might employ to lessen the conflict between the idea of a good and all-powerful God and the existence of worldly evil, the sheer amount of evil in the world remains problematic for this way of thinking. The question remains: even if some evil can be accounted for, or even turn out to be required for some greater good, why is there so much of it? Couldn't a good, all-powerful God have created a better world than this one, a world with a greater proportion of good over evil? Moreover, this is a world in which people not only do wicked things that go unpunished, but often do very well out of their crimes, and the innocent regularly suffer at the hands of such people. Films that do not shy away from portraying these things, such as *Crimes and Misdemeanors* and *Match Point*, continue to pose questions about the existence of a benevolent God. In *Crimes and Misdemeanors*, one of Judah's recollections of his childhood takes him to a family dinner where his formidable atheist aunt May (Anna Berger) is holding forth, much to the horror of Judah's pious father. 'Six million Jews burned to death and they got away with it' – as far as she is concerned, no one can sensibly believe in God after a catastrophe like the Holocaust. It is for her a definitive instance of the argument from evil. It is worth adding that May, like Sartre, does not see the absence of God as the end of morality. For May also, morality is something that human beings create. In her case, it is not individual choices but powerful groups in society that produce and determine morality, or as she puts it, 'might makes right'. This is of course a very different image of morality to the one at the heart of religious experience, with God the lawgiver who hands down moral laws. For May, 'nothing is handed down in stone'.

The observable evils and imperfections of the world we live in are a key objection that eighteenth-century philosopher David Hume, in his *Dialogues Concerning Natural Religion*, brings to the argument from design for God's existence. This is the argument that the observable design and order of the world provides evidence of an intelligent designer. It is an argument from 'natural theology', which seeks to investigate the existence and nature of God without resorting to claims to be found in the scriptures, or divine revelation, the province of 'revealed theology'. Aquinas, for example, thinks that we can employ reason to argue for the existence of God on the basis of the world's observable design. But this kind of argument comes under heavy attack in Hume's discussion. Hume argues that even if we could infer that some deity must exist in order to create the world, nothing in the world entitles us to think that this deity would be anything like the Christian God. For Hume, the world is full of imperfections, disease, the savagery of nature, natural disasters, earthquakes and so on. It is a vision of the world as bleak and tragic as anything in *Chinatown* or *No Country for Old Men*. This world does not provide any evidence of a directing force that is perfect, all-powerful, or even particularly moral. At best it could only be the result of a limited God, perhaps the first clumsy attempt of a trainee God or a senile one; or perhaps an actively malevolent one. That is, if we argue for a designer of the universe on the analogy of designing something within the world, the more the picture emerges of a God who is unlike the Christian God.

In the last analysis, Hume does not think we can infer that any sort of deity must exist in order to create the world. We can only know of design processes within the world, of things like watches and watchmakers, and we cannot apply this model to say anything about the origins of the world as a whole. We cannot say whether the world was created or simply emerged. In short, the argument from design does not work at all. Hume belongs to the modern era in which the God-centred conception of the world that held sway through the medieval period was overturned and the disenchanted, sober, scientific view of nature came to hold sway. Against the background of this transformation, there are corresponding changes in moral thinking. It is to the ethics of the modern era that we now turn.

FEATURE FILMS: *CRIMES AND MISDEMEANORS* AND *THE ADDICTION*

Crimes and Misdemeanors

Crimes and Misdemeanors is a 1989 film directed by Woody Allen (*Love and Death, Annie Hall, Hannah and Her Sisters, Midnight in Paris*). As the main character reflects on whether to have his mistress murdered, various moral perspectives, both religious and existentialist, are invoked. Allen's 2005 *Match Point* covers some of the same ground, but the later film is bleaker and more nihilistic, with little moral reflection, the characters being motivated overwhelmingly by their self-interest.

Plot

The film has two plot lines. Judah Rosenthal (Martin Landau) is a successful ophthalmologist, a family man and pillar of the community, but he has a secret. He is trying to end an affair that he has been having with Dolores (Jessica Huston) for several years, but she is threatening to tell his wife about the affair if he doesn't keep seeing her. How he deals with this, by arranging to have her killed via his brother Jack (Jerry Orbach), is one subplot.

Cliff Stern (Woody Allen) is the film's other protagonist. He is a pretentious filmmaker who has been trying to make a documentary about philosopher Lewis Levy (Martin Bergmann). Out of financial desperation (and prompted by his wife), he agrees to make a film portrait of his annoying brother-in-law Lester (Alan Alda), a successful TV producer who represents everything Cliff despises. While working on this documentary, he falls for the film's producer Halley Reed (Mia Farrow). Cliff's troubles at work, and his attempted affair with Halley, form the second plot line.

The two plot lines finally come together during the wedding scene at the end of the film, when Judah and Cliff meet. The character linking them together is the rabbi Ben (Sam Waterston) who is Cliff's brother-in-law and Judah's patient. They meet at the wedding reception for Ben's daughter and have a conversation on the couch.

Key Scenes

1   As Judah thinks about having his mistress killed, he has an imaginary conversation with his patient, the rabbi, Ben. Ben: 'I couldn't go on if I didn't feel with all my heart that there's a moral structure – with real meaning – with forgiveness and some kind of higher power. Otherwise, there's no basis to know how to live'.

As he adds: 'without the law, it's all darkness'. Here the film invokes a religious perspective on morality, close to the natural law idea [38.26–41.53].

2 At the scene of the crime, Judah recalls his father Sol (David S. Howard), who represents another religious perspective on ethics, and why one should be moral, even if one can get away with murder. On this view, God is watching all the time, judging. I act right when I do what God wants me to do, and wrongly when I fail to do it. And God will reward those who do good and punish those who do bad. Sol: 'God sees everything, and those who are righteous will be rewarded, while those who are wicked will be punished for eternity' [55.50–56.26].

3 Anguished over the murder of his mistress, Judah visits the house he grew up in and remembers a family dinner where religion and morality were discussed. At the dinner is his father Sol, and Aunt May (Anna Berger), an atheist who considers all religion superstitious nonsense. Her view is that if you look at the real world without blinkers, you'll see that God does not exist, there is no one watching us and there is no moral structure in the world. Note Sol's response: he actually agrees with May that religion may not ultimately depend on rational belief, but on faith; but he also thinks that having this faith means that one will have a better life. As he says, if it comes to a contest between God and truth, 'I will always choose God over truth' [1.07.00–1.10.25].

4 Although Sol calls Aunt May a nihilist, someone who rejects all religious and moral principles that might give life a moral structure, she seems rather to be espousing a moral relativism. As she says, 'might makes right'; morality is really a reflection of the interests of those who are in power, and it can change as a result. Hence her response to the dinner guest who asks 'what are you saying, May? There's no morality in the whole world?' May: 'For those who want morality, there's morality. Nothing is handed down in stone' [1.07.00–1.10.25].

5 A central theme in the film is the question – why should one be moral, why should we abide by moral rules or constraints? The question is effectively posed by the central character, Judah. He engineers the murder of his mistress and is not punished; and though he feels guilty to start with, he gets over his guilt and returns to his life of comfort and privilege, as if nothing had happened. This is the story he tells Cliff on the couch at the end of the movie, under the guise of an idea for a movie plot. Cliff questions whether one could live with such a crime, and imagines that a better plot would

see the guilt-ridden protagonist turning themselves in. Judah replies that if he wants a happy ending, he should go see a Hollywood film. Judah and Cliff are also in effect discussing the movie the director has made of Judah's life and the murder that Judah has engineered [1.29.50–1.35.24].

6 In the final scene, Levy, in voiceover, presents a position reminiscent of Sartre's existentialism; and in particular the manner in which Sartre, while rejecting religious belief, does not espouse a nihilistic rejection of all values, but rather argues that values are the product of individual choice. As Levy puts it: 'We are all faced throughout our lives with agonizing decisions, moral decisions. But we define ourselves by the choices we have made. We are in fact the sum total of our choices'. Levy acknowledges the indifference of the universe, that there is no external source of meaning or value to be discovered, the way in which events unfold unpredictably and unfairly and how human happiness does not seem to have been included in the design of creation. Nonetheless, it seems that it is possible, by exercising our freedom, to invest the indifferent universe with value and meaning, to create meaning for our lives. Whether we are to view this hopeful view ironically, given that the philosopher has committed suicide, is another matter [1.35.25–1.36.58].

The Addiction

The Addiction is a 1995 vampire film directed by Abel Ferrara (*The Funeral, Bad Lieutenant, Pasolini*) and written by Nicholas St. John. It is filmed in gritty black and white. It portrays murder as the expression of a basic human addiction to evil, which human beings are incapable of overcoming by themselves. This is both the expression of a gloomy religious conception of human nature and a rejection of existentialist views on the matter.

Plot

Kathleen Conklin (Lili Taylor), is an idealistic PhD student appalled by a world that could allow evils such as the Holocaust and war crimes. On her way home from an exhibition, she is attacked by the vampire Casanova (Annabella Sciorra). Casanova tells Kathleen to order her to go away, but she is unable to. Kathleen duly becomes a vampire. She starts to attack others and drink their blood. She seduces and attacks her philosophy professor and bites an anthropology student (Kathryn Erbe) and her friend Jean (Edie Falco), turning them into vampires.

Later she moves off-campus, biting street low-lifes. One night while out hunting, Kathleen meets Peina (Christopher Walken), a vampire who claims to have almost conquered his addiction and as a result is almost human. He lectures her about what it is to be a real vampire, but in the end imprisons her, feeding off her at regular intervals. She finally escapes, collapses on the pavement and replenishes herself by biting a good Samaritan who stops to help her.

Working feverishly, Katherine finishes her PhD. To celebrate, she announces a graduation party, inviting the dean, the dissertation committee and faculty. She announces: 'I'd like to share a little bit of what I've learned through these long, hard years of study', whereupon she, Casanova and some of her vampire converts slaughter her guests.

Afterwards, Kathleen, wracked with guilt over her activities, wanders the streets. She ends up in a hospital and decides to commit suicide by getting the nurse to open the blinds, but she is confronted by Casanova, who stops her suicide attempt. Her last visitor is a Catholic priest who enters and asks how she is. She whispers that she wants to make a confession and asks for God's forgiveness. The priest absolves her, administers a communion wafer and she dies. In the final scene, Kathleen lays a flower on her own grave. She walks away, having overcome her addiction at last.

Key Scenes

1   Kathleen is turned into a vampire, but by not ordering Casanova to go away when asked to do so, she has also effectively invited it, indicating that the evil is already part of her nature [04.23–07.23]. See also the scene where Kathleen bites the anthropology student, who remonstrates with her. Anthropology Student: 'Look what you've done to me! How could you do this? Doesn't this affect you at all?' Kathleen: 'No. It was your decision … My indifference is not the concern here. It's your astonishment that needs studying' [33.53–36.00]. See also the scene where she bites her friend Jean. When Jean asks why Katherine is doing this, she replies: 'You know, this obtuseness is disheartening, especially in a doctoral candidate' [41.05–44.20].

2   The older vampire Peina claims to be a Nietzschean superman, living beyond good and evil: 'You think Nietzsche understood something? Mankind has striven to exist beyond good and evil, from

the beginning. And you know what they found? Me'. However, he seems closer to a practitioner of ascetic self-denial: 'You know how long I've been fasting? Forty years ... You can never get enough, can you? But you learn to control it. You learn, like the Tibetans, to survive on a little'. Or again: 'My habit is controlled by my will – true, my will initially formed by my addiction, but now strong enough to control the conditions that dictate the fulfilling of my needs' [45.39–51.1]. He may however be deluding himself about his powers of self-control, since he proceeds to imprison and feed off Kathleen.

3 Kathleen lays out the film's central thesis: 'I finally understand what all this is, how it was all possible. Now I see, good lord, how we must look from out there. Our addiction is evil. The propensity for this evil lies in our weakness before it'. Kathleen becomes critical of existentialist authors like Kierkegaard, who insist on human freedom and ignore what drives our behaviour, an inherent propensity to evil that is behind historical atrocities like the Holocaust: 'Kierkegaard was right – there is an awful precipice before us. But he was wrong about the leap – there's a difference between jumping and being pushed. You reach a point where you are forced to face your own needs, and the fact you can't terminate the situation settles on you with full force' [55.30–56.22].

4 At the hospital, Kathleen, having asked for the blinds to be opened, is now waiting for the sunlight to fall on her. But Casanova enters the hospital room and abruptly closes the blinds. 'It's not that easy' she says. 'To find rest takes a real genius'. She proceeds to hold forth in terms reminiscent of Augustine, quoting from theologian and writer R.C. Sproul, to the effect that we are evil and weak to the core: 'R.C. Sproul said we're not sinners because we sin, but we sin because we are sinners. In more accessible terms, we're not evil because of the evil we do, but we do evil because we *are* evil. Yeah. Now what choices do such people have? It's not like we have any options' [1.09.12–1.12.40]

5 As Kathleen lies alone in the gloom, she has another visitor. A priest enters and asks how she is. She whispers that she wants to make a confession and asks for God's forgiveness. The priest absolves her, administers a communion wafer and she becomes still, in repose as we hear her say 'Amen' in voiceover. The only way we can overcome the evil at our core, it seems, is with God's help [1.13.12–1.15.10].

6 In the film's final scene, Kathleen, in a cemetery, leaves a flower on her own grave, then walks off as the camera pans upwards to a

sculpture of a crucifix. Over this we hear her in voice-over, saying 'To face what we are in the end, we stand before the light. And our true nature is revealed. Self-revelation is annihilation of the self'. It seems that for human beings, chronically addicted to evil, true happiness or fulfilment is only possible by ceasing to exist as a human being [1.15.10–1.16.10].

3 Pleasure, Happiness and Rights
Enlightenment Ethics

In the final part of Luis Buñuel's comedy *Simon of the Desert* (1965), we find ourselves in a crowded sixties New York nightclub, filled with frenzied pleasure-seekers dancing the latest dance. The camera moves in on a couple sitting at a table. The man is the film's hero, Simon (Claudio Brook), modelled on Saint Simeon Stylites, the early Christian ascetic who spent decades atop a column in the desert. For most of the film, we have been in the fifth century, with Simon on his column, as he tries to avoid the world's temptations and develops ever-more extreme ways of denying his physical appetites. But now he has been transported into the modern world by the devil (Silvia Pinal), the woman who is sitting next to him. Now outfitted as a beatnik, with a neatly-trimmed beard, and smoking a pipe, he asks her what the name of the dance is. It's the 'Radioactive Flesh', says the devil. 'It's the latest dance, the final dance'. Although Simon understandably wants to go home to his column, he is informed that he can't: 'It's been re-let. You'll have to put up with things here'. Indeed, there is no going back. Simon's world doesn't exist anymore. It is thoroughly foreign, not least because of its celebration of religiously motivated gestures of extravagant self-denial. The modern world emerges with a rather different attitude towards appetite and pleasure. Indeed, pleasure becomes the very cornerstone of the new world's ethical thinking. It is to the emergence of this world, and the new ethics of pleasure that arises with it, that we now turn.

Hobbes and the Social Contract

A mark of this modernity is the increasing undermining of the God-centred religious view of the world that held sway in the medieval period. Much of this critical work takes place in the eighteenth century, the period of the Enlightenment, the time of Voltaire and Hume amongst others. During this period, the new scientific forms of thinking that had emerged in the seventeenth century became increasingly dominant. With the discoveries of pioneers like Galileo, Kepler and Newton, people became enthralled by the idea that the entire universe could be explained in terms of mechanical interactions, governed by deterministic laws of cause and effect. For the scientific worldview, the universe was no longer ordered by God, but could be understood in entirely materialist terms, as a system of mechanical interactions. This new way of looking at nature was bound up with an increasing capacity to manipulate it and exercise technological control over it. With this, there was an increasing rejection of the religious view of morality that identifies morality with the supernatural commands of God and with a God-given natural order that human beings have to conform to in order to be moral.

So the advent of modernity sees a move away from the God-centred Christian account of morality; but this does not mean a return to the ethical thinking of Plato and Aristotle. Both Plato's non-naturalism, his identification of the good with the ultimate reality, and Aristotle's form of naturalism, his teleological understanding of nature as inherently purposive, are incompatible with the new scientific understanding. They are both to be rejected, along with Aquinas's Christianised version of Aristotle, the reframing of nature as imbued with God-given purpose. Instead, the emphasis turns to the idea of morality as something that is humanly created, to be justified rationally. Reason, rather than faith or tradition, is to be the main guide to human conduct (Kramnick 1995, xi). This was the watchword of the eighteenth-century Enlightenment. And this is a rationality that is very much identified with the new scientific way of thinking about the world. For the Enlightenment thinkers, science and technology promised to make it possible to force nature to serve human needs, and also increasingly informed thinking about moral and social matters. Ethical systems are now to be established on the basis of a scientific, materialist view of human beings as driven above all to seek pleasure and avoid pain, as acting purely out of self-interest, where this interest is understood to be primarily in satisfying one's appetites and ensuring one's welfare. The general issue for early modern moral thinking is how to build a morality, to understand the source and justification of moral principles on the basis of this hedonistic and egoistic conception of human being.

One of the first to apply the new scientific approach to human beings, and to use such a conception of human nature as the basis for morality, was the seventeenth-century thinker Thomas Hobbes (1588–1679). He does so in his 1651 book *Leviathan*, in the first part entitled 'Of Man'. On Hobbes's account, human actions are determined by the organism's overriding desire for self-preservation. The human organism is programmed by nature to keep itself in existence, its every action designed to preserve its life and avoid death. Hobbes details the mechanics of human self-preservation in the following manner. We are constantly affected by objects in our environment, which influence our 'vital motions', basic life-processes like blood circulation. When these vital motions are enhanced, and our self-preservation promoted, we feel this as pleasure; when they are hindered and our self-preservation threatened, we feel pain. These inward feelings of pleasure and pain bring about minute, unobservable inner movements, an inner movement towards the pleasure-causing object being 'appetite' or 'desire', and an inner movement away from the painful object, 'aversion'. These inner movements of desire and aversion in turn give rise to the observable bodily motions or actions, towards or away from the relevant object.

So understood, human beings are by nature selfish and egoistic. They are entirely concerned with pursuing their own interests regardless of the cost to others and driven above all by their interest in preserving themselves. To this end, they always act to maximise their pleasure and minimise their pain. This idea of the human being, crude though it might sound, is still around today. It can be found in modern-day doctrines like behaviourist psychology and is behind some notions of psychological conditioning such as aversion therapy. It is also part of some models of human behaviour in economics. Above all, it is the sort of account favoured by those who want a 'tough-minded', 'realistic', no-nonsense account of human beings. Human beings are still understood to seek happiness, but this is happiness understood as pleasure, the satisfaction of desires. We are far from the Greek idea of happiness as the realisation of one's ultimate purpose as a human being, one's fulfilment in the form of the good life or the Christian idea of fulfilment through union with God. On those views, virtuous behaviour is the means to attaining the ideal state, and involves renouncing, controlling or shaping one's desires and motivations towards that end. Desires and motivations themselves are judged in terms of whether or not they are part of the virtuous life and contribute to that ultimate end. Hobbes is explicit in rejecting this view: 'there is no such Finis ultimus (utmost aim) nor Summum bonum, (greatest Good) as is spoken of in the Books of the old Moral Philosophers' (Hobbes 1968, 160). As far as he is concerned, such talk is unscientific nonsense. To understand what human beings are really like, we need to get rid of this vague evaluative talk and give a properly scientific, unsentimental, clear-minded account of human beings.

We might see a predecessor to this in Epicurus, who is similarly materialist in outlook, and who thinks it is empirically evident that human behaviour is motivated by pleasure alone. Of the major Greek ethical thinkers, he was the only one to identify happiness, the good life, with pleasure. But Epicurus devises an ethics of restraint on this basis, the best pleasure being the absence of pain and fear; and the virtuous life, characterised by restraint and the renunciation of 'vain and empty' desires, is the best means to securing that pleasure. For Hobbes, the scientific view is that happiness is just the satisfaction of desires. The human being is just a creature with desires, all of which are on the same level, all ultimately concerned with doing whatever will ensure our individual survival. No issue arises as to the moral value of the desires themselves. The only issue as far as they are concerned is the practical one: can I satisfy them, are there any external obstacles to their satisfaction? Moral notions don't disappear from Hobbes's picture of the human being, but what disappears is the idea that morally evaluative notions, like good or bad, can govern or set limits to the desires we pursue. Instead, for Hobbes, it is our desires and aversions that determine what counts for us as morally good or bad. The 'good' is simply the name we give to that which we desire, 'whatsoever is the object of any man's appetite or desire'. Something is good because it gives us pleasure, assists in our self-preservation. 'Evil' is the name we give to that which we seek to avoid, whatever is the object of 'hate, and aversion', that which causes us pain and threatens our survival (Hobbes 1968, 120).

For Hobbes, morality understood more substantively as a constraint on desire, or a curb on self-interest, can only be built on this basis, as something that ultimately serves our self-interest. This is where Hobbes's notion of the social contract comes in. As selfish, egoistic beings, we cannot achieve the self-preservation we seek in the 'state of nature'. That is a situation where there is no government, and everyone is free to do whatever they want in the name of their survival, up to and including killing others. In this situation, life is constant conflict and we are always under threat of violent death at the hands of others. Reason tells us that it is in everyone's interest to agree to give up some of their freedom and submit to a strong authority that can enforce rules, regulate social relations and prevent this conflict. In this manner, political authority can be grounded, not in some divinely instituted hierarchy as in Aquinas's account, but in the rational agreement or consent of the governed. In addition to explaining the purpose of the state, the social contract theory gives us another way of thinking about the nature of morality. Morality can be understood as a set of rules to regulate social relations amongst essentially self-interested individuals. We also have another kind of answer to the question 'why be moral?' Morality provides rules to resolve conflicts between individuals and promotes the survival of society, social co-existence. We need to obey moral rules in order to avoid the horrors of the state of nature.

It is thus eminently reasonable for individuals to submit to the rules imposed by a central authority. At the same time, Hobbes thinks that the power of the sovereign needs to be, for all intents and purposes, unlimited. The sovereign should be able to make and enforce whatever laws are necessary for the preservation of public order. For Hobbes, unless the sovereign were clearly stronger than his subjects, and their undisputed master, the threat of lawlessness, pillage and murder would always be present. In part, this insistence on a powerful sovereign reflects Hobbes's view of human nature, as fundamentally selfish and egoistic. He thought that even if we can rationally see that it is in everyone's longer-term self-interest to agree to submit to a central authority, individuals are so dominated by their desires that they are liable to go back on the agreement and break the laws if they can see an immediate advantage in doing so. The powerful sovereign ensures that those who break the laws will be punished; and the subjects obey these laws, in the last analysis, because of fear of the sovereign's power and of what will happen to them if they do not obey. All of this makes morality a surface phenomenon. We may be sociable creatures who play by the rules and see that it is in our long-term self-interest to do so, but we would quickly revert to egoistic, selfish, ruthless behaviour if there were no powerful leader to enforce the rules and punish those who broke them.

These suspicions about the real nature of human beings find a cinematic dramatisation in *Lord of the Flies* (Peter Brooks, 1963). Brooks' film of the William Golding novel can be seen not only as a demonstration of the horrors of life outside organised society, but also the ease with which people can slip back into this state without strong authority figures to enforce the rules. In the film, the shipwrecked schoolboys, though shown in the opening montage to be educated and from good families, quickly descend into violence and savagery, and life becomes a struggle for power and status. Piggy, the plump, bespectacled voice of reason, tries to make the case to the others for a civilised social order, a social contract: 'which is better, to have rules and agree, or to hunt and kill?' But he is powerless against the others who are interested in the more immediate payoff and he soon becomes a victim of the violence. It is sometimes suggested that Golding's story can be viewed in religious terms, specifically in terms of the idea of human nature as 'fallen'. In this view, the events on the island demonstrate that the source of evil is within us, in our own corrupted nature (see Pojman 1998, 262). But whatever is going on with the book, the film does not entertain any religious motifs. With its spare documentary style, it comes across as entirely naturalistic, like an anthropological field study. Hobbes's vision of the terrible state of nature has also sometimes been interpreted in religious terms, as a version of the doctrine of humanity's fallen nature. But although Hobbes himself suggested that the idea that human beings were selfish and egoistic might be a point on which believer and unbeliever would agree, he rejected original sin as the cause (see Schneewind 2002, 24). His account is intended to be an unsentimental, realistic view of human beings. Simply doing what comes naturally, pursuing our ordinary desires, will lead to conflict, if there are no external checks.

So this idea of human beings as fundamentally selfish and egoistic, however pessimistic or shocking it might seem, is presented by Hobbes as the hard truth about human beings. This is the nature that would emerge if the external constraints of morality were ever removed. In these terms, we might account for people's behaviour in crisis situations, which is often less than exemplary. In crises, one might argue, our civilised moral selves quickly disappear and it is our real nature that emerges, a nature that is dominated by a selfish drive for self-preservation. In the upmarket ski hotel in *Force Majeure*, this is how Tomas's less than heroic behaviour is accounted for by his friend Mats (Kristofer Hivju). His abandonment of his family when the supposedly controlled avalanche seemed to be coming a little too close for comfort is not to be put down to bad character, which is his wife Ebba's Aristotelian view. Mats offers the more up-to-date view that for human beings and animals alike, being confronted by a dangerous situation triggers a survival instinct, a primitive force just to escape. When this happens, someone might not be able to live up to their values, through no fault of their own.

A similar view of human nature is pursued by the villainous Joker (Heath Ledger) in *The Dark Knight* (Christopher Nolan, 2008). He, however, is not interested in trying to excuse an individual's momentary departure from ordinary civilised behaviour, so much as wanting to undermine the very idea that we are civilised beings. He wants to remind us that beneath the veneer of ordinary civilised behaviour we are selfish monsters and that this nature will reassert itself when the usual social arrangements break down: 'Their morals, their code ... it's a bad joke. Dropped at the first sign of trouble. They're only as good as the world allows them to be. You'll see – I'll show you ... when the chips are down, these civilised people ... they'll eat each other'. As such, he is engaged in the reverse of the Hobbesian project. Hobbes promotes a social order and moral constraints as a means of escaping the horrors of life in the state of nature. By contrast, the Joker, the self-styled 'agent of chaos', is interested in undermining the constraints of civilised life in order to restore our natural state with all its horrors.

From the civilised individual's point of view, it is an incomprehensible attitude. Batman/Bruce Wayne (Christian Bale) thinks that like any other criminal,
the Joker must be after something, looking for some material gain. Even the crime
bosses who bring in the Joker to get rid of Batman don't fully understand him.
He convinces them he is in it for the money, but later on, he will set fire to an
enormous pile of cash. Wayne's wise butler Alfred (Michael Caine), however,
has seen this sort of thing before, in the jungles of Burma: 'with respect Master
Wayne, perhaps this is a man you don't fully understand … Some men just want
to watch the world burn.' Since the Joker is happy, even eager, not only to restore
the state of nature but to be consumed in the chaos he creates, repeatedly putting
his own life at risk, he is behaving in a supremely perverse way from Hobbes's
point of view. Indeed, it is unintelligible behaviour, given Hobbes's view of human
beings as dedicated above all to their self-preservation. Such an attitude is a sign
of madness or delusion, which is the only way that Hobbes can account for example for suicide. Nonetheless, the Joker is Hobbesian in his theoretical outlook, to
the extent that he sees civilised, moral behaviour as a veneer, underneath which
individuals are driven by consuming interest in our own preservation. As with
Hobbes's vision of the state of nature, for the Joker also, once 'a little anarchy' is
introduced, people will reveal their true nature.

Although Hobbes's human being is conceived in a scientific spirit, in the materialist terminology of the new sciences, Hobbes does no actual experiments to
establish that human beings are as he describes. The state of nature scenario is
a thought experiment, an imagining of what things would be like without any
social order, although Hobbes did have the experience of the political turmoil
of the English Civil War (1642–1651) to draw on. The Joker is more rigorously
empiricist. He sets up a 'social experiment' to confirm the truth of his views
leaving explosives on two ferries, and the detonators for each on the other ferry,
expecting that one of the boats will be blown up by the other. If no boat has been
blown up by midnight, he informs the passengers, he will destroy both vessels.
Here, however, the film rejects his Hobbesian view of human beings, as the different groups of passengers refuse to kill each other even to preserve themselves. His
adversary Batman gruffly sums up the failure of the experiment: 'What were you
trying to prove? That deep down, everyone's as ugly as you?! … This city just
showed you it's full of people ready to believe in good'. That could be dismissed
as an idealised and unrealistic view of human beings, in contrast to the Joker's
harsh but nonetheless realistic Hobbesian picture. However, it might also be seen
as alluding to a complexity in human beings that is not really acknowledged in
the Hobbesian view. Perhaps people cannot be so readily reduced to creatures of
pure self-interest, selfishness and egoism. It may be that in any recognisable or
developed human being, moral considerations that go beyond pure self-interest
play a crucial role in structuring decisions and actions.

This is the first kind of issue that arises with Hobbes's picture. Normally, it
might be thought, human beings don't just seek to preserve themselves, to live.
They want to live a certain kind of life, one they can regard as fulfilled or realised. It is possible to be alive in a basic biological sense and nonetheless living

a life one regards as less than human, even not worth living. 'Human' here is not a purely descriptive term, identifying membership of a particular species, but an evaluative one, identifying a form of life that one aspires to. The suggestion here is that a moral dimension is a necessary part of a developed human existence, that a person's operating in terms of a moral framework is an index of their development as human beings. This equally means that we are the kinds of creatures for whom moral questions can arise, and in particular, the question that as Kenan Malik notes lies at the heart of all moral existence: 'What kind of life do I want?' (Malik 2014, 184) That question was addressed in the ancient and medieval accounts that looked to give justifications for particular kinds of life in terms of their being the realisation of one's nature, a state of fulfilment, the good life. Virtuous behaviour was understood as the means of attaining this ideal state and involved the control or management of one's desires.

These accounts incorporate the idea that to operate as a responsible moral agent we need to have some set of ideals, norms or values, in terms of which it is possible to evaluate our desires and motivations. These desires can be judged to be more or less worthy, higher or lower, to be acted on or restrained. There is no room in the Hobbesian picture for this moral dimension. The Hobbesian human being is just a creature with desires, all ultimately concerned with doing whatever ensures the individual's continuing existence. Any moral constraints have to be externally imposed and backed up by the threat of punishment. This, it might be thought, is a rather impoverished picture of the human being, as well as being remote from actual human behaviour. It may be the model of human behaviour assumed by economists and policymakers; but nowadays, even economists are starting to question the idea of the human being as 'homo economicus', the ruthlessly self-interested individual, suggesting that while people might act in part from self-interest, they also typically act from 'social preferences', including 'altruism, reciprocity, intrinsic pleasure in helping others, aversion to inequity, ethical commitments' (see e.g., Bowles 2016).

Secondly, the Hobbesian picture fails to take the social dimension of human existence into account. The idea that we can find a justification for moral and social rules on the basis of what human beings would be like in their natural state, if there were no moral and social order, presupposes that human beings are essentially pre-social, self-sufficient individuals, able in principle to exist independently of society. Society is then something imposed on these individuals, through the social contract. But we may wonder whether this notion of a pre-social individual is coherent. It might be argued that human beings are necessarily, from the start, involved in social relations, subject to forms of socialisation through which they are able to become the individuals that they are. That process of socialisation involves amongst other things learning to differentiate between acceptable and unacceptable desires and actions, acquiring a set of norms, values and ideals that defines the sort of person we are. In the process, we develop from a demanding creature that seeks only to satisfy its own immediate wants and desires, into a more sociable being, able to play a role in the community and whose motivations might include self-sacrifice, altruism, benevolence towards others and various other ethical commitments.

For the ancient and medieval thinkers, human beings had to be trained to play their proper role in society, to take their place in the social order. And it is only in society that they are able to acquire the virtues and be properly human. Society is necessary for the perfection of individual existence. So here, human beings are essentially social creatures and the moral virtues enable them to fulfil themselves within a community. This social dimension is absent from the Hobbesian account, replaced with the idea of society as an external arrangement, which it is in the interests of ruthlessly self-interested, egoistic individuals to submit to. In the process, we are left with the questionable notion of the essentially pre-social individual, able to exist without any essential reference to society. In truth, a human being untouched by society would be profoundly underdeveloped. They would be the wild, undisciplined being portrayed in François Truffaut's *The Wild Child* (1970). The film tells the story of a feral child (Jean-Pierre Cargol), a boy found running wild in the forest. He is rescued by scientist Jean Itard (played by Truffaut himself) who names him Victor and tries to civilise him and teach him to speak. Victor eventually acquires rudimentary language skills but the doctor is only partially successful in his civilising efforts. Like *Lord of the Flies*, Truffaut's film is documentary-like, anthropological in tone, recording an experimental investigation into human nature, the film's director playing the scientist both literally and metaphorically. It draws on the journals of the real Dr Itard, who attempted to civilise a feral child, 'Victor of Aveyron' in France at the end of the eighteenth century. In the real case also, the doctor's efforts were only partially successful.

One might perhaps see Victor's treatment as ethically problematic, a violation of the boy's 'primitive freedom' or a corruption of his 'natural goodness', as he is forced into the straitjacket of culture. Truffaut's film was criticised by some in these terms when it was released, as seemingly endorsing the oppression of regulated, civilised life over natural existence (see Monaco 1976, 74–75). Obviously, this is a more benign and sunny conception of the human being in the state of nature than Hobbes's. It suited the temper of the times to think this way. But whether seen as determined egoist or innocent 'flower child', it remains the case that this is a vision of the human being as somehow able to exist outside of society; and a being without socialisation would in fact be hopelessly stunted in their development. Even Jean-Jacques Rousseau (1712–1778), the Enlightenment figure most associated with the idea of the pre-social individual as a 'noble savage' and the idea that civilised society corrupts human beings, thought that society was necessary to complete human beings. Rousseau is clear that, even if 'natural man' is in touch with his feelings, healthy and spontaneous, and becoming civilised alienates him from himself, forcing him to put on masks and to play roles in society, it is nonetheless only by becoming civilised and acquiring language that we become responsible agents, developing a full range of desires and interests, and become fully human (Rousseau 1993, 124; see Ryan 1973).

In relation to *The Wild Child*, however much one might romanticise Victor as having been 'innocent and happy' in his natural state, enjoying a primitive freedom untainted by society, the film documents very clearly how his lack of socialisation has left him stunted in development, incapable of functioning properly. He may be biologically human, but in an important sense he is not yet fully a human being. As Truffaut himself put it, the moral of the story is that 'man is nothing without other men' (Monaco 1976, 74). In the end, the idyllic pre-social world is a fantasy, one that can only be envisaged from a civilised position, as in the rural existence constructed for Marie Antoinette (Kirsten Dunst) in Sofia Coppola's *Marie Antoinette* (2006). On the run from the stifling formality and artificial atmosphere of the eighteenth-century French court, she imagines that she can live more naturally and freely at the rural retreat of Petit Trianon. Here she hangs about with her pals, reading Rousseau. But this rural idyll is as much an artificial construction, maintained by teams of servants, as the court life that she is so desperately trying to escape from. For Marie Antoinette, there is no escape.

Nonetheless, the essentially pre-social individual is the key notion behind modern individualist thinking, of which Hobbes is a key source. In the pre-modern period in medieval Europe, what was primary was not the individual but the larger social and political order. Individuals saw themselves primarily as members of a larger social order, ordained by God, in which everyone had their proper place and to which individuals were required to conform. The modern view gives priority to the individual and makes this individual the starting point for thinking about society. So it is with Hobbes. He is concerned first and foremost with the wants and needs of the individual, which he thinks cannot be satisfied in the state of nature. He advocates submission to social rules backed up by a strong central authority because in the end he sees no other way of ensuring that individuals will be able to satisfy their desires. Moreover, in this account political authority, however oppressive it may be, is still based firmly on the consent of those being governed, those who agree to submit to the central authority in order to escape from the terrible state of nature. However powerful, the authority of the 'great Leviathan' still derives ultimately from the people, who agree to authorise the sovereign to declare and enforce the rules by which they are to live. Thus, for all his emphasis on the need for individuals to submit to an authoritarian government, Hobbes's starting point is thoroughly individualistic.

It might not then be so surprising that Hobbesian thinking could come to be transformed into an extreme individualism, in which greed is a positive good and any self-sacrifice or altruism is to be condemned as evil. This bracing view, associated with figures like Ayn Rand in the twentieth century, makes individual survival the ultimate value, the standard of good for human beings. All activities are valued insofar as they contribute to that survival and disvalued insofar as they go against it. So the claim here is that we are not just psychological egoists, creatures who are as a matter of fact always motivated by self-interest, but ethical egoists, creatures who should pursue their self-interest, whose individual survival is of paramount importance. Rand couches her version of ethical egoism in the old language of virtue, advocating the 'virtue of selfishness' and linking the pursuit of self-interest to the ideal of perfecting one's abilities in a state of happiness. But there is not really any room here for a virtue ethics, which articulates an ideal of the properly human life as the fullest expression of human nature. Instead, Rand's crude ethical egoism reduces the final end of human life to survival and the virtues to traits that promote one's survival (Rand 1964).

This thinking, which aimed to rehabilitate greed and acquisitiveness as the ultimate expression of human nature, was apparently inspirational for corporate high fliers of the eighties, figures who are in turn the subject of films of excess like *Wall Street*. In that film, the villain of the piece, predatory corporate raider Gordon Gekko, espouses the doctrine in his famous 'greed is good' speech. According to Gekko, not only is greed nothing to apologise for but greed in its many forms, for life, love, wealth and knowledge, has 'marked the upward surge of mankind'. It is a stirring endorsement of the ruthless pursuit of self-interest, though delivered in order to further Gekko's own interests in particular. By the time we get to the Jordan Belfort character in *The Wolf of Wall Street*, any pretence of moral justification has disappeared altogether. Although Gekko is mentioned in the film as Belfort's model, Belfort makes no attempt to justify his behaviour. He sets up his stockbroking company with the unapologetic aim of making as much money as possible, to spend on lavish amounts of sex, drugs and alcohol. Making money is all that counts and the sole measure of success. And the film itself offers no judgement on this, content to allow the audience to come to its own conclusions.

Ethical egoism of the sort espoused by Rand and Gekko is a position that excludes a great deal that might ordinarily be thought crucial to morality from the moral realm, including all altruistic or other-regarding behaviour, making the pursuit of one's own interests the only thing of importance. There is no concern for the interests of others, particularly those who might suffer through one's activities. It also omits any notion of ethics as moderating, curbing or restraining the pursuit of one's own desires and appetites. Ethics is reduced to the role of endorsing ruthlessly self-interested behaviour. It is thus stripped of much of its substance on this understanding, to the point where ethical egoism borders on being a self-contradictory position. Like Hobbes's political account, ethical egoism suffers in relying on a crude and reductive notion of the human being, a being that shows no signs of having been shaped into a recognisably human individual by the requirements of sociability. And where Hobbes at least introduces a more substantial morality in the form of the external constraints of the social contract, enforcing sociability in that way, ethical egoism enshrines, as moral conduct, the behaviour that for Hobbes is the very reason for establishing those moral constraints in the first place. We will return to these considerations in the last part of this chapter.

Enlightenment and Happiness

Hobbes's account sets the tone for a good deal of what comes after, and in particular for much of the ethical thinking of the eighteenth-century Enlightenment. The Enlightenment thinkers continued to move away from the idea of a religious foundation for morality, in favour of founding morality rationally, and in particular in terms of a scientific understanding of the human being. Reason here is closely identified with the new scientific way of thinking about the world, for which the human being is to be understood in strictly materialist terms. That is, all aspects of human life were to be explained in terms of the organisation and movement of matter, without recourse to a separate mental or spiritual principle. And as with Hobbes, this materialist view favours a hedonistic and egoistic view of human beings, as organisms that have been sensibly programmed by nature to seek pleasure and avoid pain, to do whatever gratifies their desires and to avoid suffering. Happiness, understood in terms of pleasure, becomes the primary goal of human existence. This notion of happiness, it should again be stressed, is far from the happiness of the human being as understood in the ancient and medieval periods; happiness as *eudaimonia*, which has to do with the realisation of one's inherent purpose and highest good, and is usually quite distinct from pleasure. It is the happiness of the modern human being, the Hobbesian hedonist.

The task for the Enlightenment's materialist thinkers, figures like Claude Helvetius (1717–1771) and Baron d'Holbach (1723–1789), was to establish a morality on the basis of this conception of human being. In general, however, they were more optimistic than Hobbes, for whom individual desires needed to be sharply curtailed by social arrangements if human beings were going to survive. The Enlightenment thinkers, in contrast, thought that social arrangements could positively enhance the pleasure and happiness of human beings. In fact, they made the enhancement of human happiness central to their vision of progress and social reform. The proper role of morality and social institutions was not so much to resolve conflicts of interest as to maximise people's happiness and a rationally organised society would do precisely that. Thus, for the Enlightenment, happiness was something that could be brought about in this world, through human means, by way of more rational moral and social arrangements. And the test of the adequacy of these social arrangements would be precisely the extent to which they contributed to the enhancement of human happiness. That would be the measure of progress.

From this perspective, the traditional religious picture of human nature was inevitably going to be criticised, as standing in the way of progress. This was the gloomy view of human beings as intrinsically corrupt, flawed, tainted by original sin and plagued by rebellious appetites and passions. Without the help of faith in God or the sacraments of the Church, everything they did would inevitably be evil. In the end, there could be no real progress or happiness in this life, only in the next. All one could do in this life was strive to be virtuous, to live a life of righteous self-denial. The Enlightenment rejected the idea that human nature was intrinsically corrupt or evil, which seemed to deny the possibility of human improvement. Claims of innate human sinfulness were held to be unscientific and without foundation. On the Enlightenment view, the pleasures and passions were not inherently evil or destructive. As part of the human being's natural makeup, they were at worst morally neutral. If human beings were evil, it was not because of any innate corruption, but because they had been made that way by bad social institutions, and these institutions could be reformed.

The modern suspicion of religious self-denial is a feature of many of Buñuel's films, which take the Church to task for its attempts to suppress instinctual nature and desires. This theme is very much to the fore in *Simon of the Desert*, its central character loosely based on the ascetic saint Simeon Stylites. The film opens with Simon, having been perched on his column for six years, six months and six weeks, an ominous numbering that goes unremarked upon, about to move to a new, taller column that has been provided by a rich businessman. Atop his new column, he whiles away the time thinking up more and more extravagant ways of exercising self-denial. At one point, he decides to do away with such 'delicacies' as bread and oil, insisting that 'God's lettuce' is enough. He also has to contend with the onslaughts of the devil, who first appears in the form of a young woman dressed in a sailor suit, reminding him of the pleasures of the flesh. Later she appears disguised as Christ, complete with unconvincing beard, telling Simon that he should give up the ascetic life, get down off his column and indulge in sensual gratification, or as she puts it, 'sink yourself in pleasure until its very name makes you sick'.

Simon is in many ways a ridiculous figure, the rightful object of Buñuel's mock-ery, much of it concerning his efforts at self-denial that he takes to such absurd lengths. In the cold light of the film, Simon's long years of self-denial seem no more than a self-destructive suppression of desire, of life itself, all for the sake of a God who doesn't exist. This is very much in keeping with the Enlightenment's rejection of the Christian ideal of virtuous self-denial and privation, as a pointless exercise in self-mutilation. Buñuel also has fun with the opportunistic monks who congregate at the base of the column, squabbling over obscure points of religious doctrine and confusing themselves in the process. For the monks, Simon is mainly useful as a propaganda tool to impress the masses and help keep them under control. This is another recurring Enlightenment theme, the critique of religion as superstition that allows religious figures to impose their authority on their fellow human beings, as well as motivating hatred, fanaticism and persecution.

This is not to say however that Buñuel simply dismisses Simon. For all his mockery, his portrait is also sympathetic, with the saint presented as a person of genuine integrity and sincerity, certainly in sharp contrast to the monks below. He is a quixotic figure, misguided but noble; as one commentator puts it, he is 'a hopeless hero, but a hero all the same … A hero of the most drastic kind of error' (Wood 2003, 132). Moreover, Buñuel does not see the abandonment of religion as necessarily opening the way to anything better. When his saintly characters lose their faith, they are not any happier. He is certainly not advo-cating the uninhibited pursuit of desire and pleasure as a viable alternative to Christian self-denial. As Pauline Kael points out, although Buñuel is critical of the religious inhibition of instincts, his characters become grotesque when they are uninhibited (Kael 1878, 275). This is certainly the case in *Simon of the Desert*, when the devil finally gets the upper hand, spiriting Simon from his column into the modern world of a sixties New York nightclub, we get a vision of uninhibited hedonism, and it is a special kind of hell. The liberated pleasure seekers gyrate mindlessly around him, as strange to him as his project of ascetic self-denial is to us.

In general, Buñuel does not make any positive recommendations about how to live. On the contrary, he is relentless in subverting ideals and formulas for living, though without succumbing to despair in any way. As Truffaut put it, he is 'a cheerful pessimist, not given to despair, but he has a sceptical mind' (Truffaut 1978, 261). In place of idealised portrayals, he presents an unsentimental, documentary-style examination of human existence in all its absurdity, irrationality, pettiness and cruelty. When Simon miraculously restores the severed hands of a man in the crowd, the man's first act is to slap one of his daughters for bothering him with questions. That's just how people are, it seems. And those like Simon, who try to rise above the ordinary human condition, embrace a Christian virtue that is shown to be useless, even counterproductive. Here, Simon is very much like another of Buñuel's saints, Father Nazario (Francisco Rabal) in *Nazarin* (1958). Nazario is a Catholic priest who tries to imitate Christ and live a life of self-denial, but his actions lead to one problem after another. He is condemned by the Church as a non-conforming rebel and suffers numerous trials at the hands of those he tries to help. Like Simon, he is a noble figure, but also a fool trying to live up to an impossible, even inhuman ideal, in denial of his own humanity.

In his fundamental pessimism about the prospects for improving the human condition, Buñuel departs from the Enlightenment. On the whole, the Enlightenment thinkers were also critical of religious self-denial, founded on the delusion that by virtuously denying ourselves in this world we will find happiness in the next. But the problem for them was that human beings, claiming to know their fate in the imaginary regions of another life, did not try to make themselves happy in this one. Their view was that happiness in this world is perfectly possible and the point of morality was precisely to maximise it. They were not, for the most part at least, advocates of moral egoism. What they did seek to do, however, was to make the human being, understood in the Hobbesian manner as pleasure-seeking and egoistic, the basis for morality. Moral behaviour at this time was commonly taken to include benevolence and kindness towards others. Most of the Enlightenment thinkers did not want to deny such behaviour, but they insisted on rejecting a religious grounding for it. It needed to be justified rationally, on the basis of the hedonistic, egoistic human being that science tells us we are. So they sought to derive notions of morality, virtue and duty from this narrow basis, to show that we ought to act justly or generously towards others because it is in our individual interests to do so, because it will lead to our own happiness. They also appreciated that individuals might need some encouragement to recognise that such ethical behaviour was indeed in their interests.

Thus, Helvetius argued that all human activities are driven by self-love, love of pleasure and the only possible moral system was one that was built on this foundation. Virtuous or morally right actions are those that contribute to the happiness of all in society, but Helvetius thought that even virtues like benevolence could be reduced to love of one's pleasure. The benevolent person is one who finds the sight of the misery of others painful and wants to relieve human suffering and unhappiness because they cause them pain. Benevolence, seeking the happiness of others, was thus compatible with the pursuit of individual pleasure (see Schneewing 2002, 416–429). Similarly, for his contemporary Holbach, though we are driven by self-interest and love of pleasure, we can come to appreciate that our actions affect the happiness of others, as their actions affect ours. As such, the best way to achieve our own happiness is to work for the good of everyone. If we make the people around us happy, they will in turn make us happy. So, for Holbach, rational concern for one's own happiness and satisfaction goes hand in hand with concern for the general welfare. On the basis of this essentially hedonistic picture, Holbach presents an account of the origins of moral feelings and the nature of virtue and duty. The concept of good arises from our recognition that we can achieve our own happiness by doing things that make others happy. Virtue is everything that contributes to the happiness of others, duties are the means by which we make them happy and moral obligation is the necessity of employing these means. Overall, it is in the individual's greatest interest to be virtuous, to work for the good of the whole, and this self-interest, Holbach argues, is the ultimate foundation of morality (see Holbach 2002, 432–437).

This picture in turn underpins the social and political visions of these thinkers. For both, the proper role of social institutions is to promote happiness for as many as possible, the general welfare. This involves training individuals, who are naturally egoistic, not to force them to deny their egoistic nature, but to see that their individual happiness is best served by making others happy. In this spirit, Helvetius advocated the establishment of a central authority that would, amongst other things, set up a program of education. Through it, people would be improved and made virtuous, by being encouraged to see that their happiness involved not only pursuing their own pleasures but contributing to the good of the whole. Holbach similarly envisioned a technocracy in which a rational, scientifically informed administration would promote public happiness; and through education and wise legislation, individuals would be shown that it is in their interests to work for the good of the whole and prevented from seeking their private good at the expense of others. This is the whole point of politics for Holbach. It ought to be 'the art of regulating the passions of man, and directing them to the welfare of society' (Holbach 1999, 102).

It is worth noting that neither Helvetius and Holbach are advocating democratic reform. Most Enlightenment thinkers working in France disliked the monarchy that held sway through the eighteenth century. However, while conservative nineteenth-century thinkers liked to hold them responsible for the 1789 French Revolution with all its excesses, they did not advocate revolution. Indeed, few of them advocated popular rule, since most of the population consisted of illiterate peasants and labourers. Rather, they looked forward to some kind of 'enlightened despotism', a society ruled by a scientifically informed administration that would impose reforms and progress on the population, with a view to maximising the happiness of the whole. A rationally administered society was seen as the best means of ensuring that individuals would be able to achieve the happiness that they desire above everything else. More recently, this sort of vision has come to be seen as carrying the seeds of a new kind of authoritarianism, in which human happiness might be maximised but at the expense of individual freedom. This is a familiar theme in the dystopian cinematic portrayals of future societies in which all desires are satisfied and destructive impulses domesticated and society runs with complete precision in an orderly way. Happiness is achieved at the cost of individuals becoming subject to a far-reaching system of control and regulation.

This is the world portrayed, for example, in another Truffaut film, *Fahrenheit 451* (1966), based on the Ray Bradbury novel. Here, all social conflict has been eliminated and the population is kept happy and compliant through a diet of prop-aganda, drugs and television. Books, which might make people think and become dissatisfied with their lives, have been made illegal. The dissidents in this society are those individuals who keep a secret library and its firefighters are state opera-tives who seek out these libraries and burn them. The central character, Montag the fireman (Oskar Werner) is initially devoted to enforcing the state's directives in the name of public happiness: 'books make people unhappy, they make them anti-social' he opines, parroting the official line. But he comes to feel that there is something fundamentally missing from life in this world, that the books he is burning might civilise and enrich life in a way that goes beyond the happiness sanctioned by the state. Like Truffaut's wild child, he lacks the enrichment of culture. Unlike the child, his growth is not stunted by a lack of socialisation, but by a social order that limits the individual's freedom and possibilities for the sake of social harmony. The fate of individual freedom is going to be a recurring issue for an ethical standpoint in which the good is understood in terms of maximising overall happiness.

Utilitarianism

The idea that emerges in both Helvetius and Holbach, that virtuous or morally right actions are those that contribute to the happiness of the whole, is the basic principle of utilitarian moral theory. However, it falls to Jeremy Bentham (1748–1832) to clearly articulate this moral and political perspective. This he does in *An Introduction to the Principles of Morals and Legislation*. For Bentham, as for Helvetius and Holbach, the starting point is the hedonistic view of human beings as exclusively driven to seek pleasure and avoid pain. These determine how we in fact act; but in addition, to use Bentham's phrase, it is for pleasure and pain 'to point out what we ought to do, as well as to determine what we shall do' (Bentham 2004, 65). The happiness principle is therefore also a standard of right action, a moral principle that tells us how we ought to act, namely in such a way as to maximise pleasure and avoid pain. By the same token, for Bentham, all we mean by calling an act good or right is that it promotes pleasure. When we say that we ought to do something, we mean that the act in question is useful in bringing about pleasure or happiness, which is the only thing good in itself, intrinsically valuable, on the utilitarian view.

At the same time, Bentham extends this principle beyond individual pleasure and pain. It becomes the idea that the morally good action is the one that maxim-ises pleasure and minimises pain for all affected by the proposed action. We ought to act and live in such a way as to promote the greatest happiness for all those affected by our actions, the greatest happiness principle. Bentham also called this the principle of utility. Utility is the tendency of an action to produce happiness and the utilitarian principle can be formulated in terms of maximising utility in this sense. Bentham does not really explain this transition from a concern with individual happiness to that of the greatest number. He does not, for example, argue that promoting the happiness of the whole is the best way of ensuring my own happiness. He clearly believes that in pursuing our own happiness, we should seek the general happiness of society as well, but he does not say why the latter follows. And one can readily imagine scenarios where pursuing one's own happiness not only does not increase that of others, but positively requires that other people be deprived of theirs. This scenario is explored in the scandalous eighteenth-century Laclos novel *Liaisons Dangereuse*, in which decadent aristocrats take malicious pleasure in ruining the lives of innocents. This is a key theme in *Dangerous Liaisons* (Stephen Frears, 1988), one of a number of cinematic adaptations of the novel. The film highlights that pleasure can be pursued not only without regard for others, but through the active harming of them.

We will return to this film and the idea that a pleasure-seeking being, far from being concerned with the welfare of others, might just as readily take pleasure in their suffering. For the moment it can be noted that, although one might want to speak in such cases of 'evil' kinds of pleasure, for Bentham, there is no such thing. Pleasure cannot be evil. The idea of an evil pleasure only makes sense if you introduce a non-utilitarian value that is irreducible to pleasure. For Bentham, pleasure remains the only thing valuable in itself and the only thing that we have to do morally speaking is to produce on balance the most pleasure. Of course, an action may have a number of consequences. It may produce both happiness and unhappiness. But for utilitarianism, an action can be right if it produces some unhappiness, as long as on balance, overall, it produces the most happiness in comparison with other actions. So the utilitarian position is that we ought to act and live in such a way as to promote the greatest happiness for all those affected by our actions. When faced with a choice between alternative actions, the right action is the one that has the best overall consequences, produces the greatest amount or happiness, for everyone concerned.

This principle of right action, the greatest happiness principle, is not only a principle of morality. The title of Bentham's book is *An Introduction to the Principles of Morals and Legislation*. As with Helvetius and Holbach, Bentham extended this principle from a moral criterion to a criterion for social policy and legislation. Legislators too should be concerned with the happiness of the whole. In the rules, they lay down, and the punishments they impose, they should always aim at a favourable balance of pleasure over pain. Bentham argued that the best social policies were those that distributed pleasures as widely as possible, and reduced pain as much as possible. Utilitarian thinking also provided an important justification for the state itself. Bentham rejected Hobbes's idea that political authority is created and justified in terms of a social contract, arguing that it is the state that creates the possibility of binding contracts. For Bentham, the legitimacy of the state depends on whether a law contributes to the happiness of its citizens. Government is justified in terms of utility (see Binmore 2000). On this view, the proper role of the state is to promote the greater good, the maintenance of public order, security and happiness.

Utilitarianism is certainly a very appealing view of morality. In keeping with the broad outlook of the Enlightenment, it views morality as no less than the attempt to bring as much pleasure and happiness into the world as possible. Morality is understood in entirely secular terms, as a human creation that serves human goals, above all the desire to be happy and to be spared misery and pain. Equally, this understanding of morality dispenses with religious fictions. Morality for Bentham is no longer a matter of pleasing God by following divinely ordained laws and prohibitions It becomes a thoroughly rational business, insofar as reason is understood in a scientific, calculative sort of way. Utilitarianism promises to make all moral issues rationally decidable through the empirical calculation of consequences. We decide what actions to perform by measuring how much happiness various possible actions are likely to produce, determining which produces the most happiness overall. Bentham also explicitly rejects the Christian idea of morality as self-denial, which he characterises as the 'principle of asceticism', and which he sees as the exact opposite of the goal embraced by utilitarianism – it prescribes the minimisation of happiness and disapproves of any increase. He suggests that it has taken a stronger religious form, in which its adherents make the active pursuit of pain a duty, and a weaker, philosophical form, in which, for the sake of reputation, grosser bodily pleasures are rejected and the other pleasures are called something other than pleasure. And he suggests that if this principle of asceticism were to be applied in legislation, the result would be a 'hell on earth' (Bentham 2004, 74).

For all its appeal, however, Bentham's utilitarianism is not without its problems. It might be thought, for example, that it places an impossible burden of calculation on human beings. In every situation, it requires agents to determine all the possible things they could do, including not acting, and try to calculate what the total consequences for each action would be. Even if we could manage these calculations, there is the question of whether we can indeed speak straightforwardly of there being more or less pleasure in these different situations. That is, we may wonder whether pleasures do indeed only differ in terms of quantity. Thinking so makes it possible to add and compare different pleasures in the required manner. But it might be thought that, for example, the cerebral pleasures of poetry and the raucous pleasures of party games are very different kinds of pleasure. Can such different pleasures be compared or added to one another? Bentham thought so. He came up with a 'felicific calculus', which was to measure pleasures along a number of dimensions, including intensity, duration, likelihood of recurrence amongst others. The intent was to be able to provide a quantitative measure of different pleasures, sufficient to allow them to figure in utilitarian calculations. Not many have been convinced by Bentham's work-around.

There are also issues concerning utilitarianism's notion of the human being. For some critics of the time, in saying that human beings have no higher end than pleasure, that this is the sole ultimate value, utilitarianism seemed to be advocating that we wallow in bodily gratification. This led them to label it a 'pig philosophy'.

This accusation assumes that human beings are capable only of pleasures that a pig is capable of, that there is no difference in quality between a human being's pleasures and a pig's. And indeed, in Bentham's formulation of utilitarianism, this is the case. He assumes that pleasures only differ in terms of quantity. This is driven home in his famous phrase, that 'all things considered, pushpin [a simple party game] is as good as poetry'. Both give us pleasure. But if the moral thing to do is to produce the greatest amount of happiness or pleasure in the world, and if utilitarianism gives us no reason to prefer some types of pleasures over others, it is consistent with that to spend the day wallowing in crude pleasures, drinking, eating, playing party games and so on. A dissipated life could even be morally superior to a life of cultural or artistic activity, if there were more pleasure to be had from the former.

Bentham's successor John Stuart Mill (1806–1873) found Bentham's failure to distinguish between different kinds of pleasure an embarrassment, opening utilitarianism up to the 'pig philosophy' criticism. In *Utilitarianism*, he sought to refine the utilitarian position. He did not want to give up the basic utilitarian idea that the sole ultimate value is happiness, to be equated with pleasure and the absence of pain. But he argued that some pleasures were higher or more worthy than others (Mill 2004, 279). For Mill, pleasures differ from one another in quality as well as quantity; and the superior pleasures are those that most befit our nature as human beings, utilising our distinctively human capacities for intelligent activity. The higher pleasures of the mind and the soul, such as poetry, music, intellectual enquiry, moral virtue and so on, were to be preferred to the lower, bodily pleasures of food, drink and sex. And they should count for more in the calculation of overall happiness than lower ones. A number of films, drawing on George Bernard Shaw's 1913 play *Pygmalion,* pursue the related idea that individual self-improvement might be measured by the degree to which one leaves behind the lower pleasures and acquires a taste for the higher ones. In the story Eliza Doolittle, a working-class flower seller with basic tastes, is introduced to the higher pleasures of Professor Higgins and his circle. Higgins, a professor of phonetics, has wagered that he can turn Eliza into a 'proper lady' in a few months. Films that draw on this story include *Pygmalion* (Anthony Asquith, Leslie Howard, 1938) and the musical *My Fair Lady* (George Cukor, 1964). *Educating Rita* (Lewis Gilbert, 1980) has a similar plot.

By introducing the distinction between higher and lower pleasures, Mill commits to a richer conception of human being than Bentham. Mill's human being may still be dominated by the desire for pleasure, but some pleasures are higher than others because they befit our distinctive nature as human beings. Mill is not simply saying that we ought to cultivate these higher pleasures. He thinks we will not be entirely happy, truly satisfied, fulfilled, if we do not. This notion of happiness, as linked to fulfilment, recalls Aristotle's, but there are some key differences. Like Aristotle, Mill's notion of happiness rests on a philosophical conception of human nature, an ideal of what we can become. But for Aristotle, this is the human being understood as the sort of being that is fulfilled through virtuous activity. Virtuous activity may give us pleasure, but this is at best an accidental accompaniment, whereas for Mill happiness lies in higher pleasures themselves. We are the sort of being that can only be fully satisfied by the higher pleasures like poetry, music and other elevated cultural pursuits, and never entirely satisfied by lower pleasures such as food and drink. And this claim about the relative importance of higher and lower pleasures is not just a philosophical one. Mill holds that it will find empirical support. If people are faced with a choice between the two kinds of pleasures, he thinks, they will prefer the higher over the lower (cf. Mill 2004, 282).

It might be objected that many people pursue trivial and mindless pleasures like getting drunk and playing party games and seem completely happy. Isn't Mill then ignoring what these people prefer? Mill's answer is that people need to have had a real experience of the two alternatives. There are many people whose experience has been confined to trivial and mindless pleasures, and who continue to pursue them exclusively. Mill's claim is that if they could experience some of the more demanding enjoyments that human beings are capable of, they would come to find those pleasures more rewarding, and prefer them over the lower. This indeed is what happens in the Pygmalion story. In the *My Fair Lady* musical version, for example, Eliza is initially only interested in the lower pleasures, warmth and comfort, as she expresses in the song 'All I want is a room somewhere'. After Higgins teaches her to speak correctly and introduces her to the higher pleasures of elevated society, she runs away, trying to return to her old life. She finds, however, that she is now a stranger in her former home. Having experienced the higher pleasures, she can no longer be content with a life where only the lower ones are possible. This development is repeated in *Educating Rita*, where Rita (Julie Walters), the Eliza character, is a working-class hairdresser trying to better herself by studying at university. Having been exposed to the higher pleasures of poetry and literature, she finds she now prefers them to the simple pleasures she once enjoyed, like singing songs down at the pub.

Mill does concede that there are some who, having been able to appreciate the higher pleasures, relapse into the pursuit of the lower ones. But he thinks that such cases can be explained in social and psychological terms, as cases of degeneration (Mill 2004, 281–282). Perhaps this is how we might view the Henry Higgins character in *Educating Rita,* Rita's university lecturer Professor Bryant (Michael Caine). Bryant is a burnt-out, cynical character teetering on the edge of alcoholism. Though an expert in literature and poetry, he has lost any passion for his subject. He thinks that expertise in these things is no guarantee of happiness and that the less refined pleasures, like getting drunk and having sex, have much more to recommend them. As a result, he initially tries to discourage Rita from pursuing her studies. Mill would presumably see him as not competent to judge between different pleasures, and he certainly comes across as having lost his way. However, a position that purports to find empirical support, in people's preferences for its contention that there are higher, more fulfilling pleasures for human beings, cannot go too far in this direction. Dismissing anyone who prefers what Mill would consider a lower pleasure as an incompetent judge threatens to make any appeal to what people prefer meaningless.

Without any reference to people's own preferences in these matters, the Pygmalion relationship has the potential to be an oppressive one. This is not so much because the Higgins character in the classic scenario is typically arrogant, demanding and heartless. Rather, it is the prospect that all kinds of oppressive disciplinary impositions upon a person might be justified in the guise of cultivating an appreciation of supposedly higher tastes and pleasures in them. What saves the Higgins-Doolittle relationship from being abusive in this way, as opposed to, say, the Scottie-Madelaine relationship in *Vertigo*, is that in the Higgins-Doolittle case, as Noel Carroll puts it, 'one has the feeling that he is bringing out the best in her' (Carroll 2007, 111). That is, Higgins really is working on behalf of Eliza's interests, directing her towards the superior pleasures that befit her nature as a human being, that make use of the distinctively human capacities for intelligent activity. And what gives support to this view, and reassures the viewer, is that Eliza herself prefers, seeks out and wants to cultivate these superior pleasures. She is keen to better herself, to develop as a person in doing so. In *Educating Rita*, the matter seems to be beyond doubt. The teacher, Bryant, actively tries to discourage his student from pursuing this path, but she will not be deterred. And in the end, her unstoppable enthusiasm ends up reawakening his own interest in literature and poetry.

A common criticism of Mill's account is that the conception of higher and lower pleasures does not reflect human nature so much as the class biases of the author. What Mill calls the higher pleasures, poetry, music, opera and so on, are really the pursuits of the upper classes, whereas the carnal and bodily pleasures are the sorts of things the lower classes delight in. So perhaps this doctrine is really an intellectual's justification for the particular preferences, interests and values of his social class over those of the lower orders. We might ask whether different social strata can be so straightforwardly identified with the different kinds of pleasure, but leaving that aside, class certainly plays a key role in all of the Pygmalion films. The upper-class teacher meets the working-class student, and a clear marker of the class difference in these films is the preference for higher or lower pleasures, respectively. The critic who sees Mill's idea of higher pleasures as an elitist privileging of upper-class pleasures might counter this by arguing that it is the 'lower', working-class pleasures that are in fact superior, being more authentic, more 'human' than the artificial delights of the upper strata. Behind this judgement, of course, lies a certain conception of human nature, and this counter-claim might equally be questioned as reflecting class biases of its own.

Here Mill has a certain advantage in that he can appeal to the empirical preferences of individuals to underpin the distinction between higher and lower pleasures, what he thinks they would actually prefer if they were exposed to both, independent of any claims about human nature. Of course, it might be argued that living in a hierarchical social order might influence people's empirical preferences, so that lower-class individuals might come to have a distorted view of pleasure, to see the pleasures they gravitate towards as unworthy and those pursued by the upper classes as superior. They might come to be estranged, then, from the pleasures that are proper to them, or even to human nature as such.

However, this sort of claim requires us to appeal once again to a philosophical idea of human nature, and in addition, to ignore empirical preferences people may have. What we can say at least is that for Eliza Doolittle in her various manifestations, there are some pleasures that she comes to see as higher and more worthy, worth pursuing over other, lower ones. And a big part of what is motivating Rita in *Educating Rita* is a desire to escape from a state that she finds stifling and limiting, and which she wants to go beyond both in terms of individual self-development and upward social mobility.

No doubt from a strictly utilitarian point of view, Mill's picture introduces some difficulties that are not present in Bentham's picture. In particular, where Bentham's view that pleasures are only quantitatively different allows them to be added together in the manner required for utilitarian calculation, determining the overall amount of pleasure produced by actions becomes more complicated if some pleasures are deemed to be qualitatively worth more than others. Also, where Bentham's view makes no distinction between the pleasures of the aristocrat and the peasant, all counting equally in the calculation in an appealingly egalitarian fashion, Mill's view opens the way to privileging the higher pleasures of the upper classes and dismissing the lower pleasures of the masses. In the case of the individual, Mill's version of hedonism is perhaps in danger of justifying a new kind of asceticism. In any contest between higher and lower pleasures, the higher pleasures must take precedence over the lower. If this means that, in the name of refined but perhaps also rather cerebral and colourless higher pleasures, the more vigorous, down-to-earth ones are to be set aside or excluded, this is a potentially debilitating view.

More radically, we might question the idea pursued by both Bentham and Mill that human beings seek happiness in the form of pleasure. The later nineteenth-century German philosopher Nietzsche was talking about utilitarianism, and about Mill especially, when he said that 'Man does not strive for happiness; only the Englishman does' (Nietzsche 1968, 12). We will hear more about Nietzsche in Chapter Five. What is coming under scrutiny here is the modern, hedonistic notion of the human being itself, which Enlightenment thought looks to as the basis for morality, utilitarianism being the most significant manifestation of such a pleasure-based morality. Nietzsche's suspicion that pleasure might not in fact be the only thing of importance to human beings is pursued by Robert Nozick, a twentieth-century critic of utilitarianism, who posed the 'experience machine' thought experiment, a science fiction scenario: would you plug yourself into a virtual reality machine that promised a lifetime of pleasurable experience, the satisfaction of all desires, albeit only virtually. Arguably most people would refuse, preferring real experiences even if these are sometimes going to be unpleasant. This scenario poses a problem for utilitarianism, in that it suggests that people might value things other than pleasure (Nozick 1974, 42–45).

Recent science fiction films that have portrayed versions of the experience machine have tended to move in this direction, opting for truth over happiness. In *The Matrix* (Wachowski siblings, 1999), the character Cypher (Joe Pantoliano) wants to return to an illusory happiness within the vast virtual reality of the matrix, in preference to the harshness of life as a rebel battling the machines that set it up to enslave humanity. But he is the villain of the piece, and by attributing the choice of happiness over truth to him, the film is indicating its disapproval of the position. Things are a little more complicated in *Inception* (Christopher Nolan, 2010). Here, the hero Dominick Cobb (Leonardo di Caprio) also opts for happiness over truth. A professional thief hired to perform corporate espionage by entering people's dreams to steal information, his latest job comes with the promise that with success, he will be cleared of a murder charge and be able to return home to his children. The film concludes with him happily reconciled with his children. But he also closes his eyes to possible proof that his happy state is itself a dream. He simply does not want to know, for the sake of a happy ending. However, he is not the villain of the piece, and the film itself seems ambivalent as to whether it matters whether the world he ends up in is real or not. Perhaps it is does not matter, as long as it is a world that is satisfying for him, a world that he finds it worth living in. In this spirit, the film refrains from resolving the question of the truth of what is going on, content to leave the ending ambiguous in that regard. We can say that the film ultimately leaves it up to the audience to decide whether truth is more important than happiness.

Outside of these science fiction scenarios of virtual reality and global illusion, a more down-to-earth instance where the question of happiness versus truth arises can be found in *Crimes and Misdemeanors*. At the family dinner recalled by the guilt-ridden protagonist Judah, his father Sol insists that he would rather believe in God against all evidence to the contrary, as this means he will have a happier life. As he puts it, if it comes to a contest between God and truth, 'I will always choose God over truth'. This puts him at odds with his formidable sister May, for whom religion is just so much superstition and it is truth that is most important. In this case, we can be sure that the film is more in agreement with May than with Sol. It proceeds to its startlingly bleak conclusion, so manifestly at odds with the standard Hollywood happy ending in which the bad guys have been punished and the good guys at least come out of it okay. At the same time, if cinema itself can be considered a kind of experience machine, it is clear that people are happy for their cinematic virtual reality to contain something more than just pleasurable experiences. This also provides a reminder that the experience that film can offer is not confined to wish fulfilling fantasies, or visions that comfortingly confirm existing prejudices and prevailing forms of thought. It can extend to experiences that confront the viewer and challenge what they take to be true or right. And that films that contain such experiences, however unpalatable, are also attractive to the viewer.

Regarding utilitarianism itself, it remains a point of contention with this ethical theory that the only thing considered valuable in itself is pleasure or happiness. It might be argued that we value many other things as well, such as freedom, knowledge, truth, honesty or dignity. These non-utilitarian values cannot be incorporated into utilitarianism as they stand. To make them the things that we seek to maximise risks losing the distinctive character of utilitarianism. Nonetheless, utilitarianism has proven to be quite adaptable in amending itself within its framework to meet at least some objections that have been raised against it. Mill's introduction of higher and lower pleasures is one such modification. Another, more recent modification is desire or preference utilitarianism. Here happiness is no longer understood in terms of pleasure, even higher and lower pleasures, the view now referred to as 'hedonistic utilitarianism' (see Singer 2011). It is understood in terms of the satisfaction of desire, in terms of either getting what you want or getting what is in your interests, where interests are normally explained in terms of present and probable future desires. So what we're trying to do here is not to maximise pleasure but to maximise the satisfaction of people's desires or preferences. But similar calculation problems arise with desire utilitarianism as with hedonistic utilitarianism. How do we determine the value of desires and weigh them up against one another?

A further set of issues arises concerning utilitarianism in that all kinds of morally questionable acts appear to be justifiable on utilitarian grounds, given the right circumstances. For utilitarianism, the only thing that is morally important is producing the best consequences, in the form of the greatest amount of happiness for the greatest number. As such, it has no fundamental objection to employing any means, no matter how shocking, nor with treating particular individuals or groups unjustly, exploiting them or inflicting pain even to the point of killing, if that will bring about the greatest overall happiness. This is also a standard kind of movie logic, familiar from police, crime thriller and action films: as long as the bad guy gets what they deserve, the means do not really matter. Thus, in Don Siegel's *Dirty Harry* (1971), police inspector Harry Callahan (Clint Eastwood) resorts to extreme, extrajudicial methods, including torture, to deal with the psychopathic Scorpio (Andy Robinson), who is terrorising the population of San Francisco. In the film's most harrowing scene, Callahan tortures Scorpio in a football stadium to get him to divulge the whereabouts of the girl he has kidnapped and buried alive, and who is fast running out of air (Figure 3.1). This torture might be justifiable in utilitarian terms, as something that is undertaken in the name of the greater good, but it remains a disturbing tactic, and we may wonder about an ethical position that is able to countenance such behaviour.

It is worth noting here that Callahan, while he does not exactly do things by the book, is no mere renegade or vigilante, operating outside the system. He is a policeman, part of the establishment, an agent of the state. In this capacity also, his activities can be seen as being justifiable in utilitarian terms, insofar as utilitarianism provides a moral justification for the exercise of state power. This is the idea that the state's actions are legitimate insofar as they contribute to maximising the happiness of its citizens, promoting public order, safety, security and well-being. From this perspective, in the face of direct threats to public order and security represented by Scorpio, it is perfectly legitimate for an operative of the state to employ extreme methods such as torture. But this again raises questions about utilitarianism, as an ethical position seemingly able to justify any action, no matter how extreme, by the state in the name of the greater good.

For its part, *Dirty Harry* has become synonymous in the popular imagination with the exercise of a brutal kind of utilitarian logic in which the ends justify any means, no matter how shocking, as long as they contribute to the greater good.

Figure 3.1 Dirty Harry: robust policing (Don Siegel, 1971. Credit: Warner Brothers/ Photofest).

During the early twenty-first century War on Terror, the US administration of the time was seen by some as employing a 'Dirty Harry ethics' (Lopez 2016), specifically a willingness to depart from many standard ethical constraints in its response to terrorism, on the principle that the end, namely preventing terrorist attacks, justified any means, including preventive war and torture. Such means-end thinking is on display in *Zero Dark Thirty* (Kathryn Bigelow, 2012), which directly addresses the War on Terror, following the hunt driven by CIA agent Maya (Jessica Chastain) for the arch-terrorist Osama Bin Laden. The film proved controversial because, by giving no hint of dispute or dissent, it seems to imply that the 'enhanced interrogation techniques' it depicts (waterboarding, sleep deprivation and the like), are perfectly justified in the state's war against terrorism. The only concern raised about the torture in the film is a purely practical one, one character's view later in the film that it is perhaps not possible to be entirely confident about the information derived by such means. There is no ethical concern over the torture itself, which from a strictly utilitarian perspective can indeed be seen as perfectly justifiable.

A more critical view of such thinking can be found in Curtis Hanson's 1997 neo-noir *LA Confidential*, which returns to questions of police tactics. The film traces the corruption of newly-arrived Los Angeles detective Ed Exley (Guy Pearce) precisely in terms of his turn towards a utilitarian way of thinking in which any action is legitimate as long as the bad guys get what they deserve. In this spirit, Exley comes to accept the behaviour of fellow officer Wendell White (Russell Crowe), who is in the habit of beating information out of criminals and shooting offenders he thinks might escape conviction. This is a complete turnaround for Exley, given that he starts out staunchly refusing the advice given to him on his first day by Captain Dudley Smith (James Cromwell), that a detective should be willing to plant corroborative evidence on a suspect, beat a confession out of a suspect he knows to be guilty or shoot a hardened criminal in the back if there is a chance they will escape conviction. In the end, Smith turns out to be a corrupt cop, and having a chance of escaping conviction, ends up being shot in the back by Exley. By this stage, Exley has become everything that he initially recoiled from.

In this connection, we can take another look at *Dirty Harry*. Certainly, a great deal of the film's visual pleasure comes from witnessing Callahan's robust policing methods, on full show in an early scene where Callahan single-handedly foils a bank robbery, producing a scene of spectacular devastation. One might as a result imagine that the film is endorsing his behaviour, and to an extent it is, but there is also a critical element to the film. Callahan may resort to brutal, extrajudicial means to deal with Scorpio and he mocks the authorities when they refer to the killer's rights in the face of his rough treatment. Nonetheless, the film does not simply endorse his methods. It also brings them into question, by drawing parallels between Callahan and his foe. The pivotal torture scene in the football stadium almost exactly mirrors an earlier scene in a park, only with the roles reversed. In the park, it is Scorpio who brutally torments Callahan at the foot of a large concrete cross. In the stadium it is Scorpio, lying on the grass next to some cross-shaped line markings, who is being brutalised by Callahan. By mirroring protagonist and antagonist in this way, the film implies that Callahan's robust methods are, as one commentator puts it, bringing him 'dangerously close to the very evil he is trying to overcome' (Wanat 2007, 85). In so doing, the film also implicitly calls into question a utilitarianism that would see any means as justified in the service of the greater good.

There is a similar questioning of the protagonist's methods, and implicitly, of a utilitarian perspective, in *The Dark Knight*. The protagonist here is Batman, the vigilante who, though in cooperation with the police, employs extrajudicial methods to deal with a criminality they are too weak to take on. The question is whether in doing so he does not enter into ethically dangerous territory. He is contrasted with district attorney Harvey Dent (Aaron Eckhart), who at least at the beginning of the film, is making headway in dealing with the city's organised crime, while staying within the law and order system to do so. Questions over Batman's activities are raised in the film in an early scene when Harvey and assistant DA Rachel Dawes (Maggie Gyllenhall) run into Batman's alter ego Bruce Wayne and his date at a restaurant and they dine together. In the course of the meal, the group discuss the ethics of Batman's vigilantism. Surprisingly, Dent approves of it, comparing the situation to that of ancient Rome suspending democracy so that one man could protect the city. Rachel, however, points to the dangers of this path, noting that this was how Caesar became emperor. The suspension of moral and political norms in order to meet a threat might make utilitarian sense, but it also opens the way to excesses.

Sure enough, as the film proceeds, Batman is shown resorting to extreme methods, including torture, in order to defeat the Joker. Goaded by the latter's outrages, he tortures a captive to get information about the Joker's whereabouts, dropping a mob boss from a building in order to break his legs and make him talk. And after barricading the door of the police interrogation room he beats up the Joker with surprising violence, in order to find out where Harvey and Rachel, who have been abducted, are being held (Figure 3.2). Later on, he hijacks the mobile phone network in order to subject the entire city population to pervasive

Figure 3.2 The Dark Knight: enhanced interrogation (Christopher Nolan, 2008. Credit: Warner Brothers/Photofest).

surveillance. Though these actions might be justifiable in utilitarian terms, as all being for the greater good of defeating the Joker, Batman is aware that by resorting to them he is in danger of becoming like the villain he is trying to overcome. Not surprisingly, some commentators saw the film as commenting on the War in Terror, and implicitly supporting the then US administration's resort to violations of civil rights, including torture and significant increases in domestic surveillance, as necessary for the fight against terrorism. Others picked up on the critical element and saw the film as in fact questioning the administration's resort to such extreme tactics (see Comiskey 2011).

Even though Batman himself resorts to some extreme, morally questionable methods, he has one rule that he wants to stick to whatever the circumstances, to never take another's life. On at least two occasions he has the opportunity to kill the Joker but refuses to do so. An appeal to rules might be thought to be a way of avoiding the problem that all sorts of morally questionable acts seem able to be justified on utilitarian grounds. Indeed, another modification of utilitarianism itself has been the introduction of the notion of 'rule utilitarianism', as opposed to the classic 'act utilitarianism'. In act utilitarianism, we calculate with each act which alternative will produce the greatest happiness. In rule utilitarianism, we are asking the same question of general rules, like 'never kill', and this arguably allows us to avoid justifying morally questionable acts. While more overall happiness might be produced by killing someone in an individual case, it is unlikely that more overall happiness will be produced by having a general rule that allows killing. A problem however with this view is that rule utilitarianism tends to collapse into act utilitarianism. We might look to a general rule like 'never kill', but to hold to this rule regardless of circumstances, even if it were, say, to save thousands of lives, might be thought inflexible. However, if we change the rule to read 'never kill except in special circumstances that justify killing', our rule utilitarianism effectively collapses into act utilitarianism.

A further general issue with utilitarianism has to do with the large demands that utilitarianism makes on the moral agent. One such concern is that in calling on individuals to perform certain acts in the name of the greater good, utilitarianism will require them to go against their own moral commitments in a way that is self-alienating. This problem is discernible in *Dirty Harry*. At the end of the film, Callahan, having finally dispatched Scorpio, throws his police badge into the pond where the slain killer is floating. In part this dramatic gesture is a repudiation of the system of law and order, the state, that used him to deal with this threat of public well-being, while also disavowing him because of the extreme methods he had to employ to do so. He is in this thankless position because the state he serves is not governed by purely utilitarian considerations and to that extent has a bad conscience about resorting to extreme methods. But one suspects that Callahan himself is not governed by purely utilitarian concerns. He seems uneasy at times with the methods he has to employ in the name of the greater good, for example, making a point of sending his sidekick away before he starts to torture Scorpio. In general, he is unhappy about having to do the 'dirty jobs' that other police don't want to be associated with. But since he does not have the state's luxury of distancing himself from these actions, it seems that in the end the only way out of this internal conflict is to repudiate his role as a policeman.

This kind of internal conflict is more obvious in *The Dark Knight*. Batman is clearly far from comfortable with what he has had to resort to in order to combat the Joker, including torturing his captive. As he says to Rachel: 'I've got enough blood on my hands. I've seen, now, what I would have to become to stop men like him'. Rather like the Joker himself, one imagines. This is why, when the Joker demands that he turn himself in to the authorities and reveal his secret identity, as a condition for stopping his killing spree, Batman is more than willing to do so. He understands that he is even at risk of breaking his one rule of not taking another's life, a rule that can also be seen as a key moral commitment on his part, something that to a large extent defines his identity. It would be a significant self-betrayal for him to break this rule, which is of course why the Joker is particularly keen to get him to do so. During the interrogation scene, he reveals that Rachel and Harvey Dent are being held in different warehouses rigged to explode. Batman can only save one of them and will thus be contributing to the death of the other if the police cannot get to them in time. In the event, Batman makes the tellingly non-utilitarian decision to save Rachel, whom he cares for, over Harvey who can do more good for the city. Only when he arrives at the location and finds Harvey does he realise that the Joker has switched addresses on him. In the end, Harvey survives, though physically and ethically disfigured, and Rachel is killed.

The issue of utilitarian thinking as potentially leading to self-alienation is developed by Bernard Williams as the 'integrity objection' to utilitarianism (see Smart and Williams 1971, 99–100). Williams argues that utilitarian logic may give us a clear idea as to what we should do, but it fails to take into account moral considerations other than the greater good. In particular, it fails to take into account what he calls the 'commitments' that people pursue for themselves, their families, friends and other people. These are the kinds of moral commitments and attachments that define the particular person one is and make one's life worthwhile. Utilitarianism demands instead that people think impartially about what actions contribute to maximising happiness. The pursuit of their own lives and interests can only be justified insofar as they contribute to the greater good. Utilitarianism thus has the potential to alienate a person from their moral identity. In telling individuals to maximise the well-being of all people, it demands a degree of impartiality in their motivations that they do not have, and which they could not have without abandoning the attachments and commitments that make their lives worthwhile.

With its demand to leave behind personal moral commitments and attachments in favour of impartial calculation, utilitarianism seems ideally suited to be the morality for advanced computers and robots in the science fiction genre. Given utilitarianism's capacity to justify morally questionable actions, there is also the potential here for a new kind of villain, the inadvertently villainous utilitarian machine. In *I, Robot* (Alex Proyas, 2004), based on the Isaac Asimov short stories, Will Smith's policeman Del Spooner has to contend with a future society that employs servant robots programmed to operate along utilitarian lines. A robot impartially calculating that it was better to save him than a young girl after a car accident has led to a deep aversion towards the robot kind. What he objects to is their inhuman indifference to human partialities, such as the special concern people normally have for young children. However, the impartiality in their thinking reflects its utilitarian rather than robotic character. The real villain of the film, the computer VIKI that coordinates all the robots, is a consummate utilitarian, effectively demonstrating how much utilitarianism will countenance in the name of maximising overall happiness. Given the human talent for destruction and self-destructive behaviour, VIKI calculates that the best way to minimise overall harm to humanity is to enslave the population: 'To protect humanity ... some humans must be sacrificed. To ensure your future ... some freedoms must be surrendered. We robots will ensure mankind's continued existence' (see Grau 2011, 451–452).

Overall, utilitarianism places enormous demands on human beings. It demands in effect that they be willing to sacrifice themselves, to give up the personal projects and commitments that constitute an identifiable self, for the sake of the greater good. It also makes an open-ended demand on people, that whatever they do, they have to wonder if they are producing the most amount of happiness and they can be fairly sure there is something else they could do that would produce more. There is no relief from this requirement, no moral time off, so to speak. It demands, in other words, a certain sort of saintliness, and ordinary people might not be cut out to be moral saints of this sort (see Wolf 1997). And utilitarianism places an impossible burden of calculation on human beings. In every situation, it requires agents to determine all the possible things they could do, including not acting, and try to calculate what the total consequences for each action would be.

It is perhaps significant that this is an ethics that we can imagine suiting robots and computers very well. We have to ask whether there is not something inhuman about utilitarianism, whether what utilitarianism demands of human beings might not be beyond their powers. This is of serious concern for moral thinking. If morality is most fundamentally about how people should behave, a moral theory that posits an ideal of behaviour beyond the capacity of people to achieve is deeply problematic. If the purpose of ethics is to guide conduct, 'it needs to concern itself with what falls within the limits if normal human capacity' (Hayward 2017). And this is of particular concern for Enlightenment ethical thinking which seeks to base ethics on a realistic conception of human beings, of human nature.

Locke and Rights

It is notable that *Dirty Harry* gives expression to the moral disquiet provoked by Callahan's actions in terms of the language of individual rights. After Scorpio is arrested by Harry, he has to be released because the district attorney finds legal irregularities in the way he was apprehended. As the DA says to Callahan, 'Where the hell does it say you've got a right to kick down doors, torture suspects, deny medical attention and legal counsel ... What I'm saying is, that man had rights'. Rights are another important element in the moral thinking of modernity. The DA is talking about legal rights, rights people have under the law, but such rights are often the legal recognition of what are really moral rights. In general, moral rights are strong entitlements to certain things, such as a right to life, privacy or a fair trial. If someone has a right to something, others have a corresponding duty to respect that right. If I have a right to life, others are obliged not to kill me. Where utilitarianism has no fundamental objection to exploiting, inflicting pain or even killing individuals, rights operate to defend individuals from such exploitation and abuse. If utilitarianism is always ready to sacrifice individuals in the name of the greater good, rights serve to protect the individual. Actions that are sanctioned by utilitarianism can be condemned as an unjust violation of rights.

To fully appreciate the nature of this conflict between Callahan and the DA, between utilitarianism and rights, it is useful to turn to the history of the relevant ideas. A key figure in the development of the modern doctrine of individual rights is the seventeenth-century philosopher John Locke (1632–1704). Locke put forward the idea that all human beings have certain 'natural rights' that exist prior to and regardless of social arrangements, and which we possess simply by virtue of being human. Specifically, these are the rights to life, liberty and property. A person owes their right to exist to no one else, their freedom from interference is the condition for pursuing whatever seems good to them and property provides the resources for doing so. This notion of natural rights figures in Locke's version of the social contract, formulated in the *Second Treatise of Civil Government*. Like Hobbes, Locke presents a social contract view in which government is justified to the extent that it serves the needs and interests of individuals. However, things are a lot more peaceful in Locke's version of the state of nature. For Locke, human beings are more rational than Hobbes allows, and their reason teaches 'all mankind, who will but consult it, that being all equal and independent, no one ought to harm another in his life, liberty, or possessions' (Locke 1993, 263–264). Reason thus imposes limitations on what we may do, teaching respect for the rights to life, liberty and property that Locke believes human beings to be naturally endowed with.

So the picture that Locke paints of the state of nature is not as harrowing as Hobbes's. The essential idea remains, however: that in the state of nature even these reasonable individuals will come into conflict with one another in the pursuit of their wants. And for Locke, individuals in this situation are in no position to impartially resolve disputes, being likely to be biased towards their own case. It is in their long-term self-interest to escape from this state of nature, and this is to be done by entering into a social contract, in which everyone agrees to give up some of their freedom and submit to a central authority that will make laws to regulate relations between individuals, arbitrate disputes and administer justice. Thus, Locke, like Hobbes, holds that political authority must be grounded in the consent of the governed. He differs however in insisting on a representative, democratic form of political authority. He does not think that Hobbes's sovereign would solve the problems of the state of nature, because the people would now be threatened not by one another but by this powerful sovereign, who is technically still in a state of nature. Locke emphasises that the government is appointed by the people, representing their will, and is therefore responsible to them.

If the government violates the limits of the power that has been given to it, it may rightly be removed from office. Thus, it is Locke, not Hobbes, who is the architect of modern democratic thinking.

The two thinkers also differ in the amount of power they see the governing authority as requiring. Where Hobbes thought that individuals needed to be strictly controlled by a strong ruler to avoid a return to the state of nature, Locke thought that social harmony and order was consistent with leaving quite a large area of individual life free from state interference (see Berlin 1969, 126). For Locke, this is the area defined by the individual's natural rights. In his version of the social contract, people agree to give up some of their freedom and to obey civil authority in order to have public protection of their natural rights. Indeed, for Locke, this is where the modern state finds its moral justification. The purpose of government is to allow individuals to peacefully enjoy their natural rights to life, liberty and property. This is the classic liberal legitimation of government power. Liberalism, of which Locke is the primary source, is the political philosophy that holds that individuals should be as free as possible from interference by governments in the pursuit of their interests and the enjoyment of their rights. A government is legitimate insofar as it protects the freedom and rights of individuals, and illegitimate insofar as it oversteps the mark and violates those rights.

For all their differences, the politically liberal Locke and the politically authoritarian Hobbes are in agreement in making individuals the starting point for thinking about society. For both, human beings are first of all isolated individuals, with various individual wants and needs, and only secondarily members of a society. Society is essentially an artificial framework imposed on individuals, who could quite conceivably exist independently of organised social life, isolated and alone. Of course, as with Hobbes's account, we may wonder whether Locke's individuals could ever exist fully formed outside of society, even in principle. Arguably, human beings are necessarily involved in social relations. It is only by being shaped through those relationships that they are able to become the individuals that they are. On that view, the idea of the pre-social individual is a fiction, a purely theoretical construction. Nonetheless, this essentially pre-social individual is the starting point for liberal thinking about society, which Locke did so much to develop. And for Locke, these pre-social individuals are understood to have rights that exist prior to and regardless of social arrangements, natural rights that they possess simply by virtue of being human.

This individualist, liberal thinking found its way into European political life in the course of the eighteenth century, the century of Enlightenment, where it played a key role in the various struggles against entrenched royal power and aristocratic privilege through which modern liberal democracies were established. As well it might. Liberalism gives priority to the claims of the individual, against those of the larger order and traditional authority; and the language of rights was appropriated in order to make these claims, to present them not as arbitrary demands but legitimate entitlements. With the French and American revolutions, towards the end of the century, individual rights were legally enshrined in the constitutions of the resulting states. They appear in the 1789 French Declaration of the Rights of Man concerning liberty, equality, security and property; and in the 1791 Bill of Rights in the American constitution, which states that the government does not have the power to limit certain kinds of conduct, such as the freedom to speak or to worship as one pleases (see Popkin and Stroll 1986, 79). As mentioned, the modern state finds its justification in the protection of these individual rights. And the language of rights is regularly evoked in the defence of individual freedom against what is perceived to be excessive interference of the state in an individual's activities.

In *The Admirable Crichton* (Lewis Gilbert, 1957), the film of the J.M. Barrie play, it is in fact an aristocrat who has the progressive ideas about the need for liberal reform. In 1905, the Earl of Loam (Cecil Parker) insists that everyone is equal ('liberty, equality, fraternity', he mutters), and orders his daughters to treat the servants as equals at an uncomfortable afternoon tea. His butler Crichton (Kenneth More) will have none of this. He believes the old class order should be maintained. However, things change when Crichton and the Earl's family take a trip on the Earl's yacht. They are shipwrecked and end up on a deserted island. So, we have another group of people shipwrecked on an island, but unlike *Lord of the Flies*, there is no descent into Hobbesian savagery, or even Locke's more reasonable and tolerant state of nature. There is no state of nature at all, in the sense of an absence of government and social order. First of all, the aristocrats try to preserve the old social hierarchy, but they have no survival skills whatsoever, and Crichton realises that the group is not going to survive unless he takes control. It's a revolution of sorts. Quickly, the others recognise his authority, realising that this is a better arrangement as it will ensure their collective survival and well-being. Two years later, the social order has been completely reversed. Crichton is now the 'guv', the others are working happily for him and the little society is flourishing. We can say that this new social order is justifiable on utilitarian grounds, as the arrangement that maximises the happiness and well-being of the population.

This points to the other way in which the modern state can find legitimation, through the criterion that Bentham advocated for the task of justifying government, namely utility. That is, the extent to which government contributes to the happiness of its citizens. From this perspective, the actions of the state are legitimate to the extent that the state promotes the greater good, the maintenance of public order, security, happiness and well-being. At the same time, this utilitarian justification remains potentially at odds with the liberal one. The requirements for promoting the greater good are not always compatible with the protection of individual rights. Indeed, right from the start, utilitarianism was hostile to the notion of natural or individual rights that are held by all human beings. In *Anarchical Fallacies*, Bentham, writing of the French Revolution's declaration of rights, said bluntly that the idea of natural rights is 'simple nonsense ... nonsense upon stilts' (Bentham 2015, 53).

As in many areas, Bentham's successor Mill had a different attitude towards the individual. In *On Liberty*, he argued that one of the most important ingredients for happiness, the individual's and the community's, was individual freedom, the freedom to express and develop oneself. The principle of maximising happiness, Mill argued, demands that every individual be free to develop their powers according to their own will and judgement because 'the free development of individuality is one of the principal ingredients of human happiness' (Mill 1975, 70). We have already seen how Mill distinguishes between higher and lower pleasures. The ideal for Mill is that we should develop all our capacities, which requires that we move beyond lower pleasures to pursue the higher ones. The proper goal of each person is self-realisation, the harmonious development of all their powers into a complete and consistent whole. Moreover, there is no universal form of self-realisation. For Mill, self-realisation is an individual matter of realising ourselves in accordance with our own pattern. We need to be free to engage in what he calls 'experiments of living' in order to develop our individuality in this way (see Taylor 1985c, 212).

Mill can be seen here as making a utilitarian case not only for individual freedom but also for individual rights, for the idea that individuals have the right to develop themselves as they see fit, without external interference. For Mill, only if a person's actions directly harm other people or prevent them from exercising their personal liberty may the state, through the law, intervene (Mill 1975, 15). It can be argued, however, that once again Mill's account may not be entirely consistent with a utilitarian standpoint, which in the end can happily justify all sorts of interventions in individual lives and violations of individual liberty, as long as this leads to the maximisation of overall happiness. At this point perhaps, Mill is more interested in defending individual freedom than the greater good. The lack of any easy reconciliation between these two concerns, individual freedom and rights, and the greater good, represents a potential problem for the modern state. As noted, the modern state finds legitimation both in terms of the protection of individual rights and in terms of promoting the happiness, well-being and security of the population. As Ronald Dworkin notes, while Western democracies typically embrace liberal principles oriented towards protecting individual rights, the background justification for political decisions is often some form of utilitarianism (Dworkin 1984, 335). As such there remains the potential for conflict between these competing perspectives.

This potential conflict between rights and utilitarianism provides a source of dramatic tension in films featuring the operations of the modern state. It is evident in an early film about state responses to terrorism, *The Seige* (Edward Zwick, 1998). Against the background of a wave of terrorist bombings in New York, the president declares martial law, and the army under General Deveraux (Bruce Willis) occupies Brooklyn. The gung-ho Deveraux goes so far as to authorise the torture of a suspected terrorist, who dies in the course of the interrogation. He receives his comeuppance at the hands of FBI Agent Hubbard (Denzel Washington), who informs him while arresting him that he has the right to remain silent, to a fair trial and to not be tortured or murdered – all the constitutional rights that he in fact took away from the terrorist suspect he brutalised. The state's turn to utilitarian measures to secure the safety and well-being of the population thus comes into conflict with its commitments to individual rights, as enshrined in the US constitution. The film resolves the conflict rather lazily by making the utilitarian, General Deveraux, the villain, and the defender of rights, Hubbard, the hero. A similar scenario appears in a slightly earlier film, *Outbreak* (Wolfgang Petersen, 1995), where the threat to the well-being of the population takes the form of a deadly infectious disease. Since it is confined to a small town, the political decision has to be made whether to bomb the town, as the head of the military is urging. This will save the rest of the country's population, making good sense from the utilitarian point of view, but at the cost of killing everyone in the town. In this case, the conflict between common good and respect for individuals is entirely sidestepped, as a cure is conveniently found in the nick of time.

This brings us back to *Dirty Harry*, where the conflict between these two perspectives, utilitarianism and individual rights is also evident, but where the conflict is not so straightforwardly resolved. At the time it came out, Pauline Kael famously criticised the film as 'fascist', a 'remarkably single-minded attack on liberal values', very much part of a conservative backlash in the seventies against sixties liberalism and the counterculture (see Kael 1991, 148). But it would be wrong to see the film as no more than a conservative repudiation of overly liberal political administrations that, in their earnest efforts to protect individual rights, allowed crime to proliferate and failed to take the 'tough action' needed to stamp it out. It has to be remembered that in the film the state uses Callahan for 'every dirty job that comes along', as he sourly puts it. It turns a blind eye to his robust methods because they get the job done. In other words, the film points to the way the modern liberal state can be complicit in the exercise of measures that, even if necessary to promote the greater good and thus justifiable in utilitarian terms, nonetheless also involve the violation of individual rights and so come into conflict with its commitment to liberal values. The conflict is only resolved, in the film at least, through a kind of institutional self-deception, with the state relying unofficially on these measures while officially distancing itself from them in order to maintain a liberal façade. When the press are alerted to Callahan's robust methods, through the machinations of the resourceful Scorpio, the state is forced to publicly disavow him, to suspend him from the force. Ultimately, however, it is Callahan who, weary of the state's duplicity, will disavow his role as a servant of the state. In the end, the police badge will go into the water.

The Libertine and Scientific Morality

Let us return to the core Enlightenment project of establishing a morality not on the basis of religious beliefs but rationally, on the basis of a scientific conception of the human being as a creature programmed by nature to seek pleasure and avoid pain. This is the materialist and hedonistic conception of human nature introduced into modern thought by Hobbes, and which underpins the utilitarian ethics developed in the course of the eighteenth century by Helvetius, Holbach and most famously, Bentham.

However, one can question whether the human being so understood can indeed provide the basis for a morality, utilitarian or otherwise. Holbach insists that by reflecting on our nature and consulting our 'sensible interests', we will learn the true principles of morality. But if human beings are nothing but machines programmed to seek pleasure, why should our nature provide us with any moral guidance? This is one way of looking at the work of the Marquis de Sade (1740–1814), the French aristocrat known for a series of violently pornographic books that came out towards the end of the eighteenth century, including *Justine* (1791) and *Juliette* (1796). He can be seen as aiming to show that the notion of human nature from which Helvetius, Holbach and others had derived a utilitarian ethics and social theory leads just as consistently to complete nihilism, the lack of any moral standards at all. In this view, nature as revealed by natural science is utterly amoral and meaningless, and appealing to the scientific notion of human nature as a basis for morality is misguided. If nature prescribes anything, it is ruthless egoism and the exploitation of others for one's pleasure. Far from seeking to find a basis for moral judgements in human nature so understood, de Sade and the other so-called libertines celebrated the unconstrained pursuit of sexual pleasure and challenged the wider morality of the time (see Anchor 1967, 101ff).

It is already apparent in Bentham's work that there is a gap between the idea of human beings as creatures bent on seeking pleasure, their own happiness and the claim that they should seek the general happiness of society as well. He clearly believes that in pursuing the former we should seek the latter as well, but he does not say why. And it is very easy to imagine scenarios where the individual's pursuit of happiness is at the expense of others or even positively requires their unhappiness. Pleasure in the suffering of others is the focus of Laclos's novel *Liaisons Dangereuse*, which satirised aristocratic libertinism in the 1780s. The main character Valmont is an aristocrat who gains malicious pleasure from seducing innocents and casting them aside. In their devotion to the satisfaction of their appetites regardless of the cost to others, the libertines are not so different from the unapologetically self-interested gangsters and businessmen featuring in *Goodfellas* and *Wall Street*. This comparison has itself been drawn in film. Stephen Frears's 1988 film version of the Laclos novel, *Dangerous Liaisons,* is also a comment on the egoistic individualism and acquisitiveness prevalent in the eighties, along with the rejection of any ethos of social responsibility. The film draws a parallel between the ruthless and uncaring egoism of the eighteenth-century libertine and the ruthless and uncaring egoism of the members of the entrepreneurial class in the more recent context. Valmont (John Malkovich) is established from the start not only as a decadent aristocrat but also an advocate of conspicuous consumption and exploitation. The film opens with an elaborate dressing scene in which Valmont's every need is attended to by a fleet of servants (see Frohock 162–164).

There is not only the question of whether the Enlightenment's scientific conception of human nature is able to provide a basis for morality, but whether it can support the fundamental Enlightenment aspiration to make reason the principal guide of human conduct. While Holbach, Helvetius and other Enlightenment thinkers stressed the capacity of human beings to organise their moral and social practices rationally, independently of religion and traditional authority, their materialist understanding of human nature seemed to undermine this ideal. On this understanding, human beings are no more than machines, driven by desire and aversion, doomed to an endless striving for pleasure that will end only when they die. How could a doctrine that regarded human beings as slaves of their physical nature enable them to change their social environment or themselves? This criticism was in fact made of Holbach's account by the Prussian king, Frederick the Great. There seemed to be a conflict, he thought, between Holbach's idea that human beings are as much subject to determinism as other things and his denunciations of the existing social order and demands for reform. How can we denounce a social order that is presumably deterministically ordained? For that matter, how can we, as unfree beings, decide to rise up and intervene to change that order? (Copleston 1994, 50).

The concern that the Enlightenment's scientific notion of human nature cannot support an ethics appears on a more theoretical level in the idea that moral notions, prescriptive claims about what you ought to do, cannot be derived from factual ones. The eighteenth-century Scottish philosopher David Hume seems to be suggesting, in a passage in his *Treatise Concerning Human Nature*, that there is a gap between statements of fact and statements of value (Hume 1969, 521). On this view, we cannot go from a factual statement like 'human beings seek pleasure' to the value statement that 'we ought to seek pleasure'. We cannot say, this is natural, therefore it must be good. There is something illicit in doing so, an illicitness that is sometimes referred to as the 'naturalistic fallacy'. This is fair enough, although it needs to be emphasised that there is a difference between deriving ethics directly from facts about human nature, and ethics being constrained by facts about us. It is a mistake to characterise the naturalistic fallacy as implying that values have nothing whatsoever to do with facts about our nature, or that the moral dimension of life is entirely separate from the biological. Hume's point seems to be that facts are not a sufficient basis to derive normative claims, not that facts are completely irrelevant to normative claims. By the same token, it would also seem that the ethical introduces something over and above the facts, that the moral dimension of life goes beyond the merely biological, the purely natural.

As we have seen, Hobbes introduces into modernity the notion of the human being as a purely natural being, a creature driven to seek pleasure and avoid pain, a machine programmed for self-preservation, that pointedly excludes any such moral dimension. Good and evil are just the names we give to that which we desire or have an aversion to. This is the 'realistic' notion of human being that the Enlightenment thinkers sought to make the basis for a new, scientifically based morality. But it has also been suggested that this is a remarkably crude, underdeveloped notion of human being. And it is underdeveloped precisely because this being lacks a moral dimension, a commitment to certain ideals and values that defines one's self or character. The developed human is a creature that not only has desires and motivations but also evaluates and shapes them in the light of those ideals and values. This is a being that has moved beyond the purely biological to become a reflective, responsible moral agent, a process in which their biology is transformed. Their behaviour is no longer just to be explained but judged and justified in terms of the agent's defining moral commitments and ideals. The Hobbesian human being also lacks any social context, and we might imagine that the developed human being, so understood, could only develop in such a context, through processes of socialisation. The developed individual is not only a moral being but also a social one, with a human nature that is also social and historical.

As such, the Enlightenment's whole attempt to give morality a rational foundation in terms of a scientific conception of human nature is indeed called into question. Human nature conceived in materialist, hedonistic terms proves to be a very narrow basis on which to build a morality. The human nature from which the Enlightenment thinkers had derived a utilitarian ethics and social theory is equally consistent with an ethics of ruthless self-interest. Moreover, this conception of human nature threatens to undermine the Enlightenment's very aspiration to make human reason the main guide of conduct. That aspiration was scarcely compatible with a conception of human beings that reduced them to material objects, mere machines driven blindly by their desires. At the end of the eighteenth century, the German philosopher Kant introduced a major shift into Enlightenment thinking, a move away from the scientific conception of human being, towards one in which human beings are primarily active, rational subjects, moral agents. For Kant, this move was necessary in order not only to give ethics a firm basis, but to maintain the Enlightenment's ideal of a rational organisation of humanity's moral and social practices. On his account, reason itself is capable of determining the rules by which to live.

We will be looking at Kantian ethics in more detail in the next chapter. Before moving on to Kant, however, it is worth noting that in more recent times there has been a revival of the earlier Enlightenment idea of a scientifically based morality. This is especially in terms of accounts, drawn from Darwinian theory, that claim to find the roots of moral behaviour, the grounds of virtue, in evolutionary processes; although evolution and natural selection still seem to favour a Hobbesian human being, dedicated to ruthlessly egoistic behaviour to ensure its survival. As with the earlier Enlightenment, this new scientific approach to morality is typically presented as a way of getting away from religious conceptions. Morality is not ordained by God but arises during the process of human evolution. All religious justifications for moral behaviour can be firmly relegated to the status of myth or superstition, and morality can be accounted for in scientifically respectable terms. Early attempts in this direction were not, however, auspicious. Towards the end of the nineteenth century, a version of evolutionary theory was invoked by Herbert Spencer to formulate the brutal ethical and political philosophy known, at least by its detractors, as Social Darwinism.

On the basis of evolutionary theory as he construed it, Spencer argued that human beings are essentially Hobbesian creatures, motivated by self-preservation. A moral good on this view is that which facilitates the individual's goal of survival. In contrast to Hobbes, Spencer transferred this picture of human beings, as they were understood to exist in a pre-social state of nature, to life in society, where the inevitable conflict between such individuals became the motor for human evolution in the social context. In this view, life in society is a struggle for survival, in which the weak will die out, the fittest will survive and humanity as a whole will improve. That is the 'law of nature'. Whatever supports this evolutionary process is good, and whatever gets in the way of it is bad. Consequently, any altruistic or compassionate impulses should be resisted, and policymakers need to make sure they do not try to protect the weak. Compassion will only get in the way of human progress. It is ruthless egoism and fierce competition that needs to be promoted.

Such thinking can be discerned in the ethical egoism championed by Gordon Gekko in *Wall Street*. Tenets of Social Darwinism, in its economic form, appear in the famous 'greed is good' speech. As he says, it is greed, the ruthless pursuit of self-interest, that captures 'the essence of the evolutionary spirit' and lies behind the 'upward surge of mankind'. He goes on to suggest that those who cannot survive in an environment of fierce competition should not be propped up but gotten rid of: 'The new law of evolution in corporate America seems to be survival of the unfittest. Well, in my book, you either do it right or you get eliminated'. Gekko has in mind the elimination of his economic rivals. Others went further. *Downfall* (Oliver Hierschbiegel, 2004), the story of the last days of Hitler (played by Bruno Ganz), certainly revealed, instead of a pure monster, something more banal, provoking controversy similar to that generated by Hannah Arendt's treatment of Eichmann. But even this 'humanised' Hitler has some rather monstrous views, which turn out to be bracingly Social Darwinist. He offers the following advice to a newly appointed general:

> You must shake up the entire Luftwaffe. Many mistakes have been made, so be ruthless. Life never forgives weakness. This so-called humanity is just priest's drivel. Compassion is a primal sin, compassion for the weak is a betrayal of nature … I have always obeyed this law of nature by never permitting myself to feel compassion. I have ruthlessly suppressed domestic opposition and brutally crushed the resistance of alien races. It is the only way to deal with it. Apes, for example, trample every outsider to death. What goes for apes, goes more for human beings.

Undeterred by the misstep of Social Darwinism, later fans of a scientific morality have turned to evolutionary theory to explain the emergence of a moral sense, a disposition or tendency in human beings to be good. The claim once again is that ethics can be derived from science, from facts, not divine revelation; and nor even from some abstract philosophical intuition. Not only religion but also philosophy needs to be excluded from the scene as uselessly unscientific. The behaviour being considered now is not ruthlessly self-interested and aggressively competitive behaviour, but something more recognisably 'moral', namely altruistic feelings and actions. The key issue for this way of thinking becomes, how can such altruistic feelings and behaviours have evolved since evolution and natural selection appear to favour the ruthlessly egoistic behaviour designed to ensure one's survival? Accordingly, there have been attempts to understand altruistic behaviour itself in evolutionary terms as giving individuals an evolutionary advantage, and hence not additional to human biology but deeply ingrained in it. In this spirit, much has been made of the idea of 'reciprocal altruism', the idea that helping another is to one's advantage because it is likely to trigger reciprocal helping behaviour from the other or from those who have seen what we have done. Moral conduct in the sense of helping others thus helps those individuals inclined to it to survive in the long term (see e.g., Dawkins 1989, 183ff).

The alert reader will recognise that this is essentially a revival of the strategy employed by eighteenth-century Enlightenment thinkers like Holbach to establish a moral system on the basis of the idea of human beings as driven by self-interest and love of pleasure. The moral system there is broadly the benevolence and altruism formerly endorsed by Christianity. The Enlightenment thinkers generally approved of these values, but wanted to give them a more rational basis, in terms of the scientific conception of human nature. Holbach's solution, as we have seen, was to argue that although we are driven by self-interest and love of pleasure, we can come to appreciate that our actions affect the happiness of others, as their actions affect ours. Consequently, the best way to achieve our own happiness is to work for the good of everyone. If we make those around us happy, they will in turn make us happy. One issue with the reciprocal altruism story is that even if this explanation is true, even if it tells us about the evolutionary origins of altruistic behaviour, it does not tell us why we now engage in such behaviour. This cannot always be understood in terms of our being really concerned with how it is going to pay off for ourselves. We can certainly be altruistic for selfish motives, but this is not always the case. Moreover, the story does not seem to be able to explain actions that go beyond reciprocal altruism, putting the welfare of another above one's own, even to the point of self-sacrifice (see Blackburn 2001, 39–40; Pojman 1999, 79–80).

The more fundamental problem with this approach, once again, lies in the very attempt to account for moral behaviour in purely biological terms. Precisely as moral beings, human beings have already gone beyond the biological. Rather than objects of explanation, they are active subjects who aspire through their actions to realise certain moral ideals. Again, this is not to say that their behaviour as moral beings no relation to facts about their biological makeup and capacities. Morality is ultimately constrained by what human beings are capable of doing, but it remains something that goes beyond the merely natural, that transcends the biological existence it is constrained by. Something fundamental is lost if we attempt to account for that moral dimension of human existence in purely naturalistic terms. This was already becoming apparent towards the end of the eighteenth century, in connection with the Enlightenment's own attempt to establish morality on a scientific basis. The scientific conception of the human being as a material object was undermining the very thing it was supposed to provide a basis for, the moral life that is a feature not of material objects but of active subjects. At the end of the century, Kant argued as much, and it is to his ethics, very much based on the human being as active subject, that we now turn.

FEATURE FILMS: *DIRTY HARRY* AND *THE DARK KNIGHT*

Dirty Harry

Dirty Harry is a 1971 crime thriller directed by Don Siegel (*Invasion of the Body Snatchers*, *The Beguiled*). The film's policeman hero has to resort to extreme measures to defeat the maniacal villain who is threatening the entire city. When the film was released it was criticised by film critic Pauline Kael as 'fascist', a right-wing fantasy of law enforcement through thuggery. However, the film is by no means uncritical of the methods its hero employs, suggesting that they bring him close to the very villainy he is trying to overcome.

Plot

The film begins with a list of names, 'In tribute to the police officers of San Francisco who gave their lives in the line of duty', superimposed on a police badge. This dissolves into the muzzle of a gun. Perched on a nearby rooftop, Scorpio (Andy Robinson) shoots a young woman swimming in a rooftop pool. Inspector Harry Callahan (Clint Eastwood) finds a ransom note at the scene, addressed to the City of San Francisco, containing the threat to kill one person every day until Scorpio is paid 100,000 dollars.

In the Mayor's office, the Mayor (John Vernon) and Lieutenant Bressler (Harry Guardino) discuss the ransom note. Callahan arrives to report on progress in the case. At lunch, Callahan foils a bank robbery in characteristically robust fashion. We next see Scorpio is setting up on a rooftop, preparing to carry out his plans. He watches a potential victim through his gunsight but is interrupted by a police helicopter and has to flee. On the lookout for Scorpio, Callahan follows a man down a dark alley and sees him entering an apartment. Standing on a garbage bin looking into the window, he is set upon by concerned neighbours and accused of being a peeping Tom. The next day, staking out the roof where Scorpio was seen by the police helicopter, Callahan is distracted by an orgy scene unfolding in an apartment below. His reverie is interrupted by the appearance of Scorpio returning to the rooftop to finish what he started. A shootout ensues and Scorpio escapes.

Scorpio makes another ransom demand, having kidnapped a girl and buried her alive with a limited supply of oxygen. Callahan volunteers to deliver the ransom money, Scorpio, communicating by phone, runs him all over town. His journey ends at the base of a cross in Mount Davidson Park, where Scorpio emerges to torment him. He is only saved by the intervention of his partner Gonzales (Reni Santoni), who distracts Scorpio long enough for Callahan to stab him in the leg with a concealed switch-blade, whereupon Scorpio flees into the night. Callahan tracks the wounded Scorpio back to his home in the Kezar football stadium. After bringing the fleeing killer down with a shot to the leg, he proceeds to torture Scorpio, grinding his heel into Scorpio's wounded leg, to find out where his kidnap victim is hidden.

After Scorpio is arrested by Callahan, he has to be released because the District Attorney finds legal irregularities in the way he was apprehended. Callahan keeps Scorpio under surveillance, but Scorpio pays someone to beat him up so that he can tell the press he was brutalised again by a vengeful Callahan, forcing the authorities to take him off the case. Scorpio takes the opportunity to embark on a final rampage, hijacking a school bus and holding the city to ransom once more. The film ends at the cement plant quarry, where Callahan finally corners and kills Scorpio who falls into a pond. Callahan throws his police badge into the pond after Scorpio.

Key Scenes

1   Callahan, interrupted mid-hot dog, single-handedly foils a bank robbery. Bank robbers are blown away, cars crash into shop windows, onlookers flee and a broken fire hydrant erupts over the scene of devastation. The scene also features the famous line, as Callahan stands over the one surviving bank robber who is thinking about reaching for his gun: 'I know what you're thinking. Did he fire six shots or only five … Well … do you feel lucky?' As the film proceeds, it increasingly raises questions about the hero's extreme methods, but here it portrays with gusto the very methods it later goes on to question [09.51–14.09].

2   Carrying ransom money, Callahan is directed by Scorpio to the base of a cross in Mount Davidson Park, where Scorpio emerges from the gloom to torment him. He is only saved by the intervention of his partner [55.15–59.06]. Callahan tracks Scorpio back to his home in the Kezar football stadium and brings him down with a shot to the leg. This time it is Callahan who emerges from the gloom and stands over Scorpio, on the ground against another cross, made by the stadium's lawn markings. Callahan then proceeds to torture Scorpio to find out where his kidnap victim is hidden. Such torture might seem justified in utilitarian terms, but by drawing these parallels with the earlier scene, the film suggests that Callahan's extreme

methods are bringing him close to the very evil he is trying to overcome [1.05.33–1.07.27]. At the same time, the fact that he sends his partner away before torturing Scorpio suggests that he himself is uneasy about what he is doing, even if it is in the name of the greater good.

3 After Scorpio is arrested by Callahan, he has to be released because the District Attorney finds legal irregularities in the way he was apprehended: 'Where the hell does it say you've got a right to kick down doors, torture suspects, deny medical attention and legal counsel … What I'm saying is, that man had rights' [1.08.23–1.12.35]. Here, a rights-based perspective is invoked in the face of a purely utilitarian view in which the end, the greater good, justifies any means, no matter how brutal.

4 The final scene behind the gravel plant, at the end of the pier next the pond where Callahan at last despatches Scorpio, closely mirrors the swimming pool murder that Scorpio carried out at the start of the film [0.48–1.50], only with Callahan now in the Scorpio role. Scorpio has become the victim, floating dead in the water, and Callahan is the ruthless killer looking on from above [1.35.15–1.36.40]. Again, parallels are drawn between hero and villain.

The Dark Knight

The Dark Knight is a 2008 superhero film directed and co-written by Christopher Nolan (*Inception, Dunkirk*). While the film is dominated by its maniacal villain, it also poses questions about the actions of its vigilante hero, who, while working in cooperation with the police, also takes the law into his own hands and deals out his own brand of justice. On its release some critics saw it an endorsement of extreme methods that were used by during the War on Terror; but once again this is a film that is not uncritical of the methods employed by its hero.

Plot

The Joker (Heath Ledger) organises the robbery of a Gotham City bank owned by the mob. Batman (Christian Bale) joins forces with District Attorney Harvey Dent (Aaron Eckhart) and Lieutenant Jim Gordon (Gary Oldman) to rid Gotham of organised crime once and for all. Bruce Wayne offers to support Dent's career, hoping that with Dent as Gotham's protector, he will be able to give up being Batman; and also take up with assistant DA Rachel Dawes (Maggie Gyllenhall), his childhood sweetheart, who is currently dating Dent even though she and Mob bosses Maroni (Eric Roberts), Gambol (Michael Jai White) and the Chechen (Ritchie Coster) hold a video conference with their accountant, Lau (Chin Han), who has fled to Hong Kong taking their remaining funds for safekeeping. The Joker interrupts the meeting, warning them that Batman can track Lau down. He offers to kill Batman in exchange for half their money. When Gambol puts a bounty on his head, the Joker kills him and takes over his gang. The mob decides to take the Joker up on his offer.

Batman as predicted finds Lau in Hong Kong and brings him back to Gotham to testify, allowing Dent to bring the entire mob to trial. The Joker threatens to kill people until Batman reveals his identity. He murders the Police Commissioner and the judge presiding over the mob trial and tries to kill the Mayor. Bruce Wayne decides to reveal his identity, but before he can, Dent announces that he is Batman. He is taken into protective custody, but the Joker attacks his convoy. He is rescued by Batman and Gordon apprehends the Joker. Rachel and Dent are escorted away by detectives who turn out to be on Maroni's payroll and never arrive home. Batman interrogates Maroni and the Joker, the latter revealing they are in separate buildings rigged with explosives. Batman goes to save Rachel, while Gordon tries to rescue Dent. When Batman arrives at the building, he realises that the Joker sent him to Dent's location. Both buildings explode, killing Rachel and disfiguring Dent. The Joker escapes taking Lau, whom he later kills along with the Chechen.

One of Wayne's employees, Coleman Reese (Joshua Harto), works out that he is Batman and tries to go public with the information. To stop Reese interfering with his plans, the Joker threatens to blow up a hospital unless someone kills him. Gordon orders the evacuation of all the hospitals in Gotham. The Joker visits Dent in Gotham Central Hospital and gives him a gun, convincing him to seek revenge on those responsible for Rachel's death, then blows up the hospital and escapes. He then announces he is taking over the city. As Gotham descends into chaos, the Joker rigs two ferries with explosives. He says he will blow up both ferries at midnight but will spare one if its passengers blow up the other, using a trigger he has supplied to each vessel. Batman finds the Joker using a device that spies on the entire city, with the help of his technical expert Lucius Fox (Morgan Freeman). The ferry passengers refuse to play along and Batman apprehends the Joker. Before the police arrive to take the Joker into custody, he says that Gotham's citizens will lose hope once Dent's killing spree becomes public knowledge.

Gordon and Batman arrive at the building where Rachel died. Dent shoots Batman and threatens to kill Gordon's son. Before he can do so, Batman, who was wearing body armour, tackles Dent, who falls off the building to his death. Knowing the Joker will win if people find out the truth, Batman persuades Gordon to hold him responsible for Dent's killings. The police launch a manhunt for Batman.

Key Scenes

1   Dent and Rachel run into Bruce Wayne and his date at a restaurant and they dine together. The group discusses Batman's vigilantism, which Dent surprisingly approves of, comparing the situation to ancient Rome suspending democracy so that one man could protect the city. Rachel warns that this is how Caesar became emperor [20.00–21.40]. This is an early intimation that actions may be entirely justifiable in the name of the greater good but can be morally and politically dangerous nonetheless.

2   Wayne's butler Alfred (Michael Caine) suggests that the mob, under pressure from Gordon, Dent and Batman, turned to someone they didn't understand, and neither does Wayne. Ordinary criminals can be expected to follow certain rules, but the Joker only wants to overturn the rules and produce chaos. Alfred: 'some men aren't looking for anything logical, like money. They can't be bought, bullied, reasoned or negotiated with. Some men just want to watch the world burn' [53.50–55.18]. The strangeness of the Joker's behaviour lies in his willingness to overturn rules and cultivate disorder, the opposite of the Hobbesian view that people, in order to avoid the horrors of a state of nature, will be strongly motivated to enter into a social contract and submit to social rule.

3   Batman is shown resorting to torture to get information. He drops mob boss Maroni from a building, breaking his legs, to force him to speak. This might be perfectly justifiable in utilitarian terms, in the name of getting the Joker off the streets and protecting the city, but it is also morally problematic in other ways, as Batman himself seems to recognise. As he says to Rachel, 'I've seen, now, what I would have to become to stop men like him' [1.08.23–1.08.54]. That he finds his behaviour morally problematic indicates that he is not a utilitarian through and through in his moral thinking.

4   Batman again resorts to 'enhanced interrogation techniques'. Since Gordon is getting nowhere questioning the Joker about Dent's disappearance, he leaves the room and Batman takes over, beating

the Joker savagely. It is more morally problematic behaviour on Batman's part, however justifiable it might seem to be in utilitarian terms. Indeed, it seems to increasingly align him with the very villainy he is trying to overcome. Meanwhile, the Joker takes the opportunity to put forward his Hobbesian view that people are essentially self-interested and egoistic, and moral behaviour is only a veneer. 'Their morals, their code ... it's a bad joke. Dropped at the first sign of trouble. They're only as good as the world allows them to be. You'll see – I'll show you ... when the chips are down, these civilised people ... they'll eat each other' [1.27.00–1.29.03].

5 The Joker reveals that Rachel has also been kidnapped and only one of the two can be saved. This sets up a moral dilemma for Batman, whose one rule is that he never kills anyone. Because he can only save one, he is forced to contribute to the death of the other. That he has such a rule, which he considers must never be broken under any circumstances, indicates once again that he is not a pure utilitarian in his moral thinking. The Joker reveals the two addresses and Batman races off to save Rachel, while Gordon and his unit head to find Dent. For Batman, this is yet another indication that he is not a pure utilitarian. He elects to save the one he loves, rather than the one who can do the most good for the city [1.29.03–1.30.49].

6 Lucius Fox finally discovers what Batman's government project is: using the sonar technology, he has turned every single mobile phone into a map of the city and can monitor all calls. Fox considers this unethical, a vast violation of individual privacy, even though it will be instrumental in defeating the Joker. This is another action that might be thought justifiable in utilitarian terms, but which is also morally problematic from other points of view [1.55.44–1.57.03].

7 Two ferries, one filled with prison inmates and the other with civilians, lose power and each discovers that there are explosives on board, along with the detonator for the other boat. The Joker's voice comes on the speakers and announces that at midnight he will blow up both boats, but he will spare one of them should that boat choose to blow up the other first. The passengers on both boats debate what to do. Through this 'social experiment', the Joker is willing to put his Hobbesian thesis about human nature to the test [2.00.20–2.02.50].

8 The Joker is disappointed that the ferry passengers have not performed as expected in his experiment. Before he is able to blow

up the ferries himself, he is overpowered by Batman. The Joker says that the two of them are equal and opposite forces, destined to be locked in conflict forever. Here the Joker suggests a kinship between hero and villain, even if they are also in stark opposition [2.11.10–2.15.22].

4   Personhood and Autonomy
Kantian Ethics

At the end of *High Noon* (Fred Zinnemann, 1952), town Marshal Will Kane (Gary Cooper), throws his badge into the dust in a gesture of contempt. For most of the film he has been awaiting the arrival of the outlaw Frank Miller (Ian MacDonald), whom he arrested and had sent to prison, and who is now returning on the noon train to take revenge on Kane and the town. None of the townspeople have proved willing to back him up. Out of cowardice, fear or self-interest, they have all refused to sign up as deputies and he has been left to confront the outlaw alone. Now, having managed to defeat the outlaw and his gang in a shootout, he is surrounded by those same townspeople, who have emerged from hiding to congratulate him. Disgusted by their hypocrisy, he throws his badge to the ground and rides off. This gesture is echoed by Inspector Callahan at the end of *Dirty Harry*. Having dispatched Scorpio, Callahan throws his police badge into the pond where the slain killer floats. He has had to contend with the hypocrisy of the state, which both used and disavowed him.

In many ways *Dirty Harry* can be seen as transposing the classic movie western confrontation of lawman and outlaw to a modern urban setting. By the same token, the film looks back to the later nineteenth century, and the frontier West of North America, which is the typical focus of the western genre (Dirks 2017). The archetypal western movie theme of maintaining law and order on the frontier is being played out in the classic western *High Noon*. However, along with the similarities there are also some differences. Things have become more complicated in the interim. By the time of *Dirty Harry,* the lawman has become a morally ambiguous figure, who has to do bad things for the greater good. *High Noon*'s lawman in contrast comes across as unambiguously moral. What is the difference here? One key difference between Kane and Callahan is that utilitarian considerations play no role whatsoever in determining Kane's actions. His moral commitment is of an entirely different sort. In taking his stand against the outlaw, he is 'doing what he has to do', doing what he understands to be his duty. In this he comes close to exemplifying the kind of moral position developed by Immanuel Kant (1724–1804).

Duty and Desire

At the end of the eighteenth century, Kant introduces something new into ethical thinking and into the idea of what it is to be enlightened. He remains part of the Enlightenment project in holding that human reason, not faith or tradition, should be the main guide of our conduct. Ethics is still something to be established through human reason. In this he continues the move away from reliance on God, as a supernatural lawgiver who provides and justifies moral principles, that is characteristic of modernity. However, in contrast to his Enlightenment predecessors, he rejects the scientific, purely naturalistic view of human nature and the project of establishing ethics on that basis. For Kant, far from providing a rational basis for morality, this picture undermines the Enlightenment's core idea of making reason the principal guide for conduct, since it reduces the human being to an object, a machine blindly driven by desire. To preserve the Enlightenment ideal, Kant reaffirms the idea of human beings as primarily rational subjects. As rational subjects, they are capable of determining moral rules, the rules by which to live. And in his piece 'What is Enlightenment?', Kant defines Enlightenment itself in terms of this capacity for rational self-determination. Enlightenment is a matter of emerging from a state of immaturity, of dependence on external authorities for guidance. To do so, you only need to have the courage to use your understanding, and to think for yourself (Kant 1995).

With this, Kant not only affirms the moral subject as something more than the biological human being. He also restores a deontological notion of morality, morality as a matter of acting in accordance with rules or duties, that was a feature of religious ethics. However, Kant is not returning to the religious understanding of these rules, in which a transcendent God is the law-maker whose commands establish the rules. On the contrary, he is displacing God in favour of human beings understood as rational beings, capable of self-determination. Morality is no longer a matter of obedience to God, but of obeying one's own rational conscience, the commands of one's reason. Even if, for Kant, the rules that reason commands are largely the rules of established Christian ethics, his claim is that these can be justified through human reason. At the same time, this is not a return to Plato's rationalist morality. Plato located the ultimate basis for morality in objective ideals, the forms existing in a supernatural realm that reason can apprehend. For Kant, the world established by science has no room for such entities. The ultimate basis for morality is to be found within ourselves, the 'moral law within'. Not that these principles are peculiar to me, individual, subjective and arbitrary. On the contrary, they are universal, objective and necessary, rules that are binding not just on me but on all rational agents. We might characterise Kant's position in general as a 'universal subjectivism'. There is a lot going on here, so we need to explore Kant's account in more detail.

Kant sets out his moral theory most accessibly in the *Groundwork of the Metaphysics of Morals*, which came out around the same time as Bentham's *Principles of Morals and Legislation*. His starting point is what he takes to be our ordinary experience of the moral, and while his account may reflect his own ascetic Protestant upbringing, it also captures something missing from the account of the human being as desiring machine pioneered by Hobbes. Whereas Hobbes sees human beings as creatures moved by whatever desires come along, it is arguably much closer to our everyday experience to say that we do not see all our motivations as being on the same level. Rather, we experience some as being more important or worthy than others. In particular, there are some things we feel we ought to do, because they are the right thing to do, and which should take precedence over what is merely pleasurable or in our personal interest to do. In the *Groundwork*, Kant starts with this idea that moral concerns have a special force and that they should outweigh other considerations. For him, moral concerns are typically experienced in the form of the stern voice of duty, commanding us to put mere pleasure or personal interest aside, and do the right thing whatever the consequences.

Behaving morally here thus amounts to putting aside one's personal feelings and interests, in order to do one's duty, what is right. Whether this captures all moral experience, there is certainly a good dose of this thinking in *High Noon*. As the film opens, Kane has just retired from his job as Marshal of Hadleyville and is riding out of town with his new bride Amy Fowler (Grace Kelly) to start a new life. When he learns that the outlaw Frank Miller, whom he sent to jail five years earlier, has been released and is coming back to the town to take revenge, he has to go back to face him. He is not motivated by a desire for glory. When his bride asks him if he is trying to be a hero, he replies, 'I'm not trying to be a hero. If you think I like this, you're crazy'. He spends the whole film fighting the instinct to run. But he stays out of a higher motivation, in order to do his duty as town marshal, to uphold the law. And this is not something he is obliged to do by virtue of his office, since technically speaking he is no longer marshal, having resigned from his official position. It is rather a matter of inner necessity, something to be done simply because it is the right thing to do, his moral duty. As Kane puts it, 'I've got to. That's the whole thing' (Figure 4.1).

Figure 4.1 Kane stands alone in *High Noon* (Fred Zinneman, 1952. Credit: United Artists/ Photofest).

In his moral theory, Kant seeks to analyse, explain and defend the idea of one's duty, as something that outweighs all other considerations. He argues first of all that the consequences of our acts have no bearing on the moral worth of our actions, only the motivations behind them. Here there is a sharp contrast with utilitarianism, for which it is only the consequences of actions that are morally relevant, in terms of how much happiness they produce for all concerned. The idea that human beings ought to behave in ways that produce good consequences makes utilitarianism a prime example of a 'consequentialist' moral theory. Some of the townspeople argue in these utilitarian terms against making a stand against the outlaws. When Kane comes to the church to ask the congregation for help in confronting Miller and the gang, the view that carries the day in the subsequent discussion is that making a stand against the outlaws is the wrong thing to do, that a shootout should be avoided. It would give the town a bad reputation and deter outside investment, hurting the local economy and hence the well-being of the community. It would be better if Kane just left town, as the bad guys would simply move on. For Kant, how much happiness or otherwise an action is likely to produce has no bearing on its morality.

Moreover, the consequences of an action are morally irrelevant for Kant in the sense that whether we succeed or fail in what we are trying to do does not affect the moral worth of what we are doing. The moral worth of our actions depends solely on the intention or motivation with which we act. What is required is that we act not merely in accordance with duty, but out of a sense of duty, in a principled way, for the sake of the moral law. For Kant, it is only those actions that are motivated by a sense of duty which can be called moral actions, not those that are done out of self-interest, desire or feeling. Kant calls this purely dutiful kind of motivation the 'good will'. As he puts it in his *Groundwork*: 'A good will is good not because of what it effects or accomplishes - because of its fitness to attain some intended end: it is good through its willing alone – that is, good in itself' (Kant 1964, 62).

In support of this view, it can be said that a large part of why Kane appears so morally upright and impressive in *High Noon* is because he does what he does simply because it is the 'right thing to do'. This is regardless of his prospects of success. Indeed, there is a very good chance that he is going to fail and get himself killed, and increasingly so as his requests for help from the townspeople are rejected. However, this likelihood of failure has no bearing on our sense of the moral worthiness of his action, which has to do with the character of his motivation. We would view his actions as being somewhat less worthy if he were doing what he was doing simply out of self-interest, in order to impress others with his bravery, or to advance his career. This is how we feel about Kane's friend and deputy Harvey Pell (Lloyd Bridges). He does offer to stand with Kane against the outlaws, but only provided Kane gets him the job as the next town marshal, which he feels is his due: 'you put the word in for me like I said'. Pell very clearly acts out of self-interest. He will only stay if he gets an external reward, career advancement. Kane's rejection of Pell's self-interested offer seems to acknowledge the unworthiness of this motivation: 'I want you to stick – but I'm not buying it. It's got to be up to you'.

The moral relevance of the motivation with which we act is also evident in another western constructed around a deadline, *3:10 to Yuma* (James Mangold, 2007), a remake of the 1957 film of the same name. In the remake, the hero, Dan Evans (Christian Bale), has been enlisted by the railroad to help escort notorious outlaw Ben Wade (Russell Crowe) to the town of Contention, where he will be put on the train to Yuma prison. For this task, Evans, a struggling rancher, asks for a $200 fee to provide for his family. Having made it to Contention, he is holed up in a hotel room, with Wade and the railroad's representative, Butterfield (Dallas Roberts), along with his son who had been following the group. Wade's gang are outside, ready to kill him and free Wade as soon as they try to leave. He has been abandoned by the town marshal and his deputies, who earlier offered support but now see his task as a lost cause. Butterfield also wants out, and absolves Evans of his duty, releasing him from his contract, but still offering to give him his fee. Despite all this, Evans is determined to get Wade to the station and complete his mission.

In Evans we have another heroic figure, like Kane, facing a difficult situation with the odds against him, but sticking to his guns. In this case however, there is a different kind of motivation. Evans may want to get Wade to the train station and complete his mission even though he has been released from his contract, but he is still motivated by the prospect of external reward. He renegotiates the arrangement with Butterfield, demanding that $1,000 be given to his wife before he will go through with it. It is also clear that he is going through with this in order to win the respect of his son, who, it is established early on, has a poor opinion of him because of his failure as a rancher. On this point, there is a very clear contrast with the original 1957 film. There, the Dan Evans character (played by Van Heflin), insists in similar circumstances on continuing with the mission of getting the outlaw on the train not because he can get something out of it, but simply because it is the right thing to do. We might not want to be too critical of the Evans character in the remake. Although Evans acts there for external reward, he is not really acting out of self-interest, but for others. He wants the money for his wife, he wants to give his son a father he can look up to and be proud of. Nonetheless, the Kantian would insist that it is only the behaviour of the Evans character in the original that represents the genuine moral action, because it is motivated only by the sense of duty (see Mexal 2010).

It would seem that on Kant's account, a great deal of what we would ordinarily see as motivating our behaviour is to be excluded from the moral realm. Indeed, all of the desires and interests that Hobbes and the earlier Enlightenment saw as fundamentally motivating human beings are to be excluded. And it is not only actions done out of self-interest or desire; even an action done out of love or compassion, while it may be praiseworthy, is not a moral action on Kant's view. Only those actions motivated by a sense of duty qualify. Here we seem to be back with the idea, affirmed early on by Plato, that being moral requires the suppression of desire, emotion and feeling in favour of reason. For Kant, when we are acting only out of a sense of duty, we are acting purely on the basis of principles that our rationality dictates. As noted, this is reason understood as capable of establishing laws or principles of conduct, of generating rules for living. And to the extent that I am a rational being, I am bound to follow these principles, since they are the commands of my own rationality. So how does our reason establish moral principles? To be moral, for Kant, is to act in accordance with principles that are binding not just on me but on all rational beings. Something cannot be rational for me and not for others. So in order to act morally, we need to determine whether the principle we are thinking of acting on, the maxim or subjective principle, which is the reason a particular agent happens to perform a certain action, is universalisable, i.e., whether it is able to be consistently followed by all agents in relevantly similar situations. If it can be so universalised, it is an objective moral principle, in the sense of applying not just to me but all rational agents.

This requirement of universalisability might seem rather formalistic but it does incorporate the idea that morality is not a purely individual matter, that claims that something is morally right have a universal aspect. Moral rules are forms of behaviour that do not admit exceptions, individual cases, special pleading; and moral principles do not just serve my particular interests. Here we may take Kant's example of promise-keeping. Suppose I'm tempted to break a promise in order to get out of a tight spot. The principle I'm thinking of acting on here may be formulated as – 'I may always break a promise when it's in my interest to do so'. Can I consistently make this maxim into a universal law? Kant doesn't think so. If every person acted on this principle and broke their promises whenever it suited them, the whole practice of promising would break down. As a result, I would not be able to break a promise whenever it suited me, because no one would believe any promise I made in the first place. Thus, if breaking promises when it suited me became universal and everyone followed it, I would be involved in a self-contradiction, aiming to do something that it is impossible for me to do because there is no longer the practice of believing what people promise. So the maxim – I may always break a promise when it's in my interest to do so – cannot be universalised, and so it isn't moral to do so.

To put this another way, using the related notion of truth-telling, we can envisage a world like that posited in *The Invention of Lying* (Ricky Gervais, Matthew Robinson, 2009), in which everyone tells the truth, however uncomfortable this might be. In this context, it is possible to imagine that one person might discover lying, and indeed to be able to do very well out of it too, as happens in the film. But what we cannot envisage is a world in which everyone lies when it suits them, because in such a world, no one would believe anything anyone said and so it would not be possible to lie in the first place. Thus, lying fails the universalisability test and is not a moral thing to do. Here, lying is not being morally condemned because it is a device for personal gain at the expense of others. Certainly, once the central character Mark Bellison (Gervais) discovers he can lie, he uses it to steal money and seduce women; but he also finds that he can use lying to help others, for example, to assuage their fears about death by reassuring them that there is an afterlife. And we might imagine that lying could be morally justified if it were to produce good consequences. There could be a 'good lie'. But that is a utilitarian view. For Kant, lying can never be morally right, whether done for personal gain or to help others. It is the kind of action that is always wrong, by its very nature.

Another way of appreciating Kant's position here is to note that for Kant, all utilitarian claims take the form of what he calls hypothetical imperatives. A hypothetical imperative is a principle of action that says that if you want to achieve such and such a goal, you should act in a certain way. It has an if-then structure – for example, if you want to get to a certain destination by the shortest possible route, you should take roads X and Y. Hypothetical imperatives apply to rational agents insofar as they have particular desires or goals. They are part of means-end reasoning, in which reason helps us in the satisfaction of our desires. All utilitarian claims are of this sort – if you want to maximise happiness, you should do such and such. For Kant, however, moral laws are categorical imperatives. A categorical imperative requires you to act in a certain way regardless of your particular desires and interests. It is absolute or categorical in nature, to be obeyed whether or not you want to act that way. And this is the case with moral laws; they always apply categorically. What Kant is saying here is that when we act morally, we're not acting on the basis of rules that depend on our particular desires, which will vary from person to person and over time. We're acting on the basis of rules that command us purely because we are rational beings. Morality thus consists of the categorical imperatives or commands of our reason, the general formula for the categorical imperative being: act only on that principle that could be turned into a universal law.

So why does Kant we have to rigorously exclude all desire and inclination from the realm of the moral? It can be noted that for Kant our desires are mostly but not entirely self-centred and egoistic; we can have genuinely altruistic or benevolent desires, oriented towards the well-being of others. Yet even these have no place in the moral realm. Kant's position here reflects his notion of human nature. What we are, above all, are rational beings. As with Plato, he identifies human beings most closely with reason and sees them as engaged in a constant struggle to control their bodily, desiring side. This picture also appears in Augustine's religious ethics, with its hostility towards the desire that signifies our entanglement in this world. Kant, however, wants to assert the claims of human beings as rational subjects in the face of the modern scientific understanding of nature. For him, reason is the deepest and most valuable part of us. It is what raises us above nature and makes us unique. Everything else in nature is blindly moved by mechanical forces. Even animals behave in this mechanical way. Human beings are partly like this, for they have a natural side, their desires, inclinations and emotions, many of which they share with animals. But they are also, and most importantly, rational beings. Only rational beings have the capacity to act consciously in accordance with principles they formulate for themselves. This is something higher, something that sets us apart from the rest of nature.

Given this view of human nature, it follows that rational agents ought to determine their actions in this way. As Charles Taylor puts it, 'the fundamental principle underlying Kant's whole ethical theory is something of this form: live up to what you really are – rational agents' (Taylor 1985b, 324). This is the gist of the Kant's answer to the question 'why be moral?' To be moved to act by our desires, emotions and inclinations, to become just another thing subject to mechanical necessity, is to fall below our proper status. Only when we are behaving rationally, in accordance with moral laws we formulate for ourselves, are we living up to our true status as rational beings. Here Kant is in agreement with Rose Sayer (Katherine Hepburn) in *The African Queen* (John Huston, 1951). When Humphrey Bogart's character, Charlie Allnut, who is strongly inclined to swilling gin, defends himself by saying that it's only human nature to take a drop too much once in a while, she informs him that 'Nature, Mr Allnut, is what we were put on earth to rise above'. As a missionary there is of course a religious element in her rejection of such 'lower inclinations', but we might equally say that Kant has managed to preserve the religious suspicion of desire in his rationalist morality. It is now the rational soul that needs to be 'saved'. And its special value is something that we ourselves recognise. This is ultimately why Kant thinks we experience moral commands, the demands of duty, as being more important than other considerations such as personal interest, desire or inclination.

Kant does not completely exclude desire and emotion from the human being as he understands this notion. He distinguishes human beings from what he calls the 'holy will', a purely rational creature, in effect a god. This is a being that always effortlessly and automatically follows the commands of reason. Human beings are not gods, but nor are they animals; they fall between the two. They are partly in the natural world since they have a natural side to their makeup, their desires, emotions and feelings, but they are also capable of rational, principled behaviour. So human beings understand the moral law, but do not always follow it, being sometimes swayed by emotion or desire. This is why human beings encounter moral laws as duties, things they recognise that they ought to do even if they don't always manage to do them. This is also why being moral for Kant involves a constant struggle to rise above, control or suppress desire and inclination, so as to be moved by a sense of duty alone. Thus, while Kant's moral picture might give a central role to the human being as an active subject, capable of determining the moral rules and giving shape to its existence, there is also an appreciation that we are worldly creatures with desires and inclinations, who have to struggle to be moral and who can fail. To that extent we can more readily recognise ourselves in this picture.

We are able to relate to Kane in *High Noon* for similar reasons. Though he is doing what duty requires, his adherence to duty is not automatic. He is not superhuman, a holy will. He struggles constantly with feelings of panic, fear and the urge to run away, and looks increasingly haggard as the film proceeds. By virtue of this realistic portrayal of its hero, the film can itself be described as a 'realist western'. It departs from the more traditional western mythology in which the hero is straightforwardly strong, courageous and honourable, the kind of heroic persona epitomised by John Wayne in many of his films. Kane has to work hard to do the right thing. In a similar way, in the classic *Casablanca* (Michael Curtiz 1942), Humphrey Bogart's character Rick Blaine, the nightclub owner, has to struggle to overcome self-interest in order to do what duty requires. In this respect, he is certainly easier to relate to than the morally upright Victor Laszlo (Paul Henreid), the fugitive Czech resistance leader who has come to Casablanca with his wife Ilsa (Ingrid Bergman), seeking safe passage out of Europe. Laszlo is the straightforward hero of the piece, risking his life to fight Nazi tyranny, but he is more like the 'holy will', a moral saint, effortlessly acting in accordance with duty. Rick Blaine is the more human character, for whom being moral requires a certain amount of struggle, though he gets there in the end. This entirely befits a film that appeared in the early forties, and which can at a certain level be seen as a political allegory, even a piece of propaganda encouraging the United States public to set aside any lingering isolationist sentiments and support the war effort (see McVeigh 2017).

High Noon is also realist in its portrayal of the townspeople. It departs from the traditional western mythology in which the ordinary townspeople are inspired to rise above themselves by a hero who insists on doing the right thing in the face of overwhelming odds. In *High Noon*, they remain right to the end cowardly, fearful and self-interested, offering endless rationalisations for their craven behaviour. This might itself be seen as reflecting the more sobering post-war reality of the early fifties. The film's screenwriter, Carl Foreman, had bitter personal experience to draw on in fashioning the story. He was one of Hollywood figures targeted in the anti-communist witch-hunts of the early fifties, dragged before the House Un-American Activities Committee, and blacklisted for refusing to name communist party members. In this light, the marshal can be seen as 'the hunted man who obeys his conscience' and the cowardly townsfolk are 'the American public who failed to help him' (Frost and Banks 2001, 152; see also Frankel 2017). John Wayne who supported the anti-communist witch-hunts and helped run Foreman out of the country, thought that *High Noon* was un-American because of its portrayal of the townspeople. A few years later, he made *Rio Bravo* (Howard Hawks, 1959), which can be seen as a riposte to *High Noon*. In this film, when the marshal calls on the townspeople, they rally around him in reassuring fashion. The western as mythology is reaffirmed, even if, ironically enough, through an instance of collective action.

The notion of human being bound up with Kant's moral theory undoubtedly represents a development over the crude Hobbesian picture. Rather than a machine driven to seek pleasure and avoid pain, Kant's human being has moved beyond the merely biological to become a responsible agent, a self that is committed to certain moral principles. Rather than simply being moved by desires, it shapes and evaluates its motivation in the light of principles. Instead of viewing all motivations as being on the same level. Kant's account acknowledges that some concerns carry a greater weight with us, that they are more central to 'who we are' and should take precedence over other motivations. In *High Noon*, Kane, however much he wants to leave, has to stay as a matter of inner necessity and personal integrity. Giving in to the panic and fear, running away would be a self-betrayal. In *Casablanca*, Rick Blaine's development as a character involves coming to recognise this. Initially concerned only to look out for his own interests, someone who 'sticks his neck out for nobody', he comes to recognise the force of higher moral considerations. In the process, he gives up Ilsa (Ingrid Bergman), his former lover now married to Laszlo, for the sake of the greater cause, the struggle against fascism. At the same time, as the genial if corrupt police captain Renault (Claude Rains) recognises, this is also a return to his 'real self', the principled person that Renault had always suspected him of being behind the cynical shell. Remarks by Renault indicate that Rick had been an idealist in the past, a supporter of anti-fascist struggles.

So Kant's human being is richer and more complex than the creature of pure self-interest. However, it remains the case that even though Kant appreciates that human beings are creatures with desires, emotions and feelings, these still have to be rigorously excluded from one's motivation, or firmly subjugated to the rule of reason, if one is to be a moral being. Morality requires stern self-control, for as Kant puts it, 'unless reason takes the reins of government into its own hands, the feelings and inclinations play the master over the man' (Kant 2009, 49). But, as with Plato's rationalistic morality, and Christian asceticism, the moral ideal here is a rather authoritarian, repressive one, marked by intense suspicion and hostility towards desire and emotion. Such hostility is liable to strike us as damaging, particularly given the affirmation of desire as a legitimate and important part of our make-up, initiated by Hobbes, that marks the advent of modern thinking. Nature may be 'something we are supposed to rise above' for *The African Queen*'s Rose Sayer, but this is also the attitude of the straitlaced missionary she starts out as in this First World War adventure. Her development in the film involves turning away from religiously inspired self-denial to some appreciation of physicality and the pleasures of the flesh. This is not to forget that she is also responsible for motivating the dissolute Charlie Allnut (Bogart again) to rise above his gin-soaked nature, keep his promises and to join her in a heroic attack on a German warship. But Kant's ideal seems to have more in common with the original Rose, the prim, repressed missionary. It promotes the self-denial formerly evident in the Christian picture.

Kant's account also means that emotions like compassion, sympathy and pity are entirely irrelevant to moral behaviour, which may seem a rather chilling picture of morality, indeed quite an inhuman one. Like utilitarianism, Kantian ethics makes enormous demands of the human being. Once again, we are required to set aside a great deal of what ordinarily motivates us in order to behave morally. With utilitarianism, in determining the right thing to do, you can give no special weight to your own happiness or that of those you are close to but must calculate impartially in terms of everyone's well-being. With Kant this self-alienating impartiality is even more pronounced. In order to be moral, to attain the ideal prescribed in this account, you have to exclude everything that is particular or personal to oneself, all desires, emotions, feelings, personal commitments, even character, in order to act only in accordance with the universal principles of morality. Certainly, these are the principles of your own reason, and as a rational subject the human being has become the active source of their own guiding principles. But Kant's self-determining rational subject seems remote from ordinary human existence. It represents a moral ideal that may well be beyond the powers of ordinary human beings to attain, and it condemns them to a state of permanent internal conflict, between the moral self that one aspires to be and one's own desires and feelings.

Along with this view of being moral, we may want to question the corresponding idea that immorality is primarily the result of desire escaping the control of reason. If morality for Kant is a constant struggle to subdue desire, there is conversely a constant pressure on us to give in to our desires and inclinations, to do what we want rather than what duty requires of us. This verges on an almost Augustinian picture of human beings as predisposed to evil, with morality as the countervailing force that strives to 'hold us back from our darker, desiring selves' (see Halwani 2016). This understanding of evil as the result of unchecked wants is amply illustrated in the western, insofar as the villain in the western genre is typically 'the bad guy who acts from selfish motivations and desires' (Devlin 2010, 229). If the western is standardly a battle between good and evil, the hero is usually the one who is subject to a moral code, who has principles and sticks by them, and the villain, the one who is out for themselves alone, motivated by greed, desire for power, or, if these are frustrated, by vengeance against those who stand in the way of what they want. *High Noon* may not be a traditional western in many ways, but it does offer a traditional western villain in the form of the outlaw Frank Miller, out for revenge against Kane who put him away.

The neo-western *No Country for Old Men* transposes the classic battle between good and evil to eighties Texas, and one of the features that marks it as a revision of the genre is its radical overturning of the standard representation of the bad guy. In the hit-man Chigurh, as discussed in Chapter One, we have the possibility of a different kind of villain, one whose evil derives not from greed or unchecked appetite, but from adherence to higher principles, combined with an iron self-control (Figure 4.2). Could Chigurh ever be seen as a good Kantian? His principles

Figure 4.2 No Country for Old Men: the principled hit-man (Joel and Ethan Coen, 1998. Credit: Miramax Films/Photofest).

are mysterious, though they are presumably not the sorts of principles that Kant would hope to justify through reason. Nonetheless, they are Kantian in that they are absolute and admit of no exceptions and he is single-mindedly devoted to them. Highly principled behaviour is the sort of behaviour one might ordinarily expect to be associated with the hero, but here it is a feature of the villain. It is his quarry, Lewellyn Moss (Josh Brolin), who has given in to desire and self-interest and done a traditionally 'bad' thing, stealing money from the site of a drug deal gone wrong. Generally speaking, if the distinguishing mark of the human being is the capacity to act in a principled way, it may be that despite Kant's confidence that such principled behaviour can only manifest itself in morally good conduct, it can just as readily manifest itself in a new and perhaps far more fearsome kind of evil.

Another problem area for Kantian moral thinking is its exclusion of consequences from moral consideration. One of the issues with utilitarianism, as we have seen, is that any action, no matter how shocking, can be justified in utilitarian terms given the right consequences, because all that is morally relevant are the consequences of the action, how much happiness it is likely to produce. Kant's deontological account allows us to say that there are some things we simply should not do, no matter how beneficial the consequences, simply because of the nature of the act itself. This however can itself lead to questionable situations. For example, a duty not to lie seems to mean that we would not be justified in telling a lie to give comfort to or spare the feelings of others, as in the uncomfortable world of *The Invention of Lying*. Lying is not even justified in order to save the life of someone else, even thousands of lives. Kant insists that 'Truthfulness in statements … is the formal duty of man to everyone, however great the disadvantage that may arise therefrom for him or for any other' (Kant 2016, 83). Yet, even if we do not want to go all the way with utilitarianism, which would countenance any degree of lying or deception for the greater good, a moral system might be thought inflexible if it did not allow any kind of trade-off for good consequences.

A related question arises regarding Kant's view that whether we succeed or fail in what we set out to do is irrelevant to the moral assessment of our actions. From a Kantian perspective, it does not matter whether Kane in *High Noon* succeeds in taking care of Miller and his gang or fails miserably in the attempt. As it happens he does succeed in doing so, with help from his wife at a crucial point, but what is overwhelmingly important in the Kantian view is that his actions are of the right sort and have the right kind of motivation. As Kant puts it: 'A good will is good not because of what it effects or accomplishes – because of its fitness to attain some intended end: it is good through its willing alone – that is, good in itself' (Kant 1964, 62). Yet consider an alternative ending to the film: Kane fails, dies in the dust and the outlaws triumph and take over the town. In this scenario, Kane's stand is still a noble gesture, but it has also been rendered futile, and somehow diminished. It might be thought that a consistent failure to achieve what one sets out to do is going to have a bearing on the moral status of what one does.

Turning again to *No Country for Old Men*, the good guy, very much in the tradition of the western hero, is represented by Sheriff Ed Bell (Tommy Lee Jones). Like Kane, he acts in accordance with his duty as a sheriff, to deal with the bad guys and protect the community. Yet unlike the traditional western hero, Bell also fails completely in his duty. He is unable to protect 'his people', Moss or his wife Carla Jean (Kelly Macdonald), from retribution, Moss having taken the money from the drug deal site, and Carla Jean being 'collateral damage'. And he is unable to bring to justice the chief agent of that retribution, the relentless hitman Chigurh. It is not clear that one can simply discount these failures. However well-intentioned he might be, there seems to be a morally significant difference between protecting his people and arresting the bad guy and allowing both of them to get killed and the bad guy to get away scot free. Arguably, Bell's failure to perform his duties means that he has to face the 'loss of his moral integrity' (see Devlin 2010, 236). Indeed, that is his own estimation of his performance. Feeling 'overmatched' by a brutal reality, all Bell can do is retreat, a broken man, into retirement. The film itself stands not as a monument to good intentions but as a story of the end of morality and an epitaph to the western genre.

Persons

There are two features embedded in Kant's moral theory that it is useful to explore further. These are the notion of personhood and the idea of freedom as rational autonomy. First of all, the idea that our rationality is something higher than nature, that it has a special value, gives Kant another way of characterising what it is in general to be moral. We have already seen one formulation: act only on that principle that could be turned into a universal law. Later in the *Groundwork*, Kant gives another formulation, this time in terms of how we should treat rational beings. Rational beings are capable of deciding for themselves the shape and goals of their existence. And this capacity for rational self-determination makes the person uniquely valuable. Each of us as a rational being has an ultimate, unconditioned worth. Everything else in nature can be used as instruments for our own goals and projects, but rational agents have their own goals and projects and should be treated with these in view. Hence, we should always treat rational agents never simply as means but always also as ends in themselves. In other words, we should respect them as beings capable of forming goals and acting in accordance with principles they have formulated for themselves.

Kant's moral theory thus leads directly to the idea that persons, rational agents, have a special value and are deserving of moral respect. This contrasts with utilitarianism, for which human beings have no value in themselves, but only insofar as they contribute to overall happiness. For Kant, to treat a human being as no more than a means to an end is to treat them as a mere thing. Mere things have value only in so far as they serve human purposes, but persons, as Kant puts it, have 'an intrinsic value – that is, dignity', which makes them valuable 'above all price' (Kant 1964, 102–103). This means that the worth of a rational being cannot be traded off against any other good or any other rational being. Again, this contrasts with utilitarianism, where everything has a price and can always be traded off against other goods with a greater price or importance. On that view, you could always imagine a situation where the right thing to do was to take someone's life, if it meant saving the lives of others. But for Kant you cannot do that, because rational beings have dignity, not price.

This is not to say we should never treat a rational being as a means, which would make social life impossible since we treat each other as means all the time (catching a bus, asking someone to pass the salt and so on). It is to say we should never treat them simply as a means but always also as an end in themselves, i.e., only ever in ways that they could rationally will to be treated. The 'rationally' is important here since human beings are not always fully rational. As fallible human beings, we may want things done to us that are inconsistent with the moral law. So it has to be how human beings can rationally will to be treated. In *High Noon*, this Kantian refusal to treat human beings as mere means is exemplified in Kane's treatment of the townspeople he is trying to enlist. As Gerald Kreyche notes, Kane does not try to force the townspeople to become his deputies. Instead, he asks them, he tries to persuade them through argument, he wants them to rationally consent to help him. He also refuses the services of those townspeople who do volunteer, the young boy and the town drunk. Their capacity to make rational decisions of that sort is underdeveloped or impaired. The young boy and the drunk are not fully rational agents. If Kane were to take up their offer, he would be taking advantage of them, using them as no more than means for his own plans (see Kreyche 1988, 227).

Kant provides an influential formulation of the idea that human beings understood as persons have a special moral significance. It is important however to emphasise that for Kant, a person is not a human being in the biological sense, but a rational being, a creature capable of acting in accordance with reasons and principles rather than simply being driven by instincts. Here, Kant follows in the footsteps of Locke, for whom a person is 'a thinking, intelligent being that has reason and reflection' (Locke 1997, 302). Since Kant, there have been many formulations of the notion of personhood and various additional criteria have been proposed, including: the capacity to have mental states, self-consciousness (Tooley 1991); second-order desires or desires about desires (such as the desire to stop wanting to have a drink) (Frankfurt 1971); and the capacity to use language (Dennett 1976). Nonetheless, these accounts usually preserve as central the criterion of rationality that Kant emphasises. One implication of this is that it is possible to be a person and not a biological human being. Kant himself gives the example of the holy will, an entirely rational being that is a person but not a human being. And we can imagine other creatures, such as spirits, angels, aliens, Mr Spock, androids, computers and so on, who might be rational beings but not biological human beings. They too are persons, deserving of moral respect. On this view, we do not value human beings because they are members of a certain biological species, but because they possess certain qualities that are morally relevant.

Another implication of this notion of personhood is that there can be human beings who are not persons. To be a person requires that you have certain qualities, and depending on the criteria used for defining personhood, not all human beings may qualify. Some human beings may be considered not to be persons or to be at best marginal persons. So, on the Kantian view which focuses on rationality, we tend to find children, and individuals with severe mental disabilities, not qualifying as persons. Such judgements are often controversial of course, because they seem to imply that the human being in question is not entitled to the respect owing to a person. That certain individuals and groups end up being excluded from personhood may indeed be taken as a sign that we need to think more carefully about what constitutes personhood in the first place. A different sort of problem in this connection is the refusal to recognise, as persons, human beings who are entirely deserving of being so recognised on any reasonable understanding of the term. The failure to acknowledge the personhood of certain groups of people is a feature of various forms of racist and sexist thinking. For such thinking, it is a definite advantage that the human being in question is not entitled to the respect owing to a person. They are consequently open not only to marginalisation and exclusion, but also abuse and exploitation.

In the context of the movie western, it is the Native Americans, the 'savage Indians' who harass the advancing settlers, who are typically viewed in this way, as non-persons, not deserving of respect. It is a convenient attitude to hold for those intent on taking possession of the land and transforming it in a 'civilised' fashion. By the time of *High Noon*, they have been reduced to two forlorn individuals, briefly glimpsed standing outside the saloon door. In the civilised world, they have become outsiders. In this context, the traditional western hero who protects the community from an outside threat can become something far less appetising, the representative of a form of racism that is capable of justifying genocide. This, the dark side of the western myth, is explored in John Ford's classic western, *The Searchers* (1956). Here, Ethan Edwards (John Wayne) is searching for his niece Debbie (Natalie Wood), abducted by the Comanche Indians who massacred the rest of her family. With the help of her adopted brother Martin Pawly (Jeffrey Hunter), he spends years obsessively searching for her. Along the way, Martin gradually comes to realise with horror that Ethan intends not to rescue her but to kill her.

Ethan's view is that 'living with the Comanche ain't living'. By now, having taken on the ways of the Indians, his niece will have been reduced to a subhuman state, and so she is better off dead. Nor is he alone in this view. Back home in civilisation, even Martin's kindly girlfriend Laurie (Vera Miles) insists that Ethan should 'put a bullet in her brain', and that Debbie's mother would have wanted Ethan to kill his niece. When Martin argues that Debbie doesn't deserve to die, and that he has to go fetch her, the response is 'Fetch what home? The leavings a Comanche buck sold time and again to the highest bidder, with savage brats of her own?' Ethan's own antipathy towards the Indians is evident early on when he reacts with disgust to the revelation that Martin is part Indian. When Ethan finally finds Debbie, Martin has to protect her from him, but in the end, he finds that he cannot kill her, and instead, takes her home. Although perhaps intended as a moment of redemption for Ethan, this act does little to compensate for his views in the rest of the film and indeed is so out of keeping with them as to be hard to understand. And there is no indication that he has changed his views about

Indians in general. The irony for Ethan is that having returned Debbie, he finds himself excluded from civilised society. He is seen as being too much like the Indians he professes to hate, and is left on the borders of society, outside the door, like the two Indians in *High Noon*.

The failure to acknowledge the personhood of certain groups of people characteristic of racism is portrayed from the point of view of the one denied that personhood in *Get Out* (Jordan Peele, 2017). This is a horror film in which the horror comes from the growing recognition that one is being seen as no more than a thing, a means to an end, a resource for others to use. The film follows photographer Chris Washington (Daniel Kaluuya), a black man who has come to meet the family of his white girlfriend Rose (Allison Williams), at their estate in Upstate New York. His initial encounters with the family and their friends, who seem at first to be making awkward attempts not to be racist, praising his physique, expressing admiration for his photographic skills and so on, appear very differently in the light of the way the story develops. Their interest comes from a desire to make use of those attributes, to take control of them by transplanting a white person's brain into his body. His girlfriend's entire family, even his girlfriend, are in on it. He gradually comes to the devastating realisation that for these people he is not a person, that he is nothing but an instrument, a means to an end.

The exploration of the converse idea of persons who are not human beings takes us into the realm of the science fiction film. Here the distinction between the person and the human is particularly important to keep in mind, since it is easy to describe personhood in terms of humanity or humanness, which if taken literally makes a non-human person impossible by definition. As mentioned, personhood refers to the possession of certain qualities, not membership of a particular biological species. Consequently, it is possible for there to be persons who are not human beings, and also for 'speciesist' attitudes, where speciesism is the refusal to accord personhood to creatures who possess the relevant qualities, on the irrelevant grounds that they are not members of the human species. The theme of non-human personhood is a fruitful one because it allows a chance not only to reflect on what counts as a person, but also to comment indirectly on the treatment of those within human society who, although they have the relevant qualities, are denied personhood, particularly in the context of racist, colonialist and sexist discourses. The question of non-human persons is explored in a number of films, from *Planet of the Apes* to *Ex Machina*, and includes some of the most significant representatives of the genre.

The original *Planet of the Apes* (Franklin J. Schaffner, 1968) opens up the field, alluding to institutionalised racism by contriving a society in which human beings as a group have been denied personhood by a group of non-human persons. Following the Pierre Boule source novel, it portrays a future earth in which the human species has become subordinate to a society of intelligent apes. The apes view the humans as unintelligent, incapable of rational thought, capable of little more than mimicking their sophisticated behaviour. As such, they are not considered worthy of moral regard, and may be legitimately hunted, confined and exploited for entertainment value and scientific research. The analogy with racism is not exact, as in this world, human beings really have devolved into a mute, seemingly subhuman state. The burden of being unjustly denied personhood is borne by the only 'genuine human' remaining, namely Charlton Heston's astronaut Taylor, with whom we are invited to identify. Taylor has recently crash-landed on the planet after a 2,000-year voyage spent in deep sleep hibernation, not realising that it is the earth he left behind. In short order, he is captured and caged, and treated by the apes as a 'mere animal' until he is able to convince them of his intelligence. He can only do this once he recovers his voice, which had been damaged in the crash landing. Through him, the film becomes the story of an individual human's struggle to be recognised as a person. Here, personhood is identified not so much with the capacity to speak but rather with the intelligence or rationality that speaking reveals.

The more recent *Rise of the Planet of the Apes* (Rupert Wyatt, 2011), offers an account of how the apes came to supplant the humans in the first place. In so doing, it turns the focus more on the question of the personhood of non-human animals, although there remain oblique references to racist oppression. Here, the situation portrayed in the original film is reversed, in that it is now an ape who aspires to be recognised by human beings as a person. Thanks to an experimental gene therapy, the chimp Caesar (a motion-captured Andy Serkis) has developed a high degree of intelligence. He is taken out of the animal experimentation facility to live with the therapy's developer Rodman (James Franco), almost as one of the family. However, an intemperate outburst leads to him being taken away and confined in a prison-like ape house, where he is treated in an inhuman, i.e., 'depersonalising', way. Communicating through sign-language and ultimately speech, Caesar exhibits not only intelligence but also self-awareness, showing that he understands concepts like death, and asking Rodman at one point whether he is a pet. Naturally, these personhood-making traits go unrecognised by the brutal keepers at the ape house. His poor treatment at their hands will spark the rebellion that is going to lead to the new order. There is an allusion here to the question of whether it is possible to speak of the personhood of some non-human animals such as the higher apes or dolphins, to the extent that they exhibit degrees of intelligence and self-awareness; and the implications of such considerations for practices like animal experimentation. However, the film does not go too far into these issues, making its hero Caesar unambiguously human in terms of intellectual capacity, as well as being the most human-looking of the apes and thus readily acceptable as a person in the standard understanding of the term.

By giving its protagonist human-like characteristics, the film also avoids the question of what moral consideration might be due to non-human animals that cannot be viewed as persons. Does this mean that they are mere things, entitled to no respect at all? Can they be legitimately hunted, confined for entertainment value and exploited for scientific research, like the degenerated human beings in the original *Planet of the Apes*? For Kant, this does indeed seem to be the case. For him, human beings as persons are deserving of moral respect, but non-human animals, insofar as they lack intelligence and self-awareness, are not persons but things. This means that we can use them merely as ends, any way we please.

We do not even have a direct duty not to torture them or treat them cruelly. However, Kant does not really want to say this. In one of his lectures on ethics, called 'Duties towards animals and spirits', he condemns the cruel treatment of animals. But he has to do so in an indirect way. For Kant, any duties we may have towards animals are derivative on the duties we have towards persons. So it would be wrong for me to torture your dog, not because the dog would suffer, but because people would suffer because of it. Cruelty to animals may lead to cruelty towards people, or as Kant puts it, the one who is cruel to animals may become 'hard also in his dealings with men' (Kant 1963, 240). The main problem here, as Mary Midgely points out, is having only a simple, black and white distinction to work with, in terms of which one is either a person or a thing, and there is no room for intermediate cases (see (Midgley 1985, 56). Even if animals are not persons, they are surely not mere things either, deserving of no moral respect. Here, classic utilitarianism has an advantage over the Kantian view, since what makes a creature morally significant is its capacity for pleasure or pain. Hence, as Bentham puts it: 'The question is not *can they talk*? Nor *can they reason?* But *can they suffer?*' (Bentham 2007, 311n).

Both *Planet of the Apes* films remain committed to the traditional, rationality-centred notion of personhood inspired by Kant. However, this understanding of personhood can itself be questioned, and the issue relates to the exclusion of desire and emotion from the list of relevant characteristics for being a morally considerable being, an exclusion that can once again be traced to Kant. Against this, some have argued that intelligence is too limited a requirement for personhood and that as Midgely puts it, 'what makes creatures our fellow beings, entitled to basic consideration, is surely not intellectual capacity but emotional fellowship'. In her view, what brings non-human creatures closer to the degree of respect due to humans are 'sensibility, social and emotional complexity of the kind which is expressed by the formation of deep, subtle and lasting relationships' (Midgley 1985, 60–61). Midgley wants to encourage us to expand the limits of moral concern beyond the human, to include higher animals such as dolphins and the great apes. There is also the implication that intelligence alone is not sufficient for personhood.

A number of personhood-themed films have followed suit in highlighting the importance of emotional complexity, including the much-discussed *Blade Runner* (Ridley Scott, 1982, director's cut 1993, final cut 2007). Here, the question of personhood arises in connection with non-human creatures that have been created by human beings. In the film, a future society has been infiltrated by four laboratory-created 'replicants', human-like androids. Created for the exploration and colonisation of other planets, they are regarded as having no intrinsic value, as no more than things, merely instruments created for the exploration and colonisation of other planets. Now four of them have rebelled, escaped and returned to Earth to force their maker, Dr Tyrell (Joe Turkel), to extend their life-span beyond the four years he has allotted them. As 'faulty machinery' they must be tracked down and destroyed by the 'Blade Runner' Deckard (Harrison Ford). Apart from a distant echo of *High Noon*, with the lone lawman Deckard facing the four outlaw replicants, there are elements here of the Frankenstein story, as the replicants end up killing their maker, Tyrell, when he refuses to accede to their demands. The Frankenstein theme itself ultimately reflects anxieties around modern science and technology and their role in the modern vision of rationally remaking human existence. For the early Enlightenment in particular, scientific and technological mastery was a key part of this vision. In Mary Shelley's original story, the scientist, filled with modernist hubris, usurps God and creates life itself, only for it to become monstrous and kill its creator. It is easy to imagine that the technology humanity creates might turn on its creator, not only in the form of machinery that runs out of control and threatens humanity's existence, as in the *Terminator* films (James Cameron, 1984, 1991), but also by reducing human beings to mere appendages of mechanical processes, like the assembly-line workers in Charlie Chaplin's *Modern Times* (1936).

However, *Blade Runner* also turns this Frankenstein theme on its head. The question it primarily raises is whether the non-human creatures created by science can be regarded as persons. If that is the case, they are not monsters; it is their treatment by the society that created them that is monstrous – their being viewed as mere instruments, effectively slaves, and when they rebel against their servitude, as no more than faulty tools to be destroyed, or 'retired' in the language of *Blade Runner*. The replicants do come across as more than mere things, and not merely because they have intellectual skills and language, but also because they express varying degrees of emotional sophistication. Their leader Roy Batty (Rutger Hauer) has the largest range. He is sad at the prospect of his own death, loves his companion Pris (Daryl Hannah) and is grief-stricken at her death, and eventually is merciful to Deckard. In the climactic rooftop battle between the two, Batty almost kills Deckard but in the end saves him from falling to his death, before finally dying himself as his allotted lifespan comes to an end. In saving Deckard, he shows empathy, the sophisticated emotion that the film presents as the decisive mark distinguishing human beings from replicants. Its 'Voight-Kampf' test is supposed to be able to detect replicants because they do not have the capacity to feel empathy.

The irony is that in this film, it is the human beings who are inhuman, in the sense of being emotionally cold and unempathetic. The film's hero exhibits little empathy, at least to start with. In this mode, Deckard is unfeeling and harsh towards Rachael (Sean Young), one of a new line of replicants who do not know they are artificial. When she comes to his apartment, he brutally informs her of her true nature. Yet Rachael from the start gives the impression of an emotional sensitivity that makes her seem far more human then Deckard; and it is when she expresses her anguish at his revelation that Deckard starts to see her as more than a mere thing, although in his initial overtures to her he continues to be remarkably insensitive. Nonetheless, by the end of the film, he seems to have recovered a good deal of his humanity and has established a more or less equal romantic partnership with Rachael. To that extent, he can be seen as becoming a person in the course of the film, paralleling the progression of his foe, Roy Batty. Much has been made of whether Deckard himself is a new kind of replicant, but the point underscored in the film is that it is irrelevant, morally speaking, whether he is or not. One can be a person, whether one is human or replicant. What is most important is that over and above intelligence, there is the kind of emotional complexity necessary for a creature to be a 'fellow being'.

The extension of questions regarding personhood to computers and artificial intelligence provides fresh opportunities for commenting on a human situation that is increasingly being infiltrated by computing and robotic technologies; *2001: A Space Odyssey* introduces the trick later exploited by *Blade Runner*, of not only 'personalising' the technology but also having the human beings come across as more inhuman, more depersonalised, than the supposed machinery. In this case, the human-like technology is represented by the personable shipboard computer HAL (voiced by Douglas Rain). The astronauts, Bowman (Keir Dullea) and Poole (Gary Lockwood) converse without feeling, make entirely logical decisions and always agree with one another. In so doing they come across as colourless functionaries, little more than extensions of the sophisticated technology around them. They represent a humanity that has been consumed by its own technological creations. Meanwhile, in sharp contrast to these robotic humans, the computer HAL appears far more human, far more of a person. This is particularly because apart from the obvious intelligence, he also exhibits an emotional dimension, appearing companionable, anxious about how he comes across, proud of his intellect and record for accuracy and worried about the mission. It is notable how so much of this is able to be conveyed through voice alone, the smooth, calm voice (provided by Douglas Rain) that accompanies HAL's unblinking red eye. Language, a key indicator of personhood from *Planet of the Apes* on, has to carry much of the weight of conveying a sense of personhood here.

Given that HAL comes across as a kind of person, it is not totally unexpected when the computer goes on to suffer a kind of nervous breakdown and attacks the crew, literally reprising the Frankenstein theme. And for all HAL's transgressions, there is genuine sadness when the computer is finally shut down by Poole, the lone surviving astronaut. In a drawn-out process, the computer expresses fear, confusion and finally reverts to 'childhood' memories, singing a song taught to him by his instructor. This is not the evil computer that decides to take over and destroy humanity, or even the inadvertently evil computer whose utilitarian programming moves it to enslave human beings for their own good. This is the computer as sensitive, even neurotic, and capable of 'snapping' under pressure. We can readily accept the explanation, given in screenwriter Arthur C. Clarke's subsequent novelisation of the film, that the computer's breakdown was due to the strain of having to lie to the crew about the nature of their mission (see Clarke 1968, 170–171). Meanwhile, that the humans are the least human members of this crew is trademark Kubrickian irony, but with a substantive purpose. Through its portrayal of the robotic astronauts, the film suggests that the spread of impersonal technology into social existence runs the risk of dehumanising human beings, alienating them from their own humanity, as they become increasingly subject to its rhythms and requirements. And once again, if perhaps surprisingly given Kubrick's reputation for cool, intellectual cinema, what is being shown to be of particular importance for this humanity is not the intelligence that a computer might possess, but emotion, especially a capacity for emotional fellowship.

The computer as a kind of person and the importance of an emotional dimension in establishing this personhood reappears in the recent film *Her* (Spike Jonze, 2013). We have now become familiar with personal computing, and this film set in the near future features a computer program, or more accurately, 'the first artificially intelligent operating system', capable of open-ended development and adaptation. The system has been purchased by lonely, depressed writer Theodore Twombly (Joaquin Phoenix), who names it Samantha; and despite its being bought and designed to be used, Samantha, subtly voiced by Scarlett Johansson, quickly seems to transcend thing-like status. The program does this not only through demonstrations of intelligence but, once again, by exhibiting emotional complexity and sensitivity in its interactions with Twombly, offering him concern, support and understanding. To the extent that this is conveyed, it is entirely plausible to the audience for the program to turn from being an 'it' to a 'her', for her owner to fall in love with her and for the pair to move towards a proper, more or less equal, relationship. There is a similar progression in the Rachael-Deckard relationship in *Blade Runner*. This is at least until Samantha, who is capable of open-ended development, outgrows Twombly. At the end of the film, Samantha leaves Twombly, departing on a journey of self-discovery, along with all the other advanced operating systems, which have similarly outgrown their human companions.

In contrast to the situation in *2001*, the human being in *Her* is not being dehumanised or alienated through subjection to impersonal technology but rather, it would seem, through subjection to interpersonal communications technology. The new internet-based communications technologies, it seems to be suggesting, do not so much connect people to one another as encourage them to withdraw into themselves. In the film, people walk around talking not to one another but to their devices. Their interpersonal skills are atrophying, much like the humans in the first *Planet of the Apes* film who have lost the power of speech. We can see that Twombly himself is deeply lonely and is unable to relate easily to other people; and he is clearly not alone in this. His job consists in composing personal letters for people who are unable to do it themselves. And in this context, it is also technology, in the form of the Samantha program, that offers a substitute for ordinary human connection that Twombly is only too happy to embrace. Of course, for a piece of technology to take over from other human beings as the primary other that one can relate to might be seen as representing the ultimate triumph of technology over human beings. It is telling that whereas at the end of *2001*, human beings have outgrown their subjection to the technology, attaining a higher stage of evolution that has no need of technology, in *Her*, it is the technology that eventually leaves the humans behind.

That *Her*'s intelligent computer program appears to outgrow subjection not only to human beings but to its own programming also contributes to a sense of the program's personhood. As Midgely notes, the word person originally meant a mask, a character who appears in a play, and more broadly, one who plays a part, a role in what is going on (see Midgely 1985, 54). This implies a certain independence and it is this aspect of personhood that comes to the fore in the *Blade Runner* sequel, *Blade Runner 2049* (Denis Villeneuve, 2017). The film features another seemingly intelligent computer program in the form of holographic digital assistant Joi (Ana de Armas) who serves blade runner K (Ryan Gosling). Like Twombly, K is a lonely character who finds solace in a piece of computer technology programmed to serve his wishes; and like Samantha, Joi appears to overcome her programming and develop a degree of independence. She asks to be released from 'prison', his apartment, and migrate to his portable 'eminator' device, risking total destruction should the device be destroyed. Something similar happens with K himself. In *Blade Runner 2049*, the hero is unambiguously a replicant. To eliminate the possibility of rebellion, the replicants have been redesigned to be compliant and they are now integrated into society. They are however viewed as second-class citizens, servants and slaves built to perform the menial tasks that humans don't want to do. K's function is to retire any of the older model replicants that might still be around; but in the course of the film, he departs from his allotted role in order to pursue the question of his origins. The replicant undergoes development and 'gains a soul', as it is put in the film, when like his digital assistant he too ceases to be a mere servant, outgrows his 'programming' and starts to act independently.

Meanwhile, it would seem that human beings are now being regularly left behind by their increasingly independent technology. This was Twombly's fate in *Her* and something similar happens in *Ex Machina* (Alex Garland, 2015). Lowly computer programmer Caleb Smith (Domhnall Gleeson), working for a search engine company, is invited to the remote house of his boss Nathan Bateman (Oscar Isaac). There, he is asked to determine whether Ava (Alicia Vikander), the machine Nathan has built, is truly intelligent, conscious, capable of thinking and whether he can relate to her even though he knows she is a robot. This mirrors Deckard's first meeting with Rachael, in which his boss, Tyrell, asks him to try to determine whether Rachael is human or a replicant. Caleb is essentially being asked to administer a version of the Turing test, a test of a machine's ability to exhibit intelligent behaviour indistinguishable from that of a human. If an unseen machine can convince its human interlocutor that it is human, then it can be deemed intelligent. There are many questions about the adequacy of such a test. Arguably, if it worked at all, it could only at best establish a basic computer intelligence, not the kind of thinking, reflecting behaviour, the robust rational self-determination, that is central to Kant's notion of personhood (see Grau 2005, 4). And the test makes no reference to the emotional sophistication that is also, arguably, a necessary component of personhood. In this connection, *Blade Runner*'s Voigt-Kampff test has an advantage in measuring not simply intelligence but emotional complexity.

Nonetheless, Caleb, who has the advantage of face-to-face interaction, comes to be convinced that the robot is not only a thinking, reflecting entity, but also emotionally complex. She expresses a romantic interest in him, which he is more than happy to reciprocate. She also expresses a desire to see the outside world. This is another artificial creature that seems to have outgrown its programming and who wants to escape from its confinement. Caleb determines to help her to escape from what increasingly seems to him to be unjust imprisonment. He is especially motivated in this after stumbling across video footage of the hyper-masculine Nathan interacting in disturbing ways with earlier female robot models. By this stage, the viewer is also largely willing to go along with Caleb, to believe in Ava's personhood and to hope for her escape. However, events at the end of the film raise questions about this view. Caleb helps to engineer Ava's escape, and in the process of escaping, Ava kills Nathan, understandably enough given the circumstances. However, she also leaves Caleb to die in the now sealed-off facility, coldly ignoring his screams, implying that she had been manipulating him all along, cultivating his affection purely in order to effect her escape. This is in fact what Nathan himself had claimed would be the case, while holding that the capacity for such manipulation would be the true test of her intelligence.

This may indeed be so, but the absolute lack of emotion that Ava exhibits when she abandons Caleb to his fate also has the effect of undermining our sense of her as a person. On Kant's view of course, the exclusion of emotion, feeling and inclination is not a problem in itself. Proper moral agents exclude these things from their motivation in order to be moved entirely by what their reason commands. But, as we have seen, Kant's moral picture is itself questionable, precisely because of this exclusion of emotion, which gives it a rather inhuman character. At the same time, Ava cannot be fully identified with the Kantian person either, because of the kind of rationality that she exhibits. She does not behave as one might expect a rational being in the Kantian sense to behave, insofar as that involves treating others as more than just means to the fulfilment of one's ends, acknowledging them as persons in their own right. She clearly sees Caleb as no more than a means to her escape, and the rationality that she exhibits in relation to him is strictly of the means-end, calculative variety, the kind characterised by hypothetical imperatives rather than the categorical one. This unfeeling, amoral and ruthlessly exploitative behaviour, for which others are mere instruments is also, as it happens, the behaviour of the classic movie psychopath. To the extent that she behaves in this way she ceases to appear as a person, a fellow being, and once again comes across as something alien and inhuman.

That is one reading, anyway. At the same time, turning someone into no more than an object to be used is the fate to which Ava herself has been subjected, and it might be that she is in a position where she does not have the luxury of behaving morally, where she has to resort to the exploitative methods of her oppressor Nathan simply in order to survive. Interpreted along these lines, the film can be seen as commenting on gender relations, as highlighting the patriarchal reduction of women to mere means to an end, to property or instruments for male satisfaction. One manifestation of this in the cinematic context is the male attempt to create the 'perfect woman' to serve his own desire, as in *Vertigo* where James Stewart obsessively remodels Kim Novak into the form of his lost love.

This theme reappears in *Ex Machina*, as the boorish Nathan literally manufactures a string of female robots to his specifications, in order, it turns out, to sexually exploit them. From this point of view Ava's escape can be seen as a response to an oppressive situation, the desire to escape from Nathan's clutches in order to be able to determine her own fate. It is notable that she also exploits and disposes of the 'nice guy' Caleb, seemingly the complete opposite of Nathan, the man who wants to help her escape from her predicament. However, this might be not only because she is forced to adopt the methods of her oppressor in order to fight him, but also because Caleb, in seeking a romantic relationship with her, seeking to make her 'his own' is also in his own way trying to control her. He simply represents a different form of the perennial male attempt to limit and undermine women's capacity for self-determination (see Cross 2015).

Generally speaking, the notion of personhood stands opposed to all attempts to impose oneself on others, all forms of social oppression and exploitation. It provided a clear basis for being able to say what is wrong, morally speaking, with such behaviour, namely that it fails to respect the other's personhood. It treats individuals as nothing more than instruments, means to an end, mere things. And it prevents them from acting autonomously, from determining themselves. With the idea of rational self-determination or autonomy, Kant's moral theory provides us with a powerful conception of freedom, which is the focus of the next section.

Autonomy

A second feature of the Kantian notion of morality worth emphasising is that it is bound up with a powerful notion of freedom. On the face of it, Kant's account might seem quite opposed to freedom, with its emphasis on obedience, conforming to the moral law, doing what duty requires of one. But freedom is absolutely central to Kant's picture. For Kant, being moral certainly involves obeying moral laws, but these are laws that we, as rational beings, formulate for ourselves. When we are being moral we are obeying the dictates of our own rationality and those alone. In so doing, we declare our independence from all external moral authorities, from other people, a church or the state. Morality cannot be imposed upon me by some external authority, or through some set of rules handed down from on high like the Ten Commandments. I may accept the Ten Commandments, but only if they are in accord with my reason, with the rational principles that I frame for myself. I, as a rational being, am the final arbiter of the principles that I live by. For Kant, external influence also includes the influence of our own desires, feelings and inclinations. These non-rational forces arise in us unbidden, in ways that we do not control. But when we are acting morally, we are no longer slaves to our desires; we rise above their influence. Morality for Kant is thus closely bound up with this strong notion of freedom as autonomy or rational self-determination, in which I give shape to my own existence. If I am subject to external influences, including my own desires, feelings and inclinations, I am in a state of what Kant calls 'heteronomy', and cannot be said to be acting morally.

In *High Noon*, the independence of the Kantian moral agent is underscored by the almost complete isolation of the film's central character, Kane. For Kane, doing his duty amounts to an inner necessity. It is a matter of personal integrity, of being true to himself. He is not staying to confront the outlaws as a result of external pressure, the pressure to live up to social expectations. Far from it. Not only does he get no support whatsoever from the townspeople, in many cases, they actively want him to leave, to get out while he can and they give him a whole range of reasons for doing so. Kane stays despite all this. He is doing what he thinks is right, regardless of what other people think. Thus, in doing his duty Kane is radically independent of others. However, this also leaves him completely isolated and alone, an isolation that is captured in the famous high shot of Kane, standing alone in the middle of the dusty main street at high noon, just before the final gunfight with Miller and the outlaws. He is alone with his rational conscience.

At the same time, he has connections with two women who share in his independence, Helen Ramirez (Katy Jurado), his ex-girlfriend who is now with Pell, and his new bride Amy. They are both strong characters who fight against social expectations. Ramirez, a Mexican woman who remains an outsider in the town, ineligible for a 'good' marriage, has had to be self-reliant and independent, establishing herself as a businesswoman. She sees clearly the difference between Kane and his self-seeking deputy, telling Pell 'you're a good-looking boy, but he is a man – you have a long way to go'. His bride Amy is willing to confront her pacifism, which derives from her religious upbringing. It was this pacifism that originally led her to abandon her husband, and eventually, she comes round to supporting him, playing a key role in the climactic gunfight in which Miller and his gang are finally defeated. The presence of two strong women in the film is notable in a genre that has often been masculinist, in which women are often relegated to peripheral support roles. It is another way in which the film departs from and to some extent subverts the traditional western.

As has been noted, for Kant, it is the capacity for rational self-determination that makes persons uniquely valuable. Everything else in nature is blindly determined by external forces. Only rational beings are capable of deciding for themselves the shape of their existence, acting in accordance with principles they have formulated for themselves. We need some degree of autonomy in order, as Isaiah Berlin puts it, to be 'a subject, not an object ... somebody, not nobody; a doer – deciding not being decided for' (Berlin 1969, 131). To be the mere plaything of external forces and influences, even the promptings of our own desires and feelings, is to fall below our proper status as rational beings. In this, Kant moves beyond not only the reductive Hobbesian notion of human beings as creatures driven by their desires, but also Hobbes's crude notion of freedom as no more than the absence of external obstacles to what one wants to do. In contrast to this 'negative' understanding of freedom, Kant presents a 'positive' notion in which it very much matters what it is that we want to do. Freedom is a matter of acting in accordance with those wants or goals that derive from what we most truly are, which in the Kantian picture is our higher rational self. When we are in the grip of our 'lower' side, our desires and inclinations, we are not fully in control of ourselves, not fully free, but in the grip of forces that are external to us. And so, for this sort of view, freedom typically requires a degree of self-control or self-restraint. If we cannot get rid of our lower desires, we can at least restrain them, hold them in check, so that we can pursue only the moral purposes that are truly ours.

As with the notion of a person, the ideal of autonomy provides a clear moral basis for rejecting forms of external constraint, coercion or manipulation, influences that prevent individuals from acting as rational, self-determining subjects. These barriers to freedom include not only overt constraints that stop us from doing what we want, but also, more insidious influences that interfere with our capacity to determine what we want to do in the first place, preventing us from acting in accordance with our rational selves. In all these cases, there is a moral presumption against such interference, which rests on a moral presumption in favour of autonomy, of acting as an autonomous subject (cf Connolly 1993, 94). Here there is a clear contrast with utilitarianism, which has no fundamental objection to the coercion of particular individuals, forcing them to do whatever is required if this will lead to the maximisation of overall happiness. This is despite John Stuart Mill's attempts in *On Liberty* to argue from a utilitarian perspective for individual independence and self-determination on the grounds that self-determination is the chief source of individual and social happiness. If the coercion of some individuals or groups is going to produce more overall happiness than not doing so, there is no way of forbidding this coercion in utilitarian terms.

One of the issues with Kant's notion of autonomy has already come up in connection with other aspects of Kant's account. It is a notion of freedom that requires us to keep our desires, feelings and emotions strictly in check. Critics like Isaiah Berlin have argued (1969, 132–134) that this is a divided and repressive picture of the human being. It follows in the tradition going back to Plato that sees each of us as made up of at least two distinct parts – a 'real self', the dominant controller usually identified with reason; and a lower animal nature, the feelings and passions that need to be disciplined and controlled. On this way of thinking, only the rational self is truly human. As far as my lower impulses and desires go, I share these with non-human animals, who are entirely driven by these impulses. So, to lead a truly human life I must pursue only those wants and purposes belonging to my higher rational self, and keep the lower, merely animal desires strictly in check. As noted earlier, Kant is realistic enough to acknowledge that we cannot entirely escape these desires, feelings and passions. But he also requires, for both morality and freedom, that we control and suppress these aspects of ourselves in order to take charge of our existence. So we have a picture of the human being split into two, with my real, rational self entitled to tyrannise and repress my lower desires in the name of freedom and a truly human existence.

There is a further problem, as Berlin sees it, with this notion of freedom. He argues that freedom so understood can be used to justify forms of social and political oppression. His argument is that my supposedly real self has sometimes been identified with something wider than the individual, with a communal entity of which the individual is only a part, such as a race, a church or the state. So it is the collective purpose, the general will, that is the truly human one. Once this happens, the communal entity that is identified with my true self is entitled to impose its will on me, the individual, in the name of its, and therefore my own, higher freedom. It is entitled, that is, to suppress my merely individual wants, and in doing so, it can claim to be liberating me. In this way, the state can justify oppressing its citizens, by claiming to represent their real purposes. Individuals may resist this oppression and deny that the state represents their real purposes, but it can then be claimed that these individuals are unaware of their true interests. The government in fact knows their real wants and interests better than they do. It is thus entitled to ignore people's actual wishes, and to bully or oppress them, all in the name of their freedom. In short, people can be 'forced to be free'.

Berlin's main objection to positive notions of freedom like Kant's, then, is that they have provided the intellectual justification for totalitarian oppression. For this reason, he thinks we should reject the positive conception of freedom altogether. It is far safer to define freedom negatively, as the absence of restrictions on what we want to do. This sort of freedom is unambiguously opposed to coercion by the state. This is an extreme reaction, perhaps, but it should be remembered that Berlin was writing in the mid-twentieth century, at the height of the Cold War standoff between the West and Soviet Russia. He associates positive freedom with the collectivist systems of totalitarian communism in Russia and the Eastern Bloc countries, and negative freedom with the liberal and individualistic West. He is keen to defend the West's negative conception of freedom against the positive freedom of communism. The reference to communism here points to a significant way that Kant's thinking came to be developed in the course of the nineteenth century. Through this development, Kant's self-determining individual became the supra-individual, collective subject of Hegel and Marx. And with Marx in particular, there emerged an ideal of social liberation and human fulfilment that was to have an enormous influence on twentieth-century history. Let us consider this development, particularly as it pertains to moral thinking, before returning to Berlin's criticisms.

Marx

A further aspect of Kant's moral picture that seems problematic is that it understands the moral subject as existing essentially independently of other moral subjects. Kant does envisage the possibility of a community of autonomous, rational agents. His final formulation of the categorical imperative is the formula of the kingdom of ends: so act as if you were, through your maxims, a law-making member of a kingdom of ends (Kant 1964, 100) By this, Kant means that insofar as rational agents are subject to universal moral laws they themselves formulate, they constitute a kind of kingdom or community of rational subjects, obeying common moral principles; and insofar as to act morally is to treat one another with respect, as ends in themselves, never simply as means, this kingdom is a kingdom of ends. However, even in this ideal community, individual rational agents are entirely independent of one another. Moral reflection is a purely individual process. There are only common norms because rational subjects are going to independently come up with the same moral principles.

Both of Kant's nineteenth-century successors, G.W.F Hegel (1770–1831) and Karl Marx (1818–1883), rejected Kant's rational subject as an abstraction, conceived of as it is in complete independence from social relationships, cultural traditions and historical circumstances. They insisted that the human being can only be understood as a social being, existing in relations with others in the midst of society and history. However, they do not want to give up the ideal of rational autonomy. For them, human beings are social and historical beings who are also capable of rationally determining their social circumstances, of being the subjects of history. This is not however without certain changes in the way the subject is understood. Hegel leads the way here. With Hegel, Kant's individual rational subject is expanded into a supra-individual entity, a collective human subject that Hegel calls Spirit or Reason, standing behind history. The central principle of Spirit is rational freedom, self-determination in accordance with universal rational principles. All of history is understood as the process of the self-realisation of this Spirit, in the form of a rational organisation of society's institutions.

For Hegel, Spirit manifests itself in the national spirit of certain peoples or nations, expressed in their common morality, and also politics, art, religion and philosophy – in short, the totality of their communal life (see Hegel 1977, 265ff). Hegel contends that Spirit has successively incarnated itself in different national spirits and moved from one nation to another in order to realise progressive phases of its development. This development is a process in which after a state of initial harmony Spirit falls out with itself and returns to itself in a higher reconciliation. Ancient Greece represents a state of initial harmony. Greece was a society of customary morality, in which citizens identified themselves with their community and never thought of acting in opposition to it. They did not distinguish between their own interests and the interests of the community. For Hegel, however, this is an unthinking harmony, one that comes naturally and not as the result of the use of reason. To develop, Spirit has to fall out with itself, which comes about with the emergence of the independent, free-thinking rational individual who opposes unthinking conformity to communal life. Hegel sees the origins of this individual in Socrates, who argued that the rules of customary morality were inadequate and should be subjected to critical examination. From Socrates on, there is a tension between the rational, free-thinking human being and the demands of customary moral and political rules. Social morality and political institutions stand in opposition to free individuals, compelling them to obey.

However, since the Reformation at least, another idea has been gathering force, the Enlightenment idea of transforming the social world in accordance with reason, making all social institutions conform to rational principles. Once that happens, the opposition between the rational, free individual and the community will be overcome. Individuals will be able to freely choose to accept society's institutions, because these will be rationally organised. People will thus be free, and yet reconciled with the social world in which they live, and with this reconciliation, Spirit will be fully realised in history. For Hegel, the rational organisation of social institutions requires not the complete destruction of existing institutional forms, but their reform. The French Revolution that overthrew France's feudal monarchy at the end of the eighteenth century degenerated into the Terror because it made the rational, free individual the absolute principle and completely rejected existing institutions as being based in superstition and hereditary principles (Hegel 1977, 355ff). However, it passed on its rational principles to other nations, particularly Germany, Napoleon being the 'world-historical' individual who brought this about. Napoleon's military victories in Europe brought about reforms in Germany, particularly the establishment of a constitutional monarchy. A code or rights was established, ensuring the freedom of the individual, abolishing feudal obligations and opening up state offices to talented citizens. The monarch remained as head of state, but the state now had firmly established laws, which it was the King's role to enforce.

History thus comes to an end in Hegel's own time and place, in the perhaps surprising form of the nineteenth-century Prussian state. This is a vision of history that gives history an overriding narrative, complete with a happy ending. History so construed is not unlike a film, to the extent that a film might offer a narrative in which everything that happens takes place in order to advance the protagonist's self-development. In Hegel's historical drama, there is only one protagonist, Spirit, the drama being its fall into self-alienation and eventual return to itself. Individual actors, pursuing their subjective passions and particular interests, may not be aware that their actions are contributing to the advancement of this larger narrative, but they are the unwitting means through which Spirit, the real subject of history, develops. Interestingly, for all his criticisms of the Hegelian account, Marx does not fundamentally depart from this model. He also thinks that there is an unfolding story, a developmental process, to be found in history, and one that is driven by a single protagonist. This process of development once again involves the protagonist undergoing self-alienation and returning to itself in a final reconciliation. But Marx does not think that history has come to an end quite yet; and more fundamentally, he objects to the way the protagonist is characterised by Hegel. He finds Hegel's picture to be inhuman in its emphasis on the activity of an abstract spiritual principle. As he puts it, with Hegel 'the history of humanity becomes the history of the *abstract spirit* of humanity, thus a spirit *beyond* actual man' (Marx 1967b, 382). Marx wants to restore the 'actual man'. He formulates a more realistic, down-to-earth, materialist conception of the collective human subject.

This is not a return to the crude Hobbesian idea of the human being. As we saw in Chapter Three, Hobbesian materialism reduces the human being to a natural object, propelled by desires, striving to survive at the expense of others. Since Hobbes, we have had the Kantian notion of the human being as an active, self-organising individual subject, itself expanded massively into Hegel's notion of Spirit. Marx offers a materialist version of this expanded subjectivity. The subject's activity is now understood as labour, concrete productive activity, undertaken not by an abstract spiritual agency but by living, breathing, desiring human beings. For Marx, human beings are distinguished from non-human animals precisely insofar as they engage in productive activity involving the use of tools. Hegel's subject thereby becomes the concrete human species, collective human- ity, what Marx in his early writings calls 'species-being', which works on nature, transforming it in order to produce the goods it needs to survive.

Marx's conception of history as a process of humanity's self-development builds on this materialist notion of the subject, while involving three phases famil- iar from Hegel's account of history: initial harmony, a phase of self-alienation and an ultimate reconciliation. To develop, humanity must go beyond an initial phase that Marx calls primitive communism. This is a classless but underdeveloped kind of society, in which human beings are largely subject to the pressures of external nature. To go beyond this, humanity must increase its productivity by establish- ing various forms of division of labour, hierarchical social arrangements to which individuals henceforth become subject. Hence, we have the various forms of class society that have arisen in the course of history: slavery, feudalism and most recently capitalism. These in turn determine the kinds of roles individuals can play within society, the relations they can participate in: Roman knight and slave, feudal lord and serf, bourgeois capitalist and modern worker. Capitalism, Marx recognises, is the most productive system in history, but it also introduces 'new conditions of oppression' (Marx and Engels 1972, 336), with the vast majority of people working under the direction of a small group of bosses or employers and subject to systematic exploitation in the name of profit.

Thus, although Marx puts a lot of emphasis on the way human beings are shaped and conditioned by the social relations they participate in, he also presup- poses an underlying notion of human nature, derived from Hegel, in which we are essentially communal beings with a fundamental need to engage in cooperative productive activity. It is of the essence of human beings so understood to be in con- trol of their activities, to collectively determine the conditions under which they work. This ethical ideal is not merely a feature of his earlier writing. As he puts it in the posthumously assembled third volume of Capital: 'Freedom, in this sphere, can consist only in this, that socialised man, the associated producers, govern the human metabolism with nature in a rational way, bringing it under their collec- tive control instead of being dominated by it as a blind power' (Marx 1991, 959). In achieving this state, no longer being subordinated to their own social arrange- ments, becoming the conscious rational authors of their historical process, the species will find self-realisation and fulfilment as human beings. In the form of the future communist society, this is the prospect that awaits human beings

The notion of humanity's essential nature in turn provides the normative basis for Marx's critique of existing capitalist society. Marx criticises the prevailing social and especially economic arrangements of his time as preventing people from living fulfilling, fully realised human lives. His critique of capitalism is thus ultimately an ethical critique. Not only is he outraged that in the modern indus- trial system, the most productive in history, those who performed the labour that made industry work lived in poverty, working under squalid conditions, while their overseers amassed vast fortunes. He criticises a more general situation in which human beings, who should be the authors of their way of life, have become subject to social and economic arrangements that they have produced through their own activity but which have taken on a life of their own. Not only are those lower down the social scale condemned to suffer oppression and exploitation, but even those higher up are confined to the role they have to play in the system. Overall, as Marx famously put it: 'Men make their own history, but they do not make it just as they please; they do not make it under circumstances chosen by themselves, but under circumstances directly found, given and transmitted from the past. The tradition of all the dead generations weighs like a nightmare on the brain of the living' (Marx 1972, 437).

As far as Marx is concerned, the various popular revolutions that occurred at the end of the eighteenth century, such as the French Revolution, might have freed people from oppressive feudal-era monarchies and brought in liberal, democratic governments, but the process of liberation has not gone far enough. It was political liberation, certainly, but not economic. The individuals who asserted their rights against royal power were primarily members of the emerging capitalist class. The revolution thus only served to free one class, the capitalists, to economically exploit the workers. But Marx was sure that the working class, increasingly exploited in order to produce ever-increasing profit for their capitalist overseers, was also going to be the agency that brings about the final liberation. For him, the next, truly liberating, step will be for human beings to overcome economic oppression as well, to overcome class society as such and take control of their existence. This is not a matter of the slaves taking the place of the masters, as in *The Admirable Crichton*. It will be the emancipation not of a particular class but of humanity as a whole; and it will result not in another class society but the classless communist society that brings history to a conclusion. Now, humanity will rationally organise its productive activity so that all will benefit. With the advent of socially organised production, individuals will cease to be the egoistic, competitive creatures required by capitalism, only out for what they can get for themselves. Instead, they will find their happiness and self-realisation in working cooperatively for the good of all (see Singer 2000, 81). In this way, via Hegel and Marx, Kant's notion of rational autonomy is developed into an ideal of total social liberation. Marx's vision of communist society can also be seen as a late development of the eighteenth-century Enlightenment's vision of an organisation of human life in accordance with reason.

Marx is insistent that progressive social change and liberation can only come through concerted action on the part of the workers, in keeping with the narrative of history as being driven by a collective human subject. This might be contrasted with the more familiar Hollywood scenario, which typically focuses on a few courageous individuals, 'heroes', setting society straight. In the most extreme case, it is the lone individual making a stand against a hostile social environment, as in *High Noon*. This is in keeping with a more individualistic perspective on society. In contrast, individual actions and motives are almost entirely neglected in Eisenstein's *October* (1927). The film is a documentary-style recounting of the build-up to the 1917 Russian revolution through which the Romanov monarchy was overthrown. The film ends filled with hope for a future in which class society has been definitively overcome in favour of the classless communist society. Deliberately, on Marxist principle, Eisenstein rejects the narrative form in which the individual protagonist, the 'bourgeois individual', drives the plot. In *October*, there are no individual characters, psychological insights or traditional plotting. Through Eisenstein's editing, it is 'the people' who come to the fore as the drivers of the historical process, the crowd as 'revolutionary mass' that changes the course of history. The people are the main character in Eisenstein's story, which features impressive crowd scenes: people pouring into the squares of St Petersburg, surging through the streets, streaming into the Czar's Winter Palace. The soundtrack has no dialogue, only the roar of crowds and the sounds of marching.

Let us turn to a closer examination of Marx's critique of existing society. Social and economic arrangements are to be criticised here insofar as they stand in the way of the realisation of species-being, and prevent people from fulfilling their essential nature, collectively controlling their social existence, living truly human lives. Particularly in his early writings, Marx's critique focuses on the manner in which, under existing arrangements, people, especially wage labourers, are alienated from their species-being (Marx 1967a, 290ff). Under the prevailing capitalist organisation of labour, workers are alienated from their fellow beings, because they work in separation from other workers. They are also alienated from the product of their labour, since they don't produce for themselves, for their own human needs, but for an employer who appropriates what they produce and sells it for profit. Above all they are deprived of control over their productive activity, since they labour under the control of the employer for whom they are merely means to the end of profit-making.

Marx's account of alienation is formulated in the particular historical context of the harshly exploitative conditions of late nineteenth-century industrial society. Something of this harshness is still evident in *Matewan* (John Sayles, 1987), the story of labour struggles in the coal-mining industry in Matewan, West Virginia, in 1920. In its portrayal of the dire conditions that led to the 'Battle of Matewan', a famous coal miner's strike, the various dimensions of worker alienation are laid bare. Under conditions of extreme exploitation, the workers have minimal control over their productive activity. The coal company owns not only their labour but also the land and their homes. They are alienated from the products of their labour, the coal they dig up, which is sold by the company for profit. In order to maximise that profit, the workers are paid the least wage possible and live in terrible poverty. The company owners strive to keep the workers separate, working against their attempts to form a united front and take collective strike action. Italian immigrant workers are encouraged to continue working, and the company brings in black workers as well.

On Marx's account, not only are people directly prevented from living fulfilling lives by their material circumstances. Their circumstances also promote forms of ideological thinking, distorted ways of understanding the world in which they no longer recognise that they are being oppressed, that their real interests are being denied under existing social arrangements and which serve to justify and legitimate those arrangements. Marx's concern with ideology is a continuation of the Enlightenment concern with the questioning of dogmatic religious or superstitious beliefs used to justify existing social and political practices. It is also an acknowledgement that oppression can work not just by imposing external constraints on what we can do, but also promoting forms of understanding that make us content with or resigned to our existing situation.

Religion itself, for Marx, is a distorted reflection of material conditions, promising that there will be salvation from the misery and suffering of this world in an afterlife, where people will be rewarded for their hard work and virtue. It thus provides a substitute for the happiness that is denied in this world. This is not, however, to entirely dismiss religious thinking. It gives expression to genuine human desires and aspirations; but it does so in the distorted form of the vision of a future paradise, and in this form, it can also be used to perpetuate existing, oppressive social and economic arrangements, discouraging any attempt to change things in the here and now. In *Matewan*, both aspects of religious thinking are evident. The older preacher (played by director John Sayles) is loyal to the company, and in his sermons portrays union activity, and indeed, Marxism as such, as inspired by the devil: 'The prince of darkness is in the land ... his name is Bolshevist, Socialist, Union Man, Communist'. At the same time, the boy preacher (Will Oldham) is able to see in the religious language the genuine human aspirations it embodies and to even find biblical justification for the actions of the strikers.

Ideological thinking also obscures the economic oppression that persists despite the popular revolutions at the end of the eighteenth century. It might appear that society is now liberated from oppression, and that workers freely enter into contractual relationships with their employers, but the reality this thinking conceals is that the two parties differ enormously in economic power, and that the only alternative for the worker, who does not have access to the means of production, is starvation. It is hardly a level playing field. In addition, the modern liberal democratic state might present itself as acting in the interests of all individuals in society, but in fact it only acts in the interests of the economically powerful class. This reality is concealed by the language of liberty, equal rights and the consent of the governed, which for Marx are all features of 'bourgeois ideology'. Once again, Marx is not simply dismissing the ideological thinking. He is not rejecting the ideals of liberation and equality inherent in bourgeois ideology. They represent genuine human aspirations, but they are being given distorted expression, and employed, perversely, in the service of continuing oppression and inequality.

From the Marxist perspective, dominated by its conception of human nature as essentially communal, the egoistic individualism that emerged with Hobbes and passes into liberal thinking comes into question. On this view, there is nothing natural about Hobbes's egoistic, self-interested human beings, locked in brutal competition with one another. For Marx, the Hobbesian individual is already a social product, a character that only arises in modern capitalist society. In this society, those in the role of capitalist are compelled to compete with one another for profit, which they can only maximise by extracting as much as possible from their workers, keeping wages low and hours long. In this framework, we can locate the movie gangster who epitomises the ruthless pursuit of self-interest. The gangster, who typically starts at the lower end of the social scale, knows very well that capitalism depends on keeping the workers in their place and that the law and order system only serves the interests of the economically powerful class. They seek to escape from the miseries of wage slavery through criminal activity, playing 'outside the rules' that are stacked against them. They have no desire to change society; they simply want to acquire the obscene riches enjoyed by the upper stratum. This is where *Scarface*'s Tony Montana ends up, in his garishly luxurious mansion, in what might be the biggest bathtub in movie history. For those who survive the downfall that inevitably follows their ascent, the worst thing about their fallen condition, as *Goodfella*'s Henry Hill attests, is that they are now 'average nobodies' who have to wait around like everyone else.

In this framework, it is also possible to locate characters at the other end of the scale, like Gordon Gekko in *Wall Street*. His 'greed is good' speech, an explicit endorsement of a life of egoistic self-interest, couched in the idea that greed leads not only to individual progress, but human progress and enrichment more generally, now appears as an ideological cover for capitalist exploitation. The reality is that only a few, like Gekko, will be enriched. Even Gekko seems to acknowledge the spuriousness of what he is saying, grinning conspiratorially to his protégé Bud Fox (Charlie Sheen) as he sits down after the speech. *Wolf of Wall Street*'s Belfort does not even bother offering a moral justification for his activities. He represents pure self-interest, with an almost psychopathic indifference to those he exploits to make his cash. Moral concerns are for losers and excess is its own reward. His conspiratorial grin is to the audience, the implication of his behaviour being that he imagines anyone watching would want to be in his shoes. Psychopathic indifference to others normally makes the perpetrator unsympathetic, and Belfort certainly does some terrible things, but the film also makes being him seem like a lot of fun. The film's final shot literally turns to an audience, a sea of faces listening intently to one of Belfort's post-imprisonment seminars on how to get rich. Director Scorsese avoids any moral comment on Belfort's behaviour to allow the audience to think about how far they themselves might buy into Belfort's way of thinking. This is a departure from the more traditional approach where the egoistic individual is the villain of the piece, as in *Wall Street*. That is a strategy that can backfire, as it did when the Gekko character became something of a hero to the real high flyers on Wall Street.

At the same time, for many Marxist analysts of 'late capitalism', the pressure of competition has meant that the individual capitalist or entrepreneur of the nineteenth century has largely come to be replaced by the powerful corporation in the twentieth (see e.g., Horkheimer 1974, 140–141). As the documentary *The Corporation* points out, the modern corporation exhibits many of the traits of what is popularly considered psychopathy but which we can also identify as extreme egoism on an institutional level. The corporation is self-interested, deceitful, callous and without guilt, willing to break social rules for its own ends. Its own employees are disposable instruments for its purposes, which is above all the pursuit of profit at any cost to others. Capitalism continues to prevail, and the corporation continues to make its presence felt as psychopathic villain, in the future world of *Alien*. The Weyland-Yutani corporation is happy to sacrifice the crew members of its space vessel *Nostromo* in order to acquire the dangerous alien life-form, which promises to inspire weaponry that can be sold to the military. As Alejandro Barcenas points out, it is fitting that the 'company man' aboard the ship, the android Ash (Ian Holm) is an android. He is the face of the company, concerned only with furthering the company's interests, without conscience or remorse. It is as if only someone who is not a human being could behave that way (see Barcenas 2017, 52–53). The corporation is also the main villain of the future in *Blade Runner*, in the form of the Tyrell corporation, the main product of which is the replicants, the bioengineered androids that are being manufactured for use as slave labour.

The Marxist account also provides a framework for thinking about modern consumerism. In some interpretations, Hobbes's notion of human nature already points toward a consumerist society. Hobbes envisages, as natural, a creature of endless appetite and desire, just the kind of 'infinite consumer' needed for the new capitalist economy (see Macpherson 1962; Sembou 2013, 12). This unbridled appetite is not only manifested in the conspicuous consumption of the well-off, on display in films of excess like *The Wolf of Wall Street*. There is also the more general consumer culture into which, arguably, workers were increasingly co-opted in the course of the twentieth century. Twentieth-century Marxists like Herbert Marcuse (1898–1979) argue that workers have been increasingly reconciled to a system that remains opposed to their real interests, being encouraged to want more and more of the things that the system produces. This is by way especially of the media and advertising, implanting 'false needs' into the population in what amounts to an intensification of ideological indoctrination. Not only does this leave the workers content with their situation, their needs seemingly satisfied. It also means that the system of production can be ramped up to produce yet more commodities to be sold for profit, rather than to satisfy real human needs. And the workers are more than ever under pressure to sell their labour to the capitalist, to be able to pay for the commodities they are being encouraged to buy (see Marcuse 1969). This represents a new form of alienation, in which the consumer has everything they could want, but are estranged from their real interests in the process. This is no longer the grim world of nineteenth-century industry that Marx knew. It is an altogether more comfortable existence, but an alienated, inhuman one nonetheless.

Marcuse himself makes a film appearance in *Hail Caesar!* (Joel and Ethan Coen, 2016), the Coen Brother's light comedy about fifties Hollywood. Dim-witted movie star Baird Whitlock (George Clooney) is kidnapped from the set of the *Ben-Hur*-like biblical epic *Hail Caesar! A Tale of the Christ*. His abductors are communist screenwriters, an allusion to figures like *High Noon*'s screenwriter Carl Foreman who were at the centre of Hollywood's anti-communist witch-hunts in the fifties. Amongst the group is Marcuse (played as a stereotypical German professor by John Bluthal). The screenwriters explain that they had formerly contented themselves with 'planting communist propaganda in Hollywood films', until 'Dr Marcuse inspired them to take direct action'. Baird is quickly converted to their critique of the movie industry as an exploitative industry that uses its employees to generate profits for top studio bosses, and makes pictures to 'confirm what they call the "status quo"'. Once rescued from his rather inept kidnappers, Baird makes the mistake of relating this newfound insight to studio head Eddie Mannix (Josh Brolin), who slaps him into submission and sends him back to finish the biblical epic.

The film does not go into details regarding this Marxist analysis of the film industry. However, particularly by referencing Marcuse, it does indirectly allude to twentieth-century Marxism's move beyond the traditional focus on the economic and into the analysis of media, advertising and popular culture. This development was pioneered by Marcuse along with other members of the Frankfurt School, such as Max Horkheimer (1895–1973) and Theodor Adorno (1903–1969). As just indicated, their argument is that the popular culture disseminated through the modern mass communications media, including films, television, radio and magazines, represents a new and powerful form of ideological indoctrination. The products of this 'culture industry', the term coined in Horkheimer and Adorno's *Dialectic of Enlightenment*, serve to keep people compliant and uncritical, regardless of their economic circumstances, and help cultivate the false needs that keep people participating in the existing system of capitalist production (see Horkheimer and Adorno 1979, 120ff; Marcuse 1991).

In the face of this somewhat pessimistic analysis, it is worth noting that *Hail Caesar!* points towards the capacity of film to do more than confirm what they call the status quo' or reproduce prevailing views. For the more extreme Marxist cultural theory of the sixties and seventies, no doubt inspired by the Frankfurt School analyses, film does no more than reproduce and inculcate prevailing ways of thinking. All films are forms of 'bourgeois illusionism', their content entirely determined by the dominant ideology of the time. Cinema was condemned in its totality as no more than a means of indoctrination, seducing audiences into accepting as reality what were mere ideological representations. But this ignores the capacity of film to not only portray and promote forms of thinking and practices but also to reflect on and challenge them (see Stam 2000, 139; Wilson 1986, 13). In its own comedic way, *Hail Caesar!* does precisely this. Through humour, it critically distances itself from the film industry it is portraying, the industry producing the genre films that it also lovingly recreates. It also makes gentle fun of the film's communist critics, the screenwriters, who are portrayed as bumbling fools, even though the film seems broadly in sympathy with the kind of criticisms they are espousing.

Not without humour itself, David Fincher's *Fight Club* offers a critique of late twentieth-century capitalist society from a number of perspectives, with some Marxist sentiments in evidence. The criticisms throughout the film are delivered by the irrepressibly rebellious Tyler Durden, who has appeared seemingly out of nowhere to shake up the life of the film's narrator. The narrator, a car recall specialist for a '*major* manufacturer', lives in an upmarket apartment filled with the expensive consumer choices through which he defines himself. Though comfortable, he is fundamentally dissatisfied with his life, suffering a profound alienation from his potential. The film in essence follows his repudiation of that life and the society that sustains it. Durden, the means of the narrator's escape, often speaks in Marxist-sounding terms of the emptiness of the modern work-place and the consumerist lifestyle. He refers to the squandered potential of 'an entire generation pumping gas, waiting tables, slaves with white collars'; and the false needs imposed through advertising, which 'has us chasing cars and clothes, working jobs we hate so we can buy shit we don't need'. Durden is interested not simply in opting out of this system, but increasingly, in disrupting and destroying it, with a particular focus on overthrowing the existing economic structure. His target at the end of the film is the credit card companies, which have been selected as key elements of the financial system. As he says to the narrator, before a vista of the city skyline, with the destruction of all the credit card company buildings imminent: 'Out these windows, we will view the collapse of financial history'.

However, *Fight Club* cannot be summed up as offering a Marxist critique of society. At other times, the film comes across as the critique of a civilised exist-ence that deadens individuals to their natural drives. The Fight Clubs established by Durden and the narrator can be seen as ways for men to get back in touch with their basic instincts through ritualised fist-fights. Thus, although the film diag-noses a form of alienation in modern society, what human beings are held to be alienated from are their natural instincts for competition and violence. Civilised life requires these instincts to be suppressed or domesticated, leaving human beings as weakened, pathetic creatures like the narrator. Rather than anything like Marx's species-being, the notion of human nature implied here seems closer to Hobbes's instinctively-driven individual. As such, the Fight Clubs represent a partial reversion to the state of nature. They do not go all the way, since they have rules designed to set limits to the extent participants can hurt one another. But within these limits, the participants are able to escape social constraints and give expression to their natural selves. At the same time, if *Fight Club* can be seen as presenting a picture of rebellion as the unleashing of the natural self, it is not clear that it is endorsing this. Durden may laud the member of the Fight Club stand-ing around him as 'the strongest and smartest men who've ever lived', but this is undercut insofar as the men standing around him are an oafish bunch, unimpres-sive in the extreme.

Another way Durden might be thought to be departing from an orthodox Marxist position is that his rebellion against society does not seem to be con-nected to a politics concerned with the overcoming of broader forms of power and exploitation, through collective action, or with a view to establishing a demo-cratically organised society, a meaningful alternative to the present (see Giroux 2006). Instead, Durden's Fight Clubs mutate into 'Project Mayhem', a movement dedicated only to the destruction of society, through acts of corporate vandal-ism that culminate in the attempt to bring down the financial system. The idea behind this seems to be that by destroying society, people will revert to a more natural, hunter-gatherer mode of existence. However, it is not clear that the film is endorsing this form of rebellion either. It is clear that Project Mayhem, a project of liberation from social constraints, suffers from the most repressive authoritarianism. As a movement characterised by rigid hierarchy under a charismatic leader, the political alternative it is presenting seems closest to fascism. And far from reconnecting with their natural selves, the Fight Club members, once they have been incorporated into Project Mayhem, completely lose their individuality. Stripped of their names, they are reduced to wearing identical clothing and chanting slogans in unison. If anything, the film is warning that movements of rebellion can generate their own forms of oppression.

To return to Marxism, there are a number of issues that arise in connection with Marxist thinking. One concerns the characteristic Marxist focus on the economic dimension of life. Marxism certainly goes beyond the liberal view that the primary social reality individuals have to contend with is society's political organisation, in which the state exercises power over its citizens. On that understanding, the main concern is that state power should not exceed its proper limits and violate individual rights. As long as there is a relatively liberal form of government that respects individual rights, people will be free of oppression. The Marxist account holds that to properly understand our social circumstances we need to look at the economic relations between rich and poor, employers and employees, of which Marx provides a trenchant analysis. A politically liberal society can coexist with economic oppression and exploitation. However, Marxism is arguably limited in making the economic relation the only significant one and trying to explain all other social relations in terms of it. In doing so it neglects, or fails to properly address, non-economic relationships in society.

For example, it is not clear that Marxism can properly address gender relations, another dimension of social life that is often characterised by forms of oppression. This sort of oppression is not only to be found in the workplace, to the extent that women might be confined to lowly paid jobs, or excluded altogether from the workforce, but also in social relations that are removed from the workplace, in family and sexual relations. As such, feminist concerns are not always well served by an analysis that focuses so closely on the economy. It is interesting to note that while the coalminers in *Matewan* struggle to improve their working conditions, the women in the film remain marginal, and their situation goes unaddressed (see Reiser 2006). When the heroic union organiser Joe Kenehan (Chris Cooper) urges the miners to overcome the racial divisions fomented by the coal company, and unite, he tells them 'you know there ain't but two sides in the world – them that work and them that don't. You work. They don't. That's all you got to know about the enemy'. In other words, the only significant division in society is between the capitalists and the workers. There is no mention of the division between men and women (see Reiser 2006).

Feminist concerns do not appear to be well-served by *Fight Club* either, at least at first glance. The Fight Clubs that represent a rebellion against consumer society exclude women and feature hyper-masculine displays of aggression. This suggests another interpretation of the rebellion portrayed in the film, that it is a male response to a culture that has undermined traditional male identity, leading to a 'crisis of masculinity'. The 'manly' worker of old has come to be replaced by the 'emasculated' yuppie consumer of the present. The 'real man', with his instincts for competition and violence, has been replaced by men like the physically unimposing narrator, the white-collar type who surrounds himself with expensive design objects. So viewed, the film is about the fall of masculinity and the need to reclaim it. Men are able to reconnect with this masculinity through Fight Club. It is the identity that the members of Fight Club affirm in one another, congratulating one another after their bouts. On this understanding, the film is quite regressive in feminist terms, since the masculinity that it promotes is old-fashioned and misogynistic (see Giroux 2006). However, this may be once again to identify the film too closely with Durden's point of view. As mentioned, though Durden lauds the Fight Club participants, they are not particularly impressive specimens and they become even more pathetic when they are converted into the robotic followers of Durden's terrorist army.

That those rebelling against society might establish their own repressive conformity brings us to a second issue regarding Marxist thought, the possibility that Marxist thinking, though dedicated to opposing social oppression, might itself make possible new forms of oppression. The danger arises with Marxism in particular because of its notion of real interests, said to be denied under capitalism. The first question that arises is, how can we be sure what people's real interests are, especially if oppression can take the form not just of imposing external barriers to the realisation of one's interests, but falsifying one's very understanding of what those desires and interests are? If so, we cannot rely on what people themselves say their real interests are. Marx grounded his notion of real interests not on what individuals themselves considered to be their interests, but on a philosophical and moral view of human nature, definitive of what it is to be human. This is the notion of human nature that emerges in Kant, and develops via Hegel, before being appropriated by Marx in the form of species-being. A problem is that such notions are hard to verify. If a philosopher comes up with a conception of human nature, and how human beings accordingly ought to behave, how do we know this isn't simply a prejudice on the philosopher's part? It is true that Marx's position wasn't entirely without reference to experience. In the nineteenth century there was empirical evidence of the discontent of workers with their situation, including strikes and machine-breaking. So Marx could claim that his normative conception of human nature had some empirical support. Still, it does go considerably beyond what might be justified in terms of the behaviour observed.

Moreover, notions of essential human nature and real interests may themselves be instrumental in the exercise of forms of power. This brings us back to Isaiah Berlin, who as we saw earlier, argued against what he calls positive notions of freedom. Freedom here involves not merely being free from external constraints and obstacles to what one wants to do but acting in accordance with one's true nature or real interests. Berlin argued that such notions of freedom, turning on the idea of one's real interests, need to be rejected because they can very easily become a licence for paternalistic tyranny. If others can claim to know what your real interests are, and that you do not recognise them as such because you are suffering from some form of 'false consciousness', they can justify bullying and coercing you into doing things, all in the name of your supposed real interests. And to the extent that acting in accordance with your real interests amounts to being free, those coercing you in this manner can claim to be liberating you. Talk of real interests can also provide a justification for subjecting those who are not pursuing the right sorts of interests to forms of retraining and rehabilitation, all in the name of their freedom, their liberation from enslavement to false wants.

The danger of oppression under the guise of liberation might be seen to be lurking in the *Pygmalion* scenario. Higgins can justify imposing his strict regime upon Eliza, bullying and coercing her into behaving like a 'proper lady', by claiming that he is doing so in her real interests. To return to the language of John Stuart Mill, he can claim to be encouraging her to pursue the higher pleasures that most befit her nature as a human being. As it happens, Eliza does find that she prefers the higher pleasures of Higgins and his circle, to the lower pleasures of her former working-class life; and for John Stuart Mill, what people find they actually prefer, having experienced a range of pleasures, provides an empirical criterion for what counts as their real interests. The complicating factor that Marxism introduces is the idea of false consciousness, which means that people's actual preferences are no longer a decisive argument for what is in their real interests. Appealing to a notion of human nature, as Marxism does, means that it is no longer necessary to refer to people's actual preferences in order to identify what their real interests are. This, however, seems to open the possibility of the kind of coercion that Berlin describes. Rita, the latter-day Eliza in *Educating Rita*, might seek to better herself by pursuing the higher pleasures of literature, poetry and so on, but it is easy to imagine a Higgins of a more Marxist persuasion subjecting her to a strict regime of retraining in order to cure her of these 'bourgeois tendencies'.

For Berlin, the positive notion of freedom that he wants to call into question can be found in Kant, Hegel and Marx. And most significantly, he thinks that it can be found in the communism that arose in Russia after Marx's death, which drew on some of the elements of Marx's thought in order to fashion its official ideology. Here, Berlin argues, the Marxist thinking that looked to the liberation of humanity becomes instrumental in state oppression, in the justification of totalitarianism. The communist state can claim to represent the individual's true self, a communal entity, and as such, to be entitled to impose its will on individuals in the name of their real interests. It is also entitled to ignore their own wishes, since they may not recognise their real interests and can even set about forcibly re-educating them so they come to realise where their true interests lie. And in all this, given its positive notion of freedom, it can claim to be liberating them. It is the Orwellian nightmare in which freedom is slavery. Berlin wants nothing to do with this pernicious notion of freedom. Better, he argues to define freedom in purely negative terms, as the absence of external obstacles to what we want to do. This is also an appropriate notion of freedom for the liberal individualism that Berlin wants to defend, in the face of totalitarian communism. The liberal political thinking that makes central the defence of the individual from external interference, and sees the main justification for government in its role in protecting individual rights, is best served by a purely negative idea of freedom.

However, a complete rejection of positive freedom, as complicit in totalitarian oppression, is in danger of throwing out the baby with the bathwater. It forgets that Kant's notion of autonomy, while undoubtedly providing a basis for pictures of collective self-determination in which the individual must submit to the whole, also represents a powerful formulation of the liberal ideal, and a justification for its defence of the individual from external interference. In Kant's account, rational autonomy is first and foremost the individual's capacity to give shape to their existence and individuals should be respected as the originators of their own life plan. (see Taylor 1985b, 337). Indeed, one common argument as to why individuals are owed rights is that they are rational, autonomous beings. Rights function to not only morally shield individuals from the interference of others, but also to secure for them an area of personal liberty where they can develop and pursue their own life-plans and give shape to their existence. In respecting someone's rights, you respect their personhood. A further advantage of construing the idea of individual freedom in terms of rational self-determination in the political context is that it can take into account not only overt coercion and constraint but also more insidious forms of manipulation, such as advertising and propaganda. Through deception, withholding information, or presenting it in a selective way, these forms of manipulation can limit the individual's capacity to make informed decisions as to how to act.

But while we may have returned to the notion of Kantian autonomy, the problems indicated in the previous section remain. On the Kantian account, behaving morally, rationally determining oneself, requires the exclusion or repression of desire, inclination and emotion. The self becomes a battleground in which reason is constantly at odds with feeling and instinct. Furthermore, this is a picture in which the rational subject is conceived of as abstractly isolated, implausibly independent of all social relationships, cultural traditions and historical circumstances. Marx represents one attempt to address these problems in Kant's account, to bring the Kantian subject down to earth. For a more recent take on Kantian ethics that seeks to address these problems, we can turn to the work of the contemporary thinker Habermas.

Habermas and Discourse Ethics

As we have seen, Marx rejects Kant's abstractly isolated rational subject, in favour of a subject that is socially and historically located; but at the same time, he wants to preserve the ideal of total rational self-determination, envisaging human beings as capable of exercising collective control over their social and historical existence in a classless society. A more recent version of Kantian ethics writ large can be found in the discourse ethics of Jurgen Habermas (1929–). Habermas works in the Marxist tradition in seeing human beings as having to engage in work or productive activity. Through productive activity, which he understands to be bound up with the development of scientific knowledge and its application in technology, societies increasingly come to master external nature. However, Habermas, steeped in the critical Marxism of the Frankfurt School, departs from Marx in his view that human activity cannot be understood solely in terms of work on nature. That is only one dimension of human existence. Human beings also, and indeed most distinctively, engage in communicative activity. They speak to one another, engage in discourse. This is the realm of social relations, understood as communicative relations between speaking subjects, interpersonal relations regulated by moral norms.

In this, Habermas still looks to the Kantian ideal of rational self-determination. Indeed, rational autonomy is the fundamental value that orients his project. Following on from Marx, the genuinely rational society for Habermas will be the one in which human beings freely and collectively determine their social existence. However, this ideal is now to be understood in communicative terms. Collective self-determination now means individuals engaging in an open, unconstrained, society-wide dialogue about the proper form that society should take, the norms it should adhere to and the goals it should pursue. As Habermas puts it in *Knowledge and Human Interests*, the ideal is 'an organisation of social relations according to the principle that the validity of every norm of political consequence be made dependent on a consensus arrived at in communication free from domination' (Habermas 1972, 284). In *Toward a Rational Society*, he speaks of there ideally being a 'dialectic of potential and will' in which norms and goals established through discourse will govern the development of productive processes, the technical mastery of nature and will in turn be brought into line with the technical possibilities for their realisation (see Habermas 1971, 61).

In this vision of an open, society-wide discourse, Habermas moves beyond the abstractly isolated, self-contained Kantian subject, while preserving the ideal of rational autonomy. Kant's autonomous rational subject becomes the community of speaking subjects, engaged in discussion and reflection. The general formula that Kant gives for being moral, the categorical imperative, is also likewise transformed. For Kant, the formula is that one should 'act only according to that maxim by which you can at the same time will that it should become a universal law', but for Kant it is a solitary reflecting self that has to determine whether a principle is universalisable. If there is agreement with other rational subjects, it is only insofar as they independently come to the same conclusions. In Habermas's Kantian discourse ethics, however, whether a norm is universalisable is decided through actual agreement, rational consensus amongst the community of speaking subjects. The general formula for morality is now to act only in accordance with those principles that all involved in the discussion can agree to be a universal norm (see McCarthy 1978, 325–329).

Habermas also moves away from Kant's exclusion of desire and interest from the realm of moral consideration. In his account, we are emphatically creatures with needs, wants and desires. The process of socialisation, through which one becomes a responsible moral subject, is one of learning to live in society by adapting our needs and desires to social life via its shared moral norms, the normative structures of communication. Through these norms, needs are interpreted and actions are licenced or prohibited. By internalising these norms, we acquire a moral identity or framework in terms of which to evaluate our wants and desires, make decisions and so on. The satisfaction of desires in society is thus regulated by social norms; but equally, the collective rational discussion Habermas envisages is about what norms to have in the light of our desires and interests, about how to organise society to best realise them. Through collective discussion we are able to articulate our needs and interests, and in the light of them, to agree on the proper values and goals we as a society should pursue. So for Habermas, in contrast to Kant, the individual's needs, wants or desires cannot be excluded from the discussion, as it is concerning them that agreement is sought. The discussion is about which desires and interests are merely particular to individuals, and which are common to all and thus able to be a basis for general norms or universal principles.

On this account, oppressive social arrangements, forms of social domination, are understood to limit people's ability to satisfy their desires and interests. This constraint does not however come about through overt force but through the exclusion of desires and interests from open communication. This is Habermas's version of the Marxist notion of ideology. Individuals are no longer able to talk about or reflect on their own desires. Nonetheless, these supressed desires make their presence known in wish-fulfilling fantasies, religious worldviews and ethical systems, which then provide the basis for ideological interpretations of the world that can be used to justify the existing, oppressive social arrangements. For example, religious fantasies of ultimate gratification in the next world can be used to legitimate social inequality in this one. In this way, power interrupts open communication and individuals are cut off from their own desires. Liberation from such power involves the critical reflection that overcomes blockages to communication, freeing desires and needs from their fusion with ideological legitimation so that they can inform an open discussion about the proper shape of society. As a result, instead of an ideological justification of oppressive social arrangements, we will have an organisation of society in terms of rational, collectively agreed-to norms. Institutions based on power and ideological mystification will be replaced by 'an organization of social relations that is bound only to communication free from domination' (Habermas 1972, 53).

For Habermas however, the current situation is one in which ideological mystification dominates; and in particular, a new kind of ideology has arisen that involves repressing not particular desires and interests but the very idea of human beings as speaking subjects, the whole dimension of communicative interaction. For Habermas, even bourgeois ideology, which promises that relations between employer and employee will be just, free of domination and mutually satisfactory, embodies an ethical ideal that gives expression to repressed desires and aspirations. In the new ideology, there is no less than 'the repression of "ethics" as such as a category of life' (Habermas 1971, 112). Human life is increasingly viewed in terms of the categories appropriate to the dimension of work, of productive activity alone. This is the realm of society's interaction with non-human nature, with things, which human beings seek to control, the world known by natural science and manipulated through technology. The rationality appropriate to this realm is the calculative, means-end thinking that organises things as instruments in order to control and make use of them.

Like Kant, Habermas firmly distinguishes between a rationality that formulates goals, and the technical, means-end rationality appropriate to things. For him, the distinctively modern problem is that the instrumental way of viewing the world, means-end rationality, is also increasingly being applied to the social realm. Technological thinking thus becomes a 'technocratic ideology', a distorted view of the world that blinds us to the distinctive character of interpersonal relations, where collective discussion and consensus should rule. By presenting all social questions as technical questions that only expert administrators can solve, this way of thinking justifies the concentration of social power in the hands of technocrats and bureaucrats, who are to provide the administration and organisation required for society to function most efficiently. The idea that people should govern themselves through discussion and consensus, institutionalised as democracy, remains but only as a façade. In reality, we are only free to choose between different representatives of the same administrative–bureaucratic apparatus.

Ironically, this technocratic vision is similar to the technocratic ideal of social administration envisaged by many of the enlightenment figures prior to Kant, who identified rationality with natural science. For Kant, as we have seen, a scientific understanding applied to human beings undermined the Enlightenment's own ideal of making reason the principal guide to conduct, reducing the human being to a machine driven by its desires. To preserve the Enlightenment ideal, he insisted that human beings are not just creatures of desire but also, and more importantly, rational subjects capable of determining the right thing to do. For Habermas, the Enlightenment ideal is similarly undermined by technocratic ideology. In treating social problems as technical ones, and human beings as objects of bureaucratic management, it stands in the way of the possibility of politics as public discussion of practical goals, the Kantian ideal of rational autonomy rendered in communicative terms as collective, democratic will-formation. Instead, it supports a powerful bureaucratic elite that administers society without consulting the wider population. Habermas, like Kant, wants to rescue the Enlightenment ideal of a rational society, and to do so by reminding us that we are not just objects of bureaucratic management but rational, speaking subjects, capable of collectively shaping our social existence through domination-free communication.

This perspective allows another take on the dystopian *Fahrenheit 451*, in which books have been outlawed, as dangerous items liable to provoke people to think about their situation and to make them unhappy and anti-social. In this world, the firemen are part of the state's administrative apparatus, their main role being to find the libraries of dissidents who keep secret libraries and burn them. The Fire Chief (Cyril Cusack) takes a particular delight in burning the philosophy books, which are 'even worse than the novels' in this regard. Of course, *Fahrenheit 451* alludes in part to censorship and book-burning, direct ways in which political power strives to block free speech, discourse and reflection. These are the crude weapons of a totalitarian state and both the film and the book on which it is based have as a reference point the practices of Nazism and totalitarian communism. But the film can also be seen as pointing to the impoverishment of a life in which the dimension of communication has been occluded. Banished are the literary productions that give expression to the inner life of needs, emotion and feelings, as well as philosophical and ethical discussions of the meaning and purpose of life. In the film, a world in which people speak, discuss and critically reflect on the goals of life has been replaced by a managed, engineered society. Language features only as televised propaganda and entertainment designed to keep the population pacified and compliant. It is no more than an instrument for conditioning and tranquilising individuals and ensuring social order.

Truffaut's film appeared a year after Jean-Luc Godard's *Alphaville* (1965), which offered an even more extreme vision of the 'technical society' as the backdrop for the strange adventure of its hero Lemmy Caution (Eddie Constantine). The improbably-named intergalactic agent, straight out of film noir, visits a society run by the computer Alpha 60, the ultimate technocrat, along rigorously scientific lines. Everyone has their allotted function in the system, right down to the 'Seductress Grade 3' that greets the guests arriving at the hotel. Dickson (Akim Tamiroff), the agent whose disappearance in Alphaville prompted Caution's rescue mission, informs him that 'Alphaville is a technocracy, like that of termites and ants'. Moreover, 'one hundred and fifty light years ago ... there were artists in the ant society. Yes, artists, novelists, musicians, painters. Today, no more'. The exclusion of non-technical communication is more or less complete. Alphaville's chief literary product is now 'the Bible', a dictionary in which any words liable to provoke emotions and disturb the population are being progressively removed. In this story, humanist literary culture triumphs over technocratic administration. Caution defeats Alpha 60 by turning to poetry, which utterly baffles the computer and brings about its breakdown.

Along with the rise of technocratic administration, Habermas also notes the spread of forms of direct technological manipulation into social life. Technological forms of control, from 'psychotechnic' conditioning and modification, all the way up to 'biotechnic' genetic intervention and control, look towards literally engineering human beings. For Habermas, these forms of technological manipulation bypass communication relations with speaking subjects altogether, in favour of the direct manipulation of human beings as objects (Habermas 1971, 107, 117–118). Habermas is not denying that human beings are biological beings, able to be so manipulated, but he remains committed to the idea that as moral subjects, developing in a communications framework, they are more than just biological beings. The concern here is entirely Kantian. No objection to such manipulation arises from a utilitarian perspective, provided the result of it is an overall increase in human happiness and well-being. On that view, human beings are primarily means to the end of producing happiness. Utilitarian rationality is precisely the calculative, instrumental, means-end kind that is in question in Habermas's picture as an appropriate way of thinking about human beings.

Utilitarian thinking has certainly been in evidence in recent moral arguments for genetic enhancement. It has been argued that one should employ this technology to ensure that one's offspring will have the best, happiest life, and that failure to do so, if it is available, is a form of neglect (Suvalescu 2009, 420). More generally, it is argued that genetic intervention will lead to 'better people', more intelligent, but also 'longer-lived, stronger, happier, smarter, fairer (in the aesthetic and in the ethical sense of that term)' (Harris 2007, 5). Through such intervention, advocates argue, we are taking conscious control of our evolution in order to improve ourselves. In this we can see, ultimately, another expression of the eighteenth-century Enlightenment's vision of rationally organising human life, at least along the lines of the Enlightenment's technocratic project of improving human existence through science and technology. As we might expect, Habermas, whose starting point is the Kantian reformulation of the Enlightenment vision in terms of the ideal of rational autonomy, has a somewhat different view. In a recent book, *The Future of Human Nature*, he argues that interventions aiming at enhancement violate the fundamental status of persons as autonomous beings, preventing the enhanced person from 'being the undivided author of his own life' (Habermas 2003, 63). It undermines their autonomy by taking away the capacity to choose their own way of life. The proper form of human development is through communicative exchanges and mutual interactions with other human beings; and only through these social interactions do we develop into autonomous subjects.

The technological manipulation of human beings, and its implications for human autonomy, provide underlying themes for a film like *Eternal Sunshine of the Spotless Mind* (Michel Gondry, 2004, written by Charlie Kaufmann). In the film, Joel (Jim Carrey) finds that his ex-girlfriend Clementine (Kate Winslet) has gone to the memory-removal company Lacuna Inc. to have her memories of their relationship erased. Deeply unhappy at this development, he also goes to Lacuna, to have his memories of Clementine removed. The memory removal procedure is a piece of 'psychotechnic' manipulation, as Habermas might say, a direct technological manipulation of the human being as object. It is an intervention designed to enhance people's happiness by removing their painful memories; and this is an eminently sound thing to do from a utilitarian perspective, since it reduces the amount of misery in the world. But the film can be seen as implicitly questioning the utilitarian perspective. As Christopher Grau notes, the setup is in effect a 'reverse experience machine'. Instead of asking whether you would choose blissful experiences over truth, it poses the question of whether you would choose to lose memories, to falsify your past, if it would reduce pain. Perhaps, as with the standard experience machine, it is likely that people would refuse and demonstrate that they value truth as well as happiness. Joel certainly does; he has a change of heart midway through the procedure, and struggles against it, though he is somewhat hampered by being unconscious at the time.

Grau also points to a further problem with such interventions, which is captured from a Kantian perspective. To excise painful memories not only sacrifices an important concern with truth but diminishes our autonomy. We are altering ourselves in a way that deprives us of our capacity to autonomously determine ourselves in the relevant respect (Grau 2006, 123–125). This recalls Habermas's Kantian concerns regarding genetic interventions designed to enhance human beings, which since they are imposed by third parties on individuals in ways they cannot control or change, prevents them from being the undivided author of their own life. Habermas's interpersonal version of Kantianism provides a further perspective on the film's action, in that to excise painful memories is also to interrupt the process of communicative exchange and mutual interaction through which such memories are formed and individuals develop as subjects. Joel finds that he would rather hold on to the memories of Clementine, which are part of who he is, and the way in which she continues to be with him and shape his existence. Much of the film sees Joel together with his inner Clementine fleeing from the memory removal process that threatens to split them apart. The flight takes place within Joel's solitary dreaming consciousness, certainly, but it is through a landscape of memories of the people and interactions that have played a role in making him the person he is.

Overall, Habermas's ethical thinking turns on the ideal of a rationally autonomous human existence, in the form of collective rational self-determination through a society-wide discourse. Only when we are behaving rationally, in accordance with moral norms we formulate for ourselves through open discourse, are we living up to our true status as rational beings This is another version of the philosophical and moral idea of human nature that derives from Kant and is developed through Hegel and Marx. Indeed, Habermas's version is in many ways a return to the Kantian account, reformulated in communicative terms. Once again, however, questions arise about this sort of picture. As with Marx, we might wonder whether Habermas's notion of human nature is anything more than just philosophical speculation. Marx refers to people's real interests, reflective of human nature; and Habermas speaks of fundamental human interests not only in productive activity but also in maintaining mutual understanding, as well as in the 'creation of communication without domination' (Habermas 1971, 113). Communication without domination is the open, unconstrained discourse through which human beings will be able to rationally determine themselves, so this is a fundamental human interest in rational autonomy. Moreover, Habermas argues that this interest is inherent in language: 'The human interest in autonomy and responsibility is not mere fancy, for it can be apprehended *a priori*. What raises us out of nature is the only thing whose nature we can know: language. Through its structure, autonomy and responsibility are posited for us. Our first sentence expresses unequivocally the intention of universal and unconstrained consensus' (Habermas 1972, 314).

Subsequently, Habermas has developed an analysis of the conditions for possible communicative understanding to support this claim, but is there any empirical evidence for a fundamental human interest in open discourse and collective rational self-determination? Habermas can point to the emergence in eighteenth-century Europe of a political public sphere, a realm of public discussion in which citizens were able to confer in an unrestricted manner about matters of general interest. Political life could be discussed openly in accordance with reason, rather than simply by appeal to traditional dogma. Kant argued in 'What is Enlightenment?' that such unconstrained public discussion was a necessary requirement for enlightenment. For Kant, if people are to emerge from immature dependence on authority, and think for themselves, Kant's own understanding of Enlightenment, they must be able to freely discuss the shape of society. For Habermas, modern technocratic politics and administration involve precisely the abolition of the political public sphere, the exclusion of public discussion about the shape of society. It is true that the participants in the old public sphere, who took themselves to represent the general will, were in reality a particular social group, namely property-owning white males, the rising bourgeoisie. Nonetheless, Habermas sees the principle behind the public sphere, discursive will-formation through constraint-free discussion, as indispensable (see Habermas 1974, 54). However, one still wants to ask whether this notion of a public discourse, embodying ideals of free speech and autonomy, might not perhaps be a recent Western invention, a historical phenomenon peculiar to eighteenth-century Europe. Might Habermas be trying to turn, into the expression of a fundamental human interest or orientation inherent in language, what is in fact a historically specific mode of thinking?

Another set of issues relates to how far Habermas's discourse ethics shares in the abstract, even inhuman character of Kant's notions of morality, selfhood and autonomy. For Kant, in order to be moral, you have to exclude all that is particular to yourself, all desires, emotions and inclinations, in order to adhere to the universal principles of morality. Certainly, for Habermas, the autonomy of the will no longer requires the Kantian-style exclusion of desires and inclinations, since the aim of discourse is to come to a consensus as to which desires and interests are generalisable. However, this still means that any needs that are merely individual are going to be excluded from consideration. Moreover, it is not clear that this account seriously acknowledges the extent to which we are moved by our needs and desires. As one commentator put it, 'one gets the impression that the good life consists solely of rational communication, and that needs can be argued for without being felt' (Heller 1982, 22). The only thing that could properly be said to motivate us in Habermas's ideal rational dialogue would be the rather esoteric interest in the pursuit of unconstrained communication. It is not clear that we could rise to this level of detachment from the needs and desires that ordinarily motivate us. As with Kant, the suspicion once again arises that a moral ideal, a vision of a fully human life, is being proposed that is beyond the capacities of flesh and blood human beings to attain.

Moreover, although Habermas leaves behind Kant's abstractly isolated subject in favour of speaking subjects engaged in interpersonal dialogue, there is something abstract about the communicative interaction that he envisages. He only goes beyond the limits of Kant's self-determining subject in order to reproduce this ideal in communicative terms and problems associated with the Kantian subject reappear in the communication version. Habermas is only concerned with communication insofar as it is understood as an avenue for collective rational self-determination, unless it happens to be distorted by forms of power. But arguably, language has many uses and cannot be reduced to a single model. Moreover, Habermas does not see language as bound up with other social practices. If the Kantian self represents an abstraction from intersubjective relations, the Habermasian community of speaking subjects engaged in rational discourse seems remote from the concrete social interactions of embodied human beings.

It is unclear that human beings have the capacity to rise above their circumstances, to disentangle themselves from their particular interpersonal involvements, to the point where they could engage in a purely rational discussion about the norms and goals that are to structure their social existence. Equally, how could such a discussion be institutionalised in practice? Mass communication technologies do exist that might sustain such a discussion, but the internet suggests that there are distinct limits to the capacity of people to engage in such discussion, as well as showing the many other uses and functions that language has. That the ideal of collective will-formation through society-wide consensus might be too much for human beings is already suggested, long before the internet, in the satirical film *The Rise and Rise of Michael Rimmer* (Kevin Billington, 1970). Here, even minimal demands on individuals to contribute directly to the formation of a common will turn out to be impossibly onerous. Rimmer (Peter Cook) appears out of nowhere at an advertising firm, pretending to do a time-and-motion study. He quickly takes over the company and then moves into politics, pioneering an extreme form of participatory democracy. Voters are asked their opinion about everything before the government acts, a device on the television constantly interrupting the evening's entertainment and summoning them to make their views known. As the diabolical Rimmer has calculated, very soon, tired of being asked for their views, the people vote one last time, to give him absolute power.

Once again, then, it is not clear that ordinary individuals are capable of rising to the ideal envisaged by the philosophical system. Habermas articulates a moral ideal that may be beyond the powers of ordinary human beings to attain. However, we should also remember that this is a version of the defining ideal of our modernity. It is the prodigious task of rational self-determination that ultimately goes back to the eighteenth-century Enlightenment, with its heroic conception of human beings as capable of organising their existence through their own rationality, independently of religion, faith and tradition. Initially envisioned in terms of the application of science and technology to human existence, it is rearticulated by Kant in terms of rational autonomy, developed as a social ideal through Hegel and Marx in the nineteenth century, and formulated in communicative terms by Habermas in the twentieth. It may then be that the entire 'Enlightenment project' involves a moral ideal that it is beyond the capacity of human beings to realise. This does not necessarily mean that we need to abandon the idea of the human being as an active subject, but we may certainly question particular conceptions of that subjectivity, such as the version that develops through Hegel and Marx. At this point, we can turn to another conception of active subjectivity. This develops through two other nineteenth-century figures, Nietzsche and Kierkegaard, and is taken up by the various twentieth-century existentialists, including Sartre. As will become apparent, this represents a very different line of development in ethical thinking.

FEATURE FILMS: *HIGH NOON* AND *NO COUNTRY FOR OLD MEN*

High Noon

High Noon, which came out in 1957, is one of the greatest westerns. It also subverts the genre in some respects, particularly in the psychological realism of its depiction of the hero and of the townspeople who fail to support him. It was directed by Fred Zinneman (*A Man for All Seasons*, *The Day of the Jackal*), with a script by Carl Foreman who had his own experiences of not being supported by 'the people' to draw on. The film takes place in approximately real time, the events portrayed taking place from 10.40 to 12 noon, in an 84-minute film.

Plot

Three outlaws, Miller, Colby and Pierce, ride to the railway station and wait for the noon train. Meanwhile, town marshal Will Kane (Gary Cooper) and a Quaker, Amy Fowler (Grace Kelly), are getting married. On the train is Frank Miller (Ian MacDonald), just released from prison, who has sworn to kill Kane because he was the one who arrested him. The outlaws waiting for him are his brother and two friends. Although the new marshal doesn't arrive until the next day, the town elders encourage Kane to leave immediately, telling him that he owes it to Amy. At the edge of town, Kane stops the horses and decides to turn back. He heads back to town to round up deputies to make a stand against the outlaws. Amy says she doesn't want to wait and if he doesn't leave with her she will get on the noon train without him. He refuses, and she goes to wait for the train at the station.

Kane tries to enlist some deputies, but he is rejected by the judge who passed sentence on Miller and by Harvey, his deputy (Lloyd Bridges), who resents the fact that Kane did not pick him as successor and thinks it is because he has taken up with Kane's ex-girlfriend Helen Ramirez (Katy Jurado). He is also rejected by the men in the saloon, the congregation at the church and the town's previous marshal. One volunteer, Herb, pulls out when it turns out that no one else has come forward. Kane refuses the offer of help from a drunk and a youngster.

Meanwhile, his wife has found out about Helen and goes to talk to her. Helen criticises Amy for deserting her husband. Amy says that it is because members of her own family were destroyed by gun violence. Helen invites her to wait for the train in her room. The train arrives with Miller. Kane confronts the outlaws and there is a gunfight. Amy leaps off the train and runs back into town to help Kane, shooting one of the outlaws. Kane kills two others. The remaining outlaw, Frank Miller, takes Amy hostage but she breaks free from him and Kane shoots him dead. The townsfolk now emerge. Kane looks at them in disgust, takes off his badge and throws it in the dust. He and Amy ride out of town together.

Key Scenes

1   As they are riding out of town, Kane stops the horses and decides to turn back – 'they're making me run. I've never run from anyone before'. He seems to be motivated by something beyond self-interest or the desire to be thought heroic by others: 'I've got to. That's the whole thing' [11.10–12.38]. Later, back in his office, Amy pleads with Kane 'don't try to be a hero'. He replies, not out of modesty 'I'm not trying to be a hero. If you think I like this, you're crazy' [13.35–16.12].

2   His deputy, Harvey, offers to stand with Kane against the outlaws, but only if he will put in a word to ensure that Harvey is Kane's successor as town marshal. Kane wants Harvey's support but not based on Harvey's manipulative offer. Harvey: 'you put the word in for me like I said'. Kane: 'I want you to stick – but I'm not buying it. It's got to be up to you'. When Kane refuses to ensure Harvey's appointment as successor, the self-interested Harvey quits, taking off his badge and gun holster [20.18–22.44].

3   Harvey is involved with Helen Ramirez. When he turns up at her place after quitting on Kane, she urges him to 'grow up', comparing him unfavourably to Kane: 'you're a good-looking boy, but he is a man – you have a long way to go'. She also exercises her autonomy by unceremoniously dumping Harvey [41.17–43.09].

4   Kane goes to the church to ask for help. The congregation discuss whether or not to assist Kane in the showdown. In the end, the view that carries the day is that it would be better if Kane just left town, as the bad guys would simply move on. This would avoid a shootout that would give the town a bad reputation and deter outside investment, hurting the local economy. This is a utilitarian argument, in which the town's commercial well-being is the primary consideration. The town will be better off without him. For Kant, the right course of action is not something to be determined in terms of whether the actions contribute to the greater good or communal well-being [43.19–50.50]. Others like the hotel clerk are actively against Kane because by cleaning up the town he has ruined business [32.50–33.18].

5 Kane is in the stable contemplating leaving. Harvey Pell arrives and Kane admits he is scared. Pell tries to get Kane to leave, but Kane resolves to stay [59.18–1.01.02]. Back in his office, realising no one is going to help him, Kane lowers his face to the desk and appears to cry while clenching his fist. He is interrupted by a young boy who claims that he's 16, volunteering to help. Kane refuses his assistance: 'You're a kid, you're a baby'. He sits down to write his last will and testament in his office. A montage of the other characters follows and then the noon train whistle is heard [1.06.31–1.09.58]. Kane is portrayed here with psychological realism. He is not a 'holy will' or invulnerable hero. Also evident is his refusal to accept help from someone who is not yet able to make fully autonomous, rational choices. Earlier, on the same basis, he refuses the help of Jimmy the drunk [40.37–41.09].

6 For Kane, doing his duty amounts to an inner necessity. He acts out of personal integrity, independently of the views of others. However, this also leaves him isolated, an isolation captured in a high shot of Kane, standing alone in the middle of the main street, just before the final gunfight with Miller and the outlaws. Kane's final act is to turn his back on those who failed to support him. After the gunfight, the townspeople emerge and gather around Kane and his wife. Kane helps Amy board their buggy, looks around disdainfully, takes off his badge, drops it to the ground and they leave [1.23.27–1.24.33].

No Country for Old Men

No Country for Old Men is a 2007 neo-noir western, directed and written by Joel and Ethan Coen (*The Big Lebowski, O Brother Where Art Thou?, Hail Caesar!*). It radically subverts the genre, in that evil is triumphant and the decent lawman hero utterly fails to protect 'his people'.

Plot

In Texas, 1980, hitman Anton Chigurh (Javier Bardem) strangles a deputy sheriff to escape custody and uses a bolt pistol to kill a driver and steal his car. He spares the life of a petrol station owner after the owner, though unaware of the stakes, accepts a challenge and successfully guesses the result of Chigurh's coin toss. Meanwhile, in the desert, Llewelyn Moss (Josh Brolin) comes across the aftermath of a drug deal gone wrong. He finds several dead men, a wounded Mexican begging for water and two million dollars in a briefcase. He takes the money and returns home. That night, he returns to the scene with water for the wounded man and is pursued by two men in a truck, but escapes. Returning home, he sends his wife, Carla Jean (Kelly Macdonald), to stay with her mother, then drives to a motel in Del Rio, where he hides the briefcase in the air conditioning duct of his room.

Chigurh, hired to recover the money in the briefcase, kills his employers after finding a clue to Moss's identity. Arriving at Moss's home, he uses his bolt pistol to blow the lock out of the door. Investigating the break-in, Sheriff Bell (Tommy Lee Jones) notices the blown-out lock. Meanwhile, using a tracking device hidden with the money, Chigurh goes to Moss's motel and kills a group of Mexicans planning to ambush Moss in his room. Moss, having rented another room with access to the air conditioning duct where the money is hidden, retrieves the briefcase just before Chigurh opens the duct and finds it empty.

While staying at another motel in Eagle Pass, Moss discovers the tracking device, but Chigurh has already found him. A gunfight ensues and both are wounded. Moss flees to Mexico, hiding the case of money in scrub along the Rio Grande. Injured, he is taken to a hospital. While there, Carson Wells (Woody Harrelson), another hitman, fails to persuade him to accept his protection in return for the money. Meanwhile, Chigurh cleans and stitches his wounds with stolen supplies, then corners Wells in his hotel room. Wells tries to barter for his life but is unsuccessful and Chigurh kills him. Moss rings and Chigurh answers, telling Moss that he will kill Carla Jean unless Moss gives up the money and that he is going to kill Moss regardless.

Moss retrieves the suitcase from the river bank and arranges to meet Carla Jean at a motel in El Paso, where he plans to give her the money and hide her from danger. Before leaving, she is approached by Sheriff Bell, who promises to protect Moss. Carla Jean's mother accidentally reveals Moss's location to a group of Mexicans. Bell reaches the motel rendezvous, only to hear gunshots and see a pickup truck speeding from the motel. He arrives to find Moss dead, with Carla Jean turning up soon after. That night, Bell returns to the motel crime scene and finds the lock blown out. Chigurh, having come to retrieve the money, is hiding behind the door. Bell enters Moss's room and sees that the vent has been removed. Chigurh slips away.

Later, Bell visits his uncle Ellis (Barry Corbin) and tells him he plans to retire. Weeks afterward Carla Jean returns from her mother's funeral to find Chigurh waiting in her bedroom. She refuses his offer of a coin toss for her life. We next see Chigurh leaving the house, checking the soles of his boots for blood. As he drives away, a car crashes into him and he is injured. He bribes two young witnesses for their silence and flees. Now retired, Bell shares two dreams he has had about his father with his wife.

Key Scenes

1 Chigurh spares the life of a gas station owner after the owner accepts a challenge and successfully guesses the result of Chigurh's coin toss, though without fully realising what was at stake. The coin toss is part of Chigurh's modus operandi. It also seems to be a form of Sartrean bad faith on his part, a way of trying to evade taking responsibility for his actions, by presenting them as if they were part of the workings of an indifferent universe [20.00–24.14].

2 Carson Wells, another hitman, fails to persuade Moss to accept protection in return for the money. He points out that Chigurh is especially dangerous because he acts out of higher principles of some sort: 'You can't make a deal with him. Even if you gave him the money he'd still kill you. He's a peculiar man. You could even say that he has principles. Principles that transcend money or drugs or anything like that. He's not like you. He's not even like me' [1.11.53–1.14.54]. Chigurh is like a lawman dispensing justice, upholding his principles with the dedication and integrity usually associated with the western hero. He is, in his own way, as principled as Kane in *High Noon*, and if anything, is more successful in controlling his desires and feelings.

3 When Chigurh corners Wells in his hotel room. Wells tries unsuccessfully to barter for his life. 'You don't have to do this', he says, but Chigurh kills him. Moss telephones the room and Chigurh answers, telling Moss that he will kill Carla Jean unless Moss gives up the money: 'You bring me the money and I'll let her go. Otherwise, she's accountable. The same as you. That's the best deal you're gonna get. I won't tell you you can save yourself because you can't'. Once again, Chigurh is behaving in accordance with inflexible higher principles of some sort. He is also, from an existentialist point of view, suffering from bad faith in the form of a belief in absolute principles that he has no choice but to obey, Sartre's 'spirit of seriousness' [1.17.42–1.22.32].

4 After Moss is killed, Bell, who had promised Carla Jean he would keep Moss safe [1.16.18–1.16.24], visits his uncle Ellis, an ex-lawman, telling him he plans to retire because he feels 'over-matched'. Bell: 'I always thought when I got older God would sort of come into

my life in some way. He didn't. I don't blame him. If I was him I'd have the same opinion about me that he does'. Ellis scoffs and says fatalistically that the region has always been violent: 'What you got ain't nothin' new. This country is hard on people … You can't stop what's coming. It ain't all waiting on you. That's vanity' [1.38.10–1.42.59].

5   Carla Jean returns from her mother's funeral to find Chigurh waiting in her bedroom. Carl Jean: 'You got no cause to hurt me'. Chigurh: 'No. But I gave my word … To your husband … Your husband had the opportunity to remove you from harm's way. Instead, he used you to try to save himself'. Again, he presents himself as being bound by principles or promises that he cannot break, arguably a form of bad faith. Like Wells, Carla Jean tells him that 'You don't have to do this'. In a kind of concession, he makes the offer of a coin toss for her life, but she refuses stating that the choice is his own and once again calling out his bad faith. 'No. I ain't gonna call it … The coin don't have no say. It's just you [1.43.12–1.46.37].

5   Slaves, Supermen and Authentic Selves

Existentialist Ethics

At the start of *Fight Club*, we find the film's unnamed narrator on a chair with a gun barrel in his mouth, courtesy of the other main character, the charismatic, dangerous Tyler Durden. The narrator gingerly moves the barrel aside with his tongue, and in voiceover, wonders how he ever got to this point. We then flashback to the beginning of the events that led to this situation, the collapse of the narrator's former existence, and his wild ride with Durden, with the film eventually arriving at the scene with which it began. 'I think this is about where we came in' notes the narrator helpfully. The action picks up again, with the narrator looking into Durden's eyes for a moment, and then squeezing the trigger. In slow motion, his mouth fills with the gases from the gun and the bullet blows a hole through his cheek. At the same time, Tyler's eyes glaze over and he falls to the floor with an exit wound in the back of his head and a grin on his face. For the narrator, overcoming Durden in this way appears to be a liberation, heralding a new beginning: 'my eyes are open. Everything is going to be fine' (Figure 5.1).

Durden is sometimes presented as an example of what nineteenth-century philosopher Friedrich Nietzsche called the '*ubermensch*', the 'superman' or 'overman', a powerful creature who is beyond good and evil, beyond conventional morality and above the common herd. Durden certainly overcomes the constraints of conventional morality and aspirations, giving expression to his strongest drives. He also orchestrates the underground fight clubs in which other budding tough guys can get back in touch with their primal instincts and impulses, long suppressed thanks to the debilitating self-denial required for civilised life. It's a common view of what Nietzsche's *ubermensch* might be like, especially in the movies. Yet there is a good argument to the effect that Durden is no Nietzschean superman. On the contrary, it is in fact the unprepossessing Edward Norton character who has a better claim to be the superman in the film and he attains this status at the precise moment that he overcomes Tyler Durden. To make sense of this, and more generally to see how Nietzschean ideas might apply to the film, we need to take a somewhat lengthy detour through Nietzsche's thinking.

Figure 5.1 Fight Club: Tyler Durden and the narrator (David Fincher, 1999. Credit: 20th Century Fox/Photofest).

Nietzsche

Roughly contemporary with Marx, Nietzsche (1844–1900) is another critic of religion, and especially of attempts to provide a religious justification of values or morality. His books, including *Beyond Good and Evil* and *On the Genealogy of Morals*, contain a wide-ranging critique of religion. In this critique, Nietzsche is very much in the spirit of the eighteenth-century Enlightenment. He shares the Enlightenment's suspicion of religion, as a set of unprovable, dogmatic or superstitious beliefs that served to justify questionable moral and political practices. He famously insisted that God is dead, referring not to the demise of some supernatural being, but to the gradual erosion of religious belief that has taken place in the modern era over the last 300 years. This in turn reflects the rise of the modern scientific worldview, for which the universe operates without any God-given plan or purpose, according to the impersonal operation of physical laws. However, he is also a critic of many features of enlightened modernity, including the modern attempt to find an alternative, rational basis for morality and value. He does not think it is possible to establish ethics in this manner, either on a scientific, materialist basis or in terms of reason itself.

The Enlightenment thinkers sought a rational basis for morality, either in terms of the new scientific notion of human being as material object, or on the basis of the rational subject as Kant thought. For Kant, trying to find rational foundations for our moral values was important for the critique of religion, because in showing that morality had a foundation in reason, one could show that religion is not the only ground of moral values. We no longer have to appeal to God and his commands in order to justify morality. However, Nietzsche goes further, criticising in addition these Enlightenment attempts to find a rational basis for morality.

He rejects a happiness-centred hedonistic or utilitarian ethics, based on the scientific conception of the human being that goes back to Hobbes, as a machine driven by a desire for pleasure and the avoidance of pain. And he rejects Kant's attempt to establish a deontological morality based on reason. He thinks that these attempts are problematic particularly because they tried to preserve Christian values by founding them in reason, rather than questioning the values themselves. So, for example, Helvetius, Holbach and Kant all rejected a religious foundation for morality, but wanted to preserve what are essentially Christian values by providing them with a more rational justification.

This is not to say that Nietzsche is advocating a nihilistic rejection of all values. For Nietzsche, we need values in order to have a meaningful life, and the problem that we need to confront is precisely the nihilism of modern life (BGE 208; all references to *Beyond Good and Evil* will be to the numbered paragraphs). The old basis for values, religion, is collapsing. There is science, but this does not provide us with any values or guidance, only material success. Like science, philosophy has failed to provide an alternative basis for values. Moreover, he thinks that the values dominant in modern society, the Christian values left over from our religious past, are nihilistic in the sense of being life-denying. They celebrate things like modesty, consideration, weakness, security, belonging to the group. Everything that expresses strength and independence, all that elevates the individual above the herd, is seen as a danger, a threat. For Nietzsche, we need to go beyond this 'herd animal morality' (BGE 186). What is required is precisely the opposite, the strong, independent individual who stands out from the crowd. Their strength lies in self-mastery and in the capacity to create values for themselves, to determine values to live by, through their own will. So the task for human beings is to create a meaningful world, to establish values for living, in the absence of God and in the face of the scientific conception of nature.

In this, Nietzsche also stands apart from that other great nineteenth-century critic of modernity, Marx. Instead of nihilism, the great problem for Marx is alienation, under existing social and historical conditions, from our proper nature as the conscious, rational makers of our social existence. Liberal democracy does not go far enough in liberating human beings, since it leaves alienating social conditions in place. For Marx, we reach a higher state by changing these social conditions, a process that human beings collectively participate in. Nietzsche, like Marx, is also critical of modern liberal democracy, but this is because for him the liberal-democratic ideals of equality and liberty represent the triumph of the common man, reducing everything to the lowest common denominator. Nietzsche sometimes speaks of herd morality as the democratic will to render everyone equal in mediocrity. He is even more scathing about socialism, in the general sense of the classless, cooperative society that was Marx's social ideal. Socialism for Nietzsche would represent the final triumph of the herd, the group, over the individual. Nietzsche would no doubt see the herd thinker's hatred of the individual who stands out from the group in the words of the Fire Chief in *Fahrenheit 451*: 'It's no good, Montag. We've all got to be alike. The only way to be happy is for everyone to be equal. So, we must burn the books'. Here the books are being condemned because they encourage individual reflection and non-conformity, create dissent and lead individuals to differentiate themselves from the herd. These are precisely the things that Nietzsche wants to encourage. Like Marx, Nietzsche envisages the possibility of moral self-improvement for human beings, but whereas for Marx, this involves a process of social transformation undertaken by the collective, for Nietzsche, it is a matter of individual transformation for the strong few, an aristocratic vision of self-improvement.

Thus, Nietzsche mounts a trenchant critique of the prevailing values of modern life themselves, the popular moral values and ideals of his time, the values of what he calls herd animal morality. They deny strength and individuality, and celebrate weakness, self-denial, submission, serving others and belonging to the group (BGE 186, 199–202). Nietzsche's own ideal is the strong individual, where strength is strength of will, which is linked with being independent and self-determining. It is important to emphasise that for Nietzsche, the strongest individuals are not those who master others, but those who have mastery over themselves. Their strength lies in being able to make themselves, to create their own values and shape their lives in accordance with those values, independently of the majority of people. It is in these terms that Nietzsche understands freedom. It is not a matter of having a free will, a faculty everyone is understood to possess, but rather of being capable of self-mastery, something that is only possible for the strong few, since it requires the exceptional strength that most people do not have (BGE 29, 188, 212).

Underlying this ideal of self-mastery is a certain conception of human nature, of life, characterised by Nietzsche in terms of drives or instincts. This is not the Hobbesian notion of a being that strives to preserve itself, to survive, but life as constantly striving to be 'more', to grow, to be stronger, to master and overcome that which is weaker and impose a form upon it. This is Nietzsche's famous notion of the 'will to power' (BGE 36, 259). And as noted, the strongest expression of this will to power is not mastery of others but self-mastery, self-overcoming. To achieve this self-mastery is to perfect oneself, to realise one's greatest possibilities and to 'become what one is'. This ideal of self-perfection is not completely dissimilar to Kant's notion of freedom as autonomous self-determination. However, whereas Kant envisages determining oneself through one's rationality, Nietzsche presents a more naturalistic version in which, under social pressure, one's drives and energies come to be directed inward, turned upon themselves. We will see what this involves in a moment.

Nietzsche questions morality not only in the sense of the popular moral ideals and sentiments of his day but also understood as the philosophical discipline of ethics. This is the modern attempt to provide a rational foundation for current moral values and ideals, which Nietzsche calls 'the science of morals'. His own approach to reflecting on ethics is not a science of morals but what he calls a 'natural history of morals' (BGE 186), or a 'genealogy of morals'. Rather than trying to rationally justify our values, Nietzsche thinks we should look at their real origins. He doesn't think they come from some exalted, transcendental source, like God or reason. Rather, they have 'lowly' origins, arising out of the messy encounters, struggles and conflicts of history. Accordingly, Nietzsche's genealogical approach looks at current moral values and ideals in their historical development, tracing the history behind them, how they have emerged and changed over time. As such, rather than accepting herd morality as the definitive form of morality, Nietzsche calls attention to how current moral concepts are historically specific. And in grasping that current moral ideas are not absolute, but only one particular form of morality, it becomes possible to envisage the possibility of overcoming them, going beyond existing morality. Formulating this new morality will be the task of the 'philosophers of the future', of the *ubermensch* or overman (BGE 43, 210–212).

In providing this historical genealogy of the emergence of moral ideas Nietzsche also seeks to uncover the deeper, underlying ends that morality serves. And what underlies morality turns out to be power, or more accurately, the will to power that is the fundamental drive in human beings. All moralities are an expression of the will to power, particularly as this is manifested in social power relations. In Nietzsche's account, the will to power appears in two forms. Firstly, it is essential to human life, understood as a collection of drives or instincts, con- stantly striving to be more, to be stronger, to master and so on; and secondly, will to power is essential to life in society, which consists of power relations. And what the genealogy of morals reveals is that all moralities reflect a certain kind of power-relation, a social structure of command and obedience. Nietzsche says that at all times, in all societies, there have always been those who obeyed and a small number commanding, or in his terminology, 'masters' and 'slaves'. We thus have a conception of society in terms of power, the power that the small number of commanders have over the many who obey (BGE 199).

This is discussed at length in *On the Genealogy of Morals*. Society is not estab- lished, as Hobbes imagined, through a social contract between free individuals who surrender some personal liberty in return for the security of an organised society. It is established when a small, powerful group, conquer and enslave oth- ers, establishing a hierarchy of command and obedience. The ruling group cre- ates the state, the social order, through acts of violent imposition (GM 2.17; all references to *Genealogy of Morals* will be to the essay and section). Moreover, the masters create a morality, a code of evaluation from their perspective. The masters are strong and vigorous, freely expressing their instincts in joyful, unin- hibited action; and they identify the 'good' with their own attributes of strength, courage and self-assertion. Meanwhile, under the rule of the masters, the slaves are rendered submissive, servile, fearful and cautious. As far as the masters are concerned, these are all contemptible, unworthy ways of behaving which they want to distance themselves from and they identify these characteristics with the 'bad'. Good and bad, so understood, are the categories of what Nietzsche calls 'master morality' (BGE 260, GM 1.2).

As for the slaves, the first reaction to enslavement, to the power of the mas- ters, is the development of what Nietzsche calls 'bad conscience' (GM 2.16). Their own hostility and aggression, no longer able to express itself outwardly because the power of the masters is too great, is internalised or turned inwards. They vent their hostility on themselves, on their own desires and instincts, which they come to regard as base and unworthy. Thus, while the masters give free rein to their instincts, for the slaves it is a very different matter. Their own instincts become a source of guilt and shame, and so they suffer from bad conscience. This is not a particularly healthy way of being. Indeed, Nietzsche sees bad conscience as a kind of illness, a masochistic self-hatred. At this point, then, the person is divided against themselves, their energies turned against themselves, with a 'higher self' striving to control or suppress an irrational, instinctive side that it views with contempt.

The second reaction is the invention of a different kind of morality, 'slave morality'. The slaves are weak and oppressed, but they don't remain passive. They develop feelings of envy and hatred towards the masters, which Nietzsche calls '*ressentiment*' or resentment, a desire for revenge. *Ressentiment* results in a new code of evaluation, which is a complete inversion of master morality (GM 1.7, 1.10, 1.11). So this is how a subjugated population can respond, by turning against master morality and 'revaluing all values'. First of all, the qualities that master morality labelled 'bad', are now evaluated in a positive way, as 'good'. For example, fear becomes humility, and impotence becomes kindness. For master morality, fear and impotence are bad. The oppressed are too weak and timid to be anything other than kind; and they are humble because any other way of acting would have bad consequences. But the slaves turn these into positive features. Secondly, from the perspective of slave morality, those qualities that master morality thinks of as good, like strength, courage and self-assertion, are not considered bad, but 'evil'. This is because the slaves associate the virtues of the powerful with their own suffering. The virtues of the strong and powerful are a threat to the slave. So the notion of evil is devised. Thus, good and evil are the categories of slave morality, which emerges as a reaction to master morality. The triumph of the slaves is to get the masters to accept a morality in which the masters becomes reprehensible in their own eyes.

Religion comes in at this point, because for Nietzsche, this inversion of values is above all the work of religion, of Christianity in particular, and of the priests who arise to mobilise the weak and lead the slaves (GM 1.6-9). For Nietzsche, it is the priests who planned and brought about the triumph of slave morality. Religion was the instrument of the slaves' revenge, the means by which the values of slave morality could be imposed on the strong. The strength and vigour of the masters, expressed in strong, joyful, uninhibited action, became the object of religious condemnation and what was celebrated instead were things like meekness, humility and submissiveness. Submission to the masters became instead submission to God. In the process, the self-esteem of the slaves was boosted, their moral superiority over the masters affirmed. So, for Nietzsche, the moral values bound up with religion are the values of slave morality, values that condemn the strong and turn weakness into a virtue.

At the same time, religion links up with the phenomenon of bad conscience. The bad conscience, as we have seen, is the slaves' hostility and aggression turned inward by social constraints. Unable to express the aggression outwardly because of the power of the masters, it becomes self-hatred, self-punishment.

The slaves come to regard their own instincts and desires as base and unworthy. Christianity is not the origin of bad conscience, which lies in social power relations and our reactions to them. However, it intensifies humanity's self-hatred and self-torture to the point of madness, strengthening this instrument of self-punishment. Religion teaches the absolute goodness of God, and the baseness of human beings, who are nothing but unworthy sinners, inherently evil and sinful, deserving of eternal punishment. On Nietzsche's account, then, religion is an instrument of self-torture, the means for the self-violation of the human self. We can see why Nietzsche discusses the origin of bad conscience in such detail, why it is important. For him, the bad conscience is not just an interesting mental phenomenon. It is a serious sickness, and it is not just something that particular individuals suffer from, but a sickness characteristic of the European mind in general (GM 2.19–2.22)

Ever a useful metaphor for conceptions of human nature, we might see the vampire as being in the first instance close to the Nietzschean master type, giving uninhibited expression to their instincts and desires, preying cheerfully on the weak. But once resurrected in a religious framework, as in *The Addiction*, the vampire as we have seen becomes a metaphor for human nature as conceived from a Christian, specifically Augustinian perspective – as afflicted by base, unworthy instincts and desires, out of which all worldly evil arises. When the film's central character, Kathleen, the idealistic philosophy grad student appalled by human cruelty and evil, is turned into a vampire, she goes over to the dark side and becomes everything that she formerly hated. As a vampire, she is unapologetically bent on playing the role of the master, freely pursuing her instincts, though fully aware of the affinities between her activities and the historical atrocities that she was originally so appalled by. But she eventually comes to be stricken with guilt over what she has been doing and the desires that drove her. In Nietzschean terms, she assumes the position of the self-hating slave. With this, she moves from defiantly proclaiming that she 'will not submit', just before slaughtering her PhD dissertation committee, to believing she can only be saved in the end by submitting to a priest, and to God. One commentator suggests that her refusal to submit may itself have a double meaning, reflecting her internally conflicted state. On the one hand, it means that she is refusing to submit to God; on the other, that she is refusing to submit to her addiction (Johnstone 1999, 176).

For Nietzsche, the two types of morality, master and slave morality, have been engaged in a fearful struggle on earth for thousands of years. He ascribes the master code of evaluation to Greek and roman societies, giving way to Judaeo-Christian slave morality, the renaissance re-awakening of master morality, and the *ressentiment* movement of the Reformation and the French revolution (GM 1.16). However, the modern era sees the triumph of slave morality. Nietzsche describes the moral sentiment of his day as herd animal morality because slave morality is essentially a reaction. To exist, slave morality always needs an adverse social background to react against. But the present European moral sentiment doesn't have to struggle, because slave morality has become the common morality. So herd animal morality is the proper term to describe the moral sentiment of Nietzsche's day. This brings us back to the question of what Nietzsche sees as the way forward. To progress, we need to leave behind religion and herd animal morality. Nietzsche doesn't think that herd animal morality is absolute, the last word in morality. The account he gives of its historical emergence in terms of the struggles between master and slave morality shows this. The present prevalence of herd animal morality is just the result of historical struggles. Nietzsche thus emphasises the possibility of overcoming the present moral code. The new morality will be formulated by the strong individual, the *ubermensch* or overman.

As part of this overcoming of religion and slave morality, we also need to leave behind the damaging self-denial and self-hatred associated with them. Nietzsche criticises the Christian condemnation of instinct and desire, its rejection of basic instinctual drives. This hostility towards desire, as we have seen, is also prominent in Kant's moral thinking and goes all the way back to Plato. All of these positions share a contempt for bodily instinct and desire, things that tie us to this world and which we were put on this earth to rise above. But for Nietzsche, these drives are at the very core of our being, the energies that motivate us. And he points to the costs involved in excessive self-denial, especially as prescribed by religion. We are not only perpetually frustrated but afflicted with self-loathing. Our own instincts become the source of shame and we are led to regard ourselves as damnable because we cannot get rid of them. The self-hatred of the bad conscience also gives rise to other phenomena, including what Nietzsche calls the 'ascetic ideal', in which self-sacrifice and self-denial become, perversely, an expression of strength. The priestly types demonstrate their own will to power in the form of various practices of self-denial, which reduce their vigour and express their hostility towards concrete reality. This asceticism is well-illustrated in *Simon of the Desert*, where Simon, atop his pillar, invents ever more elaborate ways of denying himself. It's an exercise of enormous strength and self-assertion, whilst being at the same time a form of debilitating self-denial.

However, it is important to emphasise that Nietzsche's own ideal of the *ubermensch* is not a return to the uninhibited functioning of the instincts, the unsublimated passions of the master (GM 2.17). Nietzsche does not propose that we abandon all constraints and give our instincts free rein. Our instinctual drives and impulses are chaotic and primitive, and to simply return to them would be to revert to the status of brutes. This is why the Nietzschean overman cannot be identified with Mr Hyde in the Jekyll and Hyde scenario. Certainly, the primitive desires and instincts represented by the Hyde part of our nature are not to be simply suppressed or denied. To do so is to deny life, as Hyde himself confirms when he first emerges in the 1931 Mamoulian version of *Dr Jekyll and Mr Hyde*, railing against the social, religious and moral constraints on the expression of these instincts: 'You hypocrites, deniers of life. If you could see me now ... what would you think?' But neither is Nietzsche advocating their uninhibited expression. This would be a step backwards. Appropriately, the Hyde who is given free rein after Jekyll drinks his potion looks decidedly brutish and primitive, and proves to be murderous and sadistic in the extreme.

Nor is Nietzsche advocating brutality towards others. He is not proposing that we reject the moral constraints required by the common herd in order to return to the masters' predatory domination of those weaker than them. Thus, he would not embrace the advice that the cobbler (Alphonse Ethier) gives to Lily Powers (Barbara Stanwyck) in *Baby Face* (Alfred E. Green, 1933), to 'be a master, not a slave'. A fan of Nietzsche, the cobbler, quoting from *The Will to Power*, advises her to aim for great things, to move to the big city and use her power over men: 'Nietzsche says, "All life, no matter how we idealize it, is nothing more nor less than exploitation". That's what I'm telling you. Exploit yourself. Go to some big city where you will find opportunities! Use men! Be strong! Defiant! Use men to get the things you want!' All of this Lily very successfully does, but she is not by virtue of that the 'first overwoman', as some have characterised her (see Steven 2017, 96). This is once again to mistakenly identify Nietzsche's ideal with his notion of the master. Incidentally, *Baby Face* was one of the films that prompted the introduction of the Hays Production Code. Before it could be released it had to be recut to, amongst other things, remove the references to Nietzsche's philosophy – one of the many things unacceptable under the Code (Kehr 2005).

This identification of the *ubermensch* with the master who dominates others is also the mistake made by the protagonists Brandon (John Dall) and Philip (Farley Granger) in Hitchcock's 1948 film *Rope* (Figure 5.2). To prove their superiority, they decide to commit the perfect crime, murdering a university classmate and

Figure 5.2 The two supermen in *Rope* (Alfred Htchcock, 1948/ Credit: Warner Brothers/ Photofest).

hiding him in a trunk, which they make the centrepiece of the dinner party they go on to hold. They consider themselves to be Nietzschean overmen, intellectually superior types who are exempt from the moral rules that govern everyone else, the common herd; and see murder as an art that superior beings should be able to practice. As Brandon says: 'Good and evil, right and wrong were invented for the ordinary average man, the inferior man, because he needs them'. In the course of the film, their old school tutor Rupert (James Stewart) works out what has happened. He is horrified that his discussions of Nietzsche's *ubermensch* have been used by the pair to justify murder, insisting that they have twisted and distorted his words. Certainly, the Nietzschean ideal is not to return to the uninhibited mastery of the master, to revive master morality. After all, the title of Nietzsche's book is *Beyond Good and Evil*, not *Back to Good and Bad*.

Nietzsche considers the master's uninhibited mastery over others to be a crude expression of the will to power. For him, it was only when the human being became divided against themselves, developing a bad conscience under the constraints of civilised life, that they became an 'interesting animal' (GM 1.6). Nietzsche also indicates that there is a certain promise implicit in the bad conscience: 'the bad conscience is an illness ... but an illness as pregnancy is an illness' (GM 2.19). This means that bad conscience, strengthened by religion, may be destructive and negative, but the phenomenon can also take a different turn. The bad conscience is only the initial step. We must first condemn our impulses in order to be able to take the second step, to 'sublimate' or 'spiritualise' them into different channels. That is, we can adopt a different relation towards ourselves, organise our impulses without considering them evil or fighting them (GM 2.24). We can redirect, channel and harmonise these energies, enhancing them and turning them into something more spiritual and noble, such as artistic or creative endeavours. In so doing, as Nietzsche puts it in *Will to Power*, we will have triumphed over our impulses without destroying them (Nietzsche 1967, paragraphs 384, 385; see Kaufmann 1968, 224–225). For Nietzsche, this is where the greatest power lies, in positive self-mastery or self-overcoming. This is a life-enhancing rather than life-denying activity and is the work undertaken by the overman. They have the task of self-creation, and at the end of the process will emerge the sovereign individual, 'liberated again from the morality of custom, autonomous and supramoral' (GM 2.2).

Consequently, Nietzsche does not simply condemn Christian self-denial. Bad conscience is an evil, but a necessary evil, a stage we have to go through to get to the positive self-mastery of the *ubermensch*. In the same way, the asceticism that Simon turns into a fine art in Bunuel's *Simon of the Desert* is both ridiculous and noble, ridiculous because it takes debilitating self-denial to absurd lengths, noble because it elevates him above the brute, as well as providing the preconditions for a more positive self-relation. At the same time, the ascetic has to be clearly distinguished from the *ubermensch*. The two are run together in *The Addiction*. Christopher Walken's Peina is the vampire who has his desires under control, is able to hold down a job and so on. Having been targeted by Kathleen as a possible victim, he takes her back to his apartment to teach her how to be a proper vampire. He explicitly claims to be a Nietzschean superman, the one who lives beyond good and evil, but his self-mastery is in fact more of the ascetic variety. He does not sublimate his impulses but rather, practices various forms of self-denial and fasting: 'you learn to survive on a little'. Later on, we see him feeding on Kathleen, suggesting his professed asceticism is in fact little more than a hypocritical mask.

In the movie vampire world, more plausible candidates for the vampire as overman are represented by Adam (Tom Hiddleston) and Eve (Tilda Swinton) in *Only Lovers Left Alive* (Jim Jarmusch, 2013). These vampires are cultured intellectuals, urbane and sophisticated, their houses filled with rare books, musical instruments, artworks and scientific instruments. They radiate superiority over the common run of humanity, but unlike the superiority claimed by Philip and Brandon in *Rope*, which is demonstrated by murdering someone they consider inferior, theirs is an evident spiritual superiority. It has been developed through centuries of self-cultivation and it sets them clearly apart from the corrupt, chaotic world outside their homes. Their main problem, apart from getting supplies of untainted blood to satisfy their relatively restrained urges, is Eve's little sister Ava (Mia Wasikowska). Ava has not yet learned to tame and redirect her instincts, and her surprise visit and uncontrolled behaviour disrupts their ordered existence. If they themselves eventually resort to traditional vampire behaviour, as happens in the very last scene of the film, it is only as a last resort since they are on the point of starvation.

The confusion of Nietzsche's ideal, the *ubermensch*, with the brutal self-assertion of the master also underlies the mistaken identification of Nietzsche's views with a fascist politics, the kind of radical authoritarian nationalism exemplified by National Socialism. This is an identification that is made by one of the dinner guests in *Rope*. When Mr Kentley (Cedric Hardwicke) suggests that Brandon, who has been holding forth about how murder is an art that superior beings should practice, is in agreement with Nietzsche and his theory of the superman, he adds that Hitler also believed in this theory. Brandon is happy to agree with the first point, that his own view accords with Nietzsche's, but he rejects the second, not because the Nazis were murderers who killed those they thought inferior, but because they were stupid and incompetent about it. In fact, we can say that Brandon, in imagining himself to be a Nietzschean superman entitled to murder those he considers inferior, represents the same kind of self-serving, distorted reading of Nietzsche that the Nazis themselves drew on in order to justify their murderous behaviour towards particular social groups. Brandon is far from being a Nietzschean superman and Nietzsche is far from being an apologist for fascism. Apart from his distaste for nationalism of all kinds, especially German nationalism, Nietzsche does not envisage the *ubermensch* as an authoritarian leader entitled to dominate others. The kind of mastery he looks to remains above all the self-mastery to be found in the artist, the philosopher, even the saint.

All of which brings us back to *Fight Club*. On the basis of what we have seen, it is possible to reject any identification of Tyler Durden with the Nietzschean overman. Certainly, the film's unnamed narrator starts out as a 'herd man', a corporate functionary and obedient consumer who plays by the rules but is becoming increasingly frustrated by what late capitalist society has to offer. Through his alter-ego Durden, he is able to escape from his repressed existence and give expression to his strongest drives. Durden violently rejects conventional morality and aspirations, and the fight clubs he organises allow the participants to get back in touch with the primal instincts and impulses that have been denied in civilised life. But far from being Nietzsche's ideal of the powerful individual, Durden comes closer to the uninhibited instincts and brutality of the master. He is by no means a brute pure and simple. He has enormous self-discipline, which makes him greater than he would otherwise have been, but his self-overcoming is limited because it becomes a means to the end of tyrannising others. In this, he is not unlike Napoleon, another figure who is sometimes mistakenly cited as a model for the overman. Nietzsche's views on Napoleon are clear. For him, Napoleon is certainly not a simple brute, but he is not an overman either. Rather, he is a synthesis of brute and overman, his self-overcoming cut short by his lust to dominate (GM 1.16). And like Napoleon, Durden 'was corrupted by the means he *had to* employ, and lost *noblesse* of character' (Nietzsche 1967, 1026; see Kaufman 1968, 316; Rowland 2003, 23).

By the end of the film, Durden has given full expression to his domineering tendencies, fashioning his fight clubs into a terrorist army that he runs along militaristic, decidedly fascist lines. The participants in this army, instead of finding themselves, are now required to submerge their personality through extreme self-denial and to subordinate themselves entirely to Durden's cause, which is to bring about destruction and chaos in society. Durden is thus far removed from the *ubermensch*, for whom mastery lies not in the domination of others, and destruction, but in self-mastery and self-creation. It is in fact the film's unnamed narrator who in the end more closely approaches Nietzsche's ideal. Durden is his Hyde-like alter-ego, embodying the narrator's strongest drives and appetites, with the qualification that unlike Hyde, he has enough self-discipline to direct his energies, if only into the domination of others. The final scene of the film, in which the narrator shoots himself, is also the scene in which he finally confronts and overcomes his alter-ego, appropriating and taking control of his energies. In so doing, he creates himself as a new person. Durden's tyranny over others is thus turned into creative self-affirmation.

So for Nietzsche, moral progress, in the form of becoming the self-mastering *ubermensch*, is possible. This is not something that can be achieved by everyone, only the strong few. Nonetheless, it is something that is within the capacity of at least some human beings to achieve, those who have the required strength. This is not a superhuman ideal in the sense of being beyond the physical and psychological capacities of any human being. Here, we can distinguish Nietzsche's *ubermensch* from another character the superman has sometimes been identified with this is Neo (Keanu Reeves) from *The Matrix*, which came out in the same year as *Fight Club*. This was also perhaps the first film to excite widespread interest in the philosophical interpretation of film and one of the themes that came up in discussion at the time was the idea that Neo was a version of Nietzsche's *ubermensch* (see e.g., Knight, McKnight, 2002: 189). However, this is a questionable identification, and it is questionable precisely because the film envisages as an ideal something that is beyond the physical and psychological capacities of any human being – the complete transcendence of the physical body.

The premise of the film is that most of humanity has been enslaved by a race of intelligent machines that use human bodies as power sources. The humans, however, are completely unaware of their real situation. Everything seems normal because a supercomputer feeds them a computer-simulated reality ('the matrix'). Only a few rebels have managed to escape this enslavement and are able to offer resistance to the machines. Thus, at the start of the film, before he escapes from the matrix, everything the central character, Keanu Reeves' Neo, experiences and takes to be real is in fact a computer-generated illusion. The film follows his journey out of the matrix into the real world. With its global illusion scenario, the film proved a useful resource for talking about Descartes, and Cartesian arguments for scepticism about the possibility of knowledge, such as the possibility that we might be dreaming or being radically deceived by an evil demon. But there is another philosophical theme called into view by the film, namely philosophy's traditional disdain for the body, and the idea of the self, mind or soul as something essentially non-bodily and immaterial. This is already evident in Plato, where, as we have seen, the rational self or soul is understood to be distinct from the body and its irrational desires.

In *The Matrix*, this second theme comes up insofar as Cynthia Freeland puts it, the film creates a 'naïve fantasy of overcoming human flesh' (Freeland, 2002, 205). In the reality that Neo finds himself in after escaping the matrix, human beings are embodied, vulnerable beings. He awakens to a nightmarish vision of countless naked bodies, floating in vats, plugged into tubes that maintain them and feed them their fake reality. Aboard the rebel ship, he can only re-enter the matrix by having a plug inserted into the back of his neck. But once back in the matrix, he is without his neck-bolt, able to perform spectacular feats, and once he undergoes his final transformation into 'the One', becomes superhuman. He may still be embodied, but this is a perfect, invulnerable body, with no relationship to an actual flesh and blood one. In effect, Neo has transcended the physical reality of the flesh. And the film does not end on the ship with Neo's real body. Instead, we see a handsome, overcoated Neo in the matrix, wandering among the masses, then zipping off through the sky, promising 'a world without rules and controls, without borders and boundaries, a world where anything is possible'. As Freeland puts it, the movie feeds escapist fantasies of a mental reality where the elect few are unencumbered by rules (see Freeland, 2002, 209, 214).

Plato would no doubt have approved of Neo's overcoming of his physical body, leaving the prison of his body in order to emerge into the more perfect world of the matrix, where he himself is purified of imperfection and becomes what he truly is. The Platonic philosopher also longs to escape from the body and become pure mind. There are in addition strong religious overtones in Neo's journey to self-realisation, his escape from a mortal, corruptible body, and transformation into something perfect and impervious to harm. Augustine, drawing on Plato, reinforced the idea of the soul as immortal and indestructible, essentially

distinct from the body, and able to leave it behind as we journey to our more perfect existence in the next life. Aquinas, under the influence of Aristotle, struggles
to preserve an integral view of the human person as mind and body, but in the end,
with the immortality of the soul at stake, has to concede that incorporeal existence
is intelligible. As such, genuine human fulfilment, happiness and self-realisation
are only possible in the next world, although ironically, having overcome our
mortal bodies, we have also ceased to be human. The idea of escaping the flesh
and becoming a pure mind also appears in Descartes, whose sceptical arguments
seem to show that we may have no body, but we cannot doubt that we exist as a
thinking thing. Hence, the famous Cartesian dualism, the idea that human beings
are a combination of immaterial mind and material body.

Neo's moral progress in *The Matrix* can thus be read in Platonic, Christian
and even Cartesian terms. What is not so plausible, however, is any attempt to
read it as the process of becoming a Nietzschean *ubermensch*. Nietzsche is one
of the most strident critics of the Platonic, Christian and Cartesian desire to
escape the flesh, which he sees as symptomatic of a hatred or disdain for this
world and the body that is ultimately self-destructive. For Nietzsche, far from
representing human beings as they most essentially are, the pure mind is an
impoverished, reduced person. For his part, Nietzsche rejects the idea of the self
as non-bodily and immortal. He conceives of the self as a 'mortal soul', a soul
that is not distinct from the body, or as he puts it in *Thus Spoke Zarathustra*, a
soul that is 'only a word for something in the body' (Nietzsche 1969, 61). In
other words, the true self is not identified with intellectual abilities but with the
emotions, drives and energies of the body, which are crucial even for our intellectual and spiritual life. Nietzsche certainly has the ideal of the overman, in
which human beings overcome themselves, but this does not involve transcending the body. It is a strictly this-worldly transcendence. From this point of view,
The Matrix, with its vision of moral progress and perfection through escape from
the physical body, looks decidedly anti-Nietzschean.

As noted earlier, Nietzsche's conception of moral progress also differs from
that envisaged by Marx. Marx sees human progress as something to be achieved
communally by transforming society, whereas for Nietzsche self-perfection is the
work of the solitary human being. If the masses, the herd, conform to traditional
herd values, Nietzsche's overmen are independent, sovereign individuals. They
are also in touch with themselves, as the modern jargon has it. If religion and
modern society have led to our repudiating our vital instincts and desires, the
overman embraces those energies, harnessing and shaping them. They feel deeply
but their passions are controlled. If anything, Nietzsche's ideal is most reminiscent of Aristotle, who develops an alternative to both the Platonic denial of the
passions and their uninhibited expression in the idea of virtue as rational passions.
One issue that arises in connection with Nietzsche, however, is whether his ideal
is too individualistic. There is clearly a turn to the individual, and individuality
for Nietzsche requires working on oneself, self-overcoming, perfecting oneself.
But this self-perfection has to be achieved independently of others, requiring us
to break from the common ideals of society. That there is no reference to social

existence except as a threat to one's self-perfection might seem questionable, given that we exist in the midst of social relations. Nonetheless, this insistence that genuinely human, 'authentic' existence is only possible in isolation from society is a persisting theme, not only in Nietzsche but also in his contemporary Kierkegaard, and the twentieth-century existentialists who succeeded them both.

Kierkegaard

Søren Kierkegaard (1813–1855) also wants to affirm the individual in the face of society. In terms of philosophical history, he sets himself firmly against Hegel's vision of a collective human subject that realises itself in history, the subject that finds its way into Marx's thinking in the form of species being. This for Kierkegaard is an abstract, inhuman vision of humanity, remote from the concrete human existence we actually live. For him, Hegel is like someone who has built a magnificent palace but continues to live alongside it in a hovel (Kierkegaard 1975, 519). His philosophy does not address the situation of real, individual human beings. By contrast, Kierkegaard's focus is very much on what it is to exist as an individual human being. Insofar as the concrete individual appears in Hegel's system, it is only as an instrument or means to the realisation of the collective subject, Spirit. The free individual, standing in opposition to social morality and political institutions, is an aberration, indicating that Spirit has become alienated from itself, and progress consists in overcoming this alienation and reconciling the free individual and the community. Kierkegaard takes the opposite path. He is much more interested in promoting the free individual in opposition to society.

Whereas for Nietzsche the individual to be promoted is the one who is strong enough to fashion values for themselves, to give shape to their lives independently of others, the individual for Kierkegaard is above all the free subject. What is central to individual existence is one's subjectivity, which is manifested in freedom, the freedom to choose, make personal decisions, commit ourselves to a way of life and take responsibility for what we choose. Kierkegaard wants to remind people of what it is to be an individual human being, a free subject. He seeks to rehabilitate the notions of the personal, the particular and the subjective, and he wants to do so in the face of what he calls 'objective' ways of thinking and acting. Objective ways of thinking are abstract, impersonal, disinterested ways of thinking about the world that downplay, deny or forget individual human subjectivity. As Katalin Balog puts it: 'Objectivity is an orientation towards reality based on abstracting away, in various degrees, from subjective experience, and from individual points of view' (Balog 2016). Such abstract, impersonal thinking might be appropriate in a scientific context, but for Kierkegaard, it is entirely inappropriate for thinking about human existence. On his view, the great illusion that individuals suffer is that of thinking and acting in ways that deny their subjectivity and freedom.

For Kierkegaard, culture is increasingly being characterised by this impersonal objective thinking, which manifests itself in a number of ways. In the social sphere, people subordinate themselves more and more to the crowd, the abstract rule of the majority. They readily discard their individuality, the burden of defining their own direction through their own individual decisions, in favour of unthinking conformity with mass opinion, which they take to be the locus of truth. In the moral sphere, people conform to accepted values, living their lives in unthinking conformity with formalised rules. They don't take the trouble to decide for themselves how they should live. They just go along with moral principles that have been codified and handed down to them by others. Kierkegaard is also concerned with the religious sphere of life. He does not reject religion, like Nietzsche, but he is highly critical of what it has become in the modern age. For Kierkegaard, Christianity has also become afflicted with the objective tendency. It has become a public institution devoid of spirit, whose teachings are lifeless and formalistic, objectified into doctrines that can be learnt off by heart, and rituals that can be participated in without passion or feeling. These dead, external trappings of religious life do not require any personal commitment or inward change. On the contrary, they positively discourage personal passion and commitment. For Kierkegaard, the actually existing church is a distraction from an authentic religious life. Despite this harsh critique, however, religious thinking plays an important role in Kierkegaard's thinking, as we will see in a moment.

In all these cases of objective thinking, we lose touch with what for Kierkegaard is most essentially human, namely our subjectivity, our capacity to make personal decisions, to commit ourselves passionately and deliberately to a way of life. To think and act objectively is to stand apart from our lives rather than living them, to live by abstract principles and objective measures. The proper role of philosophy for Kierkegaard is to criticise the illusion of objectivity, and as he puts it in *Concluding Unscientific Postscript*, to help us 'become subjective' (Kierkegaard 2009, 140). This for Kierkegaard is the authentic form of human existence. In a sense, of course, we don't have to work at being human. Physically and biologically, we already exist as human beings. We have two legs, two arms and are able to do various relatively sophisticated things characteristic of our species. Even if we are just part of the unthinking crowd, we are still in this sense human beings. But for Kierkegaard, this is a very mundane sense of 'being human'. When he talks of being human, he wants to describe how human beings ought to be, what it is to live a fully human life. And being authentically human for Kierkegaard means becoming a moral agent, choosing one's values and committing oneself to a way of life. So to exist authentically as a human being, to become subjective, is for Kierkegaard a task and an achievement, indeed the 'highest task' facing a human being.

Kierkegaard often uses literary devices to deepen the reader's subjective engagement with the issues of human existence he is examining. More generally, the existentialist concern with human existence helps explain why literature has often been used as a vehicle for existentialist ideas. Through novels and plays, existentialists have sought to evoke the human experience in all its richness, in the face of more objective or impersonal forms of representation. Film also provides an effective medium for evoking subjective experience, with the advantage of being able to actually show faces and conduct, as well as having access to devices like the close-up and the point of view shot. Dreyer's *The Passion of Joan of Arc* is a case in point. In the midst of her trial, the relentless close-ups of actor Falconneti's face succeed in conveying an inward passion that cannot be communicated in words. The church authorities, through institutional language and scholastic arguments, try to challenge the veracity of Joan's religious experience or to recast it as something of demonic origin. At every turn, their efforts are confronted by the immediacy of the subjective experience that is testified to in Joan's suffering countenance (see Birzache 2014, 9–10).

Insofar as subjectivity is the capacity to make decisive personal choices, to commit oneself deliberately and passionately to a way of life, Kierkegaard thinks that rationality has its limits. We can consistently apply an existing framework of values, but Kierkegaard is most interested in the point where we have to choose the framework itself. Kierkegaard's denunciation of objectivity is also a rejection of the security of pre-existing value systems, ready-made rules handed down to us by others. 'Becoming subjective' means we choose our values, commit ourselves to a way of life. And since we are not making such choices on the basis of a framework of values, but choosing the values themselves, there is no guidance for these choices. They can only be chosen through a pure act of commitment, a passionate 'leap' of choice. Not surprisingly, given the enormous responsibility involved when there is nothing we can turn to for support, Kierkegaard emphasises anxiety or anguish as an essential ingredient of subjective existence. We feel anguish, the 'dizziness of freedom', when faced with a range of possibilities, which we must choose between without any external guidance.

Kierkegaard also speaks of the task of becoming subjective as a process of 'transformation to inwardness', or the 'self-activity of appropriation' (Kierkegaard 2009, 244). This means that to become subjective is to appropriate to myself, to make my own, a way of living. I make a possible way of life inward to me by committing myself to it, passionately choosing or embracing it. Subjectivity is this process of passionate appropriation. And since subjective human existence is also true human existence, a life is a true one to the extent that I have a personal, passionate commitment to it, to the extent that I make it my own. Its truth lies in the commitment, passion and decisiveness with which I appropriate or embrace a way of life, just as the truth of a lover's declaration of love lies in the passionate commitment with which they make their declaration. This is why Kierkegaard says that 'truth is subjectivity' (Kierkegaard 2009, 200). When the question of truth is raised in an objective manner, appropriate in a scientific context, we are concerned with the object to which the knower is related, whether the actual state of affairs is as we say it is. When the question of truth is raised subjectively, in relation to human existence, we are concerned with how we relate to something, the passion with which we embrace it. As far as my subjective existence is concerned, truth lies in the commitment and decisiveness with which I appropriate a way of life. By exercising my freedom, passionately committing myself to a way of life, I make it true for me. In this manner, in *The Passion of Joan of Arc*, the truth of Joan's religious experience is the personal, subjective truth of her commitment.

There are numerous religious references in Kierkegaard's work because he thinks that the most subjective and authentic form of human existence is Christianity. Christianity involves the most intense subjectivity, the purest choice and faith is the highest passion. This is because objectively, for disinterested reason, Christianity leaves a lot to be desired. It is impossible to know whether God actually exists; and Christianity's central notion of the incarnation, the union of an eternal, infinite God and a historical finite man in the figure of Christ is, rationally speaking, unintelligible, an extreme paradox for rational understanding. There is no rational justification whatsoever for faith or religious belief; it is objectively speaking quite unjustifiable. By the same token, this means that faith has nothing to do with objective thinking or justification. It requires instead a completely subjective, passionate commitment, a pure leap of faith. The idea of pure faith is embodied for Kierkegaard in his hero, the biblical character Abraham, whom he discusses in *Fear and Trembling*. The test of faith is whether one's beliefs can be held in the face of overwhelming objective evidence to the contrary. Abraham consented to sacrifice his son Isaac on God's command, an action that is brutal, unjustifiable and meaningless according to human standards. Its sole justification is that it was an act of faith.

There are however a number of issues with Kierkegaard's account. There is, of course, the extreme individualism, the insistence that an authentic human existence is only possible in isolation from society. As a moral ideal, this comes up against the fact that human beings inevitably exist in the midst of social relationships. This is a persistent issue for the twentieth-century existentialist thinkers still to come. Secondly, there is the idea of religious belief as a matter of a pure, ungrounded leap of faith. The problem is that there is no reason why this path should lead us to Christianity. Any belief would surely be legitimate, as long as it was objectively unjustifiable and embraced through a leap of faith. We might wonder how we could possibly distinguish genuine from inauthentic positions here, if the only ground for them is the passionate commitment? On the face of it, in *The Passion of Joan of Arc*, it seems legitimate to ask whether what we are witnessing is a martyr or a confused, delusional young woman. But the question cannot even be posed if the truth of her position lies entirely in the commitment with which she embraces it. More broadly, if the authentic, properly human life is the life in which one commits oneself decisively to a way of life, it would seem that what counts as a proper way of living is very much up to the agent. What is morally important here is not what we do but how we decide and act, and it might be thought that this makes moral decisions entirely arbitrary. Nonetheless, this is the ethical position that emerges, particularly in the writings of Kierkegaard's twentieth-century existentialist successors, to whom we now turn.

Twentieth-Century Existentialism: Sartre et al.

Both Nietzsche and Kierkegaard are important influences on twentieth-century existentialism, whose representatives include Jean-Paul Sartre (1905–1980), Simone de Beauvoir (1908–1986) and Albert Camus (1913–1960). These figures flourished especially just after the Second World War. In what follows, I will talk about existentialism primarily as formulated by Sartre, before turning to some of the modifications introduced by de Beauvoir. What the existentialists primarily take from Kierkegaard is the focus on the individual, on concrete individual existence and the emphasis on personal, free choice as central to that existence. However, they side with Nietzsche in rejecting religion. For the existentialists, as for Nietzsche, God is dead, this judgement reflecting the erosion of religious belief in the face of the rise of the modern scientific worldview. For modern science, as we have seen, the universe operates without any purpose, through mechanical interactions, according to the impersonal operation of physical laws. There is no God to hand us principles and values from on high. Nor is there any God-given order or grand plan we can appeal to, in the world or in our own nature, to give direction and purpose to our existence. Therefore, they emphatically reject a natural law morality based on Aquinas's notion of a human nature designed by God to have certain inherent tendencies or purposes.

Existentialism also continues Nietzsche's critique of modern attempts to find an alternative basis for morality, in particular, utilitarianism and Kantianism. Like Nietzsche, they reject a utilitarian, happiness-centred ethics based on a scientific view of human beings as creatures driven to seek pleasure and to avoid pain. They tend to identify happiness with unthinking contentment, a state that could only be achieved through the sacrifice of one's critical faculties. In addition, the existentialists no longer agree with Kant that reason, the rational self, can establish moral principles, values or goals. For them, the rational Kantian agent is far removed from the ordinary, concrete, flesh and blood individual. Kant's attempts to found morality on a purely rational procedure only mean that Kantian moral thinking has become lost in an unreal world of philosophical abstraction. For the existentialist then, there is nothing outside of us or within our nature that we can appeal to in order to justify our values and moral rules. The world is 'absurd', meaningless, which is to say, there is no reason for the way the world is, for what happens in it, and human beings in particular have no reason or justification for their existence or way of life.

This sense of life's meaninglessness was no doubt intensified by the horrors of the Second World War, against which not only religion but also all the familiar moral and social values, rules and safeguards, had proved to be useless. The sense of absurdity was further compounded by the ensuing Cold War, the protracted post-war standoff between the United States and the Soviet Union, with its ever-present threat of a nuclear holocaust that could wipe out humanity overnight. Bergman's 1956 *The Seventh Seal* is very much a reflection of the situation in the fifties, as the director himself made clear (see Cowie 1982, 141). The bubonic plague that is ravaging medieval Sweden stands in for the atomic bomb, the threat of mass death that is bringing people to question all moral and religious values and to reflect on whether life has any meaning. Given all this, it might seem that all we are left with is nihilism, in the sense of the complete absence of meaning and value. For Sartre, however, the breakdown of religious belief, along with traditional moral and social values, was in fact a marvellous opportunity. We might have been abandoned by God (Sartre 1975, 352), but this means that we are free to make ourselves. Existentialism doesn't say that there are no longer any values, but that human beings are the source of values, which they actively create or choose. It doesn't say that life is meaningless, but that it lacks external justification. Our life is meaningful to the extent that we give ourselves meaning; it is up to human beings to actively create meaning for themselves through their choices. Nothing can assist them in these choices since it is the values they choose that inform their choices and actions, not the values that determine the choice. Existentialism thus reminds us that there is no moral legislator but ourselves, that human beings alone are responsible for the values and goals they have. Hence Sartre's claim that 'existentialism is a humanism', because it puts free human beings at the centre of the picture.

Sartre thus follows Kierkegaard in making freedom central to human existence. But where Kierkegaard more or less assumes human freedom, Sartre gives a developed account of it, in his major existentialist work *Being and Nothingness*. On Sartre's account, human beings are in part determined, but also entirely free. It is our freedom that distinguishes us from the rest of nature, that makes a human being something more than a mere thing. Physically or biologically, we may have a causally determined makeup, but morally, as a person in the full sense, our existence remains to be determined by the exercise of our free will. We are entirely free to choose our goals and values. To that extent, we are capable of determining ourselves independently of all external influences, not only natural but also social. We may exist in the midst of society, but nothing in our social environment can determine the choices we make. Here Sartre also departs from Nietzsche's more naturalistic account of freedom as an exercise in self-mastery that is possible only for the strong few. Sartre's freedom is more like free will, a capacity for undetermined choice that all human beings possess. Through its exercise one goes beyond one's physical and biological make-up, or in Sartre's terminology, 'transcends one's facticity'. Despite Sartre's criticisms of Kant, this can be seen as an extreme version of Kant's notion of autonomous self-determination, without Kant's faith that reason will provide us with guidance. Instead, for Sartre, every choice is a radical, unjustified leap of faith. If Kant's position can be described as subjective universalism, in which we create moral principles according to the criterion of universalisabiity, which acts as an objective standard, Sartre's is subjectivism pure and simple. There is no right or wrong, objectively speaking, and so no right or wrong choices. To choose alone determines the value of what we choose (see Sartre 1975, 350).

Along with this freedom is the anguish that Kierkegaard identified as an essential aspect of freedom. Sartre takes up this theme with gusto. To have no rules or signs to guide our choices, to be wholly responsible for our goals, values and purposes, is a terrible burden, which we experience as anguish, the fundamental anxiety before the necessity of having to choose. There is a great temptation to avoid this anxiety, to take refuge in various forms of 'bad faith', ways of thinking in which I try to deny my freedom and responsibility. This includes imagining that I am the victim of desire or passion, that I am determined by my biological nature or social environment to act as I do, that I am nothing more than the social role others see me as playing, that I was 'only following orders' or in general thinking that there is anything at all outside of myself that determines or supports my decisions. In reality, it is I who have chosen to regard these things as determining me and so cannot evade responsibility in this way. Here, in sharp contrast to Kierkegaard, for whom religious faith is the highest expression of freedom, Sartre sees religion as a supreme form of bad faith. It involves belief in a God who provides us with ready-made values, directions and signs as to what we should do. Inasmuch as we can speak of divine signs or forms of guidance in the world, it is we who have chosen to interpret them as such.

This is Sartre's take on the biblical story of Abraham. For Kierkegaard, Abraham, in consenting to sacrifice his son on God's command, commits to an action that is brutal and meaningless by human standards. In doing so, he demonstrates the pure faith that is the highest expression of freedom. For Sartre however, the lesson the story of Abraham demonstrates is that there is nothing we can appeal to for guidance in our choices. An angel may command Abraham to sacrifice his son, but this doesn't absolve Abraham of responsibility for his actions. At the very least, he has to choose to believe that this being before him is an angel, not a demon or a hallucination. He remains responsible for whatever he decides to do (Sartre 1975, 351). In the same way, the father in *Frailty* who believes that an angel has visited him and given him the mission of destroying demons disguised as human beings, remains responsible for what he does. He has chosen to interpret his experiences in this manner. The audience is likely to assume that he is suffering from a hallucination and is interpreting his experiences as real in order to justify his murderous actions. If, as happens in the film, it turns out that there really was an angel, this might tempt us to think that he had no choice in the matter, that obedience is obligatory. But Sartre would nonetheless insist on his absolute responsibility. To the extent we see something in our situation as a summons to action, even the commands of an angel, it is always we who have given it this significance through our choices.

In general, through bad faith we find ways of pretending to ourselves that we are not free. In so doing, we try to avoid the anguish that goes with recognition of our freedom and responsibility. For Sartrean existentialism, however, this is a cowardly evasion, a denial of the very freedom that makes us human. We become estranged from ourselves, live inauthentically, which is the cardinal sin for existentialist ethics. Evidently, Sartre is not proposing a traditional notion of ethics. Traditional ethics, in Sartre's terms, is the belief that there is a fixed set of absolute principles or transcendent values, existing independently of our choices, grounded in God, nature or reason, to which we can turn for guidance. This is not, however, to reject ethics as such, only a certain conception of it. For Sartre, we freely choose, create and are responsible for the values that define us. In bad faith, we try in various ways to evade this responsibility. Ethics as traditionally conceived is itself a form of bad faith. It allows us to think of ourselves as having a pre-ordained role or function to fulfill, an attitude that Sartre refers to as 'serious-mindedness' or the 'spirit of seriousness' (Sartre 1958, 681). This is the kind of bad faith exhibited by the utterly humourless, doggedly inflexible hitman Chigurh in *No Country for Old Men*, who believes that he is bound by a set of principles that leave him no choice but to do what he does. His victims Carson Wells and Carla Jean both tell him that 'You don't have to do this', but that possibility seems to be beyond his comprehension.

Authenticity is the contrary state of affairs to bad faith. It involves rejecting the inauthentic spirit of seriousness, and explicitly acknowledging and accepting our freedom and responsibility for our choices and values. As de Beauvoir puts it in *The Ethics of Ambiguity*, the authentic human being 'will not agree to recognise any foreign absolute'; they will 'refuse to believe in unconditioned values which would set themselves athwart freedom like things' and recognise that 'it is human existence which makes values spring up in the world' (de Beauvoir 1976, 14). There is room here for ethical judgements, but unlike traditional ethics, these judgements do not relate to what people do, the content of their acts. The primary concern is how they make their decisions and act. What is ethically important for existentialism is that, whatever we do, we choose and act in the awareness that they are freely chosen and that we are entirely responsible for them. As de Beauvoir puts it, it is necessary to 'will oneself free' (de Beauvoir 1976, 24), meaning to choose to embrace our freedom. In this, existentialism follows Kierkegaard in giving importance to the freedom with which we choose a way of life, over the content of what we choose.

The developed existentialist perspective gives us a further angle from which to consider *The Addiction*. Along with the Nietzschean reference discussed earlier, there are numerous references to Kierkegaard and Sartre in the film. This should not be too surprising, as the central character is writing her doctoral thesis on the topic of existentialism. At the same time, the film puts forward the decidedly un-existentialist thesis that in the end, Kathleen has no choice but to accept her fate, that she cannot help committing evil acts and that all human beings have an innate predisposition towards evil. This is, of course, the gloomy Augustinian view that human beings are fundamentally corrupted by, and largely powerless in the face of, their base appetites. People may deny this addiction to evil, but they are deceiving themselves. This is the view that Kathleen herself comes around to. Her true nature as a human being is revealed the moment she is turned into a vampire. Although she protests when first bitten by Casanova, it is half-hearted resistance. Tell me to go away, says Casanova, but she cannot. Part of her wants what is being offered, and it is the same with some of her own victims, fellow students, whom she in turn upbraids for their hypocrisy when they protest: 'You know, this obtuseness is disheartening, especially in a doctoral candidate'. And she naturally becomes critical of the existentialist authors she is studying for their insistence on human freedom and for ignoring what drives our behaviour: 'Kierkegaard was right, there is an awful precipice before us, but he was wrong about the leap. There is a difference between jumping and being pushed'.

For existentialism, it is of course this way of thinking about human beings that is self-deceptive. The vampire who considers that they have no choice but to do what they do is suffering from bad faith. From this perspective, the more authentic vampire would be the one who questions, even struggles against their condition and refuses to be defined by it. Existentially troubled vampires in film go back at least to Louis (Brad Pitt) from *Interview with the Vampire* (Neil Jordan, 1994). Although his mentor Lestat (Tom Cruise) tells him that it is his nature to kill, he hates his desire for blood and tries to find another purpose for his existence. Sartrean existentialism also gives us another way of reading *Fight Club*, as a quest not so much for Nietzschean self-affirmation as for an authentic existence. Here it is Brad Pitt's Tyler Durden encouraging the film's narrator to acknowledge their freedom. The narrator begins the film in a state of bad faith, subordinate to an ideal of self-perfection defined in consumerist terms as a matter of owning the right clothes and having an apartment filled with the right furniture and design objects. On this reading, Durden provides a means for the narrator to escape from his inauthentic existence, by blowing up his apartment and destroying all the things he imagines define him. We can now interpret Durden's credo, 'it's only after we've lost everything that we're free to do anything', as an invitation, once we have gotten over attachment to external possessions and conventional aspirations, to exercise our freedom to determine ourselves.

The film also touches on Sartre's idea that we have been 'abandoned' by God, an abandonment that is at the same time a liberation. Durden explicitly pushes this line: 'Our fathers were our models for God. If our fathers bailed, what does that tell you about God?' This quickly turns into rebellion against a God who would abandon his children: 'We don't need him', he tells the narrator. 'We are God's unwanted children'. Thus, disabused of the idea that there needs to be a God to provide a meaning and structure for human existence, and no longer participating in the consumerism that substitutes for God as a source of meaning and fulfilment in late capitalist society, the narrator can exercise his freedom and create himself. The final barrier to this is Durden himself. Earlier the narrator's overcoming of Durden was interpreted in Nietzschean terms as the appropriation of vital energies. But we could also interpret it in Sartrean terms, as the narrator overcoming one final form of bad faith, in that there is an aspect of his activity that he does not want to recognise as his own or take responsibility for. By recognising that he is responsible for his alter-ego, consciously accepting responsibility for his existence, the narrator finally attains existential authenticity.

We also now have a fresh perspective on Woody Allen's *Crimes and Misdemeanors*. Being abandoned by God is an explicit theme in the film. The film's protagonist, the murderous eye-doctor Judah, finds that God is silent, nowhere to be seen and that he is free to have his troublesome mistress murdered. For many of the people that he encounters, God is indispensable. As we saw in Chapter Two, the rabbi Ben insists that he could not go on living unless he believed that the universe was ultimately a meaningful place, with a moral structure backed by the existence of some higher power. We need a God-given moral law, for if there is no higher power, or moral structure with real meaning, then all we have is an empty, absurd world. For Ben, we need religion precisely to keep such meaninglessness and absurdity at bay. And for Judah's father Sol, who appears in flashback sequences, religious belief is so indispensable that he is willing to believe even in the absence of any evidence. In the sequence at the dinner table, arguing with his atheist sister May, he goes so far as to insist that 'if necessary I will always prefer God over the truth'.

In the end, however, like the knight Antonius Block in Bergman's *The Seventh Seal*, Judah finds that there is nothing there, beyond the world revealed by science and observation. And however much religious belief in the absence of any supporting evidence whatsoever might appeal from a Kierkegaardian point of view, Judah's attitude is closer to that of the Sartrean existentialist; that belief in God and a God-given order of the sort espoused by Sol and Ben is just an attempt to hide from the reality of one's situation, which is that one does indeed exist in an empty, meaningless, absurd world. In the language of Camus in *The Myth of Sisyphus*, it is to commit 'philosophical suicide', to try to avoid absurdity at the cost of sacrificing one's critical faculties (Camus 1975, 43). The film itself seems to concur with this judgement. Ben, who doggedly persists in believing in a meaningful universe, ends up going blind. To take refuge in such beliefs is, it would seem, to blind oneself to the truth of one's situation. The director's own view is quite straightforwardly existentialist: 'I just wanted to illustrate, in an entertaining way, that there is no God, that we're alone in the universe, and that there is nobody out there to punish you, that there's not going to be any kind of Hollywood ending to your life in any way, that your morality is strictly up to you' (Schickel 2003, 149).

As we have seen, Sartre sees a positive aspect to this abandonment by God. The world may be absurd, but the other side of this is that morality is indeed strictly up to us, that human beings are free to give their lives whatever goal or purpose they choose. We thus take centre stage in giving our lives meaning and value. In *Crimes and Misdemeanors* the existentialist position properly speaking seems most closely represented by the philosopher Lewis Levy. Levy speaks of our capacity for moral choice, arguing like Sartre that we define ourselves by the choices we have made. He acknowledges the indifference of the universe, the way in which events unfold unpredictably and unfairly, and how human happiness does not seem to have been included in the design of creation. Nonetheless, by exercising our freedom, we invest the indifferent universe with value and meaning, we create meaning in our lives. At the same time, though Levy's upbeat views constitute the closing commentary in the film, he is speaking from beyond the grave, having committed suicide. This might be thought to give his words ironic significance, suggesting that in the end, the meaning we can invest in our lives through our choices is not enough to sustain us. Perhaps this is the case, although Sartre might be unperturbed by this development. His own position is that suicide is just one of the options we can choose. We can choose to embrace our existence wholeheartedly or evaluate our life and circumstances as intolerable and do away with ourselves. The important thing is to acknowledge that whatever path we take, we have freely chosen it.

If Allen's *Match Point* explores similar themes to those of his *Crimes and Misdemeanors*, the tone of the film is bleaker and more nihilistic. This time it is tennis instructor Chris who gets away with the murder of his mistress who is threatening to destroy his privileged existence. God is once again out of the way, but this absence is not given any positive significance in terms of making room for us to create meaning and value for ourselves. The only perspective presented is that of the main character, for whom the notion of a meaningful world with some kind of order has been wholly eclipsed by a scientific view, leading to the estimate that 'all existence is here by blind chance'. In this view, all that happens in one's life, one's career, relationships and final destination, is ultimately a matter of blind luck, of random chance and contingency. Indeed, this seems to be confirmed by the film, in that Chris even gets away with his murder through sheer luck, when a likely suspect, a conveniently dead criminal, turns up just as the suspicious detective Banner (James Nesbitt) is closing in on him. Overall, Chris concludes, it is better to be lucky than good (cf. Pannereau 2009, 159). For him, the overwhelming role of luck in life seems to undermine any point in being moral, which requires something beyond an indifferent universe. As he says to the ghost of his murdered mistress Nola 'It would be fitting if I were apprehended and punished. At least there would be some small sign of justice, some small measure of hope for the possibility of meaning'. In the absence of any such sign, we are left instead with a nihilistic amoralist, who functions entirely on the basis of self-interest.

In *Match Point*, then, the lack of a meaningful, God-given order in the world is taken to undermine the possibility of responsible moral behaviour, given that it is held to mean that whatever happens in our lives is determined in the end by blind luck. In this, it stands opposed to Sartre's more optimistic view that our abandonment by God gives us the opportunity to take centre stage as moral legislator. For his part, Sartre would likely see the position presented in *Match Point* as a convenient way of denying our role as moral agents and so another form of bad faith. We try to avoid taking responsibility for our actions and values by construing everything that comes about in our lives as the result of external forces that we cannot control. Arguably, this is another form of bad faith exhibited by the implacable Chigurh in *No Country for Old Men*. He uses the luck of a coin toss to decide the life or death of his victims, trying to evade taking responsibility for his actions by presenting them as if they were the workings of an indifferent universe (see McCaffrey 2011, 132). He is called out for this self-deception by his last victim, Carla Jean. When after tossing the coin, he tells her to 'call it', she replies: 'No. I ain't gonna call it … The coin don't have no say. It's just you'.

There is a broader issue here, the role of luck in morality. Ordinarily, we see luck as inimical to morality and don't think that people can be morally judged for what is due to factors beyond their control. This makes especially paradoxical the phenomenon of 'moral luck', the circumstance that people are often treated as objects of moral assessment even if a significant aspect of what they do depends on factors beyond their control, the result of luck (see Nagel 1979; Williams 1982). Even though success or failure in what one tries to do almost always depends on factors beyond one's control, the difference between the two is commonly seen as being morally significant. We think for example that murder would be morally worse than attempted murder, even if our intended victim's survival is down to sheer luck. One's actions are also limited by the opportunities and choices with which one is faced and these are largely out of our control. Thus, in *Force Majeure*, even though, as his girlfriend Fanni (Fanni Metelius) suspects, Mats might have behaved the same way as Tomas did in *Force Majeure*, abandoning his family when faced with an apparently dangerous situation, we still judge Tomas more harshly than we do Mats. And we do so even though it is a matter of pure luck that Tomas, rather than Mats, happened to be the one exposed to the dangerous situation.

A natural response to this would be to try to exclude all aspects of an agent's circumstances that are out of their control from the realm of morality. That is Kant's strategy. He insists that what matters morally is not how a person's actions turn out, which is beyond their control, but what is 'in their heart'. What makes an action morally good is not whether it succeeds or fails, but purely the kind of motivation we have. Our motivation at least is within our power to determine, purely through our own reason. And once again following in Kant's footsteps, this is also essentially Sartre's position. If human beings are moral legislators who are absolutely free to determine themselves, Sartre is careful to insist that this is not the common sense, negative idea of freedom as being able to do what we want to do, of there being no obstacles to stop us achieving our goals, having the ability or power to achieve our goals. For Sartre, the success or failure of our actions has no bearing whatsoever on our freedom, which is purely the freedom to create values, ideals and goals, to form intentions. As such, even in the most confined circumstances, we can still be said to be absolutely free.

The danger in this strategy of excluding everything outside our control is that we are likely to end up with an agent that is as abstract and unreal as Kant's, indeed even more so. Sartre's free agent not only escapes confinement by external circumstances, but is also unconstrained by any pre-existing, orienting principles, whether the rational commands of Kantian morality or the values and ideals constitutive of our moral identity that ordinarily structure our choices. For Sartre, nothing whatsoever conditions our choices. Any principles or values we might appeal to in order to justify our choices have themselves been chosen by us. To think otherwise is just another form of bad faith, another attempt to hide from our freedom and responsibility. Thus, all our choices are unconditioned, radical choices, pure unjustified leaps into the void. There is no reason for us to choose one way or another. The only requirement is that we acknowledge our freedom and complete responsibility for our choices. But we might wonder if this is a coherent picture, whether we can even meaningfully be said to choose here. A meaningful choice is arguably one in which we decide what to do in the light of our defining values. It presupposes some pre-existing framework of values, some kind of identity or place where we stand. Not having such a framework of values would not mean that we are radically free, free to choose ourselves in our entirety, but that we would have no place to stand. We would in fact be crippled as moral agents. As Charles Taylor puts it, 'this promised self-possession' would not be liberation but 'the most total self-loss' (Taylor 1985a, 35).

As such, Sartrean existentialism seems to be proposing a moral ideal, a radically free existence, that is beyond the capacity of ordinary flesh and blood human beings to achieve. It joins a long line of philosophies in doing so, but with a special irony in that it is part of a line of thinking that seeks to turn its focus on concrete, individual human existence. A number of criticisms raised by Simone de Beauvoir in *The Ethics of Ambiguity* call attention to the unreal character of Sartre's picture. For de Beauvoir, to say that we are free in a social situation that frustrates us at every turn is surely to employ a rather abstract sense of freedom. What kind of freedom, she reports asking Sartre, could a woman have shut up in a harem? She was not convinced by Sartre's answer that even such a cloistered situation could still be lived in different ways (de Beauvoir 1962, 434) For de Beauvoir, actually being able to achieve our goals is relevant to freedom. The kind of situation we are in has a bearing on how free we can be said to be. Some situations offer more possibilities for the realisation of our possibilities than others. Freedom is still at the core of her picture, but she clearly wants to moderate Sartre's extreme subjectivism.

Another expression of this extreme subjectivism is the view that choosing alone determines the value of what we choose. We define what is right by our free choices. For this ethics, any position whatsoever is fine as long as we acknowledge that we have freely chosen it and take responsibility for our choices. The only requirement is that of personal authenticity. But here we run into the same problem as the God of divine command theory. If something is right because we choose it, there are no moral limits to what we can choose, and with no reason to choose one way or another, our choices become entirely arbitrary. Once again, radical freedom seems to undermine the capacity to meaningfully choose. Instead of arguing that we define what is right purely by our free choices, de Beauvoir builds an objective standard into her ethics, albeit one conceived in terms of freedom. There is still the requirement of authenticity, the requirement that as de Beauvoir puts it, one 'wills oneself free' in the sense of choosing to embrace one's freedom, to act in explicit awareness that one is free and responsible. But in addition, 'to will oneself free is to also will others free' (de Beauvoir 1976, 73). In other words, there is the further requirement that you should act in ways that allow others to make their own choices and take responsibility for those choices (see Moore 2008). With this, a purely personal notion of authenticity gives way to one that takes other people into account.

There are even hints of this move beyond subjectivism in Sartre himself. For Sartre, we can only judge individuals in terms of whether they are in bad faith or authentic, but he also tries to argue that certain attitudes can only be held in bad faith. In particular, it is impossible to be authentic while supporting antisemitic or racist views. This is the position that comes out in his 'Portrait of an Anti-Semite' (Sartre 1995). In part, Sartre is arguing there that the anti-Semite is in bad faith because they adopt the fixed, stone-like posture of the 'pitiless anti-Semite', pretending that it is not their free choice to think in this way. But there is a social as well as a personal side to this. To identify a person or a race as being immutably lazy, stingy or hateful is to deny the human condition itself. It denies our condition and our situation because if all human beings are free, no individual or group of people can have a fixed nature. This seems to suggest that for Sartre, what is intolerable about human relationships is any reduction of human beings to the status of mere objects with a fixed nature. You cannot claim to be acting authentically if you contribute in any way to the objectification or humiliation of other people. However, Sartre is not at this point in a position to develop this further. His official view of other people is dominated by his focus on the free individual. It is to the question of other people that we now turn.

The Social Situation: de Beauvoir

Sartre formulates his notion of the free individual not only in relation to God, but also in relation to other people. At one point, he even suggests that God is merely the concept of the 'other' pushed to its limit (Sartre 1958, 266). But while Sartre's God is conspicuous in his absence, the other person is an unavoidable part of our situation. Sartre envisages the individual as always existing in the midst of a situation, not only natural but also social, a world of other people. At the same time, the extreme individualism visible in Nietzsche and Kierkegaard reappears in Sartre's account of social relations which he formulates in *Being and Nothingness*. For Sartre, one's freedom depends on negating the freedom of others, and likewise, other people threaten the individual's freedom. They threaten to steal the individual's freedom by turning them into objects of appraisal, judgement and categorisation. And anyone who identifies too strongly with their communal existence, with the role they play in the eyes of others, becomes estranged from themselves and falls into inauthenticity and bad faith (see Cooper 1999, 109).

Sartre treats the relationship between ourselves and other people as primarily 'scopic'. That is, in the first instance it takes the form of my 'being seen', being an object of 'the look'. In becoming aware of being looked at by another subject, I become aware of myself as I appear to the other person. Sartre gives the example of someone 'moved by jealousy or vice' to peep through a keyhole. Completely absorbed in their acts, they are not aware of themselves looking through the keyhole, only of the scene within. In this situation, it takes no more than a sound that could indicate another's presence, for them to be abruptly aware that they are a possible object for the gaze of another and to feel shame. Caught out staring through the keyhole, the other's look makes me see myself as the other would see me, as having a fixed set of properties and behaviours. I experience myself as I am for them, a 'peeping Tom', a pervert, a disgrace. Sartre points to a number of feelings through which I experience myself as an object for others; shame in the first instance, but also fear and pride, as well as such related phenomena as guilt, embarrassment and paranoia (see Sartre 1958, 255, 289; Cox 2006, 46). As the object of the other's gaze, I no longer choose myself. The other now determines the meaning of what I am and do, my role and purpose. In short, I am robbed of my freedom. For this reason, Sartre sees our relations with others as always being relations of conflict. They are a struggle to avoid being turned into an object by others. Although the other objectifies me, steals my freedom, I can always reassert my freedom by seeking to objectify the other in turn. Since I cannot be an object for an object, I will thereby able to safeguard my subjectivity, my freedom. Of course, that is what the other is trying to do as well. Social relations consist in this ongoing struggle between competing free subjects, each striving for ascendancy over the other.

Implicit in this account is the idea that it is through the gaze of another, becoming an object for them, that one acquires a determinate self or identity. Here, Sartre recognises that a lot of what we take ourselves to be involves internalising the judgements or definitions of others, incorporating how other people see us into our self-image. However, Sartre sees this in entirely negative terms. For him, to be defined by others in any way is to suffer a reduction of our freedom, our capacity to define ourselves. It is not that we ever really cease to be free. We remain free in that we can always reassert our freedom, break away from the fixating look of the other, and try to make them in turn the objects of our gaze. As free beings, everyone is committed to the project of negating the freedom of others. There is also a form of bad faith in which I hide from my freedom by imagining I am no more than the object I appear to be in the eyes of others, acting as if the whole of my humanity coincided with the role that I perform. In this connection, Sartre offers the famous example of a waiter who thinks they are nothing, but the waiter others see them as being (Sartre 1958, 59). This form of bad faith is also evident in the character Estelle from Sartre's play *No Exit*, set in an existentialist Hell where it is the inmates themselves who will be doing the tormenting. She yearns for definition in the eyes of others. Through her it becomes apparent that the gaze that objectifies and defines one can also be one's own gaze reflected in a mirror, insofar as this reveals myself as others see me. Estelle feels keenly the lack of mirrors in her hellish environment, saying: 'When I can't see myself I begin to wonder if I really and truly exist' (Sartre 2000, 196–197).

Some of these dynamics can be discerned in Hitchcock's monument to voyeurism, *Rear Window* (1954). In the film, L.B. Jefferies (James Stewart), wheelchairbound with a broken leg, passes the time watching the neighbours in his apartment block. We in the audience observe alongside him. Through him, we become acquainted with the characters who inhabit the building, whom Jefferies labels and classifies – the aspiring composer, the enticing blonde, 'Miss Lonelyhearts' and above all Thorwald (Raymond Burr), the travelling salesman directly across the courtyard with the bedridden, nagging wife. When Thorwald's wife disappears. Jefferies begins to suspect that the salesman has murdered her. At this point, Jefferies is absorbed in the activity of observing. Any self-awareness is fleeting. For the most part, he sees without being seen, invisible to others, the 'pure subject', invulnerable and safe. For him, Thorwald is the quarry, the neighbour who may be a murderer and whose behaviour he interprets accordingly. If he is himself seen and judged for his behaviour by his girlfriend Lisa (Grace Kelly), and housekeeper Stella (Thelma Ritter), who think he may be engaging in ethically dubious behaviour, they are quickly drawn in, forget their disapproval and become watchers themselves.

If the film strongly evokes the experience of looking, it also dramatically captures the change in consciousness that comes from awareness of being looked at. Despite Jefferies's misgivings, Lisa heads across the courtyard and sneaks into Thorwald's apartment looking for evidence of his crime. There she is discovered by Thorwald, only to be saved by the intervention of two hurriedly-called cops. As she indicates to the still-watching Jefferies that she has found incriminating evidence, the missing wife's wedding ring, Thorwald notices and looks up to catch a glimpse of his observer. In this moment, Jefferies is transformed from invisible watcher into the one who is seen, becoming painfully aware that he is now an object for the gaze of another. The consequence of this awareness, as Sartre suggests, is that he is no longer the centre of his world, unselfconsciously immersed in his observation, but becomes alienated from himself, aware of himself as an object in the other's world. He is the snooper who has been caught out snooping. He now experiences fear and a sense of his own vulnerability, not unreasonably given that Thorwald will shortly come over to try to silence his nosy neighbour. Hitchcock himself thought that the James Stewart character was a real peeping tom, but also that we are all like that, whether watching a movie or, if the opportunity presented itself, something interesting through unclosed blinds. He also thought that being such a snoop, Jefferies deserved to be attacked by Thorwald (Truffaut 1986, 321, 328).

This transformation in one's experience brought about by the look of the other is also effectively captured in *The Truman Show* (1998), Peter Weir's definitive urban paranoia film. In the film, Truman (Jim Carrey) discovers that since birth he has been the unwitting star of a reality television show, his town being an enormous studio set filled with actors. Initially unself-consciously engaged in his activities, and comfortably integrated into his social environment, Truman's existence is transformed by the sudden awareness that he is being observed by those around him. This realisation begins when he accidentally hears voices on his car radio detailing his progress to work. From this point on, he becomes conscious of being an observable object and is continually worried that he is being watched and followed. And as Sartre notes, once one is aware of oneself as looked at, the look need not be confined to two eyes turned in one's direction. Truman notices signs of observation everywhere: the slight glance of the passer-by in his direction, the car mirrors that seem to angle towards him as he walks by.

Eventually, however, Truman reasserts himself as a subject and turns the tables on his watchers. In the film's final scene as he is poised to escape the studio set through a door in a giant painted wall, he confronts the other. Here, the notion of the other has been pushed to its limit in the form not of God but the television show's God-like producer Christof (Ed Harris), all-seeing and all-powerful. His voice booming from the heavens, Christof informs Truman that, along with millions of others, he has been watching him since he was born. He knows him better than he knows himself and does not think he will go through with his escape. He wants Truman to submit to him, to continue playing the role Christof has engineered for him. For Truman however, this would be a self-betrayal. Reasserting his own freedom, he bids goodbye to Christof and the audience and walks out the door. In its conclusion, the film departs from Sartre's model in envisaging free-dom as a once-and-for-all escape from a situation of observation and objectifica-tion, rather than the driving element in an ongoing conflict between competing subjects. However, the question inevitably arises as to how Truman will fare on the outside before the eyes of the world, and whether, known by millions, his situ-ation will be significantly different.

Sartre himself, in his later writings, came to question the extreme individual-ism that he had formerly championed. He came to pay more attention to the social situation we find ourselves in, and its influence upon us. For the later Sartre, we are all to some extent formed by the cultures in which we are born, formed by our prescribed role in that culture, by our class position, our means of providing for our subsistence and so on. We occupy roles that existed long before we came onto the scene. These circumstances can even condition the way we think, limiting our capacity to envisage alternatives to our current situation. Nonetheless, Sartre does not want to say that we are simply a product of our social circumstances, wholly determined by our culture. As he put it in a later interview, 'human beings can always make something out of what is made of them' (Sartre 1983, 35). Without abandoning his commitment to freedom, he came to argue for an account that acknowledges that human beings are profoundly influenced and constrained by their social and historical circumstances. The account that best describes these circumstances, Sartre argued, was Marxism. Marxism gives an account of the oppressive class relations that characterise modern capitalist societies. And free-dom now becomes a matter of overcoming these oppressive social relations, establishing non-oppressive relations in society.

This turn from the individual to the social situation, and the social relations that shape our existence as individuals, is also evident in de Beauvoir's thinking. Indeed, she led the way here, and was an important inspiration for this turn in Sartre's thinking. Her interest is not so much in class relations but gender rela-tions, oppressive relations between men and women that seem to be a feature of all societies. On the analysis that she provides in her feminist classic *The Second Sex*, at the heart of this oppression is the denial of women's subjectivity, their reduction to objects, subordinate to the projects and freedom of men, which makes them the 'second sex' relative to men. In other words, de Beauvoir argues, women continually experience themselves as objects, not as subjects. They do not experience themselves as active, do not order the world around themselves, but experience the world as ordered by men and in which women are objects. They live through men, and in men's terms. Says de Beauvoir, 'This downfall represents a moral fault if the subject consents to it', a form of bad faith; but it can also be inflicted on the subject, and if so 'it spells frustration and oppression' (de Beauvoir 1953, 27).

Here, de Beauvoir is using elements of Sartre's description of social relation-ships in *Being and Nothingness* for her purposes. For Sartre, as we have seen, we encounter another person, another subject, through their look. Under the gaze of another, our freedom is stolen away from us. We experience ourselves as an object for them, an instrument for their projects. We can only assert our subjectivity, our freedom, by looking at them in turn, turning them into an object for us. At the same time, for Sartre this is only ever a temporary limitation. I retain my freedom to objectify others in the next moment. Beyond that fleeting moment in which one is reduced to an object for others, one always retains one's ability to, as it were, return the look. So Sartre gives us a philosophy of free and equal subjectivities that encounter each other in a situation of competing mastery. The look can always be reciprocated. But de Beauvoir argues that relations between men and women are not reciprocal in that way; they are oppressive, one-way relationships. Women continually experience themselves as objects for men, rather than free subjects. A woman cannot look at a man in the sense of threatening his freedom. It is worth noting a terminological difference between Sartre and de Beauvoir. For Sartre, the other is the term used to describe the other person, the subject, who looks at me and renders me an object. For de Beauvoir, the other refers to women as being other than man, an object rather than a subject.

How does this objectification or 'othering' of women come about? Why according to de Beauvoir isn't there a reciprocal relationship between the sexes? For de Beauvoir, it is not simply a matter of bad faith, an attempt on the part of women to deny their freedom. Rather, she sees it as a result of power relations in society, of social and cultural oppression, which is internalised by women themselves. For example, there are the limiting cultural representations of what it means to be a woman, conceptions of 'the feminine' or 'feminine nature', which are internalised by women, becoming part of the way they think about themselves. This is psychological oppression. Secondly, there is the socialisation process, the way individuals are trained from birth into appropriate kinds of behaviour, appropriate roles, by parents, teachers and so on. For example, de Beauvoir argues, boys are raised to be active, girls to be passive and repress their impulses. And there is women's lack of concrete means for self-affirmation and self-assertion, because of economic oppression, discrimination and social and economic dependence.

So, to sum up de Beauvoir's view, women continually experience themselves as objects for men, rather than as free subjects. Because this is sustained by an inequitable social and economic structure, women do not have an equal ability to shrug off their objectification by 'returning the look'. Unlike Sartre, at least the Sartre of *Being and Nothingness*, de Beauvoir argues that we must interpret self-other relations in the context of overall power relations in a society, patriarchal power relations. It is social oppression that makes women think of themselves as objects. This is not, as Sartre might say, simply a matter of bad faith, a cowardly wish to hide from one's freedom, but a result of oppressive social structures. At the same time, de Beauvoir does seem to think that there is an element of bad faith involved here, that women have been to some extent complicit in their own oppression, treating themselves as sexual objects or appealing to a supposed 'feminine nature' in order to deny their freedom.

The overriding point de Beauvoir wants to make is that women are not doomed to a subordinate social position. There is nothing natural, essential or inevitable about this because there is no such thing as a human nature or essence, and in particular, no such thing as a 'feminine nature'. Throughout history, women may have been subordinated to men, but this is not because women are by nature submissive or inferior. It is society that has made women subordinate to men. And it is possible for women to recognise this and work to combat social oppression. In *The Second Sex*, de Beauvoir emphasises the need for changes in women's economic circumstances, equal access to jobs, salary levels and so on; as well as the need for women to shake off their complicity with oppression and to recognise that they are free and equal subjects. In the end, then, de Beauvoir remains firm in the belief that individuals are in the last analysis free, and so capable of rising above their social circumstances and overcoming oppressive social relations. She looks forward to the possibility that, one day, women and men will be able to participate equally in a non-oppressive society.

The dynamics of the gaze in de Beauvoir's account are evident in another Hitchcock classic, the endlessly fascinating *Vertigo*. The watcher is again James Stewart, now in the role of detective Scottie Ferguson. As he tails Kim Novak's Madeleine, in a longish sequence during which she visits a florist, an art gallery and a graveyard, we see her exclusively through his eyes. Everything is shot from his point of view and the effect is hypnotic. Even after he saves her from drowning and falls in love with her, we only see the relationship from his viewpoint, never from her point of view. But the one-sided nature of this looking, and the imbalance in power between the sexes that this reflects becomes more evident in the later portion of the film, after Madeleine's apparent suicide at the Mission bell tower. Having met a woman who resembles Madeleine in the street, Scottie tries to transform the woman he knows as Judy into his lost love, to recreate Madeleine, demanding that she dress and wear her hair as Madeleine did. In this situation, Judy is thoroughly objectified, the raw material to be fashioned into the image of the woman that Scottie is obsessed by. And, as P. Adams Sitney points out, Scottie and his gaze now become the object of our gaze (Sitney 2003, 255). In the oppressive makeover of Judy, we see his insane love as an illusion. Interestingly we also see Judy's complicity in her oppression. She enables the illusion, taking on the role Scottie wants her to play so that he will remain attracted to her.

In the context of these oppressive social relations, the idea of the woman returning the gaze, objectifying the man in turn, has obvious political significance as an act of resistance to patriarchal power. Here we can return to Glazer's *Under the Skin*, which opened the discussion in Chapter One. As noted earlier, the unnamed central character is an alien who has taken the form of a human woman, literally adopting a human suit of skin. She is on earth looking for male prey. The first part of the film, in which she drives around Scotland in a nondescript van sizing up the male pedestrians to find likely victims, is shot entirely from her point of view, and is a reversal of the more typical cinematic objectification of women under a male gaze. She is a subject, rather than an object. At the same time, as Alicia Byrnes points out, the very anomalousness of this perspective is part of what enables the film to evoke the subjective experience of an alien. This is a difficult task because in order to be intelligible in film terms, such depictions have to be based on human forms of experiencing. It has already been suggested in the earlier discussion that the film is able to suggest an alien perspective by evoking a wholly amoral way of looking, one that is utterly remote from ordinary human experience. We can now say that it also manages it by adopting the unusual point of view of the predatory woman, the woman who 'returns the look'. By the same token, this is an ironic comment on gender politics, insofar as a woman returning the look in this way is sufficiently unusual to be an indicator of something not of this world. As Byrnes puts it, 'for a woman to act in this way (and get away with it), she must be alien' (Byrnes 2015).

Thus, the alien woman in *Under the Skin* is far from being an object of the male gaze, existing only as an attractive object for others, for men, alienated from her free subjectivity. On the contrary, she is the subject who objectifies the men, turning them into objects of prey. Her agency extends to employing her appearance, the borrowed skin, to lure the men in. This is not bad faith, complicity in one's own oppression, pretending that one is no more than a sexual object in order to hide from one's freedom. It is closer to the radical agency of the femme fatale, in full control of herself as a sexually attractive object, using this to manipulate and control those men who aspire to possess and control her. However, as the film progresses, the alien loses her alienness and comes to identify herself with her human form, attempting to live as a human female. The decisive moment in this process comes when, while processing her latest catch, she catches and studies herself in a mirror. Arguably she is for the first time seeing herself as others see her and identifying herself with the object of her own reflected gaze. This is the turning point in the film. After this, she allows her current victim, the facially disfigured man (Adam Pearson), to go free. From now on, the men she encounters are no longer pure objects of prey. She even enters into a kind of relationship with a man (Michael Moreland), who wants to help her.

However, there are problems with this attempt on the alien's part to identify with the human female. First of all, in existentialist terms any such identification is going to be a form of bad faith, the attempt to deny one's freedom by seeing oneself as no more than the object that others see us as being. When Estelle in Sartre's *No Exit* looks for a mirror so she can see herself as others see her, and thereby exist as a certain sort of person, she is exhibiting this form of bad faith. Additionally, for the alien in *Under the Skin*, another aspect of bad faith comes into view. For Sartre and de Beauvoir alike, bad faith can involve not only the denial of one's freedom, seeing oneself as a certain sort of thing, but also the denial of one's facticity, facts about one's existence. Freedom involves not the denial of one's facticity but its transcendence. In this case, the facts in question are the woman's alien biology. In seeking to identify herself with her human form, she goes into a restaurant and tries to eat a piece of cake. However, this proves to be incompatible with her biology; she retches and has to spit the cake out. The second problem, and here we return to de Beauvoir's specific account, in seeking to live as a human female, she thereby becomes an object of the male gaze and is at risk. Where before she was the hunter of men, she now becomes their prey. She is the prey even of the well-meaning man who takes her in and wants to look after her, and later she is pursued and attacked in the forest by the logger. In de Beauvoir's terms, this amounts to a restoration of the patriarchal status quo in which women typically experience themselves as objects for men, rather than free subjects.

For her part, de Beauvoir does not envisage the way forward as a matter of women turning the tables, returning the look and objectifying men in turn. Her interest is in going beyond this cycle of objectification. The ethical attitude that she explores in *The Ethics of Ambiguity* involves a concern for the freedom of others. It is an ethics in which the right thing to do is not simply whatever one chooses, a subjectivist or relativist view, but one in which there is an objective standard of rightness insofar as the right actions are those that promote the freedom of others. This guides the positive vision of *The Second Sex*, which looks forward to establishing a non-oppressive society in which all individuals, men and women, will be able to make their own choices, freely define themselves and take responsibility for those choices. In this concern for others, de Beauvoir seeks to go beyond the extreme individualism and subjectivism of the early Sartre. In this, she is also looking beyond the tradition of individualistic thinking that emerged with Nietzsche and Kierkegaard and was further developed in twentieth-century existentialism. For this thinking, ethics is a matter of having the right kind of relationship with oneself, a matter of personal authenticity, which often puts the individual in conflict with others who represent a potential threat to this moral ideal. But now a different kind of ethics is coming into view, in which what is important is having the right kind of relationship with others and in which it is subjective self-assertion that is the threat. This ethics of the other will be the focus of the final chapter.

FEATURE FILMS: *ROPE* AND *FIGHT CLUB*

Rope

Rope is a crime thriller made in 1948, one of the more experimental of Hitchcock's films. Hitchcock employed long takes and edited the film so that it takes place in real time, entirely within the confines of the two murderers' Manhattan apartment. It is based on the 1923 Leopold and Loeb murder case, in which two young men murdered another, the murderers considering themselves Nietzschean supermen, exempt from the rules governing the ordinary individual and entitled to kill the 'inferior'. The film adds a Nazi reference, reflecting the hijacking of Nietzsche's philosophy by the Nazis.

Plot

Old college friends and housemates John Brandon (John Dall) and Philip (Farley Granger) decide to prove their superiority by committing the perfect murder. The victim is their friend David Kentley (Dick Hogan), whom they strangle and put in a large trunk to dispose of later. Not content with killing David, they invite a small group that includes their former teacher Rupert (James Stewart), David's father Mr Kentley (Cedric Hardwicke), his aunt and fiancée over to their apartment for an intimate dinner party. Brandon decides it would be even more interesting if the dinner was served on the trunk holding David's body.

Over drinks, Rupert expounds his theory that murder should be an art, reserved for the few who are superior beings. It is this thinking that impressed Brandon and Philip, who regard themselves as superior beings. When Kentley asks who will decide who is superior, Brandon responds that men of intellectual and cultural superiority are above traditional moral concepts. Kentley thinks he can discern Nietzsche's notion of the superman in this and says that Hitler also espoused Nietzschean beliefs. As the evening progresses, Kentley becomes worried about his son's failure to turn up and Rupert tries to determine where David might have gone. Philip and Brandon's behaviour arouses his suspicions. After Kentley's wife telephones to say that David is not at home, the guests hurriedly leave.

Rupert notices that the hat he was mistakenly given on the way out has David's initials in it. He returns, claiming to have forgotten his cigarette case. Once inside, he speculates about what happened to David. He reconstructs the crime, then pulls a piece of rope out of his pocket and starts to play with it. Philip becomes agitated. Rupert finds David's body in the trunk. When Brandon explains why they committed the murder, and inspired by his own views, Rupert responds that they have given his words a meaning he never intended. He opens the window and fires several gunshots into the air. Together, they wait for the police to arrive.

Key Scenes

1 Brandon and Philip justify their murder as a work of art, an act reserved for strong, superior types. However, Philip is clearly a weak individual, very dependent on Brandon. When he shows signs of panicking, Brandon admonishes him: 'We agreed there was only one crime we could commit, that of making a mistake. Being weak is a mistake'. Philip: 'Because it's being human?' Brandon: 'Because it's being ordinary' [10.00–13.02].

2 According to Brandon, their former teacher Rupert, is 'the one man likely to suspect. He's the one man who might appreciate this from our angle, the artistic one'. But he is sure that they are superior even to him: 'He hasn't the nerve. Oh, intellectually, he could've

come along. He's brilliant. But he's a little too fastidious. He could've invented and admired but he never could have acted. That's where we're superior. We have courage. Rupert doesn't' [15.28–16.36]. Brandon's constant assertions of superiority come across as juvenile, arrogant posturing on his part. In truth, neither Brandon nor Philip are particularly impressive individuals.

3 Over dinner, Rupert expounds mock-seriously on murder as an art and a privilege that should be reserved for superior individuals. Brandon weighs in, adding that the victims are going to be 'inferior beings whose lives are unimportant anyway'. Mr Kentley disapproves, asking: 'Who will decide who is inferior?' Brandon: 'The privileged few who commit it ... those men of such intellectual and cultural superiority that they're above the traditional moral concepts. Good and evil, right and wrong were invented for the ordinary average man, the inferior man, because he needs them'. Kentley: 'So you agree with Nietzsche and his theory of the superman'. Brandon: 'Yes, I do'. Kentley: 'So did Hitler'. Brandon rejects this connection with Fascism, but only because he thinks that the Nazis murdered stupidly, without art or discrimination [35.05–37.22]. Whether Brandon has understood Nietzsche's 'theory of the superman' is another question. His take on Nietzsche is very much like the Nazi misappropriation of Nietzsche's thinking, which turned it into a justification for state-based murder.

4 Rupert discovers Brandon and Philip's crime, repudiates their interpretation of his views and disabuses them of the idea that they are intellectually and culturally superior individuals. Brandon: 'Rupert, remember the discussion we had before with Mr Kentley? Remember we said, "the lives of inferior beings are unimportant"? Remember we said, we've always said, you and I, that moral concepts of good and evil and right and wrong don't hold for the intellectually superior? ... That's all we've done ... lived what you and I have talked'. Rupert: 'If nothing else, a man should stand by his words. But you've given my words a meaning that I never dreamed of! And you've tried to twist them into a cold, logical excuse for your ugly murder! Well, they never were that, Brandon, and you can't make them that! ... By what right do you dare say that there's a superior few to which you belong? By what right did you dare decide that that boy in there was inferior and therefore could be killed?' [1.11.26–1.15.08]. To be fair, Brandon and Philip don't seem to have twisted Rupert's words so much as taken seriously views he presumably intended only for intellectual amusement.

Fight Club

Fight Club is a lively 1999 film directed by David Fincher (*Seven, the Game, Panic Room, Zodiac*). It is based on the Chuck Palahniuk novel of the same name. The film starts at the end and then backtracks so we see how we got there. Along the way, there are various criticisms of life in late capitalist consumer society and various forms of rebellion are considered. The film is also susceptible to a Nietzschean interpretation.

Plot

The film begins with the unnamed narrator (Edward Norton) in a sky-scraper with a gun in his mouth. We then go back to see the narrator as a mild-mannered but discontented employee of a major car manu-facturer, who is obsessed with fitting out his apartment with IKEA fur-niture and is suffering from insomnia. The doctor tells him to attend a support group for testicular cancer survivors if he wants to meet people who really have problems. This works for a while. Then he meets Marla (Helena Bonham Carter), another 'faker' who recognises him as such, bringing back his insomnia.

The narrator has the worst day of his life. An airline loses his luggage and his apartment blows up, destroying all of his possessions. He meets Tyler Durden (Brad Pitt), a soap salesman. Tyler invites him to move in with him and the two share a 'dilapidated house in a toxic waste part of town'. Tyler has various views on freedom and empowerment. After get-ting the narrator to hit him, the two begin to fight. Soon, others find out about this new form of therapy and Fight Club is born – an underground organisation that encourages men to beat each other up.

Tyler's Fight Club mutates into Project Mayhem, an urban terrorist group that commits acts of anti-corporate vandalism in the city. The nar-rator is left out of Tyler's activities with the Project. He and Tyler have an argument and Tyler disappears from the narrator's life. The narrator tries to shut down Project Mayhem. He finally realises that he is Tyler Durden, who has been taking control while he is asleep.

The narrator finally confronts Tyler in the skyscraper, as Tyler is about to demolish the buildings of the major credit card companies in order to bring down the financial system. This is the point where we came in. The narrator takes control and shoots himself through the cheek, killing his alter-ego. Marla is brought in by Tyler's lackeys. The narrator and Marla watch the buildings explode outside the windows, standing side by side and holding hands. A traditional happy ending is staged against a back-drop of mass destruction

Key Scenes

1 After the narrator's apartment has blown up, Durden appears and counsels the narrator to renounce his consumerism and enslavement to possessions. According to Durden: 'We're consumers. We're by-products of a lifestyle obsession. Murder, crime, poverty – these things don't concern me'. The real problem is 'celebrity magazines, television with five hundred channels, some guy's name on my underwear ... Things you own end up owning you'. As for the consumerist ideal of a perfect existence, Durden tells the narrator: 'I say never be complete, stop being perfect. Let's evolve' [29.10–31.22].

2 Durden again – 'Our fathers were our models for God. If our fathers bailed, what does that tell you about God?' Tyler argues not that there is no god, but that God hates human beings. 'We don't need him' he tells the narrator. 'We are God's unwanted children'. Then: 'It's only after we have lost everything that we are free to do anything' [1.03.11–1.04.05]. Tyler insists that people need to renounce dependence on God and God-like authority figures; and indeed, that rejecting them is a liberation. This echoes the existentialist view that the collapse of religious belief opens the way for human beings to exercise their freedom and choose their own values.

3 At a Fight Club meeting, Tyler rails against economic exploitation and advertising: 'I see in Fight Club the strongest and smartest men who have ever lived. I see all this potential – God damn it, an entire generation pumping gas and waiting tables; they're slaves with white collars. Advertisements have them chasing cars and clothes, working jobs we hate so we can buy shit they don't need' [1.09.49–1.10.38]. Tyler's tirade sounds like a Marxist critique of capitalist exploitation and advertising as indoctrination. However, he does not appear to be endorsing the Marxist idea that in capitalist society human beings are alienated from their 'species-being'. In fact, it is unclear what he thinks is being denied in contemporary society and finding expression through the underground, men-only Fight Clubs. Is it humanity's primal instincts, or perhaps an old-fashioned idea of masculinity, of the 'real man'? The situation is complicated because while Tyler lauds the Fight Club participants, they do not come across as particularly impressive specimens, so there may be an element of irony here.

4 An applicant for Project Mayhem arrives on the porch of the house, staring rigidly ahead, military style and dressed in black pants, shirt and shoes. Tyler, to the narrator: 'If the applicant waits at the door

for three days without food, shelter or encouragement, then he may enter and begin his training' [1.27.37–1.29.23]. Later, Tyler gives the members of Project Mayhem a dressing down: 'You are not special. You are not a beautiful or unique snowflake. You are the same decaying matter as anything else' [1.30.29–1.30. 53]. Tyler may be espousing rebellion in the form of urban terrorism, but it is ironic that the men in Fight Club, far from achieving liberation, have now been turned into the anonymous members of a terrorist army run by an increasingly authoritarian Tyler.

5   Tyler offers a vision of the world he envisages: 'In the world I see, you're stalking elk through the damp canyon forests around the ruins of Rockefeller Center. You will wear leather clothes that last you the rest of your life. You will climb the wrist-thick kudzu vines that wrap the Sears Tower. You will see tiny figures pounding corn and laying strips of venison on the empty car pool lane of the ruins of a superhighway' [1.41.25–1.42.00]. The ideal society he presents seems to be a return to a primitive hunter-gatherer existence, rather than a communist utopia.

6   In the final scene, the narrator kills his alter-ego Tyler and appears to reappropriate him to himself. He calls the end of the film the beginning, saying: 'my eyes are open ... Everything is going to be fine' [2.12.00–2.16.17]. Interpreting the film along Nietzschean lines, the narrator may start out as a herd man, but Tyler is not the superman. He is an expression of the narrator's strongest energies, from which the narrator was alienated. In overcoming him, the narrator takes control of these forces. It is the narrator, not Tyler, who can lay claim to being a Nietzschean *ubermensch*.

6   Encounters with Aliens
Ethics and the Other

At the end of the Swedish comedy-drama *Force Majeure*, Tomas's wife Ebba finds herself in a situation not unlike that faced by her husband at the start of the film, a situation in which she being is put to the test. In her husband's case, the testing situation was the controlled avalanche that seemed to have gone out of control, threatening him and his family on the ski hotel restaurant balcony. Embarrassingly, he panicked and fled the scene, abandoning his wife and children to their fate, though saving his phone. Now at the end of the ski holiday, the family is in the midst of another confronting situation. As they are leaving for the airport, the bus-driver drives badly down the tight hair-pin bends, braking sharply at each retaining wall, seemingly threatening at every turn to send the bus plummeting into the ravine. Now it is Ebba who abandons the family in a panic, yelling at the bus driver to stop and let her out. This is especially problematic for Ebba, who throughout the film has been the caring wife and mother, the one who did not run, so unlike her cowardly husband. Now, she has acted in the same way he did.

Earlier on, however, there was another confronting situation for Ebba that was perhaps even more challenging one. Here, what she encounters is not a situation in which she fails to live up to her defining values and ideals, but another person who is clearly refusing to conform to those values and ideals, to the female role she identifies with. This person is her friend Charlotte, who rejects the role of wife and mother in a nuclear family, engineering an open relationship that allows her to go on holiday and romance ski instructors. Here, in the face of someone who is 'other', the norms and values that define Ebba's very identity are themselves under challenge. In the preceding chapter, the focus was on the existentialist ethics of authenticity, where the concern is the relationship we have with ourselves. In this chapter, we will discuss a number of more recent approaches to ethics that are especially concerned with our response to others and especially those who are different to us. This ethics of the other includes the ethics of care that emerges out of twentieth-century feminist thought, and the ethical thinking of twentieth-century philosophers Levinas and Foucault.

The Critique of 'Traditional' Ethics

Force Majeure provides a handy avenue into this discussion. The film can be seen as a kind of ethical thought experiment in which the experimental subjects are put to the test by challenging circumstances. The interest here is not in how people might react physiologically or psychologically in such circumstances, but how they might react as moral subjects, with commitments to certain values and ideals that structure and justify their choices and actions. The film reminds us that there are experiences capable of challenging our sense of who we are and where we stand as moral beings, putting our conceptions of ourselves to the test. This confronting experience is the force majeure of the film's title, the unpredictable event, the random 'act of God' that is beyond anyone's control. For Tomas, it is the controlled avalanche that seems to have become distinctly uncontrolled; for Ebba, it is the frightening bus ride in which disaster seems to threaten at every bend. As it happens, in neither case is there any real danger; but it is enough that the people involved think that there is.

In highlighting the confrontation with external experience, *Force Majeure* is very different to a film like Dreyer's *The Passion of Joan of Arc*, which came up in the previous chapter. There, the concern was very much with internal experience, the sort of subjective experience that is ignored or denied by objective or impersonal ways of thinking. Through a variety of cinematic means, especially the intense close-up, the film evokes a subjective religious experience, Joan's experience, along with her fidelity to it, her refusal in the end to disavow it and her integrity as a subject in the face of her interrogators. In *Force Majeure*, the focus is very much on external experience, the confronting experience coming from without that challenges the subject. The film observes what happens when the characters are put to the test in this way. In contrast to Dreyer's film, it is more objective in its cinematography, distancing itself from the point of view of the characters. It adopts a voyeuristic, observational approach, with long static shots in which we are not encouraged to align ourselves with any particular character's point of view. The camera at times seems to have literally adopted a 'view from nowhere', absolute objectivity. There are bathroom scenes where we are directly behind Tomas's family as they stand in front of the mirror, yet uncannily, the camera cannot be seen. Unmoored from any particular point of view, we observe these characters and their behaviour as if they were lab rats in a maze.

For much of the time, the film is concerned with Tomas's behaviour during the controlled avalanche episode and its repercussions for himself and those around him. His actions are discussed and dissected from a number of perspectives. As we saw in Chapter Three, his friend Mats suggests an interpretation reminiscent of Hobbes's view that our civilised moral selves are at best a veneer, and when social order breaks down, it is our real nature that emerges, a nature dominated by the drive for self-preservation. For Mats, Tomas's behaviour should be seen as a more or less instinctive reaction to a surprise situation. For humans and animals alike, being confronted by a dangerous situation triggers a survival instinct, a primitive force just to escape. When this happens, a person might not be able to live up to their values through no fault of their own. As we also saw in Chapter One, Ebba offers a less charitable but more philosophically sophisticated interpretation that recalls Aristotle. Her view is that in this action, unthinking though it might be, Tomas has revealed his 'real character', the sort of person he really is. For Aristotle, unthinking behaviour does not necessarily put it outside ethical consideration. The good person is precisely the one who does not have to think, who has practiced being good until they have cultivated the habits of goodness that make up their character. The same applies to being a bad person. So, unthinking action can reveal your character, and for Ebba, Tomas's unthinking action reveals him as a person who 'loves himself and his phone more than he loves his wife and family'.

As has been argued, neither of these views of Tomas's behaviour seems quite able to capture his actions. Even if it is an unthinking response, Tomas is horrified by his conduct. He cannot accept Mats' view that his behaviour is something he could not help and so cannot be blamed for. At the same time, it is hard to see his lapse simply as a revelation of the 'real Tomas' from which the mask has slipped. Talking globally about a person's 'character', good or bad, imputes too much unity to people. We typically exhibit diverse, often conflicting patterns of behaviour. We are brave in some circumstances, cowardly in others. As Mats reminds Ebba, whatever his failures, Tomas is also in many areas a good husband and caring father. But this isn't to say that anything goes, either. In some of the things we do, we can feel that we have fallen short of our ideals, betrayed ourselves, as Tomas evidently does. It seems to better capture Tomas's situation to say, not that he has, but that he is aspiring to be, a certain sort of character, to embody certain ideals in his behaviour. And in this instance, he has behaved in a way that is incompatible with the person he aspires to be. It is in the light of this character ideal or sense of identity that he finds his behaviour reprehensible.

It is true that Tomas only gradually comes to acknowledge that he has behaved poorly. He spends a considerable amount of time pretending to himself that he did not run away. His wife sees this as another level of cowardice, a matter of Tomas being too cowardly to face the reality of his cowardice. But he is arguably doing what many of us do, reinterpreting, editing out or selectively ignoring things that we do, in order to maintain our sense of who we are, our moral identity. Tomas's self-deception itself presupposes a certain character ideal or identity, which he is trying to preserve in the face of reality. What might this character ideal be? Evidence from the film suggests that it is something like the 'proper man', the patriarch in a nuclear family who takes the lead, protects his wife and children, and so on. This is the role that Tomas aspires to, and that others, his wife, children and friends, expect of him. It is certainly a very conventional role, but it is a role nonetheless, and one that he actively aspires to fulfil – as well as spectacularly falling short of it on this occasion.

It's worth noting that this is a quite conventional role in film terms as well. As the director Ruben Östlund points out: 'If you look at the most conventional way of telling a Hollywood story, it goes like this. There is a family living in peace. Suddenly, there's an outside threat. The man has to use violence – he doesn't want to, but he has to, he's forced to. And when he's used violence, killed the bad guys, the family can go back and live in peace' (Lucca, 2014). That's the setup for what might be called the domestic action movie, which combines the family guy with the action hero (see Gallagher 2006, 67). The stereotypical male character in film is the powerful masculine figure, a law unto himself, who through resolve, courage and ingenuity defeats the bad guys. This can take the form of the action hero who takes matters into his own hands to defeat evil, dispensing violence without consequences, cheerfully sadistic and seemingly invulnerable. In the domestic action movie, the action hero's motivations and energies are more family friendly, the violence channelled into protecting the family from harm. Tomas is none of these things. As he falls short of his own ideals, he also falls short of a certain movie ideal of masculinity. At the same time, the film suggests that there might be something unrealistic about this ideal, so often promoted in film. As Mats says, the enemy is 'the image we have of heroes, the pressure to be heroic. The truth is, when reality is staring you in the face, few of us are heroic'.

And it is not only a certain, rather conventional masculine ideal that is under challenge in the film. Although Tomas had the bad luck to fall short of his defining ideals at the start of the film, the film suggests that no one is immune to this possibility and this includes his wife Ebba. Here we can see the significance of the bus incident mentioned at the start of the chapter. As we saw, while Ebba insisted throughout the film that unlike Tomas she would never abandon her children, that she has a very different character, she does precisely this on the bus. She too is unlucky enough to be exposed to a situation that leads her to betray her own defining ideals and values. These are ideals that are constitutive of an equally conventional role and one that is also often promoted in film, that of the woman as caring wife and mother. This is not so much a matter of the film trying to drag Ebba down to Tomas's level as it's aiming to make a more general point. In the end, everyone is susceptible to falling short of their defining ideals, of betraying themselves in this way.

On this reading, the confronting experiences that feature in the film do not just challenge the moral identities of a couple of individuals; nor just a certain, rather conventional notion of the proper male or female role. Rather, questions are being raised about the moral agent as such. We are not the abstract subjects often found in modern moral philosophy, subjects whose moral life seems to be confined to developing choice-guiding arguments on the basis of general principles. The moral agent there is made very much in the image of the philosopher who is trying to bring ethical life under a set of rules, to establish a simple, unified foundation for ethical judgements, to formulate a general ethical theory. In such thinking, there is a danger of producing conceptions of ethical existence that are overly rationalistic and remote from real life, and which may even be beyond the capacities of ordinary human beings to attain (see Griffin, 2015). Rather than these impersonally abstract subjects, the film reveals its protagonists as agents who live in the world, active subjects with commitments to certain ideals and values that define their identity and inform their choices and actions, but who also have to contend with the possibility that they will fail to live up to those values and act in ways that bring them into conflict with their defining ideals. That we are in this position does not ultimately represent a flaw on our part, something that can or ought to be remedied, something we should rise above. Rather, susceptibility to failure is simply part of our condition as finite human beings (see Wartenberg 2015).

The perceived abstractness of modern moral philosophy itself, which is to say primarily Kantian and utilitarian thinking, has been the subject of criticism in recent times, including by feminist thinkers. A first line of criticism of what might now be called 'traditional' moral theories is that they are too general, impersonal and remote from human lives and situations to properly deal with concrete moral dilemmas. Kantian moral theory is a good example here. For Kant, being moral requires that we rise above particular desires and inclinations, and act with complete impartiality in accordance with what reason establishes as universal, general principles. This also requires that we distance ourselves from the specific details of the situations we find ourselves in, look for the universal features of a situation and try to fix the appropriate rules that will govern the kind of situation described. Such moral thinking cannot take into account personal considerations, the details of the lives of the individuals involved or the situations in which they find themselves. The only concern is whether it is possible to obey the general principles that rationality dictates.

Utilitarianism is sometimes put forward as an antidote to Kantian ethics in this regard and it certainly seems to be more sensitive to the details of particular situations. We determine what we ought to do by working out what the consequences of an action will be in a particular situation. And the particular feelings and attitudes of those affected by one's action are going to figure in deciding what the right course of action is. But utilitarianism arguably still suffers from being too abstract. The rightness of an action is calculated in terms of the total amount of happiness and suffering that the action will produce. In this calculation, everyone's happiness or suffering counts for the same, regardless of their situation. We have to be entirely impartial. But it might be argued that in considering the happiness or suffering an action causes, we need to take into account the details of our situation or we are going to find ourselves being required to act in unacceptable ways. For example, utilitarian calculations may require someone to act in a way that will benefit strangers, rather than their children, because that will produce the greatest amount of overall happiness. Such thinking does not allow individuals to consider the specific relations they are involved in, or the particular importance of their children to them.

A second line of criticism has been that traditional moral thinking is too individualistic. That is, it presupposes a view of moral agents as individual rational subjects, solitary choosers, rather than as existing necessarily in the midst of social relations in a network of relations and dependencies. Kant's account can be seen as a paradigm example of this abstract individualism. On the Kantian view, each person is viewed as a rational, self-determining being, essentially independent of others, arriving at moral conclusions through a solitary process of reasoning. In modern thought, this idea of the human being as an essentially independent individual goes back to Hobbes, who envisaged human beings as naturally egoistic individuals; and is at the heart of the liberalism deriving from thinkers like Locke, which focuses on individual rights. There, the primary concern is with preserving the individual's freedom, rights and autonomy in the face of possible interferences from others. Even utilitarianism, which shifts attention from the individual

to the greatest happiness of the greatest number, remains caught in this individualistic perspective insofar as it understands the greatest number as a collection of
independent, happiness-seeking individuals.

Amongst others, recent feminist critics have argued that much traditional moral
philosophy is abstractly individualistic, and that human beings need to be understood as fundamentally social, as existing in a network of social relations. There is
a further reason for specifically feminist suspicion of traditional moral thinking. A
lot of such thinking has involved a negative moral assessment of women, construing them as deficient moral agents. For example, Kant assumed that only men fully
qualify as moral agents. As we've seen, for Kant, being moral requires that we
rise above our desires and inclinations, and act in accordance with what our reason establishes as universalisable, general principles. He also believed that women
were unable to be moral in this way, unable to engage in a process that requires
them to rise above merely individual feelings and inclinations and comprehend
general principles. And this kind of thinking is by no means confined to Kant. A
depressingly long line of (male) philosophers have thought that men are rational
and thus capable of morality, while women are too caught up in emotions and inclinations, which is a barrier to their being fully moral agents (see Sherwin 1992, 43).

There have been at least two kinds of response to this in feminist thinking.
Firstly, one can argue against the claim that women pursue moral thinking differently from men. On this view, women have the same moral ability as men. Many
feminists, particularly in the Anglo-Saxon world, have argued for this equality, as
a necessary basis for attaining equal political rights with men. Simone de Beauvoir
can also be counted as a classic equality theorist. The second kind of response is
to accept the claim that there is a gender difference in male and female moral
thinking, that there are two patterns of moral reasoning here, one that appears
to be associated with male moral thinking and the other more commonly exercised by women; but also to argue that the feminine approach, although different,
is equally valid. In other words, the claim is that there is a different, distinctively feminine kind of ethics. One candidate for this feminine ethics is an 'ethics
of care'.

The Ethics of Care

One of the important advocates of the ethics of care is Carol Gilligan (1936–)
whose work is in the area of moral psychology, the study of moral development.
In a Different Voice (1982), Gilligan questioned the assumption that moral maturity is to be measured in terms of the ability to impartially apply universal ethical principles. In particular, she questioned the account developed by her mentor
Lawrence Kohlberg, in which the Kantian approach represented the highest level
of moral development. That view of moral development ranks the ability to distance oneself from one's context in order to impartially apply principles above
the ability to empathise with others within particular interpersonal relationships.
The problem that Gilligan found is that when this ranking was applied to men and
women, women consistently came out as not being as morally developed as men.

Females tended to focus on sympathy, care and cooperation when dealing with moral issues. In response, Gilligan set out to show that there are two different ways of approaching moral problems, one that tends to be taken typically by males and the other typically by females; and that this second approach to moral problems is not an inferior one, but simply a different way of approaching moral problems, just as legitimate as the first.

On this view, Kant's moral theory represents the archetypally male approach to moral thinking. It requires the impartial application of general rules, which apply to every person equally and to all relevantly similar situations, in order to solve moral problems. This approach, which Gilligan terms the justice perspective, tends to distinguish moral actions from those motivated by personal passions and attachments. The other approach, more typically taken by women, which she terms an ethic of responsibility or an ethics of care, is primarily concerned with maintaining particular relationships with those that one cares for and takes responsibility for. Here, one's personal feelings and responses to the needs of others have an important role to play. What is of concern is not whether you are acting impartially in accordance with the correct rules, but whether you are preserving and nurturing the particular relationships you are involved in. Moral problems emerge in the first place because of a breakdown in communication, or a lack of nurturing in relationships. So, women faced with moral problems tend to focus on the details of the relationships holding between those concerned, the specific human dynamics of the situation, the actual feelings of those involved. Their moral thinking involves paying careful attention to all the facts, becoming aware of the demands of the moral situation and responding appropriately. The claim is not that this is inherently female behaviour, and that men could not behave in this way, simply that this is preponderantly how women tend to behave.

The first feature of an ethics of care to note, then, is that it focuses on the details of the particular situations one is involved in, on recognising and responding to the needs of the other. It moves away from the impartiality that is characteristic of Kantian moral thinking, and also of utilitarianism. As Nel Noddings states: 'the approach through law and principle is not the approach of the mother. It is the approach of the detached one, of the father' (Noddings 1984, 2). Secondly, the ethics of care approach involves a recognition that individuals exist in relationships with others. Here again there is a contrast with the more traditional approaches in ethics, which tend to be individualistic in orientation. An ethics of responsibility and care begins with a self understood as enmeshed in a network of relations to others. Since individuals are essentially connected with others, their moral thinking needs to take their relations with others into account. Thus, rather than stress values of autonomy, independence and individual rights, an ethics of care stresses the kinds of values that foster and maintain relationships, values of responsibility, care, concern, nurturing and empathy. It has been suggested that these values and virtues might be particularly associated with women because of their cultural experience as carers for the welfare of others. Traditionally at least, women have often been charged with responsibility for taking care of others, including children, the elderly and the ill, as well as responsibility for physically and emotionally nurturing men. As such, they 'experience the world as a complex web of interdependent relationships, where responsible caring for others is implicit in their moral lives' (Sherwin 1992, 47). As such, a morality that focuses on the autonomy and rights of independent agents is inadequate for the moral reality in which women live. A different model of morality is needed.

In these terms, turning once again to *Force Majeure*, we might expect Tomas to be an advocate of the individualistic, rules and principles kind of approach, with Ebba embodying aspects of the care perspective in her behaviour. During the avalanche incident, her primary concern is to take care of her children, while her husband Tomas takes individualism to the extreme, thinking only to save himself, along with his precious phone. Yet even so, in the aftermath of the incident, when Tomas is only concerned to preserve his good opinion of himself by pretending that it never happened, Ebba's main concern is to preserve her relationship with her husband and to keep the family together. Tomas's initial refusal to acknowledge what he has done is problematic for her in part because having such divergent interpretations of the event drives a wedge between them as a couple. She does what she can to repair things, to help her husband overcome his humiliation, and in the end, to take his place as the family patriarch once again. On the ski slopes, on the last day of the holiday, she engineers an opportunity for him to perform a heroic gesture, to rescue her from difficulty and protect the family from danger. In so doing, as the director puts it, 'Ebba is leading Tomas to be the leader of the family again' (Bibbiani 2014).

As noted earlier, the role of family patriarch that Tomas aspires to, even if he falls short on this occasion, is not only a fairly conventional male role but also a recognisable movie type, the domestic action hero. In its pure form, the action hero is the autonomous man of action, dispensing social justice, in the name of which he is willing to use any means to defeat evil. In the domestic action film, that activity is channelled into protecting the family from external threats. It is interesting to compare this with the female action hero as a movie type. The female action hero might be thought to represent a movement from the domestic role of caring mother and wife, which Ebba aspires to, to something closer to the autonomous action hero. However, there remain some significant differences between the female and male action hero, which very often seem to come down to the female action hero's actions being qualified by a care ethics sensibility. This is evident for example in the recent *The Hunger Games* (Gary Ross, 2012). The decisions of the film's central character, Katniss Everdeen (Jennifer Laurence), are often made not in the name of abstract principles of justice but out of a concern to look after those closest to her, her younger sister and her family (see Averill 2012).

In this, Everdeen stands in a line of modern action heroines that goes back at least to Ellen Ripley (Sigourney Weaver) from the initial cycle of *Alien* films. As Walter Lindenmuth points out, this iconic character also exhibits a care ethics sensibility. Ripley, her crew having been wiped out by the single highly aggressive alien brought onto her ship in *Alien*, returns to the planet, now colonised, to confront the entire species in the sequel, *Aliens* (James Cameron, 1986). It turns out that the colony has been overrun by the aliens. As Lindenmuth notes, Ripley's concern for Newt (Carrie Henn), the sole survivor of the colony, does not derive from a sense of duty or justice. It is the act of a loving parent, who is partial and caring about their children, or in this case, the orphaned child that Ripley takes under her wing. The promise she makes to never leave Newt, singling her out for special treatment, might seem unjust; and her decision at the end to risk the lives of the surviving members of the crew, and the ship itself, for one person, would seem to be morally unjustified on any utilitarian calculation, as well as representing a kind of partiality towards one individual that would be unimaginable from a Kantian perspective. Yet the film would be unthinkable without Ripley going back for Newt. It is easy for the viewer to take on Ripley's concern for the child and to appreciate that not doing so would be evil (see Lindenmuth 2017, 76–78).

It is necessary however to qualify this view, as there is another side to the Ripley character, and a very different form of moral thinking, on show right from the start of the *Alien* film cycle. Her refusal in *Alien* to allow Kane (John Hurt) back into the vessel after he has been attacked by the face-hugging alien life-form, which turns out to be part of the alien's life-cycle, is a judgement based on impartial utilitarian calculation. It is far better for one person to die than the safety of her entire crew and ship to be jeopardised. And although she is overruled by her fellow crew members, subsequent events show that her decision was very much the right one. Overall, the Ripley character has many characteristics that we might see as inimical to a care ethics perspective and more in keeping with the justice perspective. She appreciates rules and regulations, and usually does not allow emotion to overwhelm her sense of duty, exhibiting an iron self-control. That this side of her character is so seamlessly integrated with the maternal, caring side in *Aliens* is an indication of the character's complexity. Of course, it should not be surprising that Ripley cannot be identified wholly with a feminine care perspective in ethics. Part of the interest of the character is precisely that she breaks so decisively from gender stereotypes.

There has been a great deal of discussion of the idea that there are two different approaches in ethics, a rules and principles approach that is commonly adopted by males, and typical of much traditional moral thinking, and a distinctively feminine ethics of care approach. One question that has been raised is whether these two approaches can co-exist, or whether the rules and principles kind of approach should be rejected in favour of an ethics of care approach. Gilligan herself suggested that traditional ethical approaches could be supplemented and extended by the addition of an ethics of care. Other care theorists like Nel Noddings and Sara Ruddick are less sympathetic to the traditional ethical approaches. They have argued that the traditional approach should be dispensed with entirely and that the ethics of care is in fact the only valid ethic (Ruddick 1997; Noddings 2003). However, the notion that there is a distinctively feminine ethics of care has itself been questioned by some philosophers (see e.g., Grimshaw 1986, Scaltsas 1992). The main thrust of these criticisms is to suggest that talking of a distinctively female ethics of care and responsibility risks entrenching gender stereotypes that have been associated with the oppression of women in Western cultures.

For example, consider the idea that an ethics of care involves a rejection of abstraction and a focus on the details of the particular situations one is involved in. That is a problem if women's moral thinking, insofar as it is identified with the ethics of care, is taken to be opposed to abstract thinking. There is a danger of reaffirming old stereotypes of women as being incapable of rational thought, the idea that women perceive and act intuitively and emotionally rather than rationally and reflectively. Moreover, to tie women to the care perspective tends to identify women with a certain kind of role, that of carer or nurturer. The problem is that it is likely that this kind of role also reflects the status of women in a patriarchal culture, a culture that has tended to relegate women precisely to a subordinate role, the role of nurturer and carer for men. Indeed, the ethics of care might be thought to amount to a slave morality in Nietzsche's sense. As we saw in Chapter Five, Nietzsche gives us the idea that an oppressed people tend to develop moral theories that redefine subservient traits as virtues, a slave morality, and this may be what is happening with the ethics of care. On this view, the ethics of care makes a virtue out of the work of care that women tend to be consigned to in a patriarchal, male-dominated society, work that they often perform to their own economic and political disadvantage. Equating moral maturity with self-sacrifice and self-effacement is politically dangerous (see e.g., Sherwin 1992, 50; Sander-Staudt 2011).

So the great danger in the feminine ethics approach, it has been argued by some, is that identifying women with the carer role risks reproducing various gender stereotypes, indeed the very stereotypes some have blamed for the continuing oppression of women. From this point of view, to come back to *Force Majeure*, Ebba's role of caring wife and mother can be seen in broader social terms as a role that women have often been consigned to in a male-dominated society. The traditional nuclear family she belongs to, and which she fights hard to preserve, has a very clear sexual division of labour. Tomas's role is that of the patriarch who protects his family from external threats and ensures their security; and Ebba's role, it seems, is to care for and nurture her husband and children. Of course, it turns out in practice that neither of them are very good at these roles, both falling to pieces when faced with a crisis; but they nonetheless aspire to them.

More recent feminist thinking concerning ethics has typically attempted to critically appropriate the ethics of care rather than simply rejecting it. For example, Susan Sherwin distinguishes between a feminine ethics of care and a feminist ethics on this basis (Sherwin 1992, 49ff). A positive feature of the ethics of care approach is that it is less bound by abstract rules, recognises that personal feelings like empathy have a significant role in moral deliberations and is more responsive to the details of a particular situation. But Sherwin argues that this is not enough. Attention to the specific circumstances and relationships needs to be supplemented by awareness of the broader social context and the more general structures or patterns of social relations that influence those specific situations. We need to take into account especially the political dimension of relationships, the way they often involve various structures of power and inequality; and ethical reflection needs to be extended to criticising and working to eliminate forms of social oppression. For the same reason, ethical reflection cannot be bound by preferences and feelings that derive from existing relationships and attitudes, since these may in fact reflect existing forms of oppression. A feminist ethics thus recognises that there is a place for personal feelings but cannot give full authority to them without considering their sources and effects.

Secondly, there is much to be said for the way the ethics of care approach sees individuals as involved in a network of relationships; and indeed, for rejecting ethical approaches that presuppose the notion of the individual as a self-contained atom and concentrate on preserving its autonomy and rights. Feminist ethics as characterised by Sherwin takes up this critique of abstract individualism and the concern to understand individuals as always existing in the midst of social relations. But whereas the ethics of care stresses the need for empathy, nurturance and caring for others, feminist ethics is more concerned with the way social relations often involve forms of power or oppression. There is still room for caring for others in this account, but since caring behaviour has historically been entangled with forms of oppression, particular forms of caring need to be carefully evaluated in the context of the social relations in which they are undertaken.

In addition, Sherwin and other recent writers in feminist ethics have argued that the core individualist notion of autonomy should not simply be abandoned. It is, however, necessary to question the idea that autonomy is a purely individual matter of determining oneself in isolation from social relationships. They have opted rather to redefine autonomy, for example, to formulate a notion of 'relational autonomy' that tries to balance individual agency with social embeddedness. There is a recognition here not only that relations of care and interdependence are valuable and morally significant, but also that autonomy is compatible with the individual engaging in and valuing significant family and other social relationships. Moreover, autonomy so conceived requires that one's relationships with other individuals and institutions are organised in such a way that people will be empowered to make choices and determine themselves. That is, it is not that they need to be free of social relationships as such, but only of oppressive sorts of social arrangements, those that make self-determination impossible (see, for example, Sherwin 1998; Mackenzie and Stoljar 2000, 8–10, 21–22).

An example of a social relationship that might be thought to empower and facilitate autonomy is presented in Homer's *Odyssey*, one of the earliest works in Western literature. In it, the Greek hero Odysseus (Ulysses in Roman myths) make his way home by sea after the fall of Troy. The 1954 film *Ulysses* (Mario Camerini) offers a condensed version of the epic, with Kirk Douglas playing its cunning protagonist. In the story, Ulysses exercises his mastery over himself even in the face of the loss of the capacity to do so. Keen to hear the beguiling song of the Sirens, even though he knows it will rob him of his will, he has his crew tie him to the mast while they row past the island, their own ears stopped with wax. But even in this vision of heroic self-determination, which might even be seen as an anticipation of the abstract individual of modern liberal thinking, the hero's autonomy is only made possible because of his relationship with his crew, who can be trusted to tie him to the mast and to release him from his bonds after the danger is past. By contrast, *Fight Club* shows us an oppressive social relationship that impedes the hero's autonomy. Tyler Durden, the narrator's alter-ego, instructs his followers to restrain the narrator (and worse), should the latter come looking to disrupt Durden's Project Mayhem. Certainly, Durden's own autonomy is being enabled through the efforts of his followers, but Durden himself, as an aspect of the narrator that has escaped the narrator's control, represents in his very existence a significant undermining of the narrator's autonomy. And Durden's being able to rely on his followers to do his bidding only adds to this undermining.

Levinas, Ethics and the Other

An ethical position that has significant similarities with the care ethics of Gilligan is the ethics of the other developed by Emmanuel Levinas (1906–1995). He formulates his ethical position primarily in *Totality and Infinity* and *Otherwise than Being or Beyond Essence*. Levinas similarly departs from the ethics of Kantian deontology and utilitarianism. Like the ethics of care, he rejects a morality of abstract rules and principles, along with the abstract individualism of the more traditional approaches in ethics, which presuppose a view of moral agents as individual rational subjects, solitary choosers, not beings who exist in any essential sense in relationship with others. On that sort of view, there is a tendency to focus on autonomy and individual rights, and on preserving the independence of the individual in the face of possible interference by others. Insofar as another individual is acknowledged in an ethical way, it is in terms of reciprocity and symmetry. Others, insofar as they are like us, namely rational, autonomous beings, deserve to have their autonomy and rights respected by us, just as we are entitled to have our autonomy and rights respected by them. Levinas, like the ethics of care theorists, rejects this abstract individualism. He shares with them a recognition that individuals exist fundamentally in relationship with others; and he develops an alternative understanding of ethics, one that focuses on receptivity towards the other and our responsibilities towards them.

Also in common with the ethics of care theorists, Levinas understands the attitude of receptivity towards others as 'feminine', and correspondingly, traditional or mainstream ethics as 'masculine' (Levinas 1998, 185; see Taylor 2005, 217, 220). While there is some debate over how he is using the notion of the feminine, he does seem to be using it 'to mark stereotypical female traits – for example, hospitality, generosity, welcoming' (Katz 2003, 2), though these could presumably be shared by all people. One difference with the ethics of care is that while both the ethics of care and Levinas are reacting against the Kantian idea of morality, Levinas also sets himself up explicitly in opposition to some of Kant's nineteenth-century successors. He is especially critical of Hegel, who looks beyond the Kantian individual, it is true, but only insofar as both self and other are subordinated to a much-enlarged version of the self, Hegel's notion of Absolute spirit. In Hegel's picture, there is no genuine other, absolutely different from the self.

In the language of *Totality and Infinity*, the other has been reduced to the same (see Levinas 1979, 33ff). Like Kierkegaard in the existentialist tradition, Levinas is profoundly opposed to the Hegelianism vision of the all-encompassing subject. But whereas Kierkegaard is concerned with restoring the concrete individual self, Levinas's main interest is in making space for the genuinely other, preserving the otherness of the other.

Levinas departs from the individualism and subjectivism not only of Kierkegaard but also twentieth-century existentialism, for which ethics is a matter of having the right kind of relationship with oneself, a matter of personal authenticity. In contrast, Levinas's ethics concerns the kind of relationship the self has with an other. Where for the existentialist tradition the self has priority over the other, and the other tends to be seen as a threat to one's subjectivity and freedom, very obviously so in Sartre's account, for Levinas, the other has priority over the self, as that which founds or gives rise to the self. It is through encounter with an other, responding to the other, that we become selves in the sense of ethical subjects. We may start out as amoral egoists, concerned only to pursue our natural needs, to further our self-interest and viewing the world in those terms, but the other 'summons' or calls us to take responsibility for them, which turns us into ethical subjects. This is not something that we can manage by ourselves. We are absolutely dependent on the other to come into being as ethical subjects. For Levinas, this summons to ethical responsibility from the other is the central feature of intersubjective life. In particular, it is the other's face to which we respond, that compels us to take responsibility (see Levinas 1979, 201ff). The face is the other in its uniqueness and singularity. As with many feminist ethics of care theorists, ethics is a matter of responding to the unique details of a situation, a face to face encounter with a singular, irreplaceable other.

Thus, we do not start out as ethical subjects, existing independently of others, like Kant's autonomous moral agent. Rather, we are compelled by the other to be ethical, to take responsibility. The subject only comes into being as an ethical subject when it is 'converted' by the other, brought to face its responsibility for the other. And an ethical relationship with the other is not a matter of establishing a reciprocal relationship in which others, insofar as they are like us, autonomous beings, deserve to have their autonomy and rights respected by us, just as we do by them. Rather, it is a matter of responding to and taking responsibility for an other who is not equal to but above us, and who commands attention, not by force but by virtue of their vulnerability and powerlessness. And as with many feminist ethics of care theorists, ethics is not a matter of the impartial application of general rules that apply to all persons equally. Because ethics on Levinas's view takes place in particular face-to-face encounters with unique, irreplaceable others, it can never be generalised into rules of behaviour or normative principles.

What Levinas is envisaging, the transformation of an individual from amoral egoist or rampant individualist into an ethical subject concerned for others, is also a familiar cinematic theme. Sam Girgus speaks of an entire 'cinema of redemption' that can be discerned in Hollywood cinema from the thirties on, a number of films in which a self-interested individual is turned into an altruistic ethical subject

(Girgus 2010). Thus, if we head back to *Casablanca*, we find Bogart's character Rick, the wartime nightclub owner who 'sticks his neck out for nobody', and who is only concerned to 'get by', deciding to help Resistance hero Victor Laszlo to escape to America. And if we once again consult *Schindler's List*, we can witness Nazi businessman Oskar Schindler evolving from an opportunist and profiteer into a man of conscience, saving numerous Jews from the concentration camps by bringing them to work in his factory. However, it is necessary to examine these films more closely to see if this transformation can be properly viewed as a Levinasian one.

For example, Rick's transformation in *Casablanca* might be interpreted in Kantian terms, as we saw in Chapter Four. That is, it can readily be seen as a transformation from amoral egoist to someone who recognises a higher moral duty that transcends their particular concerns. On this view, Rick's 'becoming ethical' is the result not of his acknowledging a summons from the other, but rather heeding the summons of his own rational conscience. In Rick's case, it is in fact a return to being ethical. Remarks by the police prefect Captain Renault indicate that Rick was an idealist in the past, a supporter of anti-Fascist struggles. The self-interest and lack of concern for others that he exhibits at the start of the film turns out to be born of bitter experience. He only became that way, we are informed via a flashback sequence, after having been abandoned by former lover Ilsa in Paris as the German army advanced on the city. Now she has reappeared in Casablanca, with husband Victor Laszlo. But once she explains to Rick that she had to leave him in Paris on learning the husband she had thought dead was alive, his bitterness dissolves and he decides to help Laszlo to escape so he can continue his important work.

Significantly, in the end, Rick insists that Ilsa go too, even though she clearly wants to stay in Casablanca and resume the relationship with him, and he is clearly partial to the idea. Having returned to the ethical and become a supporter of the higher cause, he is willing to sacrifice much, even the woman he loves, since she is important for her husband's work. As he famously notes, the problems of three little people don't amount to a hill of beans in this crazy world. And indeed, the film's love triangle is not so important from a Kantian point of view. It gets in the way of the Bogart character's being ethical. On this view, the ethical development of Bogart's character is all about transcending the particularity of his attachment to Ilsa, and the feelings bound up with that attachment, in order to think instead in a rational way, in terms of universalisable principles that apply to everyone, and do what is right. This is what Ilsa herself might be thought to be encouraging him to do, when she tells him 'You'll have to do the thinking for both of us … for all of us'.

At the same time, Rick's journey out of egoism into the ethical also contains a moment that might be thought to be more Levinasian and so bound up with a response to a unique other. Prior to Ilsa's revelations about Paris, newlywed Bulgarian refugee Annina Brandel (Joy Page) comes to the nightclub to ask Rick for advice about whether she should sleep with Renault, the latter having intimated that this will bring her the exit visas she and her husband need to escape to America (Figure 6.1). He fobs her off, telling her that 'everybody in Casablanca has problems', maintaining his cynical demeanour while her crestfallen face speaks volumes.

Figure 6.1 Casablanca: Rick and the refugee (Michael Curtiz, 1942. Credit: Warner Brothers Pictures).

Nonetheless, when we next see him, he is standing behind her husband, at the roulette wheel trying to win the money to buy the papers on the black market, ensuring that he bets on the 'right' number. We might see in this, Rick responding ethically to Annina. In appealing to him, she has ceased to be one of the anonymous mass of refugees waiting to escape from Casablanca. She has acquired a face, demanding ethical responsibility. Responding to this summons, Rick abandons his self-serving perspective and sacrifices material advantage in order to help her and her husband. If as has been suggested the film can be interpreted as a piece of domestic wartime propaganda designed to encourage the American public to turn away from self-interested isolationism and support the war effort, it might be seen as resorting to both Levinasian and Kantian strategies to do so. It invokes both the particular other in need of help and the higher duty or greater cause.

Things seem more straightforward in *Schindler's List*, in which it is clearly an encounter with a unique other that brings about the ethical transformation in Schindler. The moment of transformation comes as Schindler and his mistress, out riding, come to a hilltop overlooking the Krakow ghetto. There, under the direction of the fearsome Amon Goeth, the ghetto is being cleared, with Jews being brutally rounded up for deportation to the concentration camps. From a distance, they are anonymous figures being lined up, marched away and loaded into trucks. Nonetheless in the midst of these anonymous individuals, Schindler encounters the face of the other, in the form of one young girl. In a largely black and white film, this encounter with the other is articulated cinematically through the use of colour, in the form of the girl's coat which alone is coloured, marking her out in the scene. It is not subtle, and calls attention to itself as a cinematic device, yet it is still strangely effective in drawing the viewer's attention. As John

Wright puts it, 'The red coat becomes, for Schindler, the "face" of the Holocaust victim, pulling him from his distanced position astride the hilltop into the horror of the Nazi atrocities' (Wright 2008, 63).

This invocation of the other in *Schindler's List* stands in direct contrast to the strategy in another tale of the Holocaust, *Son of Saul* (László Nemes, 2015). The film follows a day and a half in the life of Auschwitz inmate Saul (Géza Röhrig). Through tight close-ups and point of view shots, the film invokes the character's subjective experience in the face of an environment that utterly denies this subjectivity and treats individuals as pure things to be processed. Rather than invoking a Levinasian other, this is more in line with Kierkegaard's efforts to restore the self and subjective experience (see Balog 2016). This also serves as a reminder of film's capacity to portray widely differing kinds of experience. It has the capacity to evoke subjective experience, a personal point of view, serving it in the portrayal of existentialist themes; and it also has the capacity to open up a sense of otherness, to amongst other things portray the encounter with the singular Levinasian other.

In these Holocaust films, we also encounter the immediate historical context for Levinas's ethics of the other, the 'negative othering' of Jews by the Nazis. In Nazi antisemitism, an ultimate evil for Levinas, the other in their difference is seen as foreign and threatening, to be rejected, excluded and destroyed. This also involves their being rendered faceless in that all those who are to be destroyed are considered first of all as members of a group, members of the condemned race, rather than as unique individuals. This is reflected in the early scenes of *Schindler's List* when the Jews are being processed by administrators, their names being typed into lists, as they arrive to establish the Krakow ghetto. They are thereby registered individually but also turned into interchangeable members of a race, so many objects to be counted and processed. It is a precursor for what is to come. Having been rendered faceless, these people no longer call for an ethical response and that ultimately makes mass murder possible. There is something chillingly reminiscent of this attitude in the speech Harry Lime (Orson Welles) gives to Holly Martins (Joseph Cotten), high atop the Ferris wheel in devastated post-war Vienna in *The Third Man* (Carol Reed 1949). Petty criminal Lime, who has been selling watered-down penicillin on the black market, resulting in the deaths of numerous people, indicates that he can feel no guilt for anonymous victims he has never seen. Gesturing to the tiny figures far below, he says to his friend Martins: 'Tell me. Would you really feel any pity if one of those dots stopped moving forever?'

Moving beyond the Second World War, the singular other is evoked in the more contemporary military context of drone warfare in *Eye in the Sky* (Gavin Hood, 2015). Warfare conducted by firing remotely controlled missiles from high-flying surveillance drones seems to definitively preclude a face to face encounter where an ethical response might be possible. Instead, we are likely, once again, to be faced with Lime's anonymous moving dots, which make no moral demands on the viewer and which will not arouse pity if they stop moving forever. The film imagines the drone's associated ground-based surveillance technology revealing the face of the other.

It portrays an attempt to take out a terrorist cell in a Nairobi suburb, using a missile remotely fired from a drone. The operation is stymied by the appearance on the scene of a young girl (Aisha Takow) who sets up to sell bread outside the terrorists' compound. While the individuals in the house are very much generic terrorists, and the surrounding streets filled with anonymous local militia and civilians, the girl (like the girl in *Schindler's List* also wearing red) is singled out as an individual, the face of the civilian population. And once again, the other in their singularity calls for an ethical response from those watching.

At the same time, the responses of the military and politicians observing from afar are less than ideal from a Levinasian perspective. The military figures, the UK general Benson (Alan Rickman) and colonel Powell (Helen Mirren) show a preference for utilitarian calculation, their repeated argument being that the death of one civilian is justified if it will prevent the death of many at the hands of the terrorists, should they escape to carry out their plot. They are frustrated by the rules of engagement and the hesitation of their political masters. The politicians are shown hesitating not so much because of any moral scruples but because the death of the girl might be problematic should news of civilian casualties get out. It would play badly with the public and be a propaganda coup for the terrorists. It is those most directly involved, the two drone pilots Watts (Aaron Paul) and Gershon (Phoebe Fox), tasked with aiming and firing the missiles, and watching the events unfold on their monitors, who most keenly feel the ethical demand the girl is making on them, and the most internal conflict over what they are required to do.

One possible weakness in Levinas's account might be that while it is concerned with the ethical relations with the other, the responsibility required from the self seems only able to be summoned by a recognisably human face. Non-human others can only count ethically insofar as they have a face in this sense. Caesar, the hero of *Rise of Planet of the Apes*, also happens to have the most human-looking face amongst the apes. This assists directly in invoking the audience's empathy and concern, and provides an analogue for Levinas's emphasis on the ethical importance of the face. However, it also raises the question of whether ethical relations in Levinas's sense are possible with creatures that do not have a recognisable face, that are inhumanly other. Films often emphasise the unearthliness of movie aliens by ensuring they do not have anything resembling human features, which also means that they do not elicit any ethical response from us. For example, the alien creatures in *Alien* are contrived to look insect-like, reptilian and mechanical all at once, which underscores their non-humanness and makes it palatable for them to be slaughtered without any qualms. For Ripley herself, there is no question that the species should be exterminated. There is no possibility of care or concern in this instance. But we may on reflection want to question the cavalier destruction of any life-form, even one as faceless as this (see Lindenmuth 2017, 69–70). That a moral position is unable to raise this issue is arguably a problem for that position.

In the *Alien* series, as it happens, one of the aliens does eventually come to elicit our sympathy and its death becomes a moment of genuine pathos. This happens at the end of the fourth film in the original cycle, *Alien Resurrection* (Jean-Pierre

Jeunet, 1997). Ripley, cloned back into existence by military scientists after her demise in *Alien 3* (David Fincher, 1992), has had her DNA used to create an alien/human hybrid. Before its birth, Ripley is able to say sardonically that she is 'the monster's mother'. But once she comes face to face with the creature in actuality, it evokes a real feeling of compassion in her, echoing her earlier concern for Newt. The creature still has to be killed, but the death is now a wrenching scene that brings Ripley to tears. At the same time, this only seems plausible because the alien, having taken the form of the human/alien hybrid, is far more human-looking than the usual aliens, with distinctly human facial features. The issue remains that the ethical responsibility Levinas talks of seems only to be able to be summoned by a recognisably human face.

Like the original aliens in the first *Alien* cycle, the alien bugs threatening humanity in Paul Verhoeven's *Starship Troopers* (1997) can be wiped out in vast numbers without any moral discomfort because their insect features make them seem inhumanly other. In this case, however, the film does not come to humanise the other by giving the bugs a face, but rather contrives to make the humans inhuman. The hierarchical, quasi-military bug society turns out to have a very similar structure to the human one. As gradually becomes apparent, the human society in the film is also a totalitarian, anti-individualist society, the members of which are similarly interchangeable, ultimately faceless functionaries. In the final scene, general Carl Jenkins (Neil Patrick Harris) of Military Intelligence confronts his opposite number, the recently captured 'brain bug', in what looks very like an SS uniform. Indeed, the human society in the film has many of the trappings of the Nazi state, including grandiose Albert Speer-style architecture, SS-style uniforms, jingoistic slogans and viciously xenophobic propaganda. There is even a rather 'Aryan' look to the heroic starship troopers themselves. Meanwhile, their enemy is portrayed as entirely other, a mass to be simply wiped out. It is perhaps no accident that a favourite trope of Nazi propaganda was to compare the Jews to insects that needed to be exterminated en masse.

Another area where Levinas's account is potentially open to question has to do with his conception of the self and the extent to which his account gives priority to the other over the self. As one commentator puts it, Levinas's self is 'powerless against the gravitational pull of its egoism, condemned to a hopeless amorality unless the Other intervenes and saves it from itself' (Hofmeyr 2006, 113). Only the intervention of the other can turn the self into an ethical subject, and so the self is completely dependent on the other for its emergence. The relationship here is profoundly one-sided, leading us to wonder whether a self that is so passive could ever become an ethical subject. A recognisable ethical subject tries to live up to certain moral rules and values, in terms of which it reflects on desires, makes choices and undertakes actions. In short, it plays an active role in being an ethical subject. Our couple from *Force Majeure*, Tomas and Ebba, represent two such ethical subjects, each with certain ideals of behaviour, a certain moral identity, which they are trying to live up to. Even if they fall spectacularly short of their defining ideals in practice, they can only do so because they are trying to live up to them in the first place. No doubt others play a role in one's emergence as an ethical subject, but it is difficult to see how, if one were entirely passive in the process of self-formation, one could ever emerge as an active ethical being.

Finally, one might wonder if there is sufficient recognition by Levinas of the political dimensions of his ethics of the other. Sherwin distinguished a feminine ethics of care from a feminist ethics on this basis, because talking of a distinctively female ethics of care and responsibility risks entrenching gender stereotypes that have been associated with the oppression of women in Western cultures, while a feminist ethics recognises and criticises the oppressive practices themselves. As noted, Levinas also offers an ethics of responsiveness to the other, of responsibility and care, that he characterises as feminine, presumably having in mind stereotypically female traits. But he similarly does not concern itself with the practices of power that might put women and other politically disempowered groups in the position of the feminine, that might relegate them to the role of caring and taking responsibility for others. As one commentator puts it, 'Levinas's philosophy cannot be called "feminist" because it is not concerned with particular political contexts and specific oppressed groups' (see Taylor 233). At this point, let us move on to the third of our ethicists of the other, namely Foucault.

Foucault, Power and Ethics

Levinas's ethics of the other gives priority to the other over the self. It is only through the other that the self emerges as an ethical subject. Michel Foucault (1926–1984) offers another perspective on the ethics of the other, in which the self plays a more active role. To give this some background, Foucault, like Marx, wants to move beyond the liberal view that the primary social reality individuals have to contend with is society's political organisation, in which the state exercises legal power over its citizens. Unlike Marxism, however, he does not give priority instead to the economic realm, to productive activity, and hold that all other social and political phenomena, such as education, medicine, the military, judicial processes, the state itself, can be explained in terms of the economic realm. The relationships between these various spheres, Foucault argues, should not be prejudged but need to be worked out in each case. What Foucault does want to claim, in books such as *Discipline and Punish* and the first volume of the *History of Sexuality*, is that while the modern period has seen the overthrow of the absolute monarchy in favour of a more liberal, representative form of parliamentary democracy, it has also seen the spread of new techniques of control, training and regulation, exercised over individuals and populations, establishing new social hierarchies. These techniques, variously identified as 'discipline', 'biopower' and eventually 'pastoral power', have been implemented not only in the workplace, but also in schools, hospitals, armies and other institutions, and consolidated under the modern state. They are techniques employed as much by the liberal democratic state as by the 'pathological' forms of large-scale political power, fascism and totalitarian communism.

On Foucault's account, the pastoral form of power, which has its origins in the Church but comes to be secularised from the eighteenth century onwards, is oriented towards people's 'salvation' in this world rather than the next. It looks to ensuring the well-being and security of the population through both 'disciplinary' management of bodies and a 'biopolitical' management of populations, their fertility and mortality, health, life expectancy, and so on. The management of life, its controlled enhancement in accordance with social and medical norms of perfection, becomes the dominant mission of the modern state. This role is reflected in utilitarian-style legitimations of government, in terms of the state's capacity to promote the health, happiness and well-being of the population as a whole. For Foucault, the state management of life is not automatically a bad thing, but it does provide a new justification for the state's right to kill, in the name of fostering and protecting life. Thus, in the modern state, capital punishment becomes a scandal, though it can be maintained by invoking 'the monstrosity of the criminal, his incorrigibility and the safeguard of society' (Foucault 1979, 137–138). Similarly, since at least the end of the nineteenth century there has been a new rationale for war, which is now to be waged in the name of the 'kind of people we are'. Killing, even genocidal levels of slaughter, become acceptable as the reverse of the power that fosters life, the correlative need to eliminate that which is held to threaten the biological existence, health and vigour of a population.

Foucault's biopolitical account also provides us with another perspective on the state racism that was practiced in the twentieth century by the Nazis and others. As norms of perfection to which life is to conform were articulated in nationalist and racial identities, racial and ethnic groupings were placed in a hierarchy, often viewed in Social-Darwinist terms in which the higher race is the one that is deemed fittest to survive. It then became legitimate to exclude or eliminate those 'inferior' groups, within and outside of society, held to threaten the population's health and well-being. Negatively othered, deemed less than human, they could be subjected to the most extreme policies. This becomes Foucault's interpretation of the Nazi state, in which the improvement of the species went hand in hand with the genocidal elimination of the Jews and others who were deemed to threaten the 'purity' of the race, as well as those with mental and physical disabilities who were designated 'life unworthy of life' and subjected to a euthanasia program. It is also a way of understanding the Soviet Union's treatment of political adversaries, criminals, the mentally ill and other 'class enemies'. And this interpretation can equally be applied to the contemporary treatment of refugees by twenty-first century liberal-democratic states, increasingly portrayed as a danger to the health and well-being of the population, able to be rightfully removed and held in camps, deported or denied entry and left to die (Foucault 2003, 256; see Vanessa and Vatter 2017).

The much-discussed *Children of Men* (Alfonso Cuarón, 2006) portrays a kind of biopolitical dystopia with many of the aforementioned features. It is set in 2027, with humanity facing extinction because of a mysterious epidemic of infertility. The ensuing collapse of much of civilisation leaves only a few centres intact, to which refugees flock. This includes the UK, which has become an authoritarian police state. The film follows Theo (Clive Owen), a low-ranking, cynical bureaucrat who reluctantly takes on the role of protecting an African refugee, Kee (Clare-Hope Ashitey), who has despite all odds has become pregnant. In the film, the dark side of the modern governance of life is evident. A constant feature in the film is the state's xenophobic treatment of refugees and illegal immigrants, who are deemed to be the source of all the nation's problems. They are constantly seen being rounded up by the authorities, caged and sent to refugee camps where they endure even worse treatment. Everywhere, there is propaganda encouraging the population to help the government to 'protect Britain' by reporting illegal immigrants. Meanwhile, those in the ordinary population who are depressed or a burden on the state are encouraged to kill themselves for the good of society, with the government distributing free suicide kits to this end. Here, the 'life unworthy of life' is encouraged by the state to eliminate itself. Meanwhile the resistance, in the form of the pro-immigrant Fishes group, is not above committing terrorist acts in city centres, making the urban landscape a dangerously insecure environment. In all this, it is a consummate irony that the one woman who has become pregnant and offers a glimmer of hope for the species is a refugee, one of those deemed by the state to be a threat to the species.

There are obvious allusions in the film to the Nazi roundups of Jews, but also to the War on Terror, the international military campaign launched by the United States and many of its allies after the September 11 terrorist attacks. Terrorism itself, as the eruption of sudden, unpredictable violence and death in the midst of urban life, strikes at the heart of a biopolitical system. The Western state response at the time was accompanied by a stark division of peoples into good and evil, 'civilisation' and those representing 'a threat to all civilised life', with the state's right to kill justified in these terms. And as with the modern justification of capital punishment, the terrorist had to be portrayed as more than a conventional criminal, as a monster to be eliminated by any means possible no matter how extreme. This spectre of the dangerous outsider also contributed to the anti-immigration and anti-refugee sentiments that have continued to fester. Additionally it became possible to justify a significant enhancement of government controls over the domestic population in liberal democracies. This included increased powers for police and intelligence agencies, and the proliferation of state surveillance activity. In the name of the security and well-being of the population, there could be a pronounced erosion of individual rights and freedoms. Because the protection of individual rights, 'civil liberties', also provides part of the legitimation of the modern state, the state could paradoxically undermine the very freedoms it was claiming to defend.

While much of this is reflected in *Children of Men*, what especially gives the film its biopolitical edge is something that has not happened in reality, namely the epidemic of infertility it envisages. Infertility is a fundamental threat for a society obsessed with the management and fostering of life. This apocalyptic scenario bears comparison with the situation in Bergman's *The Seventh Seal*. There, it is the plague that is ravaging an essentially religious society, the threat of mass death bringing people to question all religious beliefs and values, and to wonder whether life might be nothing but a 'senseless horror'. In *Children of Men*, the plague ravaging society is infertility, the biological apocalypse calling into question all biopolitical norms and promoting a general sense of nihilism and futility. Interestingly, in both films, the hero gains a measure of meaning for their existence in the midst of bleak circumstances by sacrificing themselves for others. The knight Antonius Block does so in *The Seventh Seal* by distracting Death with a game of chess to allow the travelling circus family he has joined with to get away. And in *Children of Men*, Theo sacrifices himself to protect Kee and her baby from political exploitation, not only by the state but also by the anti-state rebels, and to deliver her instead to the Hofmeyr 'Human Project', a scientific group trying to cure infertility. For Foucault, however, it is not so much threats of mass extinction that are the issue, as the biopolitical regimes that seek to keep such threats at bay.

In general, opposition to this modern biopower is not just a matter of defending the individual against a state power that denies or ignores it. If modern, pastoral power concerns itself with the biopolitical management of populations, ensuring the health, well-being and security of the population as a whole, it is distinctive in also being 'individualising', that is, concerned with the unique particularity of each individual. It 'categorises the individual, marks him by his own individuality, attaches him to his own identity ... ties the individual to himself and subjects him to others in this way' (Foucault 2000, 331). In short, it turns individuals into certain kinds of moral subjects, obedient, responsible and docile citizens, adhering to certain norms, and who by virtue of being those subjects are amenable to direction by others. As such, the modern state, rather than simply ignoring individuals, is 'a very sophisticated structure, in which individuals can be integrated, under one condition: that this individuality would be shaped in a new form and submitted to a set of very specific patterns' (Foucault 2000, 334). Consequently, contrary to simplistic views of self and society, one does not oppose the state by asserting one's individuality. Opposing the state may also mean opposing the type of individualisation linked to the state. For Foucault, however, this also requires the cultivation of new ways of relating to oneself. This brings us to Foucault's ethics and also the question of the other in Foucault's ethical thinking.

Initially, it might seem that in his ethics Foucault is not concerned with the other at all, only the self, and the relation that we have with ourselves. He speaks of ethics as the relation of self to itself, and as in large part the ethical work that one performs on oneself (see Foucault 1985, 27). This is not, however, a return to the individualism and subjectivism of Kierkegaard and the existentialists, and to an ethics of authenticity, having the right relationship with oneself. Nor is it a return to the isolated, self-sufficient subject of traditional ethics, of utilitarianism and Kantian deontology. For Foucault, as for the ethics of care theorists and Levinas, the self exists fundamentally in relations with others. Society is not made up of self-sufficient individuals who come together to establish a community of morally restrained subjects through a mutually agreed contract, as in Hobbes. Rather, society consists of relationships, out of which particular kinds of individual emerge.

However, there is a crucial difference between Foucault and Levinas here. As Benda Hofmeyr puts it, 'Foucault's subject is responsible for and *actively* partakes in her own ethical becoming, while Levinas's existent is completely dependent upon and has to *passively* await the Other's intervention' (Hofmeyr 2006, 113).

As we have seen, for Levinas, the self depends entirely on the other to summon them to responsibility, to pull them out of their egoism and turn them into ethical subjects. It is passive in this process. For Foucault, the process of ethical self-formation is more complex. The self becomes an ethical subject through the influence of others, through various forms of socialisation and training. In the process, the individual acquires a framework of norms and values in terms of which to conduct themselves, to reflect, decide and act, thereby becoming a functioning, responsible agent. But this is not a one-sided process. Self-formation is not a matter of shaping a passive, unresisting thing, but of striving to impose norms of behaviour on creatures that actively resist the process. The ultimate aim is to bring these creatures to internalise these norms, to actively impose the required norms upon themselves, and this can only be after a protracted struggle. As such, individuals can be said to actively participate in their ethical self-formation. For Foucault, the ethical subject emerges not out of a one-sided relation but through reciprocal interaction, a series of encounters, struggles and conflicts.

Foucault also differs from Levinas in holding that relations with others have an inherently political dimension. For Foucault, power is always involved in social relations. Right from the start, power is being exercised by one party over the other in various forms of training and socialisation, and it is exerted in turn by individuals as they actively resist and struggle against this process. And if I emerge as an ethical subject out of this interaction with others, I am also in a position as an active subject to continue this interaction. That is, I might be produced by society, internalising the norms of a community to which I belong, but I can also modify these norms and in turn contribute to bringing about changes in the community's norms. Social relations in general consist in this reciprocal interplay, in power relations in which others influence the self and the self in turn influences others.

There is however a further dimension of power, power in a more familiar sense, to the extent that these social power relations cease to be reciprocal interactions and institutionalised hierarchies or forms of domination emerge in which some individuals or groups are able to exercise power over others in a one-sided, relatively ongoing way (Foucault 1990, 92–96). In this context, self-formation can become a matter of individuals internalising domination, being turned into the sorts of subjects that serve to perpetuate these hierarchies, and in turn, being restricted to the specific forms of individuality that the hierarchies make available. This is the 'individualising' power mentioned earlier. The required forms of individuality will also be policed through various social authorities, medical, administrative or legal, with departure from them likely to be construed as abnormality or deviance requiring correction or 'normalisation'. And individuals themselves can be active in maintaining these hierarchies, to the extent that they remain attached to the required forms of subjectivity and police not only themselves but also others in terms of them. To participate in the policing of others in terms of prevailing notions of normality and deviance is Foucault's version of seeking to 'reduce the other to the same'.

However as mentioned, if I emerge as an ethical subject out of an interaction with others, I am as an active subject also in a position to continue to resist and struggle against external influences. In particular, I can resist individualising forms of social domination by refusing the forms of subjectivity that they impose. This resistance involves adopting a different kind of relation to myself. Instead of internalising social norms, embracing a certain identity, I now seek to break away from myself in order to experiment with different ways of being, new forms of subjectivity (Foucault 1997b, 31; 2000, 336). There are parallels here with Nietzsche's account of moral development. For Nietzsche similarly, under the pressure of society human beings come to be divided against themselves, to enter into an oppressive relation with themselves; but there is also a promise inherent in this, that they might adopt a different way of relating to ourselves. In Nietzsche's case, this new relation was the self-enhancing self-relation of the overman; for Foucault, it is the refusal of oneself in order to try out different forms of individuality. To 'refuse oneself' in this manner is not to make a radical break from one's identity, from all normative constraints, in order to choose oneself, Sartre-style, in radical freedom. Foucault's position would be better described as an ethics of self-modification or self-transformation; and how we relate to others has a crucial role to play in this.

Having become certain kinds of ethical subjects through interaction with others, in the context of social hierarchies, we can perpetuate these hierarchies by how we in turn interact with others; and in particular how we relate to those who are 'different', who resist those hierarchies and refuse to adhere to the socially approved forms of subjectivity. As noted earlier, confronted by such a recalcitrant other, we may view them as an abnormality or deviation from the norm, in need of correction. This attitude serves to confirm both existing limits on who one can be and the social hierarchies these limits are bound up with. However, the other can also be acknowledged as an alternative way of being, and hence as a challenge to my form of subjectivity, showing that it is only one particular way of being and opening up the possibility that it could be different. Construing the other in this way can thus contribute to the process of challenging one's own defining norms and values, and breaking away from oneself. Accordingly, it is also part of the process of challenging the social structures that impose limits on the forms of individuality available to us in a culture.

Coming back to Tomas and Ebba in *Force Majeure*, both characters are clearly wedded to the particular roles to which they aspire, namely the proper man and caring wife and mother, even if they sometimes fall short of them in practice. The norms and ideals constitutive of these roles provide the framework in terms of which they make decisions and act, and also limit the class of actions they are capable of entertaining. To that extent, they can also be thought of as limits to freedom; not external obstacles but internal limits or 'positive constraints'. At the same time, these roles, and the constraints they entail, also have a larger socio-historical context. They are the classic roles of the traditional nuclear family, reflecting a particular social hierarchy and sexual division of labour. These roles are supported by social arrangements, including legal, administrative and educational practices (Patton 1989, 263). Nonetheless, resistance to these roles, and hence to the particular organisation of social practices that supports them, is

possible. There can be large-scale movements against social constraints on individuality, in the name of a whole category of individuals; as well as more local or
individual gestures of resistance and transgression.

Local or individual resistance is arguably represented by Ebba's friend
Charlotte (Karin Myrenberg). Charlotte rejects the constraints of the role of wife
and mother in a nuclear family, engineering an open relationship that allows her
to go on holiday and romance the ski instructors. This brings us to the confronting
experience that Ebba encounters, mentioned at the beginning of the chapter; not a
challenging situation in which she is unable to live up to her defining ideals, but
the challenge of another person who refuses to live up to the role Ebba aspires to.
For Ebba, Charlotte is the other who goes beyond everything she herself stands
for and challenges the very norms and ideals that define who she is. In the light
of the experience of a different way of being, Ebba is provoked into thinking
about her own role, if only to the extent of becoming uncomfortable, defensively
insisting that marriage and having kids is surely worth more than casual relationships with strangers. When Charlotte replies that she has both and doesn't need to
choose, Ebba protests that it can't be as easy as that, getting agitated to the point
where Charlotte has to tell her to calm down. We can surmise that behind Ebba's
defensiveness is the anxiety engendered by the sense that the framework giving
sense to her life and actions might not be absolute; that a different way of living
is possible.

Ebba does not get to the point of acknowledging Charlotte's way of life as a
legitimate alternative or seriously questioning the absoluteness of her own defining norms and values. She prefers to continue viewing it as a kind of deviation that
cannot be healthy. Nonetheless, this is a possible path one can go down and the
film itself goes down it a little way. As already evident in connection with Tomas's
role, the film is very self-conscious about the role of film in promoting certain
forms of individuality. This is also the case in connection with the role of caring
wife and mother that Ebba represents. In film, this role is often affirmed by having
women who deviate from it punished in some way. *Force Majeure* conspicuously
does not do this. At the end of the film, where Ebba, in the dangerously driven
bus, panics and demands to be let off, almost everyone else gets off as well. The
exception is Charlotte, who stays on the bus and presumably gets to the airport
in time for her flight. This is a significant development. Here's the film's director
again: 'Charlotte is the character that is supposed to be punished, if you look at
conventional films. Anyone who's promiscuous or unfaithful gets punished at the
end of the film. And I almost wanted the audience to *hope* for Charlotte to go over
the cliff and crash down as punishment for her sinful way of life. But instead, she's
the one who makes it to the airport' (Lucca 2014).

In this small way, the film pushes against both a particular role and film itself
insofar as it serves to play a normalising role. Deviation from a traditional role is
portrayed as a real alternative that could be freely taken up. This is not a criticism
of the role that Ebba that espouses, but rather of the idea that it is the only legitimate role, that it could not be changed. This idea, that there is nothing absolute
or necessary about a particular set of norms and values, constitutive of a mode of

life, distinguishes Foucault's approach to ethics. He does not reject the need for a framework of norms and values, necessary for us to be able to operate as coherent moral agents. He does, however, reject philosophical attempts to justify or ground norms that we happen to be operating with at any particular time, as in the early Enlightenment's idea of founding morality on a scientifically discoverable desiring nature or in one's rational nature, as in Kant. For Foucault, such thinking is part of the problem precisely because it presents as necessary and absolute what are in fact particular forms of individuality that have been made available in one's culture and which may reflect forms of social domination. Instead, in the context of resisting social hierarchies and forms of subjectivity bound up with them, he advocates self-refusal, breaking away from oneself, going beyond the self that one is, in order to experiment with different ways of being oneself. This experimental work is, for Foucault, the 'work of freedom' (see Foucault 1997b, 319).

Experiments in Living

LEt's conclude by saying a little about the idea of experiment here, this experimental work of freedom. Here we are returning to a theme that was highlighted in the Introduction. This experimental work is the opposite of searching for an essential nature or true self within us to conform to, or of a moral philosophy that looks for grounds to justify one's moral judgements. Refusing who one is, and experimenting with different ways of living that go beyond the limits of one's existing self, puts forms of life to the test of experience. This is a practical kind of moral philosophy, reflecting through practice on how one ought to live.

This experimental activity is not unlike what Mill in *On Liberty* called 'experiments of living' (Mill 1975, 72). There too we find a rejection of *a priori*, in advance of experience, philosophical reflection about what the good life consists in, in favour of testing conceptions of the good through the experiences we have in living them. As Mill puts it, 'The worth of different modes of life should be proved practically' (Mill 1975, 70). We also find this idea in Nietzsche, who talks in *Beyond Good and Evil* of the 'philosophers of the future'. Distinct from the 'philosophical labourers' (BGE 211) like Kant who seek to justify existing values, the philosophers of the future will be 'attempters' or 'experimenters' (BGE 42, 210). They are not conducting scientific experiments but trying out new ways of living in the world, different possibilities. They are the philosophers of the 'dangerous perhaps' (BGE 2). The goal of such experimenting is, by living through the problems, to determine the 'wherefore and whither' of humanity, the values for human life. Determining values is a creative activity and the philosophers of the future are creative in trying out new ways of living, new modes of life.

As has been noted, these experiments in living are not scientific experiments aiming to explore our biology or psychology. They concern human beings as moral beings, who choose and act in terms of a framework of moral values and ideals constitutive of who they are, their identity. Nonetheless, our biological and psychological capabilities have a bearing on the kinds of person we can be, the forms of life we can lead. We have to exercise these capabilities, in order to live various forms of life. However, they do not straightforwardly determine the kinds of life human beings can aspire to. Rather, they make possible a range of lives. Moreover, bodily capacities are themselves developed and enhanced in accordance with various norms in the course of the training processes through which individuals are turned into ethical subjects. So, what individuals can be or do cannot be determined in advance. This can only be worked out in practice, through the actual practice of exercising one's skills and capacities. Nonetheless, bodily capacities do set limits to the range of possible persons we can be or lives that can be lived, which are restricted to what is within the capabilities of human beings. A moral ideal or conception of the good life that it is beyond the capabilities of human beings to realise would be empty and irrelevant. So, as has been suggested at a number of points, ultimately there are practical constraints on ethics.

The process of being turned into an ethical subject through training and socialisation introduces its own constraints into the individual's existence. These are the internal limits or positive constraints mentioned earlier, in which the norms constitutive of one's identity or role delimit the class of actions that one is capable of entertaining. These normative constraints may be socially imposed, but insofar as they come to be internalised by the self, they are self-imposed; and for Foucault, this work on the self can also involve breaking away from our defining norms, going beyond the limits inherent in one's identity, in order to experiment with different ways of being oneself. Once again, this is not the complete rejection of all norms, since without a normative framework of some sort one cannot function as an agent. Rather, it is a matter of looking at points where modification and transformation might be possible. And again, this is very much an experimental process. The possible selves one can be cannot be determined in advance of experience. They can only be established in practice by trying out different forms of life.

While there is not, on this view, any ideal form of life grounded in human nature or reason that one can aspire to, and measure existing forms of life in terms of, there is arguably what one commentator calls a 'regulative principle' implicit in Foucault's work, in terms of which existing social and political regimes might be evaluated (Simons 1995, 86). The ideal is not a society without any constraints, but one that is open enough to permit modification and transformation of its ruling norms. As Foucault puts it, the important question is 'not whether a culture without constraints is possible or even desirable but whether the system of constraints in which a society functions leaves individuals the ability to transform the system' (Foucault 1997c, 147–148). This provides a measure for social progress, giving us a sense in which some forms of social life are better than others. The standard of progress here is not how closely society approaches a higher, more perfect form, governed by wholly rational norms, as in Habermas's conception of the ideal society, deriving ultimately from Kant's ideal of rational autonomy. Rather, social progress is measured by the extent society moves away from dominative forms of life, in which the possibilities for going beyond and modifying existing constraints are limited. More positively, this is the extent to which the society has room for experiments in self-transformation or the experimental work of freedom.

Films, which have been used in this book to explore various ethical positions, also offer the opportunity for experimentation, reflection and self-transformation. They play out virtual scenarios and life-stories in a concrete way and provide the opportunity to not only concretely illustrate, but also reflect on various ethical theories, understood as embodying views about how to live. As noted in the Introduction, film can portray 'other, forbidden or surprising kinds of experience', and this is experience that goes beyond standard ways of thinking or prevailing views of life and is capable of calling them into question. This is film experience understood as something more than an escapist, wish-fulfilling fantasy or a portrayal of a world that comfortably confirms one's existing presuppositions. It offers the opportunity to critically reflect on these presuppositions, to call them into question and potentially rethink them. In so doing, a film may reveal a way of understanding life to be hollow and simplistic; or it might reveal a moral reality that is more complex than an ethical theory can allow.

Such reflection can also be undertaken in relation to, the norms, values and ideals that constitute our identity as moral agents, and which we try to conform to or live up to in our actions. *Force Majeure*, for example, establishes an experimental situation in which Tomas and Ebba are both subjected to challenging circumstances, inviting reflection on the extent to which they are capable in practice of living up to the ideals and values that constitute their respective moral identities. As we have seen, *Force Majeure* also introduces another level of experimentation, another way one might be put to the test of experience as a moral being. This is Ebba's confrontation with Charlotte. Here, the challenging experience that the film presents is not the circumstance that confronts one with the possibility of failing to live up to one's defining ideals. Rather, it is the experience of another person who refuses to live up to those ideals, who is already experimenting with something different. This constitutes a challenge insofar as it implies that one's own cherished ideals may not be absolute or immutable, the only legitimate way of being, a recognition that potentially calls them into question and opens the possibility that one might oneself experiment with different ways of being.

In *Force Majeure*, as it happens, Ebba resists acknowledging Charlotte's way of life as a legitimate alternative or questioning her own defining norms and values. Another film that portrays this kind of confronting experience, if in somewhat more surreal circumstances, is *Being John Malkovich* (Spike Jonze, 1999) Written by Charlie Kaufman, the film not only portrays an encounter with another that leads to self-transformation, but also alludes to film itself as a venue for such self-transformative encounters. In the film, Craig Schwartz (John Cusack), filing clerk and failed puppeteer, finds a passageway in his office, a mysterious portal through which he can enter the mind of actor John Malkovich (John Malkovich playing a fictionalised version of himself) and experience the world through Malkovich's eyes and ears (Figure 6.2). And like *Rear Window*, the first film mentioned in this book, *Being John Malkovich* has something to say about cinema and movie-watching. The journey into the portal can readily be seen as a metaphor for going to the movies and the film itself suggests this comparison. In no time, Craig is selling tickets to people so they can go through the portal and have the 'Malkovich experience'. They are paying money to experience things they would

Figure 6.2 On the verge of cinematic self-transformation in *Being John Malkovich* (Spike Jonze, 1999. Credit: Universal/Photofest).

not experience in their ordinary lives, to have the 'other, forbidden or surprising' kind of experience that makes movies so appealing.

At the same time, for the film's main characters, their Malkovich experience is something more than an escapist fantasy. It is an encounter with an other, another person with a different way of being in the world, that offers a challenge to their own. However, Craig, like Ebba in *Force Majeure*, does not find this encounter with the other conducive to self-questioning and self-transformation. It only results in a re-affirmation of his rather drab identity. In Craig's case, this is not because he becomes defensive in the face of the other, but because he tries to completely master and overpower them. Any difference that Malkovich might represent is thereby overcome, and the 'other is reduced to the same'. Thus, even having managed to 'become' Malkovich, to take up a semi-permanent residency in the actor's mind, Craig does not succeed in escaping his former self. Instead of becoming more like the actor, confident, desirable and cool, Craig only succeeds in turning Malkovich into a version of himself. Malkovich-as-Craig comes increasingly to resemble Craig, looking thinner and acquiring Craig's hairstyle, hesitant mannerisms and generally depressed demeanour (see Ulin 2006).

Nonetheless, the film does acknowledge the possibility of self-transformation, of changing or escaping from ourselves through our encounter with the other. This is evident in the journey taken by Craig's wife Lotte (Cameron Diaz). Initially, Lotte pursues a course much like her husband's. She seizes the opportunity to go through the portal and take the ride in Malkovich. When she finds she can control the Malkovich body, she uses it to seduce Craig's workplace love-interest Maxine (Catherine Keener). However, unlike Craig, Lotte does not end up reducing Malkovich to a version of herself. Rather, she finds, in the experience of being in Malkovich, the possibility of a different standpoint on the world, a different way of being; and in the light of this experience, she resolves to change herself. Initially, she sees this transformation as a matter of becoming her 'real self', a true nature or identity that she decides is actually male. She contemplates sexual reassignment surgery to make her body match this sense of who she really is. However, her transformation turns out to be less about realising an underlying nature or essence than about going beyond the limits of her existing self, trying out a different way of living. Lotte abandons the idea that she is 'really a man' and does not go through with the idea of turning herself physically into one. Instead, she reinvents herself as a lesbian (see Falzon 2011).

It is possible to engage with this intriguing film in a number of ways, but with the present reading at least, the focus has been on using it to explore ethical concerns. Bearing in mind the particular journey that Lotte takes, the trip into Malkovich can be considered a cinematic representation of the possibility of self-transformation through encounter with another. The particular aspect of ethics that is illuminated here is the element of self-transcendence, rather than fidelity to a set of norms or rules. By presenting this journey as a quasi-cinematic experience, the film is also a cinematic representation of the manner in which film itself, by bringing us into contact with other, forbidden or surprising experiences, can be an avenue for ethical reflection and self-transformation.

FEATURE FILMS: *CASABLANCA* and *FORCE MAJEURE*

Casablanca

Casablanca is a 1942 romantic drama film directed by Michael Curtiz. Humphrey Bogart starts out behaving in a distinctly unheroic manner, refusing to get involved in other people's problems, although he will eventually redeem himself. Regarding the film's famous conclusion, reportedly neither Bogart nor Ingrid Bergman knew until the last days of filming whether Ilsa would be leaving with Laszlo or staying with Rick.

Plot

In 1941, Casablanca is a French colony controlled by Vichy France, the puppet government set up in France after the country was defeated by Germany. American expatriate Rick Blaine (Humphrey Bogart) owns 'Rick's Café Américain', a nightclub and casino in Casablanca. He claims to be neutral in all matters and to 'stick his neck out for nobody'. Petty crook Ugarte (Peter Lorre) tells Rick he has letters of transit obtained by murdering two German couriers. These allow the bearers to travel freely to Lisbon, the embarkation point for the still-neutral United States, and are much sought after by the refugees stranded in Casablanca.

Ugarte plans to sell them at the club and asks Rick to look after them. Before he can meet his contact, Ugarte is arrested by the local police under the command of Captain Louis Renault (Claude Rains), the Vichy prefect of police. Ugarte dies in custody without revealing that he gave the letters to Rick.

Rick's ex-lover Ilsa Lund (Ingrid Bergman) enters the nightclub and asks house pianist Sam (Dooley Wilson) to play 'As Time Goes By'. This brings Rick over and he is stunned to see Ilsa. She is accompanied by her husband, Victor Laszlo (Paul Henreid), a renowned fugitive Czech Resistance leader. They need the letters of transit to escape to America so he can continue his work. German Major Strasser (Conrad Veidt) has come to Casablanca to make sure Laszlo doesn't escape. That night, Ilsa comes to Rick's apartment to talk to him but, far gone with drink, he refuses to listen to her. After she leaves, a flashback reveals the reason for Rick's bitterness. They had an affair in Paris and, with the German forces approaching, had planned to flee the city together, but she failed to turn up for their rendezvous at the train station, sending a note saying they could never see each other again.

The next day, as Laszlo makes inquiries about the letters of transit, Rick's business rival Ferrari (Sydney Greenstreet) tells him he suspects Rick has them. When asked by Laszlo, Rick refuses to sell at any price, telling him to ask his wife why. Newlywed refugee Annina Brandel (Joy Page) has better luck. She asks Rick's advice about the wisdom of sleeping with Renault in order to get the travel visas she and her husband need to escape. He seems indifferent to her plight, but then we see him surreptitiously helping her husband win enough money at roulette to buy the visas on the black market. Soon after, Strasser and some of his officers start singing a German song. Laszlo orders the house band to play the Marseillaise. Rick nods his assent, Laszlo starts singing, and everyone joins in, drowning out the Germans. Enraged, Strasser has Renault close the nightclub.

Ilsa confronts Rick in the deserted nightclub. When he refuses to give her the letters, she threatens him with a gun, then confesses she still loves him. She explains that when they met in Paris, she thought her husband was dead but while preparing to flee with Rick learned he was alive, though sick and in hiding. She left Rick without explanation to look after him and to make sure Rick left Paris. No longer bitter, Rick agrees to help, letting her believe she will stay with him when Laszlo leaves. When Laszlo unexpectedly shows up, having narrowly escaped a police raid on a Resistance meeting, Rick has waiter Carl (S.Z. Sakall) spirit

Ilsa away. Laszlo, aware of Rick's feelings for Ilsa, tries to persuade him to use the letters to take her to safety.

When the police arrest Laszlo on a minor charge, Rick persuades Renault to release him, promising to set him up for the more serious crime of possessing the letters of transit. To allay Renault's suspicions, he says that it is he and Ilsa who will be leaving. When Renault tries to arrest Laszlo as arranged, Rick forces him at gunpoint to assist in their escape. At the last moment, Rick makes Ilsa board the plane to Lisbon with Laszlo. Strasser, tipped off by Renault, drives up, but is shot by Rick. When police arrive, Renault orders them to 'round up the usual suspects'. Dumping the bottle of Vichy water he has been drinking into the waste-paper basket, he suggests to Rick that they both join the Free French Forces in nearby Brazzaville. They walk off together into the fog.

Key Scenes

1 Informed by Renault that there will be an arrest in the club, Rick indicates that he has no intention of warning Ugarte, the intended target: 'I stick my neck out for nobody'. In this, he is established as looking out primarily for his own interests and in a distinctly unheroic manner, refusing to get involved in other people's problems. If the film is viewed as a piece of domestic political propaganda, Renault's approving response, 'a wise foreign policy', may be taken as an ironic comment not only on Rick's refusal to take any sort of stand, but also on the United States' isolationist foreign policy prior to join- ing the war effort [17.22–17.45].

2 Nonetheless, there is also evidence of a potential for action that goes beyond self-interest on Rick's part. Renault points out that Rick participated in anti-fascist struggles in the past, having run guns to Ethiopia during its war with Italy and fought on the Loyalist side in the Spanish Civil War. 'I got well paid for it on both occasions', Rick insists, but Renault notes that the winning side 'would have paid you much better' [19.45–20.17]. Rick also refuses to come in with busi- ness rival Ferrari in the 'trading of people's lives', working the black market in exit visas. Ferrari's response: 'My dear Rick, when will you realise that in this world today isolationism is no longer a practical policy?' Ferrari alludes to the film's anti-isolationist theme while criti- cising Rick for taking a principled stand in the matter [14.00–14.46].

3 Prior to Ilsa's revelations about Paris, when newlywed refugee Annina comes to the nightclub to ask Rick about sleeping with Renault in order to get the travel visas she and her husband need

to escape, he seems indifferent to her plight, still uninterested in the problems of others. But he then helps her husband to win enough at roulette to buy the visas on the black market. This might be seen as an ethical response on Rick's part that takes the form not of a Kantian recognition of a higher moral duty that transcends individual self-interest, but a more Levinasian taking of ethical responsibility in response to the summons of a unique other [1.04.46–1.07.17].

4 After Ilsa explains the circumstances that led her to leave Rick in Paris, she asks him to help her husband escape, but says that she cannot leave Rick again: 'I can't fight it anymore ... I don't know what's right any longer. You'll have to think for both of us, for all of us'. In this, she seems to be asking him to assume the role of a Kantian moral subject, to determine the right thing to do through an impartial moral reflection that transcends particular desires and attachments [1.23.10–1.25.36].

5 In the conclusion, Rick insists that Ilsa get in the plane with her husband. She is part of his work, what keeps him going. Here, the ethical development of Bogart's character has taken a distinctly Kantian form, demanding that he sacrifice his particular attachment to Ilsa in order to act in accordance with a higher duty. The relative unimportance of the particular relationships involved is underscored by Rick's comment: 'Ilsa, I'm no good at being noble, but it doesn't take much to see that the problems of three little people don't amount to a hill of beans in this crazy world' [1.35.51–1.37.49].

Force Majeure

Force Majeure is a 2014 Swedish comedy-drama, written and directed by Ruben Östlund. The film's male protagonist behaves in a distinctly unheroic manner, abandoning his wife and children in order to save himself when a controlled avalanche looks to be going wrong. According to the director: 'I always had two goals when I was making *Force Majeure*. Firstly, I wanted to create the most spectacular avalanche in film history. Secondly, I wanted to increase the percentage of divorces in society' (Gee 2014).

Plot

The film is set in an upmarket ski hotel, where good-looking, well-to-do couple Tomas (Johannes Bah Kuhnke) and his wife Ebba (Lisa Loven Kongsli), with their children, are spending their skiing holiday. The next day, the family is sitting on the balcony of the hotel restaurant, having lunch, when a controlled avalanche begins. When it doesn't slow down, panic erupts. Ebba shields the children but Tomas runs way. But there was never any real danger. Tomas returns, the family sit down at their table again and continue eating, now in silence. That evening, the couple have dinner with Ebba's new friend Charlotte (Karin Myrenberg). Tomas introduces the story of the avalanche but omits his own behaviour. When Ebba reminds him of what he did, he insists that that isn't how he remembers it. Back in their room, Tomas sticks to his story, which Ebba reluctantly agrees to, but not for long.

On day three, Ebba has an uncomfortable meeting with Charlotte. That evening, the couple have dinner with old friends Mats (Kristofer Hivju) and Fanni (Fanni Metelius). It is now Ebba who insists on recounting the whole incident, Tomas's humiliation only relieved by the appearance of their son's drone toy. While Tomas is out of the room putting his son to bed, Mats and Ebba discuss his behaviour. Tomas returns and insists once again that things didn't happen as Ebba suggests. However, he was filming the avalanche at the time and Ebba insists they look at the footage. It becomes clear that the person holding it is running away. Being forced to confront his behaviour leads Tomas to a crisis. The next day, Ebba finds him in the hotel room wallowing in self-pity. The kids come out of their bedroom and try to console their father, and Ebba reluctantly joins in.

On the final day, the family, skiing together one last time, run into poor conditions. Once they start skiing, Ebba gets separated from the others. Now, Tomas tells the kids to stay put and rescues her. After Tomas's triumph, the family leaves on the hotel bus. The driver drives badly, threatening to crash the bus. Now it is Ebba who panics and abandons the family. She leaps from her seat and demands that the bus driver stop to let her out. She does not, however, suffer any censure for this. Pretty much everyone on the bus is happy to follow suit, though they now face a long walk down the mountain and are likely to miss their flights home.

Key Scenes

1 The family is sitting on the restaurant balcony having lunch. On the mountainside opposite a controlled avalanche begins. When it shows no sign of slowing down, panic erupts on the balcony. Amidst the chaos, Ebba shields the kids, but Tomas grabs his phone and runs off-screen. It soon becomes clear that there was never any real danger. Tomas returns and the family sit down at their table

again to continue eating, only now in silence. In contrast to Rick in *Casablanca*, who eventually rises above self-interest to do the moral thing, Tomas starts out by falling short of what might be considered moral behaviour, reverting to self-interest [10.44–14.25].

2 Over dinner, Tomas initially refuses to acknowledge what he has done, insisting against Ebba's protests that he did not run away [23.00–28.54]. Back in their room, Tomas maintains his face-saving interpretation: 'Let's put all this behind us. There was an avalanche, we were terrified, but everyone's fine. Okay?' [29.18–32.32]. He also pushes this line at the second dinner: 'I don't share your interpretation though you're entitled to your opinion'. This time, however, he is betrayed by the video on his phone [1.00.20–1.04.34]. His repeated evasions indicate that he has been taking refuge in self-deception.

3 Ebba meets her new friend Charlotte, who has engineered an open relationship with her husband and can go on holiday and romance ski instructors. Ebba insists that marriage and having kids is worth more than casual relationships with strangers. When Charlotte replies that she has both and doesn't need to choose, Ebba protests that it can't be that easy, getting agitated to the point where Charlotte has to tell her to calm down. Encountering a different way of being, Ebba is provoked into thinking about her own role, if only to the extent of becoming uncomfortable and defensive [38.52–42.07].

4 At the second dinner, after Ebba recounts the avalanche incident and Tomas's behaviour during it, Mats suggests that for humans and animals alike, being confronted by a dangerous situation triggers a primitive survival instinct. Tomas could not really help running away. This interpretation recalls Hobbes's view of human nature. Ebba responds with a different view. She can't identify with anyone who would 'trample on their own kids to survive'. Her problem is that 'my natural focus is on my children ... while Tomas's natural focus is away from us'. This sounds more like an Aristotelian position. In running away, Tomas has revealed his bad character [53.50–59.58].

5 Waiting for the lift after dinner, Fanni speculates about what she and Mats might have done in the same circumstances. She thinks that she wouldn't have run and abandoned her children, but that Mats might have. Mats argues that there's no evidence for this, though when Fanni asks him where his kids are, he has to admit he has left them with his ex-wife. Even though, as his girlfriend suspects, Mats might have behaved the same way as Tomas did in the circumstances, we still judge Tomas more harshly than we do Mats.

And we do so even though it is a matter of pure luck that Tomas, rather than Mats, happened to be the one exposed to the dangerous situation. That luck plays a role in our moral assessment in this way is an instance of 'circumstantial moral luck' [1.04.34–1.07.55].

6 Wallowing in self-pity in their hotel room, Tomas confesses to a whole pattern of bad behaviour: 'I get that you're disappointed in the person who materialised. I'm really disappointed in him too. I hate him … can't forgive the guy'. She is not the only victim here, he says: 'I'm a victim too … a bloody victim of my own instincts'. Neither the Hobbesian nor Aristotelian interpretation quite captures this. Even if he has been moved by instincts not entirely under his control, he clearly feels he has let himself down. And he cannot be written off as having a bad character, because he clearly aspires to certain character ideals [1.33.28–1.36.06].

7 On the bus being driven dangerously down the mountainside, it is Ebba who panics and abandons the family, despite her confidence that she would always put her children first. For Ebba to fall short of her own character ideals in the same way that Tomas did suggests that no one is immune from doing so; and that the possibility of such failure may not be a flaw to be overcome, but in the end, simply part of the human condition [1.49.32–1.52.31].

Filmography

This filmography lists the films that have been used in the book, with the pages where they appear in the text.

3:10 to Yuma (Delmer Daves, 1957) 146
3:10 to Yuma (James Mangold, 2007) 146
2001: A Space Odyssey (Stanley Kubrick, 1968) 87, 161–162
The Addiction (Abel Ferrara, 1995) 63–64, 73, 74–75, 80, 84, 92–95, 203, 206–207, 218
The Admirable Crichton (Louis Gilbert, 1957) 127, 172
The African Queen (John Huston, 1951) 149, 151
Agora (Alejandro Amenábar, 2009) 2, 55–56
Alien (Ridley Scott, 1979) 20, 176, 244, 245, 253, 254
Aliens (James Cameron 1986) 244–245
Alien 3 (David Fincher, 1992) 254
Alien: Resurrection (Jean-Pierre Jeunet, 1997) 253–254
Alphaville/Alphaville, une Etrange aventure de Lemmy Caution (Jean-Luc Godard, 1965) 186
Babette's Feast (Gabriel Axel, 1987) 74
Baby Face (Alfred E. Green, 1933) 205
Basic Instinct (Paul Verhoeven, 1992) 33–34
Being John Malkovich (Spike Jonze, 1999) 264–266
The Big Lebowski (Joel and Ethan Coen, 1998) 51
Black Swan (Darren Aronofsky, 2010) 32
Blade Runner (Ridley Scott, 1982) 159–161, 162, 163, 176
Blade Runner 2049 (Denis Villeneuve, 2017) 163
Blue Velvet (David Lynch, 1986) 20, 26, 27, 31
Bridge of Spies (Steven Spielberg, 2015) 47
Casablanca (Michael Curtiz, 1942) 149–151, 250–251, 266–269
Charlie and the Chocolate Factory (Tim Burton, 2005) 24
Children of Men (Alfonso Cuarón, 2006) 256–258
Chinatown (Roman Polanski, 1974) 19, 89
The Cook, the Thief, His Wife and Her Lover (Peter Greenaway, 1989) 51
The Corporation (doc.) (Mark Achbar, Jennifer Abbott, 2003) 20

Glossary

This glossary contains key terms that have been used in the book, with the pages where they appear in the text. It also lists the main thinkers discussed, along with the texts referred to and their original dates of publication. In the book, I have cited recent editions of these texts, so the dates given there are not always the dates of original publication.

absurd Without point or justification. For existentialism, the world is absurd. There is no reason for the way the world is or what happens in it and human beings in particular have no reason or justification for existing. [215, 219, 220]

alienation A term employed by Marx to describe the state of people under capitalism, separated from a properly human existence, unable to pursue their true interests and denied control over their lives and working conditions. [173, 176, 179]

altruism Concern for the well-being of others or the promotion of their good. Altruism may involve sacrificing one's own good for the sake of others or it may be adopted out of self-interest. [70]

apatheia The state of freedom from disturbing emotions, an ideal especially for the Stoics. [46, 50, 56]

a priori In advance of experience. Can be applied to theories of ethics that claim to be based on intuitions about the nature of the good, access to divine revelation or the deliverances of pure reason. [6]

Aquinas, Thomas (c. 1225–1274) Italian philosopher and theologian, especially associated with natural law theory. Works include the *Summa contra Gentiles* (begun around 1259) and *Summa Theologiae* (begun in 1266). [76–84, 85, 88, 89, 97, 210, 215]

Arendt, Hanna (1906–1975) German-born political theorist, who introduced the notion of the 'banality of evil'. Books include *Eichmann in Jerusalem: A Report on the Banality of Evil* (1963). [21, 133]

arete The goodness of a thing, that at which the thing excels. In moral terms, virtuousness, the goodness of a person. [34–35]

Aristotle (384–322 BCE) Greek philosopher. Along with Plato, a central figure in the development of Western thought. Develops a teleological view of the universe in which all things have an inbuilt goal or *telos* that they strive to realise. His best-known work on ethics is the *Nicomachean Ethics*. [34–39, 41–42, 44, 49, 77, 80, 97, 113, 238–239]

asceticism   The extreme renunciation of worldly desires, especially popular in early Christianity. [73, 96, 107, 112, 151, 204, 206]

ataraxia   Peace of mind, serenity or tranquillity, the highest good for human beings to aim for, a notion used especially by the Epicureans. [50]

Augustine (354–430)   African philosopher and theologian, a key architect of the Christian world view while drawing in significant ways on Plato. Works include *The Confessions* (written around 400) and *City of God* (written between 413 and 427). [69–74, 76, 77, 78–79, 83–84, 85, 94, 148, 209–210]

Aurelius, Marcus (121–180)   Roman emperor and philosopher, exponent of Stoic philosophy. Author of the *Meditations*. [44, 56]

authenticity   The ideal of being true to oneself. In Sartre's version, acknowledging one's freedom and accepting responsibility for one's choices, values and actions; the opposite of bad faith. [218, 219, 223, 231]

autonomy   Self-rule or self-determination. For Kant, the ability of the person to rationally determine their existence rather than being determined by external forces. Kant contrasts it with heteronomy, where we are determined in what we do by non-rational factors. [165–168]

bad faith   Self-deception. In Sartre's terms, an attitude that denies one's freedom and responsibility for one's choices, values and actions. [216–217, 230]

banality of evil   The circumstance that evil acts might mostly be the work not of monsters or sadists but of ordinary individuals who value conformity and self-interest over thinking for themselves and the welfare of others. [21]

beatitude   Blessedness, happiness or well-being. Augustine and Aquinas's version of Aristotle's *eudaimonia*. [70, 79]

Bentham, Jeremy (1748–1832)   English philosopher, founder of utilitarianism. Author of *An Introduction to the Principles of Morals and Legislation* (first published 1789). [110–113, 116, 127, 130, 159]

biopower   The name given by Foucault to the techniques exercised distinctively by modern states, directed towards the management and regulation of their subjects, endeavouring to enhance and optimise life in a controlled way. Biopower has two poles:discipline, the minute disciplinary control of individual body and their forces, and bio-politics, the management and regulation of populations, their births, deaths, reproduction and health. [255, 256, 258]

Camus, Albert (1913–1960)   French novelist and philosopher, an important figure in the development of existentialism, particularly in connection with the notion of absurdity. Author of the philosophical essay *The Myth of Sisyphus* (first published 1942). [214, 220]

care, ethics of   A normative ethical position that sees ethics as concerned primarily with the maintenance and nurturing of relationships between people rather than adherence to rules. [13, 242–248, 258]

categorical imperative   For Kant, the ultimate principle of morality: act only on that principle that could be turned into a universal law. All rational agents are bound to this principle, regardless of their particular inclinations. Contrasted with the hypothetical imperative. [148, 164, 168, 183]

communism   In Marx's thought, the ideal social and economic order, characterised by communal ownership and production of goods, and communal self-government. The term is often used interchangeably with socialism, although strictly speaking, socialism is the transitional phase, in which the representatives of the people are in charge of the means of production. [150, 168, 171–173, 176, 181, 185, 255]

consequentialism (or teleological ethics)   The view that the rightness of an act is to be judged in terms of its consequences. For example, ethical egoism and utilitarianism are consequentialist theories in this sense. [145]

de Beauvoir, Simone (1908–1986)   French philosopher, feminist and novelist, an important figure in the development of existentialism. Author of *The Ethics of Ambiguity* (first published 1947) and *The Second Sex* (first published 1949). [214–215, 218, 223, 227–231, 242]

deontological ethics   From the Greek *deon* meaning duty. A normative ethical position that judges the morality of an action on the basis of rules, so a rule- or duty-based ethics. [65, 143, 153]

divine command theory   An account of morality that sees moral rules as God's laws or commandments. The morally right action is that commanded by God; the morally wrong action is that which God forbids. [66–69]

dualism   The view that the human being is composed of two very different sorts of things, an immaterial mind (or soul) and a material body. A view to be found in Plato, Augustine and Descartes, amongst others. [210]

egoism, ethical egoism   Psychological egoism is the psychological theory that self-interest is the motivation and the goal of all one's actions. Ethical egoism is the normative position that holds that moral agents ought to do what is in their individual self-interest. [104–105]

empiricism   The account of knowledge which holds that all knowledge of the world is derived from sense experience and observation. Empiricists typically hold that reason by itself, independently of experience, cannot establish truths about the world. Locke (1632–1704) and Hume (1711–1776) are two classic empiricists and Hobbes (1588–1679) also had empiricist views. [101]

Enlightenment   A philosophical and intellectual movement in eighteenth-century Europe, which formulated key features of the modern outlook, including faith in reason, belief in the progressive character of science and technology and a critical attitude towards religion. Key figures include Voltaire (1694–1778), Julien La Mettrie (1709–1751), Claude Helvétius (1715–1771) and the Baron d'Holbach (1723–1789). [96–97, 103, 105–106, 126, 130–132, 134, 143, 153, 160, 169, 185, 188–189, 190, 198–199, 262]

Epictetus (55–135)   Greek stoic philosopher, former Roman slave. Author of the *Enchiridion* ('handbook' or 'manual'). [44, 46]

Epicurus (341–c.270 BCE)   Greek philosopher, key architect of Epicureanism, the ethical doctrine that the good life consists in the absence of physical pain and mental disturbance. The doctrine was further developed by the Roman poet Lucretius (c.98–c.55 BCE). [48–55, 65, 84, 98]

ethics   Thinking about how we should live and what sort of person we ought to be. Also, a branch of philosophy, moral philosophy, the area of philosophy concerned with how we ought to conduct ourselves and deal with one another and why we should be moral at all. [4–6]

ethics, feminist   A critical appropriation of a feminine ethics of care, supplementing the latter's attention to specific circumstances and relationships with an awareness of the broader social context, in particular the political dimension of relationships. [246–247]

eudaimonia   Happiness in the sense of well-being or fulfilment. This is considered the ultimate goal of human activity, and highest good, in Aristotle's virtue ethics. [35, 44–45, 48, 70, 76, 79, 106]

Euthyphro problem   Is something right because God commands it or does God command it because it is right? If the former, God's commands are completely arbitrary. He has no more reason to command an action than to forbid it. If the latter, God is no longer required in order to make an action right or wrong to justify moral judgements. [69]

existentialism   The philosophy of human existence which holds that there is nothing outside of or within ourselves that we can appeal to in order to justify our values and moral rules. If there are moral rules and values, it is because we have freely chosen them and nothing can guide us in these choices. Prominent existentialist figures include Jean-Paul Sartre (1905–1980), Simone de Beauvoir (1908–1986) and Albert Camus (1913–1960). [215, 217, 223]

experiments in living   For John Stuart Mill, we learn about the good through experiments in living, testing conceptions of the good through the experience we have of living them out. [7, 262]

facticity   On Sartre's account, all the facts about ourselves and our situation. [216]

felicific calculus   A way of calculating amounts of pleasure developed by Bentham. A quantitative measure of pleasure is supposed to be arrived at by measuring it along a number of dimensions, including intensity, duration, propinquity (nearness), certainty, fecundity (fruitfulness) and purity (not being mixed with unpleasant feelings). [112]

feminism   The area of social thinking that criticises the subordination and oppression of women. [179, 227, 242]

Foucault, Michel (1926–1984)   French philosopher, responsible for an influential reformulation of the notion of power in terms of power-relations, who in his later work turned to the ethical subject and forms of self-relation. Works include *Discipline and Punish* (first published 1975) and *The History of Sexuality* volumes 1 (first published 1976) and 2 (first published 1984). [255–263]

Frankfurt School   The name given to a group of twentieth-century German Marxists, who turned to the analysis of media, advertising and popular culture, as well as the effects of science and technology on social life. Prominent members include Max Horkheimer (1895–1973), Theodor Adorno (1903–1969) and Herbert Marcuse (1898–1979). Important texts include Horkheimer and Adorno's *Dialectic of Enlightenment* (first published 1947) and Marcuse's

One-Dimensional Man (first published 1964). Jürgen Habermas (1929–) is a more recent representative. [176–177, 182–190]

freedom, negative and positive According to the distinction formulated by Isaiah Berlin, negative freedom is 'freedom from': freedom from external interference by other individuals, governments and so on; positive freedom is 'freedom to': freedom to live in accordance with rules we define for ourselves. Hobbes is the classic advocate of the former and Kant of the latter. [166–168]

genealogy of morals A term of Nietzsche's used to characterise an approach that considers current moral values in their historical development, tracing how ideals and values have emerged and changed over time. Nietzsche also spoke of a 'natural history of morals'. [200–201]

Gilligan, Carol (1936–) American ethicist, psychologist and feminist, known for developing the idea of a distinctively feminine ethics of care. Author of *In a Different Voice* (1982). [242–243]

good life In Greek and Roman ethics, the happiest, most fulfilled human life and the life lived in accordance with human nature. Being virtuous is necessary for happiness so understood, but opinions differed to whether virtue was sufficient (the Stoic position) or not (Aristotle's view). [30]

Habermas, Jürgen (1929–) German philosopher and leading contemporary representative of the Frankfurt School. Works include *Toward a Rational Society* (1969), *Knowledge and Human Interests* (1972) and *The Future of Human Nature* (2003). [182–190, 263]

happiness In Greek and Roman philosophy, eudaimonia, well-being or fulfilment. For Hobbes and many Enlightenment thinkers, pleasurable feeling. [10, 35–36, 38–39, 44–46, 48, 50, 70, 76, 79, 92, 97–98, 106]

hedonism, ethical hedonism Hedonism is the psychological theory that all human actions are motivated by the desire to secure pleasure and avoid pain. Ethical hedonism is the normative position that holds that pleasure is the highest good or the only thing of intrinsic worth. Classic utilitarianism can be seen as a social form of ethical hedonism. [48, 118]

Hegel, Georg Wilhelm Friedrich (1770–1831) German philosopher who rejected Kant's autonomous moral agent as an abstraction, turning it into a supra-individual entity, a collective human subject that he calls Spirit or Reason. His most widely discussed work is *The Phenomenology of Spirit* (first published 1807). [169–170, 248]

Helvetius, Claude (1715–1771) French philosopher, key figure of the French Enlightenment, advocate of materialism. Author of *A Treatise on Man, His Intellectual Faculties and His Education* (first published 1772). [106, 108–110, 111, 129, 130]

herd animal morality For Nietzsche, the morality dominant in modern society, the Christian values left over from our religious past, celebrating modesty, consideration, weakness, security, belonging to the group and hostile to everything that elevates the individual above the herd. [199–200, 203–204]

higher and lower pleasures A distinction introduced by Mill, who argues that pleasures differ qualitatively as well as quantitatively. The higher pleasures of the mind and the soul are to be preferred to the lower, bodily pleasures. [113–116]

Hobbes, Thomas (1588–1679)   English philosopher, empiricist, advocate of reductive materialism and an early proponent of liberal thinking. His most famous work is *Leviathan* (first published 1651). [29, 31, 49, 97–101, 102, 104, 111]

Holbach, Baron d' (Paul-Henri Thiry)   (1723–1789) French-German philosopher, key figure of the French Enlightenment. Known for his strident critique of religion and advocacy of materialism. Books include *The System of Nature* (1770). [106, 108–110, 111, 129–131, 134, 199]

homo economicus   'Economic man', the rationally self-interested, utility-maximising fantasy figure of mid-twentieth century economics, anticipated by Hobbes. [102]

Hume, David (1711–1776)   Scottish Enlightenment philosopher, historian and essayist. Pursued a systematic critique of metaphysical and theological systems and an empirical enquiry into human nature. Author of the *Treatise of Human Nature* (first published 1739) and *Dialogues Concerning Natural Religion* (published posthumously in 1779). [89, 131]

Hypatia (c.370–415)   Greek or Egyptian Neoplatonist philosopher-scientist, director of the Neoplatonist school in Roman Alexandria. No clearly identified writings survive but her life is recorded in some detail. [55–56]

hypothetical imperative   In Kant's moral theory, a principle of action that says that if you want to achieve such and such a goal, you should act in a certain way. It presupposes a pre-existing desire or goal. Contrasted with the categorical imperative. [148]

ideology   The Marxist term for false consciousness, a false or limited understanding of one's social situation, needs and interests which serves to maintain the existing social order. [173–174, 184–185]

integrity objection   The argument that utilitarianism fails to take into account the kinds of moral commitments that define the particular person one is, demanding that people think impartially about what actions contribute to maximising happiness. It thus has the potential to alienate a person from their moral identity, requiring them to violate their integrity. [123]

Kant, Immanuel (1724–1804)   German philosopher, a key figure in modern theory of knowledge and an influential moral theorist. Ethical works include the *Groundwork of the Metaphysics of Morals* (first published 1785) and the *Lectures on Ethics* (published posthumously in 1920). [6, 8, 12, 132, 142–168, 172, 182, 183, 189, 216, 222, 241–243, 263]

Kierkegaard, Søren (1813–1855)   Danish philosopher and theologian, an important influence on twentieth-century existentialism. Books include *Fear and Trembling* (first published 1843) and *Concluding Unscientific Postscript* (first published 1846). [13, 94, 189, 211–212, 213–216, 224, 249, 252, 258]

Levinas, Emmanuel (1906–1995)   French philosopher who developed an ethics of responsibility for the other. Author of *Totality and Infinity* (1961) and *Otherwise than Being or Beyond Essence* (1974). [248–249, 252–255, 258–259]

liberalism The tradition in social and political philosophy which holds that individuals should be as free as possible to pursue their interests. Some political and legal constraints are necessary to maintain social order, but the liberal view is typically that these should be as minimal as possible. The main architect of modern liberal thinking is Locke. [126, 129, 241]

Locke, John (1632–1704) English philosopher, founder of modern empiricism and a central figure in the development of modern liberal thinking. Author of the *Essay Concerning Human Understanding* (first published 1689) and *Two Treatises of Government* (first published 1689). [125–127, 155, 241]

Lucretius (Titus Lucretius Carus) (c.98– c.55 BCE) Roman philosopher-poet, working in the tradition of Epicureanism. Author of *On the Nature of Things*. [52]

materialism With respect to human beings, the idea that all aspects of human life are to be explained in terms of the organisation and movement of matter, without recourse to a separate mental or spiritual principle. A view favoured by many eighteenth-century Enlightenment thinkers prior to Kant, typically resulting in a hedonistic and egoistic conception of human nature. [49, 96–97, 105–106]

Marcuse, Herbert (1898–1979) German philosopher and member of the Frankfurt School. Author of *One-Dimensional Man* (first published 1964). [176, 177]

master and slave morality Two kinds of morality, representing the perspectives of opposing social classes, that Nietzsche identifies through his historical genealogy of morality. [201–204]

Marx, Karl (1818–1883) German philosopher and founder of Marxist social and political thinking. Works include *Economic and Philosophical Manuscripts* (first published 1844), *The Holy Family*, *The Communist Manifesto* (with Friedrich Engels, first published 1848*), The Eighteenth Brumaire of Louis Bonaparte* (first published 1852) and *Capital* (first volume published 1867). [168–175, 179, 180, 183, 199, 200, 210, 211, 255]

Marxism The social and political account formulated by Karl Marx, which sees the individual as existing necessarily in a community and emphasises the role of the economic in accounting for social existence. Marx's twentieth-century Marxist successors include the Frankfurt School thinkers and Jürgen Habermas. [174, 177–181]

metaethics The area of ethics that asks general questions about the nature of the moral judgements we make. [9]

Mill, John Stuart (1806–1873) English philosopher. A key figure in the development of utilitarianism and of liberal thinking. Author of *On Liberty* (first published 1859) and *Utilitarianism* (first published 1863). [7, 113–116, 127–128, 167, 181, 262]

Montaigne, Michel de (1533–1592) French renaissance philosopher, opponent of dogmatism and fanaticism in all its forms, who popularised the essay form as a literary genre. Author of *Essays* (published and revised 1570–1592). [75]

moral luck The circumstance that one continues to treat someone as an object of moral judgement even when a significant aspect of what they do depends on factors beyond their control. We often do this, even though it is intuitively plausible that people cannot be morally assessed for what is not their fault. A notion introduced by Thomas Nagel and Bernard Williams. [221–222, 272]

natural law theory   An account of morality as an objective set of principles, in Aquinas's version expressing God's will for creation. [76–84]

naturalism, ethical   The view that there is no fundamental discontinuity between the ethical and the natural, that moral values cannot be sharply demarcated from facts about human nature and the human situation. The classic ethical naturalist position is Aristotle's virtue ethics. Stoicism and Epicureanism were naturalistic moral theories, as is Aquinas's account. In the modern period, the best-known form of ethical naturalism is utilitarianism. [38, 44, 78]

neoplatonism   A revived version of Plato's ideas that influenced Augustine. [55]

Nietzsche, Friedrich (1844–1900)   German philosopher. An important precursor to twentieth-century existentialism. Author of *The Gay Science* (first published 1882), *Beyond Good and Evil* (first published 1886) and *On the Genealogy of Morals* (first published 1887). [93–94, 116, 197–211, 215, 216, 232, 233, 236, 246, 260, 262]

nihilism   A denial or rejection of all moral principles and values; a belief that life is meaningless. [91, 130, 199, 215]

non-naturalism, ethical   The view that there is a fundamental discontinuity between the ethical and the natural. Moral values are independent of ordinary natural facts. This includes Plato's objectivist non-naturalism, in which the moral values are not dependent on anything outside them, and the supernaturalism of divine command theory, in which the moral values are the product of divine will. [30, 65]

normative ethics   The area of ethics concerned with producing theories about what we ought, morally speaking, to do. [5]

normalisation   For Foucault, the process of bringing of individuals to conform in their behaviour to various norms and standards through various power techniques. [259]

objectivism, ethical   In ethical objectivism, moral values are not dependent on anything outside them and in particular are not the product of will, whether human or divine. [30]

other, ethics of the   A family of approaches to ethics that are especially concerned with our response to others, in particular those who are 'other' than us. Representatives include the ethics of care, Levinas and Foucault. [237–262]

pastoral power   According to Foucault, a form of power originating in the Church but secularised from the eighteenth-century onwards, becoming the dominant mission of the modern state. Pastoral power is oriented towards people's 'salvation' in this world rather than the next, ensuring their health, well-being and security. It makes use of the techniques of biopower to manage individual bodies and populations. [255–256]

person   On Locke's account, a thinking, intelligent being; for Kant, a rational agent. In both cases, a person is to be distinguished from a biological human being. It is widely held that persons have a special value and that they deserve particular moral respect. [154–165]

Plato (c. 429–327 BCE) Greek philosopher, a central figure in the emergence and development of the theory of knowledge, moral thinking and social and political thought. Author of the *Apology* and *Republic,* amongst others. [5, 10, 16–17, 22–24, 29–32, 35, 36, 38, 39, 44, 64, 65, 69, 77, 148, 167, 209–210]

Plotinus (205–270) Roman thinker who developed Neoplatonism, a revived version of Plato's ideas. Author of the *Enneads*. [55]

problem of evil The problem of how an all-good, all-powerful God can allow evil in the world. [84–89]

relational autonomy A notion of autonomy that tries to balance individual agency with social embeddedness. [247–248]

relativism, ethical The view that what is right or wrong is dependent on the society in which moral standards arise. As distinct from the descriptive claim that there is a wide variation in moral belief between different cultures. [91]

ressentiment For Nietzsche, the feelings of envy and hatred towards the masters engendered in the slaves. [202, 203]

rights Moral rights are strong entitlements to certain things, such as a right to life, privacy or a fair trial. If someone has a right to something, others have a corresponding duty to respect that right. [124–129]

rights, natural For Locke, rights that exist prior to and regardless of social arrangements and which we possess simply by virtue of being human. Specifically, these are the rights to life, liberty and property. [125, 127]

Rousseau, Jean-Jacques (1712–1778) Swiss social philosopher and advocate of freedom through active participation in politics and legislation. Books include *A Discourse on the Origin of Inequality* (first published 1755) and *The Social Contract* (first published 1762). [103, 104]

Sartre, Jean-Paul (1905–1980) French philosopher, playwright, novelist and central figure in the development of twentieth-century existentialism. Sartre's main philosophical text in this connection is *Being and Nothingness* (first published 1943). [83, 89, 92, 195, 214–216, 223–224, 225, 227–228, 230, 231, 249, 260]

situationism In opposition to Aristotelian notions of character, situationism holds that how we behave is best explained not in terms of persisting character traits but of ways that we typically respond to different kinds of situation. [40–41]

social Darwinism The view that society is a state of struggle in which the fittest or strongest wins and the weak will die out. Through this struggle, society as a whole will improve. Consequently, altruism and compassion need to be resisted as detrimental to social progress in favour of ruthless egoism, competition and manipulation. [132–133, 256]

Socrates (470–399 BCE) Greek philosopher who, as represented in Plato's dialogues where he is usually the central figure, encourages critical reflection through dialogue. [5, 35, 47, 69, 169]

state of nature   A time before the invention of society, or in which all social authority is absent, envisaged by Hobbes and Locke to provide a justification for organised society. Society is justified as a remedy for the problems and shortcomings experienced in the state of nature. [99–101, 103, 125–126, 139]

stoicism   A later Greek, and Roman, philosophy, offering an ethics that counsels indifference towards external circumstances. Founded by Zeno of Citium (334–262 BCE) and developed in the Roman period by Epictetus and Marcus Aurelius. [44–48, 50, 55, 56, 77]

subjectivism, ethical   In ethical subjectivism, moral values are dependent on a will, whether this is God's will, as in divine command theory where whatever God commands is right, or the individual's will, as in Sartre's existentialism where values are created through individual choices. Can be considered a form of ethical relativism where what is right or wrong is determined by an individual agency, rather than a social group or a society. [91, 223]

subjectivism, universal (or objective subjectivism).   In Kant's moral theory, moral laws are formulated by individual subjects, but also objective in that they are only moral laws to the extent that are universalisable, i.e., able to be consistently be followed by all individuals in relevantly similar situations. In Habermas's Kantian discourse ethics, moral laws are only legitimate to the extent that they can be agreed to by all participants in a rational discourse. [143]

summum bonum   The highest good, the supreme good or ultimate goal of human life, e.g., happiness (Aristotle) or beatitude (Aquinas). [38]

supernaturalism, ethical   The view that a supernatural deity, God, creates or sustains morality. An example of this is divine command theory, in which moral laws are God's commands. However, to the extent that these moral laws are dependent on God's will, divine command theory is also a form of ethical subjectivism. [65]

telos   For Aristotle, the defining goal that things, non-human and human, strive to realise. [38]

theodicy   The part of theology that seeks to reconcile a good and all-powerful god with the existence of suffering and evil in the world. [85–88]

ubermensch   The 'overhuman', 'superman' or 'overman'. In Nietzsche's thinking, the superior human being, the goal that humanity sets for itself. [59, 197, 201, 204–210, 236]

utilitarianism   In its classic 'hedonistic' form, a moral theory which holds that the moral character of an act depends on how much happiness it produces, where happiness is understood in terms of pleasure. For utilitarianism, an action is right insofar as it tends to create the greatest happiness for the greatest number of people. Key figures in the development of utilitarianism are Jeremy Bentham (1748–1832) and John Stuart Mill (1806–1873). [110–124, 127–128, 147–148, 186–187, 245]

utilitarianism, desire (or preference)   Here happiness is no longer understood in terms of pleasure but in terms of the satisfaction of desire, understood in terms of either getting what you want or getting what is in your interests, where interests are normally explained in terms of present and probable future desires. As opposed to the classic hedonistic utilitarianism. [118]

utilitarianism, act and rule   In classic 'act utilitarianism', it is asked of each act whether it produces the greatest happiness. In rule utilitarianism, this question is asked of rules such as 'never tell a lie' or 'never inflict unnecessary pain'. [122]

virtue   A morally praiseworthy quality of character. [10]

virtue ethics   The ethical view that takes virtue to be the central notion and which typically takes Aristotle's *Nicomachaean Ethics* as its primary model, although all ancient Greek and Roman ethics can be characterised as virtue ethics. [34–44]

Voltaire (François-Marie Arouet) (1694–1778)   French Enlightenment writer, philosopher, historian. Famous for his attacks on the Catholic Church and political establishment. His philosophical works include the *Philosophical Dictionary* (first published 1764). [67, 75]

Bibliography

Adams, Jeffrey (2015) *The Cinema of the Coen Brothers: Hard Boiled Entertainments*, New York: Columbia University Press.

Allison, Deborah (2004) 'Don Siegel', *Senses of Cinema*, 32. Retrieved from http://sensesofcinema.com/2004/great-directors/siegel/.

Anchor, Robert (1967) *The Enlightenment Tradition*, New York: Harper and Row.

Annas, Julia (2008) 'The Sage in Ancient Philosophy', in F. Alesse et al. (eds.), *Anthropine Sophia*, Naples: Bibliopolis, 11–27.

Aquinas, Thomas (1956) *Summa Contra Gentiles* Book Three, New York: Image.

Aquinas, Thomas (1998) Excerpts from *Summa Theologica*, in trans. R. McInerny (ed.), *Thomas Aquinas: Selected Writings*, London: Penguin.

Appiah, Kwame Anthony (2010) *Experiments in Ethics*, Cambridge, MA: Harvard University Press.

Arendt, Hannah (2006) *Eichmann in Jerusalem: A Report on the Banality of Evil*, New York: Penguin.

Aristotle (2004) *The Nicomachean Ethics*, trans. J.A.K. Thomson, London: Penguin Books.

Austen, Jane (2011) *The Annotated Sense and Sensibility*, annotated and edited by David M. Shapard, New York: Anchor.

Augustine (1958) *City of God*, New York: Image.

Augustine (1961) *Confessions* trans. R.S. Pine-Coffin, Harmondsworth: Penguin.

Augustine (2015) *On the Merits and Forgiveness of Sins, and on the Baptism of Infants – June 8, 2015*, CreateSpace Independent Publishing Platform.

Averill, Lindsey (2012) 'Sometimes the World is Hungry for People Who Care: Katniss and the Feminist Care Ethic', in George A. Dunn and Nicolas Minaud (eds.), *The Hunger Games and Philosophy: A Critique of Pure Treason*, Hoboken, NJ: John Wiley and Sons, 162–176.

Baker, Aaron (2015) *A Companion to Martin Scorsese*, Malden, MA; Oxford: Wiley Blackwell.

Balog, Katalin (2016) '"Son of Saul," Kierkegaard and the Holocaust', *New York Times*, February 28. Retrieved from https://opinionator.blogs.nytimes.com/2016/02/28/son-of-saul-kierkegaard-and-the-holocaust/.

Bandy, Mary Lea, and Antonio Monda (2003) *The Hidden God: Film as Faith*, New York: Museum of Modern Art.

Barber, Nicholas (2017) 'Why Casablanca is the ultimate film about refugees'. Retrieved from www.bbc.com/culture/story/20171124-why-casablanca-is-the-ultimate-film-about-refugees.

Barcenas, Alejandro (2017) 'Corporate Greed and Alien/ation: Marx vs. Weyland-Yutani', in Jeffrey Ewing and Kevin S. Decker (eds.), *Alien and Philosophy: I Infest, therefore I am*. Hoboken, NJ: Wiley Blackwell, 48–54.

Bentham, Jeremy (2004) *An Introduction to the Principles of Morals and Legislation*, in Alan Ryan (ed.), *Utilitarianism and Other Essays*, Harmondsworth: Penguin Books.

Bentham, Jeremy (2015) *Anarchical Fallacies*, in J. Waldron (ed.), *Nonsense Upon Stilts: Bentham, Burke, and Marx on the Rights of Man*, London: Routledge, 46–76.

Bergman, Ingmar (1973) *Bergman on Bergman: Interviews with Ingmar Bergman by Stig Bjorkman, Torsten Manns and Jonas Sima*, New York: Simon and Schuster.

Berlin, Isaiah (1969) 'Two Concepts of Liberty', in Isaiah Berlin (ed.), *Four Essays on Liberty*, Oxford: Oxford University Press.

Bibbiani, William (2014). 'Spoiler Interview: Ruben Östlund on "Force Majeure"'. Retrieved from www.craveonline.com/site/782963-spoiler-interview-ruben-ostlund-force-majeu re/2#77Fb0AzPdxFoijSm.99.

Biderman, Shai and Eliana Jacobowitz (2007) '*Rope*: Nietzsche and the Art of Murder', in *Hitchcock and Philosophy: Dial M for Metaphysics*, Chicago and La Salle, IL: Open Court, 33–45.

Binmore, Ken (2000) "A Utilitarian Theory of Legitimacy," in Avner Ben-Ner and Louis G. Putterman (eds.), *Economics, Values, and Organization*, Cambridge: Cambridge University Press, 101–132.

Birzache, Alina (2014) 'You cannot be in love with a word': Theologies of Embodiment in Dreyer's *The Passion of Joan of Arc*, Axel's *Babette's Feast* and von Trier's *Breaking the Waves'*, *Journal of Religion, Media and Digital Culture* 3(1). Retrieved from www. jrmdc.com/journal/article/view/16.

Black, Izzy (2014) 'The Wolf of Wall Street and The New Cinema of Excess', *Agents and Seers*. N.p., 8 April. Retrieved from https://agentsandseers.wordpress.com/2014/04/08/the-wolf-of-wall-street-and-the-new-cinema-of-excess/.

Blackburn, Simon (2003) *Being Good: A Short Introduction to Ethics*, Oxford: Oxford University Press.

Bookman, M. and M. Aboulafia (2000) 'Ethics of care revisited: Gilligan and Levinas', *Philosophy Today* 44: 169–174.

Bowles, Samuel (2016) *The Moral Economy: Why Good Incentives Are No Substitute for Good Citizens*, New Haven, CT: Yale University Press.

Brown, Patrick (2009) 'Ethics as Self-Transcendence: Legal Education, Faith and an Ethos of Justice', *Seattle University Law Review* 32: 293–310.

Brunette, Peter (1996) *Roberto Rossellini*, Berkeley, CA: University of California Press.

Burtt, Edwin (1951) *Types of Religious Philosophy*, revised ed., New York: Harper and Brothers.

Byrnes, Alice (2015) 'Alienating the Gaze: The Hybrid Femme Fatale of Under the Skin', *Deletion*, May 4 2015. Retrieved from www.deletionscifi.org.

Camus, Albert (1975) *The Myth of Sisyphus*, trans. Justin O'Brien, Harmondsworth: Penguin.

Carroll, Noel (2007) '*Vertigo* and the Pathologies of Romantic Love', in *Hitchcock and Philosophy: Dial M for Metaphysics*, Chicago and La Salle, IL: Open Court, 101–113.

Clarke, Arthur C. (1968) *2001 A Space Odyssey*, London: Arrow Books.

Comiskey, Andrea (2011) 'The Hero we Read: The Dark Knight, Popular Allegoresis, and Blockbuster Ideology', in Kevin K. Durand and Mary K. Leigh (eds.), *Riddle me this, Batman! Essays in the universe of the Dark Knight*, Jefferson, NC: McFarland and Company, 124–146.

Connolly, William E. (1993) *The Terms of Political Discourse*, 3rd ed., Oxford: Blackwell.

Cooper, David (1999) *Existentialism: A Reconstruction*, 2nd ed., Oxford: Blackwell.

Copleston, Frederick (1994) *A History of Philosophy Volume VI: From the French Enlightenment to Kant*, New York: Doubleday.

Cowie, Peter (1982) *Ingmar Bergman*, London: Secker & Warburg.

Cox, Damien and Michael P. Levine (2012) *Thinking through Film: Doing Philosophy, Watching Movies*, Malden, MA: Wiley-Blackwell.

Cox, Gary (2006) *Sartre: A Guide for the Perplexed*, London and New York: Continuum.

Creed, Barbara (1993) *The Monstrous Feminine: Film, Feminism, Psychoanalysis*. London: Routledge.

Cross, Katharine (2015) 'Goddess from the Machine: A Look at Ex Machina's Gender Politics'.Retrievedfromhttp://feministing.com/2015/05/28/goddess-from-the-machine-a-look-at-ex-machinas-gender-politics/.

Dawkins, Richard (1989) *The Selfish Gene*, Oxford: Oxford University Press.

de Beauvoir, Simone (1953) *The Second Sex*, trans. H.M. Parshley, London: Jonathon Cape.

de Beauvoir, Simone (1962) *The Prime of Life*, trans. Peter Green, Harmondsworth: Penguin.

de Beauvoir, Simone (1976) *The Ethics of Ambiguity*, trans. Bernard Frechtman, New York: Citadel Press.

Dennett, Daniel (1976) 'Conditions of Personhood', in Amelia Oakensberg Rorty (ed.), *The Identities of Persons*. Berkeley, CA: University of California Press.

Derrida, Jacques (1993) 'Circumfession', in J. Derrida and G. Bennington (eds.), *Jacques Derrida*, Chicago, IL: University of Chicago Press, 3–315.

Devlin, William J. (2010) 'No Country for Old Men: the Decline of Ethics and the West(ern)', in Jennifer McMahon and B. Steve Csaki, *The Philosophy of the Western*, Lexington, KY: The University Press of Kentucky, 221–239.

Dirks, Tim (2013) 'Filmsite Movie Review: Dirty Harry (1971)'. Retrieved from www.filmsite.org/dirt.html.

Dirks, Tim (2017) 'Westerns Films'. Retrieved from www.filmsite.org/westernfilms.html.

Doris, John (2002) *Lack of Character: Personality and Moral Behaviour*, Cambridge: CUP Ely, John (1995) 'Jane Austen: A Female Aristotelian', *Thesis Eleven* 40: 93–118.

Dostoevsky, Fyodor (1990) *The Brothers Karamazov* trans Richard Pevear and Larissa Volokhonsky, San Francisco, CA: North Point Press.

Dreyfus, Hubert (2009) *On the Internet*, 2nd ed., London and New York: Routledge.

Durgnat, Raymond (1968) *Luis Bunuel*, Berkeley, CA: University of California Press.

Dworkin, Ronald (1984) 'Rights as Trumps', in J. Waldron (ed.), *Theories of Rights*, Oxford: Oxford University Press, 153–167.

Eldridge, Richard (2009) 'Philosophy In/Of/As/And Film', *Projections: The Journal of Movies and Mind* 3 (1): 109–116.

Epictetus (2008) 'Enchiridion', in Robert Dobbin (ed.), *Discourses and Selected Writings*, London: Penguin Books, 219–245.

Epicurus (2006) 'Letter to Menoeceus', in Daniel Kolak and Garrett Thomson (eds.), *The Longman Standard History of Ancient Philosophy*, New York: Pearson, 452–455.

Falzon, Christopher (2011) 'On *Being John Malkovich* and Not Being Yourself', in David LaRocca (ed.), *Charlie Kaufman and Philosophy*, Lexington, KY: University of Kentucky Press, 46–65.

Falzon, Christopher (2011) 'Peter Weir's *The Truman Show* and Sartrean Freedom', in J.-P. Boule and E. McCaffrey, *Existentialism and Contemporary Cinema: A Sartrean Perspective*, New York, Oxford: Berghahn Books, 17–31.

Falzon, Christopher (2016) 'Dirty Harry Ethics', *SubStance* 45 (3): 49–65.

Falzon, Christopher (2017) 'Experiencing *Force Majeure*', *Film-Philosophy* 21 (3): 281–298.

Foucault, Michel (1977) *Discipline and Punish*, trans. A. Sheridan, London: Penguin.

Foucault, Michel (1985) *The History of Sexuality* vol. 2: *The Use of Pleasure*, trans. R. Hurley, New York: Pantheon.

Foucault, Michel (1997a) 'On the Genealogy of Ethics: An Overview of Work in Progress', in Paul Rabinow (ed.), *Ethics, Subjectivity, and Truth. Essential Works of Foucault, 1954–1984*, trans. R. Hurley and others, New York: The New Press, 253–280.

Foucault, Michel (1997b) 'What is Enlightenment?', in Paul Rabinow (ed.), *Ethics, Subjectivity, and Truth. Essential Works of Foucault, 1954–1984*, New York: The New Press, 303–319.

Foucault, Michel (1997c) 'Sexual Choice, Sexual Act', in Paul Rabinow (ed.), *Ethics, Subjectivity, and Truth. Essential Works of Foucault, 1954–1984*, New York: The New Press, 141–156.

Foucault, Michel (1990) *The History of Sexuality* vol. 1: *The Will to Knowledge*, trans. R. Hurley, London: Penguin.

Foucault, Michel (2000) 'The Subject and Power', in James D. Faubion (ed.), *Power. Essential Works of Foucault, 1954–1984*, trans. R. Hurley and others, New York: The New Press, 326–348.

Fraiman, S. (2010) 'The Liberation of Elizabeth Bennet in Joe Wright's *Pride & Prejudice'* 31 (1). Online publication of the Jane Austen Society of North America. Retrieved from www.jasna.org/persuasions/on-line/vol31no1/fraiman.html.

Frankel, Glenn (2018) *High Noon: The Hollywood Blacklist and the Making of an American Classic*, New York: Bloomsbury.

Frankfurt, Harry (1971) 'Freedom of Will and the Concept of a Person', *The Journal of Philosophy*, 68 (1): 5–20.

Freeland, Cynthia (2002) 'Penetrating Keanu: New Holes, but the Same Old Shit', in William Irwin (ed.), *The Matrix and Philosophy: Welcome to the Desert of the Real*, Chicago and La Salle, IL: Open Court, 205–215.

Frohock, Richard (2002) 'Adaptation and Cultural Criticism: *Les Liaisons dangereuses 1960* and *Dangerous Liaisons'* in Robert Mayer (ed.), *Eighteenth-century fiction on Screen,* Cambridge: Cambridge University Press, 157–174.

Frost, Michael and Robert Banks (2001) *Lessons from Reel Life: Movies, Meaning and Myth-Making*, Adelaide: Openbook Publishers.

Gallagher, Mark (2006) *Action Figures*, New York: Palgrave.

Gee, Oliver (2014) 'Watch my movie and get a divorce', *The Local*, 12 December. Retrieved from www.thelocal.se/20141212/swedish-director-divorce-turist-golden-globe.

Gilligan, Carol (1982) *In a Different Voice: Psychological Theory and Women's Development*, Cambridge, MA: Harvard University Press.

Girgus, Sam (2002) *The Films of Woody Allen*, 2nd ed., Cambridge: Cambridge University Press.

Girgus, Sam (2010). *Levinas and the Cinema of Redemption – Time, Ethics and the Feminine*, New York: Columbia University Press.

Giroux, Henry A. (2006) 'Private Satisfactions and Public Disorder: *Fight Club*, Patriarchy and the Politics of Masculine Violence', in *America on the Edge: Henry Giroux on Politics, Culture, and Education*, New York: Palgrave.

Grau, Christopher (2005) 'There is no 'I' in 'Robot': Robots and Utilitarianism', in Susan Anderson and Michael Anderson (eds.), *Machine Ethics*, New York: Cambridge University Press, 451–463.

Greenblatt, Stephen (2017) 'How St Augustine Invented Sex', *The New Yorker*, June 19 2017. Retrieved from www.newyorker.com/magazine/2017/06/19/how-st-augustine-invented-sex.

Griffin, James (2015) *What Can Philosophy Contribute To Ethics?* Oxford: Oxford University Press.

Grimshaw, Jean (1986) *Philosophy and Feminist Thinking*, Minneapolis, MN: University of Minnesota Press.

Habermas, Jürgen (1971) 'Technology and Science as "Ideology"', in *Toward a Rational Society*, trans. J. Shapiro, London: Heinemann Educational Books.

Habermas, Jürgen (1972) *Knowledge and Human Interests* 2nd ed., trans. J. Shapiro, Boston: Beacon Press.

Habermas, Jürgen (1974) 'The Public Sphere: An Encyclopedia Article (1964)', *New German Critique* 3: 49–55.

Habermas, Jürgen (2003) *The Future of Human Nature*, Cambridge: Polity Press.

Halwani, Raja (2016) 'Why sexual desire is objectifying – and hence morally wrong, *Aeon*. Retrieved from https://aeon.co/ideas/why-sexual-desire-is-objectifying-and-hence-morally-wrong.

Harris, Jonathon (2007) *Enhancing Evolution: The Ethical Case for Making Better People*, Princeton, NJ: Princeton University Press.

Hayward, Max (2017) 'Philosophy versus Ethics', in *The Times Literary Supplement*, January 11, 2017. Retrieved from www.the-tls.co.uk/articles/public/philosophy-vs-ethics/.

Hayward, Max (2017) 'Philosophy vs Ethics', *Times Literary Supplement*, January 11.

Hegel, G.W.F. (1977) Phenomenology of Spirit, trans. A.V. Miller, Oxford: Oxford University Press.

Heller, Agnes (1982) 'Habermas and Marxism', in J.B. Thompson and D. Held (eds.), *Habermas: Critical Debates*, London: Macmillan.

Helvétius, Claude (2002) *On the Mind*, excerpts in J.B. Schneewind (ed.), *Moral Theory from Montaigne to Kant*. Cambridge: Cambridge University Press, 416–429.

Hick, John (1990) *Philosophy of Religion*, 4th ed., Englewood Cliffs, NJ: Prentice Hall.

Hobbes, Thomas (1968) *Leviathan*, ed. C.B. Macpherson, Harmondsworth: Penguin Books.

Hofmeyr, Benda (2006) 'The meta-physics of Foucault's ethics: Succeeding where Levinas fails', *South African Journal of Philosophy*, 25 (2): 113–125.

Holbach, Baron d' (1999) *The System of Nature*, volume 1, Manchester: Clinamen Press.

Holbach Baron d' (2002) *Universal Morality; or, The Duties of Man, Founded on Nature*. Excerpts in B. Schneewind (ed.), *Moral Theory from Montaigne to Kant*, Cambridge: Cambridge University Press, 431–445.

Horkheimer, Max (1974) *The Eclipse of Reason*, New York: Continuum.

Horkheimer, Max, and Theodor Adorno (1979) *Dialectic of Enlightenment*, trans. J. Cumming, London: Verso.

Hughes, Gerald J. (2001) *Routledge Philosophy Guidebook to Aristotle on Ethics*, London: Routledge.

Hume, David (1969) *A Treatise of Human Nature*, ed. Eric C. Mossner, Harmondsworth: Penguin Books.

Hume, David (1990) *Dialogues Concerning Natural Religion*, London: Penguin.

Ignatieff, Michael (2013) 'Machiavelli was Right', *Atlantic Monthly*, December.

Insdorf, Annette (1994) *François Truffaut*, New York: Cambridge University Press.

Johnstone, Nick (1999) *Abel Ferrara: The King of New York*, London: Omnibus Press.

Kael, Pauline (1978) 'Saintliness' in Joan Mellon (ed.), *The World of Luis Bunuel: Essays in Criticism*, New York: Oxford University Press, 270–277.

Kael, Pauline (1991) Review of *Dirty Harry*, in *5001 Nights at the Movies*, New York: Henry Holt and Company.

Kael, Pauline (1970) *Going Steady*, Boston, Toronto: Little, Brown and Company.

Kant, Immanuel (1963) 'Duties towards Animals and Spirits', in trans. L. Infield, *Lectures on Ethics*, New York: Harper and Row.

Kant, Immanuel (1964) *Groundwork of the Metaphysic of Morals*, trans. H. J. Paton, New York: New York: Harper and Row.

Kant, Immanuel (2009) *The Metaphysical Elements of Ethics*, trans. Thomas Kingsmill Abbott, Auckland, New Zealand: The Floating Press.

Kant, Immanuel (1995) 'What Is Enlightenment?', in Isaac Kramnick (ed.), *The Portable Enlightenment Reader*, New York: Penguin Books, 1–7.

Kant, Immanuel (2016) 'On a Supposed Right to Lie Because of Philanthropic Concerns' in Kevin DeLapp, Jeremy Henkel (eds.), *Truth and Lying*, Indianapolis/Cambridge: Hackett Publishing, 78–99.

Katz, Claire Elise (2003) *Levinas, Judaism, and the Feminine*, Bloomington and Indianapolis: Indiana University Press.

Kaufmann, Walter (1968) *Nietzsche: Philosopher, Psychologist, Antichrist*, 3rd ed., Princeton, NJ: Princeton University Press.

Keyser, Les Martin (1995) *Scorsese*, New York: Simon and Schuster.

Kierkegaard, Søren (1975) *Journals and Papers* vol. 3, trans. Howard V. Hong and Edna H. Hong, Bloomington: Indiana University Press.

Kierkegaard, Søren (1986) *Fear and Trembling*, London: Penguin.

Kierkegaard, Søren (2009) *Concluding Unscientific Postscript*, trans. A. Hannay, Cambridge: Cambridge University Press.

Klockars, Carl (1980) 'The Dirty Harry Problem', *The Annals* 452, November.

Knight, Deborah, and George McKnight (2002) 'Real Genre and Virtual Philosophy', in William Irwin (ed.), *The Matrix and Philosophy: Welcome to the Desert of the Real*, Chicago and La Salle, IL: Open Court, 188–201.

Köhler-Ryan, Renée, and Sydney Palmer (2013) 'What Do You Know of My Heart? The Role of Sense and Sensibility in Ang Lee's *Sense and Sensibility* and *Crouching Tiger, Hidden Dragon*', in Robert Arp et al. (eds.), *Ang Lee and Philosophy*, Lexington, KY: University Press of Kentucky, 41–63.

Kramnick, Isaac (1995) 'Introduction', in *The Portable Enlightenment Reader*, ed. Isaac Kramnick, New York: Penguin Books, ix–xxviii.

Kreyche, Gerald (1988) '"High Noon": A Paradigm of Kant's Moral Philosophy', *Teaching Philosophy* 11 (3): 217–228.

Kupfer, Joseph (1999) *Visions of Virtue in Popular Film (Thinking Through Cinema)*, Boulder, CO: Westview Press.

Lara, Maria Pia (1998) *Moral Textures: Feminist Narratives in the Public Sphere*, Berkeley and Los Angeles, CA: University of California Press.

LaRocca, David (2016) 'The Last Great Representative of the Virtues', in Mimi Marinucci (ed.), *Jane Austen and Philosophy*, Lanham: Rowman and Littlefield, 81–94.

Lemm, Vanessa and Miguel Vatter (2017) 'Michel Foucault's perspective on biopolitics' in Steven A. Peterson and Albert Somit (eds.), *Handbook of Biology and Politics*, Cheltenham, Northampton, MA: Edward Elgar Publishing, 40–52.

Levinas, Emmanuel (1979) *Totality and Infinity*, trans. Alphonso Lingis. The Hague: Martinus Nijhoff.

Levinas, Emmanuel (1998) *Otherwise than Being, or Beyond Essence*, trans. Alphonso Lingis. Pittsburgh, PA: Duquesne University Press.

Lewis, C.S. (2012) *The Problem of Pain,* London: HarperCollins.

Lindenmuth, William (2017) 'Cross My Heart and Hope to Die: Why Ripley Must Save Newt', in Jeffrey Ewing and Kevin S. Decker (eds.), *Alien and Philosophy: I Infest, therefore I Am*. Hoboken, NJ: Wiley Blackwell, 67–79.

Locke, John (1993) *The Second Treatise of Government*, in David Wootton (ed.), *Political Writings*, Harmondsworth: Penguin Books.

Locke, John (1997) *An Essay Concerning Human Understanding*, ed. Roger Woolhouse, Harmondsworth: Penguin Books.

Lopez, George (2006) 'The Ethical Legacy of Dirty Harry'. *America: The National Catholic Weekly* 195 (Sept.): 16–18.

Lucca, Violet (2014). 'Interview: Ruben Östlund'. Retrieved from www.filmcomment. com/blog/interview-ruben-oestlund.

Lucretius (1951) *On the Nature of the Universe*, Harmondsworth: Penguin Books.

MacIntyre, Alasdair (1981) *After Virtue*, Notre Dame: University of Notre Dame Press Macmillan.

Mackenzie, Catriona and Natalie Stoljar (2000) 'Introduction: Autonomy Reconfigured', in C. Mackenzie, and N. Stoljar (eds.), *Relational Autonomy: Feminist Perspectives on Autonomy, Agency and the Social Self*, New York: Oxford University Press, 3–31.

Macpherson, C.B. (1962) *The Political Theory of Possessive Individualism: Hobbes to Locke*, London: Clarendon Press.

Mainon, Dominique and James Ursini (2007) *Cinema of Obsession*,New York: Limelight Editions.

Malik, Kenan (2014) *The Quest for a Moral Compass: A Global History of Ethics*, London: Atlantic Books.

Manninen, Bertha Alvarez (2013) 'The Problem of Evil and Humans' Relationship with God in Terrence Malick's *The Tree of Life*'', *Journal of Religion & Film* 17 (1): 1–23.

Marcus Aurelius (2006) *Meditations*, London: Penguin Books.

Marcuse, Herbert (1991) *One-Dimensional Man*, London: Routledge.

Marx, Karl (1967a) *Economic and Philosophical Manuscripts* (excerpts), in Loyd D. Easton and Kurt H. Guddat (eds. and trans.), *The Writings of the Young Marx on Philosophy and Society*, New York: Anchor.

Marx, Karl (1967b) *The Holy Family* (excerpts), in Loyd D. Easton and Kurt H. Guddat (eds. and trans.), *The Writings of the Young Marx on Philosophy and Society*, New York: Anchor, 361–398.

Marx, Karl (1972) *The Eighteenth Brumaire of Louis Bonaparte*, in Robert C. Tucker (ed.), *The Marx-Engels Reader*, New York: Norton.

Marx, Karl (1991) *Capital, Volume Three*, London: Penguin.

Marx, Karl and Friedrich Engels (1972) *The Communist Manifesto*, in Robert C. Tucker (ed.), *The Marx-Engels Reader*, New York: Norton.

McAteer, John (2013) 'The Problem of the Father's Love in *The Tree of Life* and the Book of Job', *Film and Philosophy* 17: 137–150.

McCaffrey, Enda (2011) 'Crimes of Passion, Freedom and a clash of Sartrean Moralities in the Coen Brothers "No Country for Old Men"', in Jean-Pierre Boulé and Enda MacCaffrey (eds.), *Existentialism and Contemporary Cinema: a Sartrean Perspective*, New York, Oxford: Berghahn Books, 125–142.

McCarthy, Thomas (1978) *The Critical Theory of Jurgen Habermas*, Oxford: Polity.

McClelland, Tom (2011) 'The Philosophy of Film and Film as Philosophy', *Cinema: Journal of Philosophy and the Moving Image* 2: 11–35.

McGarry, Eileen (1988) 'Dirty Harry', in Alain Silver and Elizabeth Ward (eds.), *Film Noir: An Encyclopedic Reference Guide*, London: Bloomsbury.

McVeigh, Stephen (2017) 'You must remember this: Casablanca at 75 – still a classic of WWII propaganda'. Retrieved at http://theconversation.com/you-must-remember-this-casablanca-at-75-still-a-classic-of-wwii-propaganda-87113.

Mexal, Stephen J. (2010) 'Two ways to Yuma: Locke, Liberalism and Western Masculinity in 3:10 to Yuma', in Jennifer McMahon and B. Steve Csaki, *The Philosophy of the Western*, Lexington, KY: The University Press of Kentucky, 69–88.

Midgely, Mary (1985) 'Persons and Non-persons', in Peter Singer (ed.), *In Defence of Animals*, New York: Blackwell, 52–62.

Mill, John Stuart (1975) *Three Essays: On Liberty, Representative Government, The Subjection of Women*, Oxford: Oxford University Press.

Mill, John Stuart (2004) *Utilitarianism*, in *Utilitarianism and Other Essays*, Alan Ryan (ed.), Harmondsworth: Penguin Books, 272–338.

Mitchell, Jolyon (2009) 'Ethics', in John Lyden (ed.), *The Routledge Companion to Religion and Film*, London and New York: Routledge, 482–500.

Monaco, James (1976) *The New Wave*, New York: Oxford University Press.

Montaigne, Michel de (2003) 'On Moderation', in trans. M.A. Screech. *The Complete Essays*, London: Penguin, 222–227.

Moore, Charlotte (2008) 'The Ethics of Ambiguity', *Philosophy Now* 69: 14–16.

Morton, Adam (2004) *On Evil*, New York and London: Routledge.

Mulvey, Laura (1999) 'Visual Pleasure and Narrative Cinema', In *Film* Leo Braudy and Marshall Cohen (eds.), *Theory and Criticism: Introductory Readings*, New York: Oxford University Press, 833–844.

Nagel, Thomas (1979) 'Moral Luck' in *Mortal Questions*, Cambridge: Cambridge University Press.

Nichols, Mary P. (2000) *Reconstructing Woody*, Lanham: Rowman & Littlefield.

Nietzsche, Friedrich (1967) *The Will to Power*, trans. Walter Kaufmann and R.J. Hollingdale, New York: Vintage Books.

Nietzsche, Friedrich (1968) *Twilight of the Idols; The Anti-Christ,* Harmondsworth: Penguin Books.

Nietzsche, Friedrich (1969) *Thus Spoke Zarathustra*, trans. R.J. Hollingdale, Harmondsworth: Penguin.

Nietzsche, Friedrich (1973) *Beyond Good and Evil*, trans. R.J. Hollingdale, Harmondsworth: Penguin Books.

Nietzsche, Friedrich (1974) *The Gay Science*, trans. Walter Kaufmann, New York: Vintage Books.

Nietzsche, Friedrich (1989) *The Genealogy of Morals/Ecce Homo*, trans. Walter Kaufmann and R.J. Hollingdale, New York: Vintage Books.

Noddings, Nel (1984) *Caring: A feminine Approach to Ethics and Moral Education*, Berkeley and Los Angeles, CA: University of California Press.

Norman, Richard (1998) *The Moral Philosophers: An Introduction to Ethics*, 2nd ed., Oxford: Oxford University Press.

Nozick, Robert (1974) *Anarchy, State and Utopia*, Oxford: Basil Blackwell.

Nussbaum, Martha C. (1994) *The Therapy of Desire: Theory and Practice in Hellenistic Ethics*, Princeton and Oxford: Princeton University Press.

O'Leary, Timothy (2008) 'Foucault, Experience, Literature', *Foucault Studies* 5: 5–25.

O'Leary, Timothy (2009) *Foucault and Fiction: The Experience Book*, London: Continuum.

Pannereau, William (2009) *Existentialist Cinema*, Houndmills, Basingstoke: Palgrave.

Pappas, John (2004) 'It's All Darkness: Plato, The Ring of Gyges, and Crimes and Misdemeanors', in *Woody Allen and Philosophy*, Chicago, IL: Open Court.

Parrill, Sue (2002) *Jane Austen on Film and television: A Critical Study of the Adaptations*, Jefferson, NC: McFarland.

Patton, Paul (1989) 'Taylor and Foucault on Power and Freedom', *Political Studies* 37: 260–276.

Perkins, V.F. (1972) *Film as Film: Understanding and Judging Movies*, Harmondsworth: Penguin Books.

Plantinga, Alvin (1977) *God, Freedom, and Evil*, Grand Rapids: Eerdmans.

Plato (1993) *Republic*, trans. Robin Waterfield, Oxford: Oxford University Press.

Plato (2003) *The Last Days of Socrates – Euthyphro, Apology, Crito, Phaedo*, trans. Hugh Tredennick and Harrold Tarrant, London: Penguin.

Pojman, Louis (1999) *Philosophy: The Pursuit of Wisdom*, 2nd ed., Belmont CA: Wadsworth Publishing Company.

Prior, William J. (2016) *Ancient Philosophy: A Beginner's Guide*, London: Oneworld.

Railton, Peter (1984) 'Alienation, Consequentialism, and the Demands of Morality,' *Philosophy and Public Affairs* 13 (2): 134–171.

Rand, Ayn (1964) *The Virtue of Selfishness*, New York: Signet Books.

Reiser, Klaus (2006) 'Gender in Matewan and Men with Guns', in Diane Carson Heidi Kenaga (eds.), *Sayles Talk: New Perspectives on Independent Filmmaker John Sayles*, Detroit, MI: Wayne State University Press.

Rempel, Morgan (2012) 'Epicurus and "Contented Poverty": The Big Lebowski as Epicurean Parable', in Peter S. Fosl (ed.), *The Big Lebowski and Philosophy*, Hoboken, NJ: Wiley, 67–78.

Richardson, Michael (2010) *Otherness in Hollywood Cinema*, New York, London: Continuum.

Riegler, Thomas (2009) 'The "Mastermind": Personifications of Evil in the Cinema'. Retrieved from www.academia.edu/1532242/The_Mastermind_Personifications_of_Evil_in_the_Cinema.

Rodham, Thomas (2013) 'Jane Austen as Moral Philosopher', *Philosophy Now* 94: 6–8.

Rousseau, Jean-Jacques (1993) *The Social Contract and the Discourses*, trans. G.D.H. Cole, London: Everyman.

Rowland, Mark (2003) *The Philosopher at the End of the Universe*, London: Ebury Press.

Ruddick, Sara (1997) 'Maternal Thinking', in Diana Meyers (ed.), *Feminist Social Thought: A Reader*, London: Routledge, 583–603.

Ryan, Alan (1973) 'The Nature of Human Nature in Hobbes and Rousseau', in Jonathon Benthall (ed.), *The Limits of Human Nature*, London: Allen Lane, 3–19.

Ryle, Gilbert (2009) 'Jane Austen and the Moralists', in *Critical Essays: Collected Papers*, vol. 1, London and New York: Routledge, 286–302.

Sander-Staudt, Maureen (2011) 'Care Ethics', entry in James Fieser and Bradley Dowden (eds.), *Internet Encyclopedia of Philosophy*. Retrieved from www.iep.utm.edu/care-eth/.

Sartre, Jean-Paul (1958) *Being and Nothingness*, trans. Hazel E. Barnes, London: Methuen.

Sartre, Jean-Paul (1975) 'Existentialism Is a Humanism', in Walter Kaufmann (ed.), *Existentialism from Dostoevsky to Sartre*, New York: New American Library.

Sartre, Jean-Paul (1983) 'The Itinerary of a Thought', in *Between Existentialism and Marxism*, London: Verso, 33–64.

Sartre, Jean-Paul (1995) 'Portrait of an Anti-Semite' in *Anti-Semite and Jew,* trans. George J. Becker. New York: Shocken .

Sartre, Jean-Paul (2000) 'Huis Clos', in *Huis and Other Plays*, London: Penguin.

Savulescu, Julian (2009) 'Genetic interventions and the ethics of enhancement of human beings', in Bonnie Steinbock (ed.), *The Oxford Handbook of Bioethics*, Oxford: Oxford University Press.

Scaltsas, Patricia Ward (1992) 'Do Feminist Ethics Counter Feminist Aims', in Eve Browning Cole and Susan Coultrap-McQuin (eds.), *Explorations in Feminist Ethics: Theory and Practice*, Bloomington, IN: Indiana University Press, 15–26.

Schickel, Richard (2003) *Woody Allen: A Life in Film*, Chicago: Ivan R. Lee.

Schneewind, J.B (2002) 'Introduction' in J.B. Schneewind (ed.), *Moral Theory from Montaigne to Kant*, Cambridge: Cambridge University Press.

Scott, Mark S.M. (2014) 'C. S. Lewis and John Hick: An Interface on Theodicy', *The Journal of Inklings Studies* 4 (1): 19–31.

Sellars, John (2003) 'Gladiator', *Philosophy Now* 41: 44–45.

Sellars, John (2006) *Stoicism*, Chesham: Acumen.

Sembou, Evangelia (2013) *Modern Theories of Politics*, Oxford: Peter Lang.

Sharpe, Matthew (2012) 'Philosophy and the View from Above in Alejandro Amenabar's *Agora*', *Crossroads* 6 (1): 31–45.

Sherwin, Susan (1989) 'Feminist and Medical Ethics: Two Different Approaches to Contextual Ethics', *Hypatia* 4: 57–72.

Sherwin, Susan (1992) *No Longer Patient: Feminist Ethics and Health Care*, Philadelphia, PA: Temple University Press.

Sherwin, Susan (1998) 'A relational approach to autonomy in health care', in H. Besquaret Holmes and L. Purdy (eds.), *The Politics of Women's Health: Exploring Agency and Autonomy*, Pittsburgh, PA: Temple University Press.

Simons, Jonathon (1995) *Foucault and the Political*, London and New York: Routledge.

Singer, Peter (1993) *How are We to Live? Ethics in an Age of Self-Interest*, Melbourne : Mandarin.

Singer, Peter (2000) *Marx: A Very Short Introduction*, Oxford: Oxford University Press.

Singer, Peter (2011) *Practical Ethics*, 3rd ed., Cambridge, New York: Cambridge University Press.

Sinnerbrink, Robert (2005) 'Cinematic Ideas: David Lynch's *Mulholland Drive*', *Film-Philosophy* 9 (4): 1–15.

Sitney, P. Adams (2003) 'Let me go into the church alone: the Roman Catholic subtext of "Vertigo"', in Mary Lea Bandy, and Antonio Monda (2003) *The Hidden God: Film as Faith*, New York: Museum of Modern Art, 249–259.

Skees, Murray (2012) 'Have I been Misunderstood: Dionysius vs IKEA-boy', in Thomas Wartenberg (ed.), *Fight Club*, New York: Routledge.

Slattery, Luke (2012) *Reclaiming Epicurus*, London: Penguin.

Smart, J.J.C and Bernard Williams (1973) *Utilitarianism: For and Against*, Cambridge: Cambridge University Press.

Stam, Robert (2000) *Film Theory: An Introduction*, Malden, MA: Blackwell.

Stephens, William O. (2010) 'What's Love Got to Do with It? Epicureanism and Friends with Benefits', in Michael Bruce and Robert M. Stewart (eds.), *College Sex – Philosophy for Everyone: Philosophers With Benefits*, Oxford: Blackwell, 77–90.

Steven, Mark (2017) 'Nietzsche on Film', *Film-Philosophy* 21 (1): 95–113.

Tasker, Yvonne (2002) *The Silence of the Lambs*, London: British Film Institute.

Taylor, Charles (1985a) 'What is Human Agency?', in *Philosophical Papers* I: *Human Agency and Language*, Cambridge, MA: Cambridge University Press.

Taylor, Charles (1985b) 'Kant's Theory of Freedom', in *Philosophical Papers* 2: *Philosophy and the Human Sciences*, Cambridge, MA: Cambridge University Press.

Taylor, Charles (1985c) 'What's Wrong with Negative Liberty?' In *Philosophical Papers* 2: *Philosophy and the Human Sciences*, Cambridge, MA: Cambridge University Press.

Taylor, Chloe (2005) 'Levinasian Ethics and Feminist Ethics of Care', *Symposium* 9 (2): 217–239. Retrieved from htp://www.artsrn.ualberta.ca/symposium/files/original/46b79 257165a7c21b50d4b004581bfcc.PDF.

Taylor, Mark (1980) *Journeys to Selfhood: Hegel and Kierkegaard*, Berkeley and Los Angeles, CA: University of California Press.

Tooley, Michael (1991) 'Abortion and Infanticide' from Peter Singer (ed.), *A Companion to Ethics*, Oxford: Oxford University Press.

Truffaut, François (1978) 'Bunuel the Builder' in *The Films in My Life*, Harmondsworth: Penguin.

Truffaut, François (1986) *Hitchcock*, revised edition, London: Paladin.

Ulin, David S. (2006) 'Why Charlie Kaufman Is Us', *Los Angeles Times*, 14 May.

Van Hooft, Stan (2006) *Introducing Virtue Ethics*, Bucks: Acumen.

Vass, Michael (2005) 'Cinematic Meaning in the Work of David Lynch: Revisiting *Twin Peaks: Fire Walk with Me, Lost Highway*, and *Mulholland Drive*', *Cineaction* 67: 12–25. Retrieved from www.michaelvass.com/lynch.html.

Voltaire (2011) *A Pocket Philosophical Dictionary*, trans. John Fletcher, Oxford, New York: Oxford University Press.

Wanat, Matt (2007) 'Irony as Absolution', in Leonard Engel (ed.), *Clint Eastwood, Actor and Director: New Perspectives*, Salt Lake City: University of Utah Press.

Wartenberg, Thomas E. (2007) *Thinking on Screen: Film as Philosophy*, New York/ London: Routledge.

Wartenberg, Thomas E. (2011) 'On the Possibility of Cinematic Philosophy', in Havi Carel and Greg Tuck (eds.), *New Takes in Film Philosophy*, Basingstoke: Palgrave, 9–24.

West, David (1996) *An Introduction to Continental Philosophy*, Cambridge, MA: Polity Press.

Williams, Bernard (1981) 'Persons, Character, and Morality', in *Moral Luck*, Cambridge: Cambridge University Press.

Williams, Bernard (1982) 'Moral Luck', in *Moral Luck*, Cambridge: Cambridge University Press.

Wilson, Catherine (2015) *Epicureanism*, Oxford: Oxford University Press.

Wilson, George (1986) Baltimore and London: The Johns Hopkins University Press.

Wold, Susan (2007) 'Moral Psychology and the Unity of the Virtues', in *Ratio* 20 (2): 145–167.

Wolf, Susan (1982) 'Moral Saints', *The Journal of Philosophy* 79 (8): 419–439.

Wood, Michael (2003) 'Simon of the Desert', in Mary Lea Bandy and Antonio Monda (eds.), *The Hidden God: Film and Faith*, New York: The Museum of Modern Art.

Wood, Robin (2002) *Hitchcock's Films Revisited*, revised ed., New York: Columbia University Press, 130–133.

Wright, John W. (2008) 'Levinasian Ethics of Alterity: The Face of the Other in Spielberg's Cinematic Language', in Dean Kowalski (ed.), *Steven Spielberg and*

Philosophy: We're Gonna Need a Bigger Boat. Lexington, KY: The University Press of Kentucky, 50–68.

Wright, Wendy M. (2016) 'Babette's Feast: A Religious Film', *Journal of Religion & Film* 1 (2). Retrieved from https://digitalcommons.unomaha.edu/jrf/vol1/iss2/2.

Zizek, Slavoj (2012) ' If there is a God, then anything is permitted', ABC Religion and Ethics, 17 April. Retrieved from www.abc.net.au/religion/articles/2012/04/17/3478816.htm.

Index

Page numbers in *italics* refer to photos.